MEMOIRS OF A JEWISH REVOLUTIONARY

Hersh Mendel

MEMOIRS OF
A JEWISH
REVOLUTIONARY

With a Preface by
Isaac Deutscher

PLUTO  PRESS

First published in English 1989 by Pluto Press
11 – 21 Northdown Street, London N1 9BN

Distributed in the USA by Unwin Hyman Inc
8 Winchester Place, Winchester
MA 01890, USA

Translation copyright © 1989 Robert Michaels

First published in Hebrew as: *Zikhroynes fun a Yidishn Revolutsioner*
Copyright © 1959 I.L. Peretz Library, Tel Aviv

Published in German as: *Erinnerungen eines jüdischen Revolutionärs*
Copyright © 1979 Rotbuch Verlag, West Berlin

Preface to the Yiddish edition copyright © Tamara Deutscher
Translator's note copyright © 1984, 1987 Robert Michaels
Grateful acknowledgement is made for permission to reproduce the following:
Selection from *Writings of Leon Trotsky 1934-35* reprinted by permission of
Pathfinder Press copyright © 1971 and 1974 by Pathfinder Press; exchange between
J.S. Hertz and Hersh Mendel from *Unser Tsait* 1960-1 reproduced here in translation by
permission of *Unser Tsait* and J.S. Hertz; exchange between Hersh Mendel and
Leon Trotsky from *International Information Bulletin* No. 1, 1935, reproduced by
permission of the Socialist Workers Party, New York.

Photographs reproduced by permission of J.S. Hertz; S. Fischer Verlag, Frankfurt am
Main; Progress Publishers, Moscow; Institut für Marxismus-Leninismus, Berlin;
Państwowe Wydawnictwo Naukowe, Warsaw; Tamara Deutscher. Every effort has been
made to trace copyright holders. Any omissions will be rectified in subsequent editions if
requested.

British Library Cataloguing in Publication Data

Mendel, Hersh
    Memoirs of a Jewish revolutionary.
    1. Mendel, Hersh   2. Jews—Poland—
    Biography   3. Jewish radicals—Poland
    —Biography
    I. Title
    943.8'004924   DS135.P63M465

ISBN 0-7453-0264-5

CONTENTS

Translator's Note

The following edition of Hersh Mendel's memoirs was translated from Nele Löw-Beer's and Jakob Moneta's German translation and checked line for line against the Yiddish original. Isaac Deutscher's preface to the original edition, on the other hand, was translated from the Yiddish and checked against the German translation. Substantial discrepancies between the Yiddish and German translations of Deutscher's Polish-language preface are duly noted in the present edition.

Aside from the footnote on page xviii by Isaac Deutscher, the footnotes in this translation have either been taken from the German edition (denoted by the abbreviation "GE") or added by the present translator (as denoted by the abbreviation "trans.").

Several errors in dates appear in Hersh Mendel's text, which, in keeping with the author's wishes, have been corrected for this edition. In his reply to a critic, which appeared in the Bundist journal *Unser Tsait (Our Times)* Nos. 1-2, January-February 1961,[1] the author remarks: "1. In regard to three inaccuracies in the dates: these mistakes are indeed mine and are truly regretable. I noticed them earlier, but it was already too late to correct them. When the book is translated, the errors and the dates will be set straight." The critic, J.S. Hertz, notes in his very unfavorable and rather idiotic review "Remembered or Invented"(*Unser Tsait* No. 11, November 1960[2]) that the author mistakenly refers to the newspaper in which Peretz published his article imploring the Jewish workers to go to the synagogue as *der Moment*. The article appeared, according to Hertz, in *Haynt* (page 88). He further notes that Hersh Mendel incorrectly refers to the "Cominform" in place of the "Profintern" (page 97). Hertz points out that Hersh Mendel errs in writing that the latter's first trial took place in March 1912 (page 106). He also insists that Hersh

---

[1] See Appendix 1.
[2] For Hertz's review, which manifests a Fundamental social-democratic belief in bourgeois legalism, see Appendix 1.

Mendel errs in stating that Mickiewicz, the chairman of the purge commission in Moscow, was Jewish (page 271). In referring to the date of Lyova Sedov's death as August 1938 (page 319) as well as in stating that Adolf (Rudolf Klement) was murdered in July 1939 (page 321), Hersh Mendel is in error.

Italicized words and phrases in this edition which convey emphasis are the author's own. In keeping with English style and usage, however, foreign words, particularly those in Yiddish, Hebrew, Russian and Polish, have been italicized by the translator. Likewise, newspaper names and titles of literary works appear in italics.

In the one and a half years I have spent translating and producing this book, I have received a great deal of aid from many quarters. In particular, the staff of the East Europe Reading Room of the Staatsbibliothek in West Berlin devoted a great deal of time in helping me decipher, define, and transliterate various Russian and Polish words. Their thoroughness and readiness in helping me to smooth out some of the rough edges is much appreciated. The YIVO Institute in New York City as well as a certain professor in Tel Aviv, whose name I have unfortunately forgotten, supplied me with the names of the Polish Trotskyists' various publications. It was also this same professor who led me to J.S. Hertz's review of Hersh Mendel's book as well as Hersh Mendel's reply to it. Special thanks goes to Wolfgang Plum of Delta Schnelldruck GmbH in West Berlin, who placed his typesetting equipment and shop at my disposal and who was always ready to offer his advice on various technical matters.

Lastly, I would like to thank my dear friend Jeff Pott for reading and editing the proofs. It is largely due to his helpful and very necessary editing work that the present translation has assumed the shape which it has. The responsibility for this translation, its strengths as well as its weaknesses, naturally rests with the translator.

West Berlin, 17 May 1984

In preparing this volume for publication, a number of additional acknowledgements are in order. I wish to thank the Staatsbibliothek Preussischer Kulturbesitz, Berlin, for permitting me to photograph pictures from books in its collection and for the general use of its own reproduction department. Elena S. Danielson, assistant archivist at Stanford University's Hoover Institution, was very helpful in putting me on the track of some of the publications of the Polish Left Opposition and for providing me with the register of Boris I. Nicolaevsky's collection of papers of Leon Trotsky and Lyova Sedov.

For his encouragement and his recognition of the importance of these memoirs, I thank Holger Behm of Rotbuch Verlag in West Berlin. Warmest thanks go to members of the international Spartacist tendency for encouraging me to publish this book and for suggesting prospective publishers. It is the Spartacists' socialist program and their dedication to preserving and enriching the Trotskyist archival heritage which generally inspired this translation. (For their review of Hersh Mendel's book, see "Memoirs of a Revolutionary Jewish Worker", *Spartacist* English-language edition No. 41–42, Winter 1987–88.)

Finally, if it weren't for the perceptive eye of Gloria Rom, certain inconsistencies and blunders may have made their way into the finished work.

It is a great honor to be able to present to English-speaking readers Hersh Mendel's remarkable *Memoirs of a Jewish Revolutionary*. For its honesty, its revolutionary passion, its portrayal of a relatively unknown chapter in the history of socialism, this work is unsurpassed in the working-class literature of our time. It stands out as a forthright statement of the yearnings and struggles of thousands upon thousands of nameless and faceless Jewish, Polish and Russian revolutionaries whose life's work was devoted to and culminated in the great Russian Revolution. Indeed, the fact that Hersh Mendel wrote these memoirs almost two decades after he broke from Marxism testifies to the power of the Bolshevik idea of socialist world revolution and the depth of his dedication to it.

Memoirs of a Jewish Revolutionary is a book about Poland the oppressed and Poland the oppressor. From tsarist-ruled pre-independence Poland to the post-independence Poland of the dictator Pilsudski, Hersh Mendel was an enemy of all forms of nationalism. Born of East European Jewry, an essentially stateless people which lived at the transnational junctures of modern history, this revolutionary could with equal venom condemn Russia's rape of Poland and Poland's rape of West White Russia and the

Ukraine. To Hersh Mendel, who in turn identified himself as a Jewish, a Polish and a Russian socialist, the only solution to the crisis facing mankind in the Twentieth Century was the brotherhood of peoples.

The topicality of this internationalist message bears special importance today for Poland, for not too many years ago this country was on the verge of a social counterrevolution under the clerical-nationalist leadership of Solidarność. A pro-imperialist movement which even today is steadily eulogized by the Western bourgeois media, Solidarność harked back to the "independent" (i.e. capitalist and anti-Soviet) Poland of the interwar years—the Poland of anti-working-class terror and extensive peasant land hunger, the Poland of anti-Semitism and national oppression. In Hersh Mendel's day this regime was reviled the world over; in answer to it he and his comrades fought for internationalist unity and the organization of the Polish working class to spread the Russian Revolution westward—to Poland, to Germany and beyond. Not the anti-communist, anti-Russian nationalism of a Solidarność, but the internationalism of a Lenin, a Trotsky, a Rosa Luxemburg or a Hersh Mendel will lift Poland out of the cycle of economic crises and free it from its Stalinist stranglehold.

Great changes are taking place in the Soviet Union today. With the inauguration of Gorbachev's program of *Glasnost* (openness) and *Perestroika* (restructuring) the working class faces a campaign of increasing labor discipline, the institution of market-orientated decentralization and the attendant problem of future layoffs. At the same time, however, a vibrant intellectual ferment has taken hold, and there is increasing interest throughout Soviet society to uncover the truth about the distortions, the gaping holes and the lies of the Stalin era. It has been reported that young people have taken an interest in books of quotations from Lenin and, most notably, Trotsky. It is in this situation that Hersh Mendel's memoirs could find a very appreciative and receptive audience. Also in the light of continuing anti-Semitism in the Soviet state apparatus and the resurgence of traditional anti-Semitism as symbolized by the fascistic Pamyat (Memory) movement, *Memoirs of a Jewish Revolutionary* could well serve to remind Soviet Jews that it was precisely the October Revolution which pledged to emancipate their parents, grandparents and great-grandparents. As a reaffirmation that the defense of Russian Jewry was central to Bolshevism, these memoirs could undoubtedly play a role in impelling many Jews to reconsider their faith in the bogus "let my people go" rhetoric of US imperialism and Israel and put such Cold War Zionists as Natan Sharansky in their proper, historical perspective.

Glasnost and *Perestroika*, as the Spartacists have stressed, is directed toward improving relations with the West in the futile hope of convincing the imperialists—centrally the United States—to disarm. Historically, it was this program of renouncing world revolution in favour of "peaceful coexistence" with the capitalist powers that formed the political basis of Stalinism and which played a key role in the degeneration of the Soviet workers' state. Against the Stalinist bureaucracy and its dogma of "Socialism in One Country", Trotsky called for a political revolution in the Soviet Union, a revolution which would oust the parasitic bureaucratic caste while defending the planned economic foundations created through the Russian Revolution. Indeed, Hersh Mendel abandoned this necessary defense of the Soviet Union. In his later life he ceased dialectically to distinguish between defense of the *economic* gains of the revolution and defense of the usurpatory, privileged Stalinist *political* regime.

In response to the annihilation of the Communist movement in Poland by Stalin and of virtually the entire Polish Jewish population by the Nazis, Hersh Mendel finally abandoned Marxism. In embracing Zionism following World War II, he adopted as his own the theory of the Zionist Ber Borochov which held that there must first exist a Jewish territorial homeland before the Jewish workers could mature sufficiently to fight for socialism. How erroneous this view seems when one considers Hersh Mendel's own decades-long work among the Jewish workers in the land of his birth! But the founder of the Polish Trotskyist movement, if in error in later years, remained true to a key tenet of his earlier beliefs: the brotherhood of peoples. Readers of Yiddish will find evidence of this in a work which Hersh Mendel published in Paris in 1949 titled *An Entfer Unzere Kritiker (A Reply to Our Critics)*. While defending "proletarian Zionism", he categorically denounces terrorist acts against innocent Arabs and insists that with the economic flowering of the Near East as a result of economic competition from Israel the developing Arab proletariat will be a "natural ally of the Jewish working class in the struggle for socialism".

The Zionist establishment of Israel has of course borne different fruit than that desired by Hersh Mendel. From its "conquest of the land" policy in the late 1920s and 1930s to its present-day construction of settlements on the West Bank, Zionist colonization has led to the economic dislocation, political disenfranchisement and geographical dispersal of millions of Palestinian Arabs. Nor has the Zionist movement spared Jewish socialists. From its collaboration with the tsarist secret police against Jewish revolutionaries to the Israeli-organized massacres in 1982 at Sabra and Shatila,

Zionism has consistently shown itself to be an enemy of human freedom. Now, thanks to the courageous exposé of Israel's huge arsenal by Mordechai Vanunu, who faces the death sentence today for his humane act, it is clear that Zionism's historic anti-communism and expansionism, in conjunction with the anti-Soviet war plans of the US bourgeoisie, can well lead to another, a worldwide, holocaust. Anti-Sovietism and anti-Semitism go hand in hand, a fact symbolized by the visit of the American president and the West German chancellor to the site of SS graves at Bitburg on the fortieth anniversary of the defeat of Nazi Germany.

Hersh Mendel was right to call for the alliance of Jewish and Arab workers. In the Near East today this internationalist alliance, once forged, must fight for socialist revolution and for a bi-national workers' state embracing both Palestinian Arabs and Hebrew-speaking Jews. To this end, it is hoped that *Memoirs of a Jewish Revolutionary* will one day find its rightful place in translation alongside the works of Arabic and Hebrew literature.

Robert Michaels , San Francisco
14 December 1987

Preface to the Yiddish Edition

I would like to draw the attention of the Israeli reader to the following book—an extraordinary document from the field of working-class autobiographical literature. Regretably, I have not had the opportunity during the last decades to go through the Hebrew and Yiddish literature, and I do not know if it is rich in such works. I can say with certainty, however, that there are not many documents of this type in the world literature. Prior to the year 1939 the memoirs by the worker Yakov Voitshekovsky had a colossal echo in Poland. They in fact deserved attention; in Polish literature they occupied a special place. Although not without class consciousness and proletarian passion, Voitshekovsky was not a revolutionary. The memoirs by Hersh Mendel—the author will most certainly allow me to use his old, revolutionary pseudonym—is the work of a worker-revolutionary who, in the course of several decades, played a significant role in the Polish workers movement. More than that, Hersh Mendel's experiences had an international dimension. Even prior to World War I he was part of the Polish and Russian emigré community in Paris. He took part in the Russian Revolution as a fighter in the October uprising in Moscow and as one of the first volunteers in the Red Army. In 1920 he was a member of the Military-Revolutionary Committee of the Communist Party of Poland, the task of which was to technically prepare an uprising in Warsaw at the rear of Pilsudski's army, while the Red Army advanced on the gates of the Polish capital. He played a serious role in the struggle of the White Russian peasants and workers against Polish oppression. He led the Jewish workers of the Communist Party of Poland. He was an insider in the Communist International's organization in Moscow and was a witness and unwilling participant in the Stalinist collectivizations. In the prison holes of Poland and Austria he fought for his revolutionary dignity, and on more than one occasion he resorted to so sharp a weapon as the hunger strike. And finally, for one long decade—a time of great events, a time loaded with political tragedies—he found himself as a comrade and disciple in Leon Trotsky's circle of activity. What a life full of richness and content, notwithstanding the disappointments with which it was accompanied!

In simple, unpretentious language, which does not vie for literary effect, Hersh Mendel tells about his life. In this simplicity the working-class character of the author finds expression; he remains true to himself throughout and is worlds apart from any sort of pomp and pose. In addition, his high spiritual culture also comes to life. For Hersh Mendel is a worker-intellectual, one of the most educated whom I have had occasion to know in a number of countries in the course of almost 35 years. He differentiates himself from one category of so-called worker-leaders in this: for him, the struggle for the interests of the working class—in his best years, at any rate—was connected with the stubborn formation of his world view and with his incessant drive to take on the great problems of social life.

In his parents' dark, little attic abode, in the prison cells of tsarist Russia, in Pilsudskiite Poland, at the Lenin School in Moscow and in discussion circles of the underground movement, he avidly absorbed everything which classical Marxist literature—the economic, historical, philosophical—and which world literature could offer him. To this child of horrible Jewish poverty, a small piece of knowledge was always dearer than a little crumb of bread.

The first Russian Revolution of 1905 was like a bolt of lightning on the horizon. By its glow, Hersh Mendel read the works of Marx, Engels, Kautsky and Plekhanov. He read Tolstoy's novels, Mickiewicz's poems and Peretz' dramas. "Had it not been for the Revolution of 1905," he says on the first page of his memoirs, "there is no doubt that I would have sunk in the swamp of the underworld of Smocza Street." From that time on, every great historical watershed was also a watershed in his spiritual life. Hersh Mendel's memoirs, therefore, are not simply a description of his political struggle; rather, they are also a sketch of his stirring fight to scramble his way out of the dregs of his youth to the heights of the thought of his time. The unity of theory and practice was not a hollow phrase for him as it is for many others. For him, this was a necessity of life. He purchased it with hunger and lifeblood; he wanted and needed to understand what he was fighting for, and to fight for that which he understood.

The grimness of life accompanied Hersh Mendel in his wanderings and manifested itself in various forms. In the first place, it manifested itself in the gruesomeness of the capitalist system, with its social and national oppression. It manifested itself in the elemental severity of the Russian revolutionary storm; in the torment of Soviet society, which writhes in the contradictions of the transitional era; and finally in the Stalinist degradation of the workers movement. This is not to mention the European inferno under Hitler's occupation. In each of these phases, the grisliness of social reality dug its claws into Hersh Mendel's personal existence and into the lives of those who were nearest and dearest to him.

Merciless destiny, however, was unable to blunt his extraordinary sensitivity and the nobility of his feelings. To the contrary, it fortified his compassion, sympathy and solidarity with the abused and humiliated. Hersh Mendel does not actually talk about this character trait of his directly. As if unwillingly, he blurts it out when describing events and scenes. Example—when, with the eyes of a child, he looks at his sick and dissipating mother, who suffers from successive fainting spells. Example—when, as a political prisoner during a hunger strike, he is beaten to the point at which he is no longer able to feel his own pain, but in a remaining flash of consciousness is amazed by the bestiality of the hangmen, who have tortured a fellow prisoner (a White Russian peasant) to whom he is chained. Or example—when, as a Communist in Moscow, he is sent to a village in order to participate in the collectivization and is mortified at the sight of the senseless savagery to which the Russian peasant has fallen victim. Sensitivity to injustices and suffering guides the step of this revolutionary. It delineates his political attitude and forms the backbone of his heroic character.

I hope that the reader will not view the foregoing description as exaggerated. For Hersh Mendel is very much an authentically heroic individual. He was seen by his comrades and friends as a figure from a storybook, quite literally as a legend in the reality of prewar, Jewish working-class Warsaw. He is conscious of his heroism, but he is able to speak of it with humor and almost with self-irony. At times, his sense of humor dictates scenes to him which are reminiscent of a Hašek or Chaplin. But "literary" humor it is not; rather, it is almost unconscious, for it is derived from the depths of truth. In order to be convinced of this, it will suffice to read over Hersh Mendel's description of his conduct during the

October uprising, when he thrusts himself into the defense of the Moscow Soviet and takes up his post without even knowing how to fire a simple handgun. The charm of these memoirs, among other things, consists of this: there is an intertwining of pathos with humor, which the reader will not find on just one page alone.

At various times in earlier years I asked myself the question: which of Hersh Mendel's character traits were fundamental in his coming to play a leading role in the communist movement? At first glance, he did not possess a single one of the assets which distinguishes a leader. He was not a good organizer; for work of this nature he was much too absent-minded and "romantic." Yet as few others, he would kindle, enthrall, recruit and draw into the underground work a great many young and old comrades. A speaker he wasn't; he possessed neither the talkativeness nor the gestures of an orator. Nevertheless, masses of workers at rallies and trade-union gatherings listened with bated breath to him, as to few others. Nor was he a theorist. Yet his theoretical thought had an exciting impact on people. As an autodidact, he knew a number of European languages. Yet he did not master a single one of them. In fact, he is only able to speak Yiddish. On more than one occasion, however, I heard him speak in circles of Polish writers and intellectuals, making do with a fantastic mixture of broken Polish and broken Russian. Downright odd was the first impression one got from hearing him speak. But after a few minutes, those present let his peculiar "pogrom" against both languages pass in one ear and out the other, while listening to the wonderful speaker with ecstasy and esteem.

Without the help of normal means of expression his thoughts, so to speak, sufficed to propel his listeners. What was it in Hersh Mendel which attracted men from such different backgrounds? It was the high tension between thought and will which one gleaned from him, the flame of revolutionary spirit which flickered in him and which gave itself over to others.

Hersh Mendel is a human flame; he embodies the revolutionary nature of the Jewish worker of yesteryear, of whom Lenin was wont to say: with his blood he "oiled the wheels and gears of the revolution."

I initially referred to the international dimension of Hersh Mendel's political experience. But from Moscow as well as from Rostov, from

Berlin as well as from Paris, Hersh Mendel returned each time to
"Murdzhel," to our old Muranów district in the very heart of Jewish
working-class Warsaw. It was there that he was in his own element;
there he restored his psychological balance. There too he revived his
energies and entered the fray with new impetus. There he found his
own tenor again, a tenor which harmonized with the voice, the experiences, the feelings of the Jewish proletarian vanguard. That vanguard,
in turn, used to fill out the best portion of his own nature. Indeed,
it is from this that his memoirs derive their value as a historical document. We have here not only a self-portrait of Hersh Mendel, but rather of the fighting Jewish-Polish workers in general.

Unfortunately, this worker is a thing of the past. For the new generation of Jewish readers in Israel, apparently, he is not merely remote;
rather, I fear that he is an unknown and incomprehensible figure. I hope
that the following pages will draw him nearer. From the very depths of
misery and oppression, this worker gained and demonstrated his sense of
pride and his astounding courage. Shut within the confines of the Jewish
quarter's narrow streets, in his musty and dwarfish cellar workshops, his
thought came to embrace the broadest world horizon. [1] With the fiber
of his body and soul he experienced the destiny of the Russian Revolution. He passionately absorbed the "storm over Asia," the social upheav-
al in faraway China. He was deeply alarmed by the portents of catastrophe seething in the life and death conflict between the German workers movement and Hitler. And in precisely the same way he experienced
firsthand the rise and collapse of the People's Front both in France and
Spain. In his hopeless isolation and powerlessness he did, however, as
an internationalist, sense his relationship to all of these issues and never
lost his hope. Such a man as this was not to be found in those years
merely in the person of the author of these memoirs. Such men were
our own comrades: the Nathans, Itzhaks, Daniels and so many other
nameless dreamers and fighters for the revolution. Those vital human
flames, which were extinguished in Hitler's ghettos and gas chambers,
also included the likes of Mania Shumik, Hersh Mendel's wife, who was

---

[1]   This sentence in the German translation, which was corrected against Deutscher's Polish original, reads
     as follows: "Shut within the confines of the Jewish quarter's narrow alleys and its musty and dwarf-
     ishly tiny cellar workshops, often without contact to his Polish neighbors on the other side of the street,
     his world of ideas nevertheless embraced the broadest horizon." (trans.)

a simple worker from a small shtetl, a worker of strong character and intelligence.

A quarter of a century has passed since I had the good fortune to work in their surroundings. In the intervening years I have become acquainted with a number of other environments in various countries in Europe and America, but nowhere have I again found this broad, political horizon, this devotion to ideals, this sacrifice, this courage, which animated the Jewish worker of past generations in East Europe. I know just how much poorer the world became when the heart of that worker ceased to beat. Perhaps the new Israeli reader will sense at least an echo of that pulse upon reading Hersh Mendel's book. By way of this echo, perhaps, he will feel the depths of the traditions of the old Jewish workers movement and internalize something of it as his own.

I do not want to leave the reader with the impression, however, that I am in agreement with Hersh Mendel's present conceptions. Regretably, our political paths have veered apart. I will not discuss here our differences regarding the Jewish national question, for this question does not fall within the scope of the topics which Hersh Mendel touches on in his book. (The reader, presumably, will at least acquaint himself with the dispute over this difference of opinion through the polemical commentaries which the Israeli press has recently devoted to my position on the policies and perspectives of Israel and the Jewish question in general.) It would also be pedantic of me to correct certain details of Hersh Mendel's story where his memory has led him astray.[2] I cannot conclude this preface, however, without a short critique of Hersh Mendel's attitude toward the Soviet Union and his views regarding the history of the Russian Revolution. For this attitude and these views have a negative impact on the last part of his personal account, particularly when he describes our common struggle in the ranks of the Communist opposition in Poland.

"Following our expulsion from the party," says Hersh Mendel, "we found ourselves in a tragic contradiction.... We already knew that we had nothing but the worst to expect from the Stalin regime...but psychologically, we were not prepared to completely break with it." Hersh

---

[2] I merely wish to note that Hersh Mendel exaggerates when he speaks of my ostensible willingness to make sacrifices in supporting comrades and friends.

Mendel also sees Trotsky's own tragic contradiction in the "politically
unfathomable" position of the latter, who, even in the midst of the grimmest struggle against Stalin and Stalinism, "did not renounce his policy
of the unconditional defense of the Soviet Union" against the capitalist
countries.[3]

Hersh Mendel maintains today that this position is absurd, and the
fact that Trotsky so stubbornly clung to it is simply interpreted by him
as... psychological inertia. The reader gets the impression that according
to Hersh Mendel the October Revolution ended with a complete social
and moral crash, that there is absolutely nothing remaining of its con-
quests which is worthy of being defended. In other words, the victory of
Stalinism simply means the triumph of the counterrevolution, which has
continued up until the present day.

This was not our view when, with Hersh Mendel, we undertook the
struggle against Stalinism in the Communist Party in Poland. Nor is this
my view today, more than a quarter of a century later. We were convinced that in spite of all the crimes and absurdities of Stalinism, the
main conquest of the October Revolution remained untouched—social-
ized property in the means of production. To be sure, this by itself is not
socialism; it is, however, its principle precondition and makes it possible
for Soviet society to develop toward socialism. We saw a contradiction
between this progressive side of the Soviet Union and the bureaucratic
Stalin regime, which inhibited, to some degree pushed back and crip-
pled the development of Soviet society, or which forced the society to
pay for its every step forward with inhuman and unnecessary sacrifices,
exacting from all social classes a heavy tribute in favor of the privileged
bureaucracy. We saw this double character, this contradiction between
progress and reaction, in all aspects of Stalinism. In defending the Soviet Union we defended, according to our conception, the socialist elements of its social structure not only against its class enemies, but against
the Soviet bureaucracy itself.

I do not believe that this position was derived both by Trotsky and
by us from psychological inertia or from subjective or political schizo-
phrenia. Rather, the double-sidedness of our view of the Soviet Union

---

[3] This sentence in the German translation reads as follows: "He senses the same tragic contradiction
as well in the 'politically unfathomable' stance of Trotsky who, even in the midst of the grimmest struggle
against Stalin and Stalinism, held fast to 'his policy of the unconditional defense of the Soviet Union'
against the capitalist states." (trans.)

reflected the objective double-sidedness of Soviet reality. We endeavored to grasp this reality as fully as possible, not to force it into rigid, one-sided, dogmatic formulas. Not us, but rather the facts, spoke with the language of contradiction. And this could not especially surprise us Marxists, for our convictions were rooted, for better or worse, in dialectical philosophy. Without a doubt, we made mistakes—Trotsky as well. We sometimes viewed the one, sometimes the other side of this contradictory reality too sharply and too definitely (or again, not sharply and clearly enough). From the perspective of several decades, it seems to me that these partial mistakes sprang more from underestimating than from overestimating the progressive character of the USSR's social structure. Nevertheless, our principled stance was correct. Even our partial mistakes had their grounds. They derived from the fact that we undertook the struggle in an epoch when the dark sides of Stalinism were at their strongest, in the years when the policies of the Comintern facilitated Hitler's victory and when we were tormented by the nightmare of the purges and the Moscow Trials.

Trotsky, as Hersh Mendel says, defended until his last breath his "double-sided" view of the Stalinized Soviet Union. He spent the last year of his life, the year 1940 (following the deaths of all his sons and daughters, and after the Stalinist assassin, on assignment, had already entered his own house), sharply polemicizing against those Trotskyists who—like Hersh Mendel today—reproached him for not combating Stalin consistently enough. Unflinchingly, he maintained that in the war between the USSR and Finland, the workers movement was obliged to defend the USSR, in spite of Stalin's truly bear-like clumsiness and brutality toward the Finns.[4] Today, Hersh Mendel sees in this position Trotsky's weakness. I, on the contrary, see in this Trotsky's moral greatness as a revolutionary and a splendid example of his heroically clear-sighted view of the world, a view unsullied by emotions.

It seems to me that "freed" from our double-sided position, Hersh Mendel has fallen into a narrow, emotional anti-Stalinist dogmatism, which repudiates his own glorious, revolutionary past and which is divorced from reality. Today, in the era of the Cold War, this anti-Stalinist dogmatism is in fashion. I am certain, however, that with Hersh Mendel it is not a case of going along with the trend. No man is less yielding

---

[4] In the German translation this sentence reads: "Unflinchingly, he maintained that in the war between the Soviet Union and Finland, the workers movement was obliged to support the Soviet Union..."(trans.)

to the ruling social opinion and the political fashion than the author of these memoirs. His anti-Stalinist dogmatism springs from the purest motives.[5] It is an outcry of disappointment and pain from a participant in the October uprising who cannot and will not forget the Stalinist slaughter of those who led and participated in the uprising; and from a Jew who is incapable of forgiving the wrongs to which the Jewish people have been subjected by Stalinism. Indeed, these wrongs may neither be forgiven nor forgotten. But Hersh Mendel, so to speak, has hardened in his pain and has turned his back on reality, a reality which has not become hardened, a reality which will push ahead and defeat—although again, not without contradictions and complications!—the reactionary side of Stalin's legacy and develop the progressive side.

What is expressed in Hersh Mendel's hardened pain is his solitude. Ah, if the author of these memoirs could only find himself once again in the surroundings of the Muranów district as it was—among our Nathans and Itzhaks, in our old trade unions, in the midst of the Jewish masses pulsing with the warmth of life and revolutionary passion! He would once again feel his connection with the torrential stream of reality and regain his ideological balance and the clarity of his vision. Unfortunately, that environment no longer exists—our "Murdzhel" bled to death and perished under the ruins of the Warsaw Ghetto. And Hersh Mendel— flesh of its flesh and blood of its blood—is not one of those who is able to transplant himself in different soil.

And yet, I believe that he has not lost his feeling for the historical dialectic of the revolution. It is only necessary that the dialectic liberate itself from its present muddle in order to become more transparent. This is not, incidentally, the first time that political and human disappointment have driven Hersh Mendel along the false path of emotional subjectivism. With frankness and humor, he himself tells us how, shaken by the betrayal of the Second International in 1914 and embittered toward Marxism, he sought a way out and consolation in anarchism; and how, enthralled by the Russian Revolution and attracted to Lenin's ideas, he then made the journey back from anarchism to Marxism.

I only wish that he could live to see the radical recovery of the workers movement once again and a new healing storm which will clear the air

---

[5] In the German translation this sentence reads: "His anti-Stalinist dogmatism springs from the purest revolutionary motives." (trans.)

of our times. At present there is indeed no lack of recovery symptoms!
And through its influence, I wish he could once again make a turn: this
time from anti-Stalinist dogmatism to Marxism.

And in this hope, I recommend to the reader, despite all of my reser-
vations, this beautiful book.

Isaac Deutscher
London, 14 November 1958

MEMOIRS OF A JEWISH REVOLUTIONARY

PART 1

My Childhood

*F*rom the world of literature, we are familiar with many sketches of
the lives of children who had no childhood, whose childhood
years from the first days on were devoid of joy, affection, brightness
and warmth.

This is the kind of childhood which the Jewish children from Smocza
and Gesia Streets in Warsaw had. Such children often grew up to become socialist fighters, something which happened when good fortune
was on their side and they accidentally came into contact with a revolutionary environment. They then began to grasp the social causes under-
lying this terrible injustice. They then connected the wrongs they suffered
personally with the wrongs they saw all around them, which are the
product of a definite social system. They became revolutionaries. But
most of the children later turned out to be wanton human beings, human
beings without a grain of social morality who were ready for any adventure. Victor Hugo once wrote about such children. One could always
find thirty of them who were ready to storm any conceivable barricade
without knowing why or wherefore. Life has no great value to such people; downhearted, they are ready for anything. It is just this environment which forms the topsoil of the underworld. My childhood dreams
tended in this direction too. But brighter times came, which set my life
on a different course. Had it not been for the Revolution of 1905 there is
no doubt that I would have sunk into the swamp of the Smocza Street
underworld.

I do not have anything to say about my first childhood years; they
completely lose themselves in the abyss of darkness. They offered neither a single moment of joy nor light. I will begin with my later boy-
hood, with events which have buried themselves deep in my memory,

events I have been able to scrutinize and which I reflected about at great length later in my life—during my long years in prison.

In the years 1902 to 1903 we lived at Gesia Street 39. We had already been living there a long time, but these are the years which are fast in my memory.

The courtyard at Gesia 39 was very large, and the building was rented out to many tenants. It goes without saying that almost all of them were poor. The sensation of the courtyard was a Jew who had the rank of a senior policeman. He wore a long beard, and when he died everybody continued to praise him. Why? Because a man who had not shaved off his beard was ever and always a Jew.

There was a gate in the corner of this large courtyard which led to a smaller courtyard. The WC, which all the tenants shared in common, and the garbage bins too were located there. Whenever you went anywhere near it you were assaulted by a stench so terrible that you walked by but quick. Near the corner of the courtyard there was an entrance to the building; this led up to the third floor and that's where we lived. A long, narrow hallway led to our apartment. When I was arrested in 1912 and taken to Warsaw's Pawiak, with its dark, long corridors illuminated by oil lamps the whole day through, I was reminded at once of the corridor at Gesia 39.

When you opened the door to our abode, it was hard to tell just what lay in front of you: a room, a kitchen or a continuation of the long, dark corridor. The room was long and dark. There was a window at the end of it—simply a hole in the wall which had obviously been designed in such a way that not one single ray of light could beam in from outside.

The room had a door to the left, which opened up to a tiny cubicle. This was my father's workshop, which he was but seldom seen to leave. There were six of us in the apartment: my father and mother, three sons and my only sister. There were once ten children, but six of them had died.

My father was a large man, broad-shouldered and healthy, who wore a long, black beard. In later years, as he went grey from suffering, he looked like one of the apostles. I saw such faces again years later in the Orthodox paintings hanging in the Moscow museum.

My father never conversed with us kids. In general, he was an exceedingly taciturn man, and besides, he did not have much time to talk because he was always working. On Saturday nights he would immediately dive into his work for another entire week following the *havdalah*. [1]

No matter how late I came home and every morning when I woke up, he was always in his small workroom. It seemed to us kids as if he worked all the way through from the close of the Sabbath to the lighting of the candles on Friday evening without taking any breaks.[2]

My father's trade was fulling, a branch of the tanning industry. This sort of work was hard and dirty. I simply never understood how he was able to work so hard so late into the night. He had no clothes to change into for the Sabbath and he went to pray wearing his filthy work suit.

It originally astonished me that my father kept so persistently silent. But it later became clear to me that it was the yoke of a difficult life which made him so. Despite how hard my father worked, we lived in our hovel in great want, so much so that my mother became ill from it. She contracted a serious, chronic ailment.

In his family my father was the one and only worker. Everybody, therefore, treated him with contempt. My grandfather was one of those who had studied the holy scriptures; he was the owner of a house on Wołynska Street. Already more than 60 years old, he married once again because he did not want a simple worker saying *kaddish* for him.[3] My father's entire family refused to forgive him for being a worker. Why he became a worker I never learned. I only knew that he felt ashamed and dejected, and that because of this he suffered and kept his thoughts to himself.

In contrast to my father, my mother was small and weak. The wig which she wore covered her completely. I have often asked myself where she got the strength to carry it on her head.[4] Despite her frailty she was the head of the family, and the children loved her dearly. However, her serious illness oppressed all of us. Any excitement at all and she fell into a faint. We would attempt to revive her by massaging her temples, but it was occasionally some minutes before she regained consciousness. Quite often, it seemed as if she would never come to again at all.

My older brother Shlomo bore a strong resemblance to my father. He was a big, healthy, honest worker. In later years, after he got married, he made a good and warm father. But back in those days, his life was full

---

[1] *Havdalah* is the ceremony differentiating the holy Sabbath from the profane weekdays. (GE)
[2] The lighting of the candles announces the beginning of the Sabbath. (GE)
[3] Prayer said by a mourner, generally a son, for a dead parent. (trans.)
[4] Strictly orthodox Jewish women cut their hair short after getting married and wear wigs. (GE)

of contradictions. On one hand, he was an honest proletarian who worked together with my father; on the other hand, however, his friends came from the underworld. I later understood why. In our life stamped with great want, immersed in hard work and lacking the elements of education and culture, the underworld seemed to be a world of freedom. All proscriptions imposed on things by tradition, law and morality were of no value to my brother and his peers. They risked and led wanton lives, they were afraid of nobody, and this is what attracted the children from the cellars and attics. My brother too landed himself in this environment and it came to dominate him. When my father came home from the tradesman on Friday evenings and paid out the weekly wage to my brother, his friends were already waiting for him. We knew that they were not on their way to the synagogue to pray, but rather to their favorite pubs and taverns. My brother would run through his money on Saturdays, pawn his Sabbath suit on Sundays and get it out of hock again by the time the following Sabbath rolled around.

I turned nine years old in 1902 and entered the Talmud school located at New Miła Street 63. Instruction there was free. I cannot remember one single joyful hour. Obviously, my teacher did not know very much about education. He loved to hit the bottle and had a red nose. The teacher's wife did a bit of a business on the side as a vendor and sold candy and cookies to the children. Everything cost a groschen. Although the teacher held a whip in his hand, he seldom used it. His lessons were given to several of us at once; he would recite something and we would have to babble it back. Since we were all supposed to hear him, he screamed at the top of his lungs and we screamed in return. Was I a good pupil? Yes, I believe so, for the teacher never once scolded me. And on Sabbath, when I was taken to grandfather's in order to hear him read that weeks's excerpt from the Torah, he always honored me with a glass of wine. When my father took me out of school and made me his helping hand, my uncle came running (and he never came otherwise, by the way, because my father was a worker), ripped open the door and roared: "Moshe, you've committed a great sin. You've dragged Hersh-Mendel away from his studies. You'd better know that there's a storm on the loose in heaven." That said and done, he slammed the door. From that time on, we never saw him again at our house. I gather from all of this that I wasn't a half-bad student, even though I quickly forgot everything I had learned at the *heder*.

Instruction at the Talmud school lasted the entire day, with a break in the afternoon. I always went home for lunch with my heart pounding away. My mind was not on eating; I was preoccupied with the thought, would my mother have one of her fainting spells or not? I was overjoyed whenever she wasn't feeling faint, and that small piece of bread with herring was a festive occasion for me. Whenever I found her on the verge of collapsing, however, I was unable to swallow a single bite. I was used to getting home from school at seven o'clock in the evening, having a bite to eat—bread with a pickle or herring—and going to help my father until late in the night.

Working with him as I did, under the faint glow of the small petroleum lamp which threw off hardly any light, I yearned for something which could give me a little joy and brightness. Quite often I tried to get away and go off to school on Saturday afternoons. The kids gathered there and sang and danced on the tables. But that did not satisfy me either. So I looked for something else: each Saturday I fought brawls with Polish kids. And they were not always the aggressor.

In those days, I was deeply envious of my brother and his friends. They went out on Sabbath with walking sticks in their hands and drove around in droshkies. This kind of daring appealed to me. My dream at the time was to grow up fast so that I too could drive around on Saturdays in a droshky without being afraid of anyone.

My sister, who was older than I, was very beautiful and her character was similar to my mother's. She did not have particular capabilities. There was no question whatsoever of sending her to work, for this would have made the blotch on the family all the blacker. It goes without saying that she did not receive any education either; everybody thought it was unnecessary. She therefore did the same thing that all other poor girls did; she went dancing every Sabbath in the dance hall where she met her boyfriends and girlfriends. But even they were unable to affect one single change in our difficult lives.

Only later, after I became a revolutionary and an activist in the Bund, did I learn that by 1903 this organization had already created a widely-branching network of workers' circles in Warsaw. There were also Zionist groups, but they were unknown to us on Gesia Street. No ray of light had as yet reached us, no sound had as yet broken through. We were still living in deepest darkness.

Spring Approaches

In the year 1904 our material situation began to improve. There were two reasons for this: first, the war with Japan; and second, the beginning of the strike movement.

We experienced practically nothing of the war with Japan. It played itself out in faraway Manchuria, while we in Warsaw lived at the other end of the Russian empire. In general, nobody said a word about it in our home. There were merely events of a minor character which reminded us of the fact that a war was on. Across the way from our gate on Gesia Street was a large barracks. A regiment from Volhynia was quartered there. From time to time soldiers from these barracks would march off to the front and the word would go around that they were off to the war against Japan. It may be that the war did not get much mention in our home because none of the members of the family were of draft age. Not only did we not perceive it as something bad; to the contrary, it was due to this war that our material situation improved appreciably. My father prepared leather for military boots, and because it meant more work he took on two additional workers. In later days, when I studied the history of the Russian revolutionary movement, I was able to ascertain that it was not only for our family, but rather for Russia as a whole that an economic upswing had set in. And in the Marxist literature the question was posed: in an economically ascending situation such as this, how is a revolution possible?

Leon Trotsky asserted that the conditions for revolutionary struggles are better for the working class in periods when the economy is on the rise. In crisis times the worker conducts a struggle of despair, while in times of economic revival he is filled with a greater sense of pride. He improves his material situation, and through this a sense of dignity arises which propels him into revolutionary action.

But all of these problems were still foreign to me at the time; I only saw that we had taken on new workers and that our earnings were better.

The second reason for the improvement in our material situation was the strike movement. Traces of this movement in the workers quarters were there for all to see, although nobody in my family had as yet been on strike. Neither my brother and I as helpers went on strike, nor did the other two workers belong to the vanguard of the strikers. Yet our wages were increased. This was explained by the specific conditions in our branch of industry, with its many small workshops employing between three and six workers. Since the trade union wanted to be certain that the workers were in fact receiving the stipulated wage rates, they also established a rate which the master artisans were to demand from the tradesmen. In order to avoid competition, tradesmen were not permitted to parcel out work to another master. Given this arrangement, it was not only the workers who profited from the strike, but rather the masters as well. That went for my father too, who, like all other masters in this branch of the economy, benefited from the new rates.

The improvements in my family's material situation were very quickly tangible. My father now got out of his dirty work pants when Sabbath rolled around and put on a pair of Saturday trousers. They bought me a Saturday suit. We no longer boiled a pot of water on the stove on Friday nights in order to deceive the neighbors into thinking that our Sabbath dinner was in the making. No longer did my father say the *kiddish* over *hallah*. [5] My mother was now able to prepare the Sabbath like all other housewives. It was no longer a day of sighs and tears, but rather a day of joy and rest. We even began to put some thought into a better apartment. My brother had gotten engaged, my sister too was grown up, and we needed a prettier apartment so that my brother's bride and my sister's future bridegroom could come to visit without us feeling ashamed.

In comparison to the apartment on Gesia Street, our new apartment at Pawia Street 51 was paradise: one large room with a big window and, in addition to that, a large kitchen too. Half of the kitchen was partitioned off for my father's workshop. It was bright and warm all around us, although the new apartment had one big drawback: the WC and the garbage bins were located on either side of the window. But we were so happy about the spaciousness and brightness of our new apartment that we didn't pay it any heed. My brother got married at the end of 1904 and that gave us even more room in our abode.

Our cultural level also improved. We began buying a newspaper each day, for we wanted to know what the situation at the front was. The

---

[5]   *Kiddish* is the Sabbath blessing over wine. When one is too poor, however, to buy wine he recites the benediction over hallah, or braided egg bread. (trans.)

radical transformation of our lives did not come at one stroke, but we did sense that something had changed for the better. At the age of twelve I was already a good—yes, even a qualified—worker. I was already capable of filling in the slot of an adult. During work my brother would tell stories the likes of which I had never before heard. In general, he loved to tell about the heroic deeds of his friends from the underworld, but all of a sudden his narratives began to go off in new directions. And it was this which pointed to the moral watershed in my brother Shlomo's life.

He told us that in Russia secret groups had formed whose members stemmed from the imperial court itself. They had taken it upon themselves to murder the emperor, kill the ministers and the rich and distribute everything to the workers. It was just the primitive form of this tale which made so enormous an impression on me and captivated me so. During this same period, boys from our courtyard came around and sang a song whose every stanza ended with the words: "Beat the pig, the great hero." This was a satire against the tsar who had been defeated by the Japanese. But this song made a strong impression on me. I was astonished that such people actually existed who dared to call the emperor himself a pig. And when my father got himself all worked up over these songs and drove the gang away, it only elevated their significance for me even more. It was in this way that my longing for the underworld melted away, for what significance could the dream of a Sabbath stroll with a walking stick in my hand or the dream of a forbidden droshky ride have in comparison to the idea of giving the tsar a thrashing?

Such moral transformations had not only taken hold of my brother and me; my sister's whole world changed as well. It used to be that the friends whom she brought home were simple girls who had no other interest than to go out dancing. All of a sudden she began bringing home a totally new set of friends, who were something else again. They naturally went dancing every Sabbath as well, but their conversations had nevertheless begun to touch on other subjects. They talked about politics, about strikes and above all sang revolutionary songs. The first song I heard them sing was the old Bundist *Shvue*.[6] What an impact the *Shvue* had on me. Moreover, it was the first revolutionary song I had ever heard.

---

[6] *Di Shvue*, the *Oath*, was a Bundist hymn. Its opening line is:
"Mir shvern, mir shvern, mit blut un mit trern..."
"We swear, we swear, with blood and with tears." (GE)

So it was perfectly natural that I conceived of Bund and revolution as one and the same thing.

The revolutionary, socialist mood forced its way through the smallest crack, turning our feelings, our whole way of thinking around and around. But just the same, things old and familiar stayed the way they were. It still took several months before everything radically changed, before my brother and his friends decided to go over to the side of the workers.

In the meantime, my brother's old friends from the underworld still came around. After work they got together to play cards. What was interesting was that we all loved this bunch. My father and mother, both honest working people, used to be brought to tears whenever one of them ran amok, that is, was arrested during a robbery. Even I, filled to the brim with revolutionary thoughts though I was, felt attached to them. Maybe it was because we found them ready to lend a hand in moments of danger.

A Polish woman and her husband, a Russian, were neighbors of ours. She did the laundry for us. Practically every time she brought the laundry back, her drunk and brawling Russian husband came along too. He would try to pick a fight and rant and rave. Other Poles lived in the same building, big anti-Semites. Whenever my sister brought her girlfriends and boyfriends home, the Poles would often throw rocks through our window. On one occasion, in the middle of one of the Russian's typical commotions, he was joined by these Poles, and together they proceeded to beat down the door and smash the windowpanes. Just then my brother came home, saw what was up and ran off to fetch his friends. Bursting in like a storm, they got down to business and dealt the attackers their share of well-placed blows. Nobody ever bothered us again. The gang came around every single day to see if we were being left in peace. Who knows how long our love for the revolution would have coexisted with our friendship toward the underworld had events not intervened which forced us to take a stance: for the revolution—or for the underworld.

In 1904, when the strike movement began to spread, the workers' struggle against the underworld sharpened. The reason for this was that a particular group within the underworld, the "tribute collectors," had come into being. Each Friday, when the masters paid out wages to the workers, the "tribute collectors" were on the lookout for them and demanded their cut. The workers paid them a "tribute," as this duty was called.

They were a terrible plague, these "tribute collectors," a real pestilence. They were genuine parasites and the workers were afraid of them because they were forced to yield to them a part of their wages.

When the strikes began, the masters bribed the "tribute collectors" to go out and terrorize the workers and force them back to work. It was a matter of course that wherever the workers were on strike they immediately exchanged blows with the underworld. At the beginning the workers went back to work from fear, but as time went on, as the strike movement became a mass phenomenon, the conflict with the underworld became stronger and ever more exacerbated. And by no means solely among simple workers, but rather among the trade-union organized as well. The underworld was too primitive to understand the new order—the immense power which had grown out of the working masses—and they had no desire to abandon their privileges. This led to a situation in which the struggle against the masters became at the same time the struggle against the underworld. The fight deepened and sharpened from day to day until it came to open, mass-scale confrontations.

That is what happened during the first great strike, in which the workers from every calling laid down their tools and streamed into the streets in order to have it out with the underworld. One of these pitched battles in the year 1905 lasted several days. That time, the workers laid waste to all the bordellos, beat the fences bloody and tracked down the underworldniks where they lived with the aid of drawn-up lists. Not seldom were pimps and thieves thrown from windows. They were forced to quit the center of Warsaw and to dig themselves into the old town along the Vistula, where it was in fact difficult to get at them. That's why they called their refuge "Port Arthur."[7]

At the beginning, the police stayed neutral in these battles. They thought that the workers would be beaten. When it later turned out, however, that the workers were winning, the police came out on the side of the underworld and together with them arrested the workers in droves. It worked like this: a military patrol led by a policeman combed the streets, while one of the underworldniks—with a revolver in his hand— accompanied them and pointed out which of the workers to seize. This dragged on until 1907—that is, until the complete victory of the reaction.

---

[7] Port Arthur, scene of the rout of the tsarist fleet in the war with Japan, 1904. (trans.)

I remember a discussion we had at home about which side to be on: the side of the workers or the side of the underworld. My brother and brother-in-law (my sister's husband) were unable to manage with the dilemma. To go with the workers, they maintained, would mean having it out with their own brothers. Going against the workers was also out of the question because the workers were fighting for the welfare of all the working masses and, therefore, for them as well. For months on end they were unable to arrive at a decision as to which side they were on.

But as it turned out, little by little the workers were winning. The revolutionary movement was embracing ever broader layers of the workers and the people as a whole. A change then came not only over my brother and brother-in-law, but over all of those who were regular visitors at our home. Everybody came out on the side of the workers movement; they became socialists. Later on, a part of them were to participate actively in the struggle. My brother remained a devoted socialist his whole life long.

Spring

The spring which came with the ascent of the revolutionary movement was not to be the great spring which brought freedom to the popular
masses of Russia. Spring was exceedingly short and enveloped in fog.
Everything ran in circles of confusion: freedom and fight-outs, semilegality and pogroms. It was a spring full of terror.

As early as the beginning of 1905 we children lived in hope and expectation. I say we children because I already had two friends at the time—
two schoolboys who lived in the same building as we did. I can hardly
figure out how we befriended one another. The most intelligent one was
Shlomo. He read a great deal and understood more than we did. Somewhat later it came out that his father had a small mechanical device at
home which he used to "wash" postage stamps. We learned of it when a
fire broke out there. Shlomo stole laundered stamps from his father and
sold them. That's why he always had pockets filled with money. He also
took us to the theater or to the café where he bought us cheese cake and
coffee. Even in good times, such delectable morsels as these were never
to be had at home.

I am not merely introducing my friend Shlomo here because of the
good things he gave me, but also because of the beautiful stories he used
to tell me too. He also explained how things stood with the revolution,
in his childlike manner of course.

When Bloody Sunday, that famous demonstration led by Father
Gapon, took place in January 1905, we were strongly agitated by it. Of
course we did not know who Gapon was. My friend Shlomo tried in his
way to make the events comprehensible to me. Gapon had merely
dressed up as a priest, he told me; he had been dispatched to the workers, grown himself a long beard in order to be effective and after the victory of the revolution was going to be the president of Russia. Shlomo
brought me a small photo of Gapon which was for sale at the time. To
this day, I do not know who produced it, the revolutionary movement
or a private concern.

In the course of the innocent exchanges which we struck up about our
sympathy for the revolution, differences of opinion arose. My two
friends, the schoolboys, dreamed of going to Petersburg, joining the stu-

dents' organization and helping to murder the ministers. My dreams went in a wholly different direction. The leaders of our trade union were Bundists. My sister's friends also. My brother and brother-in-law were friends with Bundists. So I naturally resolved to become a Bundist too.

Meanwhile, the general strikes began. The October general strike was not the first one that year. In the course of 1905 we had several such strikes in Warsaw. I can remember that committees sprang to life in every street. In any case, there was one such committee on Pawia Street. During the period of the general strike, foodstuffs were collected in the shops and distributed to the needy. When I witnessed how the small shopkeepers doled out their goods without a single word to the contrary, I grasped that they had already become reconciled to the thought that you had to tax yourself for the revolution. Whatever the case may be, they had no other choice. They had more respect for the revolution than for the government. Collecting and distributing the foodstuffs took place during the day. In the evenings people stayed home and played cards. It was impossible to go out at night. During the day groups of workers traversed the city smashing the gas lanterns which illuminated the streets. That's why nights in Warsaw were enveloped in darkness. But this did not terrify anybody. The terror only began later—during the days of the pogrom scare. These first days, however, were something else again—the darkness of the night catalyzed our slumbering hopes and filled us with joy. You knew one thing: the revolution demanded darkness by night. Only the tsarist reaction was afraid of the dark.

This is how the time elapsed. By day my brother helped smash lanterns and went to demonstrations; by night everybody stayed home and played cards.

The October general strike lasted much longer than the previous strikes, and hunger took hold of our household with a vengeance. Day by day the street demonstrations grew larger until news arrived that the tsar had published a manifesto addressed to the people, which promised freedom for all.

What overwhelming joy ruled the streets that morning following the appearance of the manifesto; scarcely anyone stayed home. We had lots of Polish neighbors on Pawia Street, and the courtyards were given over to mass meetings. The fighting units of the PPS[8] marched together

---

[8]   Polish Socialist Party (trans.)

with the throngs of demonstrators—guns in hand. I remember great mass demonstrations of Jewish workers as they weaved their way through every street in Warsaw. Whether other organizations besides the Bund took the lead in these demonstrations I do not know. I was always there but I never noticed any demonstrations other than those lead by the Bund.

I can no longer remember how long the general strike continued after the manifesto was published. I only know that for quite a few days following that, nobody went back to work. I wished that it would go on as long as possible. The whole thing was something particularly special for us children. You felt at home in the street. Whoever experienced the Russian Revolution of February 1917, with its mass street meetings in Petersburg and Moscow, can form a picture of what the streets of Warsaw looked like in October 1905. With one difference of course: whereas the streets of Russia in the year 1917 were filled with soldiers fraternizing with the people, there wasn't a single soldier to be seen in Warsaw in October 1905. They were kept locked away in the barracks. As for Polish policemen, only very few of them participated in the demonstrations.

This atmosphere of joy lasted a few days until the police opened fire on a demonstration at Theater Square. Many were killed or wounded. Now you knew that freedom was not yet assured, that tsarism still had the power to turn and attack. It also became clear now just why the soldiers had been confined to barracks.

The thoughts running around in my head were a welter of confusion and I was no longer able to figure out what was happening. On one hand, the revolution had won; on the other, workers were being shot at again.

The situation grew even more ominous when we got wind of the fact that a wave of ghastly pogroms was sweeping Russia and all the towns and shtetls where the Jewish people lived. Nevertheless, it seemed as if freedom had won the day, for the workers kept coming to the hiring halls again and again without interference by the police. Economic strikes were conducted, party proclamations were freely distributed and party newspapers sold—and nobody stood in the way. I was too young to take it all in. The situation was peculiar: everybody was exuberant about the revolution but feared the morrow at the same time. Later, I was able to gather from studying the history of the Russian Revolution that all the political parties at the time were experiencing these mixed feelings of joy and terror. It was exactly this feeling which was expressed in the proclamations and political resolutions. But for me, a thirteen-year-old boy, it was simply an instinctive feeling of fear. This fear only grew when, by way of the frequent calls put out by the National Democrats, the pogrom atmosphere reached us Jews in Warsaw. I only came to know who the Polish National Democrats *(endecja)* were much later. They wanted to live in peace with tsarism because they believed that the tsar was only striving for expansion in the Far East. They therefore believed that tsarism was less dangerous to Poland than Germany, for Germany's aim was to conquer the lands of East Europe. The National Democrats also saw in the power of tsarism a bulwark in the struggle against the working class at home.

This would become clear to me in years to come, but in 1905 it was beyond my comprehension. I thought that the pogromists would have to come from Russia, that when they had finished their work there, the tsar would send them to us in Poland. I had come to the conclusion that they would have to come from Russia, that they could not be indigenous Poles, because there were also Polish workers participating in the self-defense organizations. On Pawia Street there were more Polish workers organized for self-defense than Jewish workers. The Polish workers continually assured us that Poland was not Russia and that there would be no pogroms here.

Every courtyard had its committee; our courtyard was no exception. During the night the gate was locked. The self-defense groups stationed themselves at specific points while scouts took to the streets. I remember that from time to time, whenever the alarm sounded, the self-defense groups threw themselves into specially readied droshkies at the snap of a finger and hurried off to meet the threat. Aside from the active self-defense groups, there were also auxiliary groups composed of all the occupants of the apartment house, especially the Jewish ones. They were armed with whatever was at hand: axes, hatchets, knives. Men from every calling came armed with the tools of their trade. My father too was in one of these auxiliary groups. After the gate to the courtyard was locked, they stood at the entrance and waited. Their assignment was to defend the gate in case of attack.

Whole nights I stood beside my father and looked up at him—my father with an axe in his hand! I knew that he would never raise it against anybody should it come to that, any more than the other Jews would. I had the feeling that we were in fact defenseless; should an attack come, god forbid, we would all be murdered. I walked around, my heart burdened, even though there were groups of workers in the street, who were ready for battle. It was already clear to me at the time that the workers/self-defense squads would only be able to defend us against pogromists. What would happen, however, if behind the pogromists stood the police? Would the workers/self-defense groups put up resistance? I was tormented by these thoughts and felt a great fear that went hand in hand with the new feeling of freedom.

Downhill

In 1906 it became clear that the revolution was going rapidly downhill. In the summer of that year elections to the First Duma took place, but we did not take any notice of them because the workers did not participate in the vote. The sole representative whom the Poles elected was a reactionary. In the year 1906 I still knew nothing about the discussion which was taking place among the Russian Marxists dealing with the role of the Duma. The Mensheviks hoped to convert the Duma, step by step, into a normal parliament. The Bolsheviks, on the other hand, sought to turn the Duma into a revolutionary tribune in order to prepare a new revolution. The only thing I felt was that it kept growing darker and more sinister, that everything was falling apart.

Things at home also took a turn for the worse, and by the end of 1906 there was a real catastrophe brewing. But before I sketch what this difficult moment of my life looked like, permit me to say a few words about another subject.

I have often been reproached for having never paid any attention to my personal life, to my own existence. Whenever I hear these barbs it makes me melancholy to think that this was as good as predetermined by fate. Not only my life, but the life of my whole family was ever and always determined by political conditions. Whenever the slightest gusts of freedom began to blow, the streets of poverty and want became brighter and our abode homier. And whenever material conditions improved, faces looked brighter too. In 1906, when the hard times of reaction set in, our family life was destroyed. When the First World War broke out, practically everybody in my entire family died a grisly death. The truth is, there was a big difference between me and the other members of my family. The whole of life inflicted itself on them from outside; both at the moment of the revolutionary upswing as well as in the hour of defeat they were passive. For me it was the reverse: I was an active participant in the events, I chose my way consciously. But my free and conscious choice was determined by the events as well.

When I became a revolutionary I soon came under the influence of *Russian* Marxism. Marxism achieved its most revolutionary expression in Russia on the basis of Russian reality. Not only the Bolsheviks, but the Mensheviks as well were much more revolutionary than any of the Social Democratic Parties of West Europe. The primary causes for this lay in the history of the Russian revolutionary movement.

As early as the second half of the 19th Century, when the Russian students' revolutionary circles passed over from work of a purely cultural nature to revolutionary struggle against the tsarist order, they were thoroughly aware of just how weak their forces were. They relied on their moral steadfastness, even though they knew that they would die in the course of the unequal struggle. No matter how their organizations and political views may have differed from one another, the members of each and every group were bound by the same moral credo: "If you enter the revolutionary ranks, then you must give up your personal life. Give your entire life to the revolution."

The critical stance which Marx assumed toward the fighting methods of such Russian revolutionaries as Bakunin and Nechayev is well known. But it was with admiration and respect that he wrote about the heroic struggles of the Narodniks, and it was from the Narodniks that the organizers as well as the theoreticians of the first Marxist circles in Russia came. One simply has to cite such names as Plekhanov, Deutsch, Zasulich and Axelrod. Lenin was proud of the revolutionary tradition of the old generation of Narodniks. Both wings of Russian Marxism, the Bolsheviks as well as the Mensheviks, were permeated by this revolutionary idealism.

When I became a Bundist in 1911 I found an environment which was dominated by this moral credo through and through. Everyone, no matter how young they were, dreamed of giving their lives for the revolution. And this is how they remained. I cannot remember one single comrade from those days who left the workers movement in order to establish himself in private life. This goes for those who remained loyal to the Bund as well as for those who went over to other workers parties.

I have dwelt a bit upon the revolutionary morality of Russian Marxism in order to make it clear why I, a worker from Smocza Street, never thought of my personal life. Such was the environment in which I received my revolutionary training. I believe that the situation was exactly the same in the other Jewish-socialist parties. It was not without cost that the second wave of immigration to *Erets Yisroel*[9] brought such cadres along

---

[9] Palestine (trans.)

with it. My personal life was a part, but only a part, of my activities as a socialist.

I have already mentioned that the material conditions of our household deteriorated in 1906. There were two main reasons for this: first, the Russo-Japanese War came to an end and there was no longer any demand for leather to manufacture military boots for the army; second, the trade we were in was modernized. Better quality leather had been produced which had to be worked up with new tools. But my father did not have the money to buy new tools. The illegal trade union grew weaker and weaker. The tradesmen began driving down wages. In a word: we got it from all sides.

My older brother had to look for work abroad and I filled in his place. Since I did not know the work as well as he did, I worked every day until eleven or twelve o'clock at night. No way was I going to let my father's home go to ruin. It filled me with sadness to see how he had gone grey from worrying and how my mother had begun to fall sick again.

I was already fourteen years old at the time and a real worker. I decided to go to the hiring hall. The truth is, there was not much left over at the hiring hall in those days; not too many workers showed up any more. But I decided to become an active member of the trade union.

One fine day I set out. But nobody at the hiring hall wanted to talk to me. After all, I was a "proprietor's son." I noticed that the workers treated one another to cigarettes, so I bought a pack the next day and went back to the hall. Surely, I thought, the workers will talk to me when I offer them cigarettes. But nobody wanted to take them. They thought I had turned up to spy on them and report it all back to my father. Many of them had legitimate gripes—my father still owed them money for work they had done. I felt that they simply wanted to drive me away. Humiliated and despairing, I walked out the door and decided never to go back.

For some time after that, I was caught between fire and water. Without knowing it, I had ended up doing my father a real injustice. The workers had humiliated me, my father insulted me, and it all cut to the quick.

By the beginning of 1907 the trade union had already been seriously weakened. It no longer had any strength left to conduct joint strikes. But there were still strikes in individual workshops where the tradesmen were seeking to drive down costs. In such cases, the tradesmen handed over the work to different masters. These masters, for their part, kept mum about where their work commissions were coming from.

On one occasion my father brought home one of these workloads. It made me utterly sick to my stomach, but when I took a look at his grey beard and my mother's pallid face, I didn't have the heart to report them to the hiring hall. Great want was really the master of our house. By accident, a group of strikers happened to come by and asked whether we had perhaps taken on their work. My father told them no. But as they left, I called them back and showed them where the goods were. Enraged, my father swung at me with all his might, striking me on the nose. Blood flowed. Looking on, the workers said that they would not get mixed up in a conflict between father and son. I felt miserable and had to take off to bed. Crying, my mother screamed at my father that he had killed me.

I cannot remember my father ever striking any of us children—most certainly not me. What could he have against me? Ever since childhood I had worked hard. My father was a devout man, but it is noteworthy that he never forced me to pray. He knew that this meant lost time for me, that I had wanted to go forward with the work. But it seemed that he had invested great hopes in the new work, and I had destroyed them.

The next day I got to work on it. Neither my father nor I said a word about what had transpired between us. Despite everything, we loved one another immensely.

All my efforts to save him came to naught. Lacking work, we also went without our daily bread. Our landlord threw us out into the street. With sack and pack, we were forced to move into a tiny room at narrow Miła Street 11. It was hard to find work. The trade union was completely in shambles, the hiring halls dissolved themselves. That was in the year 1907.

After looking for work in Warsaw for the longest time, my father took to the province, to the small towns of Lithuania. The center of the tanning trade was located in those parts at the time. My brother set out for London. I found work in Warsaw and became the family's one and only breadwinner. My sister married and moved with us into our tiny room. When her baby finally arrived, it grew awfully tight in that minuscule attic of ours. Due to the stuffy air, my mother came down with choking spells, most of the time at night. Thus we went down to the street late at night after the gates had already been locked and sat ourselves down on the steps of a shop. That's how my mother slept through the night—lying on the stone doorstep with her head in my lap. At dawn, we went back to our hovel and then I took off for work.

I do not know whether anything else exists which binds people so closely together as common want. I began to develop special feelings for my
mother. I loved her as only a son can. Whole days and nights I thought
about her, and it gave me the shakes whenever I saw her face so much as
contort. I was really ready to give my life just to see her break out in a
smile. In return, my mother bestowed her love on me too. Her maternal
love was without bounds—not only for me, but for everything around
me as well. Later, during my years as a Bundist, she was a mother to
every Bundist in Warsaw, above all to those who lived illegally.

Household cares, hard work and my feelings for my mother in no
way weakened my longing for socialism. To the contrary, I longed for it
more and more with each passing day. I was dying to meet socialists, to
talk with them, to find in them consolation and to hear of their
thoughts and hopes for a new revolution. But I didn't know where to
meet them. I was determined to go out and look. It was simply impossible that there were no more socialists left in the world!

I had heard that socialists wore long hair, black broad-brimmed hats
and black shirts. I took to the streets in search of people who looked like
this. I walked around for hours but met nobody to fit this description.
Later, I was told that they had gone into hiding, that they had disguised
themselves with Jewish hats and long coats so that nobody would be
able to recognize them. I ran into lots of Jews in Warsaw who wore long
coats, but how was I to determine which of these were religious men and
which were disguised socialists?

In those sad times, my sole source of socialist nourishment revolved
around the speeches which the famous Social-Democratic deputy Tseretelli gave in the Duma. I read them in spiritual rapture. Years later, when
I became a pupil of Lenin's and familiarized myself with his critique of
Tseretelli's speeches (particularly his critique at the London Congress of
the Russian Social Democrats in 1907), my heart sank. I was conscious
of the role which Tseretelli's speeches had played in my life.

The situation at home grew worse and worse. My sister and her husband moved out. My father was in Lithuania in search of work. My
mother, my younger brother—he was six years old—and I were left
alone at home.

One evening before Sabbath my mother took my younger brother
to visit her sister. I was alone in our little room. It must have been
sometime during those difficult days of unemployment. There was no
money in the house; mother could not have had more than ten ko-

pecks left. This was just enough for a loaf of bread. I went downstairs to buy bread for the Sabbath and walked past a newspaper kiosk. There I saw a little book by Andreev entitled *The Seven who were Hanged*. I asked how much it cost, and when the vendor told me twenty kopecks, I stood there in a quandary. I did not have more than ten kopecks in my pocket. How astonished I was when she suggested lending me the remaining ten. Had she perhaps detected that I had spent my whole fortune? It's hard to tell, but I spent a peculiar Sabbath full of melancholy and exaltation. I cried my eyes out but I felt happy. Andreev's story would come to play a great role in my life. I already knew that I would become a socialist fighter. I was certain that nobody could divert me from this course—come what may. I loved and cherished each of the five revolutionaries in this book and each of the seven who awaited their deaths by hanging. I would have sacrificed my life for any of them. The girl Mussia, the youngest, had the strongest effect on me. I cried; how happy I was to know that there were people in the world like these seven, and in the ranks of the revolution no less. Just as they had demanded the right to die with the courage shared by all great martyrs of the revolution, my innermost yearning was that I be worthy of carrying on the struggle for which they had so heroically, so honorably and so beautifully given their lives.

In times to come, during my long years in prison—particularly in those difficult moments when I never imagined I would make it—I thought about Mussia and about how, as a prisoner, there could be no giving in to the enemy. One had to be honorable and steadfast.

The Fog Grows Denser

It grew dark and foggy in tsarist Russia in the second half of 1907. It was like being on a ship making its way through the thickest of fogs on a dark night. You stand there and look; you want to see some sign, some glimmer of light. But all your efforts are in vain. The darkness crushes you and fills you with a kind of stifling fear. The ship itself seems to be borne by a dark power. So enveloped in darkness was the whole of Russia, a darkness which sowed so much terror that it scared you to death.

In the June days Stolypin sent the Duma packing and launched his provocations against the Social-Democratic fraction. The entire press publicly accused the government of starting the campaign, but the reaction already felt so sure of itself that they were no longer constrained to pay heed to public opinion. I was strongly moved by these events, for Tseretelli was condemned to hard labor. I was no longer able to hear his speeches, the only voice which had broken through the silence surrounding me, which awakened my hopes and brought me consolation. In the Third Duma, left Cadets such as Radishchev and Shingarev repeatedly came out most militantly against Stolypin. The speech by Radishchev in which he said that the future generations of Poles would remember such sad days as the period of Stolypin's "neckties"[10] made a strong impression on me. This speech of his sought to brand Stolypin as an executioner. But these men were not the deputies for me, for they sometimes came out against the revolutionary movement as well.

By the end of 1908 things had changed somewhat. My father returned from his "exile" in Lithuania. He had been in search of work for over a year and had found practically nothing. He came home thoroughly crushed and thoroughly grey. Great want was again the rule. My earnings were hardly enough for my mother, my younger brother and myself, and with my father's return lean times began in earnest.

My father was unable to get a job in Warsaw at the time, so he went out of his way to find work for me. There were workshops in those days where one worked year-round and earned better pay on top of it. If I

---

[10] nooses (trans.)

managed to come by one of these jobs, we would be able to live modestly. Thus my father went out, combed the workshops and found me such a job. I do not know whether the master really needed somebody or if he took me on simply out of sympathy for my father.

I relished working there, not only because I earned well and was able to drive away the hunger at home, but also because the factory plugged me into an environment which seemed as if created to lead me into the socialist movement.

The master was an enlightened and intelligent man, the sole intelligent master in his trade. The room where we worked was large, bright and clean. Until then I had never seen such a workshop in our branch of industry. The production was of good quality and therefore the wages were higher than in other small factories. Unlike elsewhere, where the workday lasted until late in the night, we worked from seven in the morning until seven in the evening.

The workers there were also a special breed. Mainly they were former socialists whose interest in socialism had already waned. They rather reminded one of Andreev's portraits: tired men who longed for the quiet of family life, but in whom some trace of socialist tradition remained. In any case, they were intelligent and refined. Our conversations at work revolved around cultural questions. We talked about literature, and a recurring theme was the Revolution of 1905. I got along quite well with my co-workers.

There were also young workers employed there who would have the good fortune in days to come to participate in the socialist movement. One of them, Shmelke, became an active Bundist and because of this was exiled to Siberia. Years later in the Ukraine, he joined the Communist movement together with Rafes. Another one, whom we nicknamed Little Avremel, was a Bundist as well and went to Russia. I do not know what became of him. A third, another Bundist named Itshe, would become a Communist in Germany in later years. When I met him again in 1934 he was a Brandlerist.

We also had a one-legged Bundist working there. He had lost his other leg in a demonstration in 1905. He was an odd chap: a fiery revolutionary, a dedicated socialist, but an altogether primitive soul. He obviously had a different view of himself. He constantly gave talks on scientific and philosophical subjects. It was from him that I first heard a lecture on Darwin, but I couldn't say whether it was comprehensible or not. I doubt that he had ever read any of Darwin's works. And if he had, it is doubtful whether he had understood them. Most likely, he had once heard that Darwin was of the opinion that mankind stems from a man-like creature. And in order to explain this theory to us in a simple and tangible form, he told us that if mankind stems from an animal, that animal must stem from another, smaller sort of animal. This proves that man descended from the flea. We had fun just listening to him and laughing. His philosophical lectures were no more penetrating. It goes without saying that he considered himself a historical materialist. He popularized Marx's well-known dictum, "Being determines consciousness," and also interpreted it in his own peculiar way. Whenever he expounded the theory of historical materialism, he began with the following words: "Don't believe for a minute that you, I and everybody else are particular people. We are one person, only with lots of feet, heads and hands." It was naturally difficult to imagine such a man, but we forgave him everything.

His methods of propaganda were on the same level. His favorite example of all was to compare mankind to straw. His explanation went something like this: "Take a blade of straw, you can tear it; but take a bundle of straw, you can turn it into a mattress and sleep on it. This is how it is with the worker too—alone he's weak, bound up with the trade union he's strong." Though this contained a grain of truth, it was hard to grasp all the same just what was supposed to come out of comparing a mattress to a trade union. Despite it all we liked him immensely and treated him with respect. We never forgot that he had lost a leg for the revolution and that he was ready to give his whole life for it. He was personally acquainted with Dzerzhinsky. The two of them had been together in Siberia. Later on, when he traveled to Russia, Dzerzhinsky often lent him a helping hand. His name was Benjamin; we called him Benjamin Boydem.[11]

I was able to breathe more freely in this environment. My mood improved tremendously. And even when news arrived that Azev[12] had been unmasked as a provocateur and that a number of revolutionaries had committed suicide in response out of shame and disappointment, I reacted totally differently. To be sure, I knew next to nothing about the party of the Socialist Revolutionaries, for in those days I had yet to run into anyone who belonged to it. I only knew that this party carried out

[11] *Boydem*, literally "attic", is a nickname here for a man with his head in the clouds.
[12] Evno Asev, leader of the Socialist Revolutionary Battle Organisation and police informer. (trans.)

political terror. The exposure of Azev as a provocateur proved to me that the days of darkness were drawing to a close, that the betrayers had been gotten rid of. It was a sign that the revolutionary movement had come into its own. Admittedly, it took a long time—we still had two years to wait—but I was full of hope.

Meanwhile, I worked peacefully and contentedly. The workers at the factory often sang revolutionary songs, songs which scoffed at religion. Frequently, they also gave me books to read. I cannot imagine why the first of these dealt with venereal disease. They probably thought that I must be forewarned.

Then something important happened, something which changed my life. In the first days of spring in the year 1911 I sensed a peculiar sort of disquiet among the workers. They were whispering among themselves, they were agitated. I was the only one nobody talked to, even though I was already eighteen years old. Shortly thereafter, everything was clear: they were organizing a strike. The master in our shop was gung ho and helped out by giving advice. Practically the entire strike committee was composed of workers from our workshop and Avremel was elected the committee's leader. In the meantime, the organizing got underway.

I have already mentioned that the masters as well as the workers were able to improve their own situation through a workers' strike. And it was just then that they were in need of an improvement. Like the workers, they too had knocked themselves out and suffered from want. Thus they placed their small factories at our disposal in order for us to hold illegal meetings. The workers from the small workshops in the area all gathered in one of the larger factories. A handful of workers stayed outside and kept watch. That's how meetings took place, how we decided to strike and how the strike committee was elected.

Preparations went on for weeks, and then when June rolled around we hit the bricks.

My First Strike

The strike, which finally broke out in June 1911, evoked admiration, terror and enthusiasm. Ever since 1907 you hadn't heard a word about strikes. The brush makers and tanners trade unions in Lithuania did conduct strikes during that period, but in Warsaw it had been quiet. With our strike in June 1911 we broke through the frightening stillness of the years of reaction, and it was just for this reason that the strike not only had economic significance. It was the signal for a new era of political struggle. The fear of Stolypin's executioners began to dwindle and the revolutionary forces, little by little, closed ranks.

Why was it that precisely my branch of industry was called upon to be the harbinger of the new epoch? It seems to me that there were three factors at play here. The first was the general improvement of the economy taking place throughout the whole of Russia; the second was that the number of fullers was quite small, some 200 in all; and the third was that the fullers were employed in larger workshops, so that it was easier for them to organize.

Since this strike only broke out after long years of reaction, it was hard and bitter. Both sides demonstrated toughness, and it lasted for six weeks.

The strike was only in its first few days when we got a visit from two leaders of the Bund who had come by to assist us in the fight. This was natural; even though the Bund had already developed politically toward Menshevism, their principles of organization were similar to those of the Bolsheviks. I would say that the Bund was Trotskyist at the time—only in reverse. On political questions Trotsky's standpoint approximated Lenin's; only on organizational questions was he of another opinion. The Bund, on the other hand, was already Menshevik-minded in ideological matters, but resembled the Bolsheviks in terms of its organizational structure.

Of all the socialist parties in the then Russian empire, only the Bolsheviks and the Bund recognized the principle that the trade unions must come under the sway of the party.[13] The stamp of our association, with

---

[13] Hersh Mendel uses the formulation: parteyishe prof. fareynen. (trans.)

which we sealed our signatures, in fact bore the inscription: "trade union of the Warsaw fuller workers under the leadership of the Bund."

The two comrades whom the Bund sent to us were Bernard Goldstein and Leyzer Levin, or Leyzerke as we called him in those days. Leyzer Levin became the de facto propagandist and organizer of the strike. He traveled to the small towns of Lithuania, where the tanning factories were located, in order to collect money. If I remember correctly, we also received support from abroad.

Leyzerke's appearance—the broad-brimmed hat, the black shirt and the long hair—corresponded to the archetype of the revolutionary socialist whom I had looked for in the streets of Warsaw in 1907. He was a good speaker with his rich Yiddish, although something of a phrasemonger and a windbag. These two character traits of his only struck me later when he began a speech to simple workers with the words: "The famous philosopher Spinoza once said...". Later on, this in fact made everyone smile. One could tell that Leyzer liked to play himself up and shock people. I idolized him at the time on account of his beautiful speeches, his flaming revolutionary phrases—and also because I didn't understand him whenever he spoke of philosophy.

Leyzer brought us a great deal of money during the strike, and we distributed it among the strikers. Each week strike benefits were paid out which amounted to between one and three rubles, depending on the size of the family. Without the aid which Leyzer handed out it would not have been possible to go on striking for six long weeks.

This strike was my first revolutionary trial. Although I was confined to the turf of the economic struggle for the time being, my occupation with political matters as well was not long in coming.

I have already described how the masters also profited from our strike. That is why they frequently helped us out and placed their workshops at our disposal for our illegal assemblies. But as the strike dragged on, their support collapsed. They were all immensely poor and received no money from our strike fund. Finally, without the workers, they began to perform the work by themselves. Every master had a family—a wife and children—which he was able to put to work for the duration of the strike. In so doing, approximately half the workers' normal finished output could be produced. This, of course, posed a great danger and the strike threatened to backfire. We had to take extraordinary measures in order to shut down the works.

All of the workers in our branch of industry were mobilized to go around and make sure that nobody was working. From morning until night the workers stayed in the small workshops and kept an eye on the masters. But the latter found a way out: at ten o'clock at night, when the caretakers shut the gates and the masters were certain that nobody would disturb them, they got down to business.

We had to find a way to put a stop to the work. Thus a group of young workers was organized which took over the task of controlling the night work. (We were in fact known as the "night workers.") Our assignment was difficult and dangerous. We were to prevent the masters from working at night. But how? The gates were closed and the caretakers were in the main bribed. And another particularly difficult problem presented itself too.

In the intense summertime heat, when the larger families were afraid of suffocating in the confines of their small apartments, many people went into the stairwells to sleep. They set up camp there for the night and slept through to the morning. Whenever we climbed the stairs in the nighttime darkness in order to tear open the doors and prevent anybody from working, we also confronted human bodies. The shrieks and howls were dreadful—as were the thousand curses with which they greeted us.

The worst of it, however, were the locked gates. How were we to open them? At the beginning, we simply fooled the caretakers. When we rang the bell and the caretaker opened up, we elbowed our way in and put a stop to the work in the master's shop. But the caretakers got wise to our tricks and refused to open the gates as long as we were unable to say whom we wanted to see. Giving the master's name was naturally out of the question. So we went around during the day and jotted down the names of the other occupants. But this ploy collapsed too. The masters kept on working and the situation became catastrophic. We then resolved to take the most extreme measures.

With axes hidden beneath our jackets, we did our nighttime rounds and simply hacked our way through the gates. We then took these same axes, opened the doors to the small workshops and often destroyed the goods in the process of production. We only resorted to this, however, when it came to particularly obstreperous masters.

This night work really did me in. Additionally, my shoes were quickly worn out and I was ashamed to walk the streets during the day. I kept strictly to "night work." The police also started to mix in. They began looking for me, and I was forced to leave home and sleep elsewhere. I spent my daytime hours with one of the masters who had stuck by the strike. How ashamed I felt to be going around practically barefoot. Not only did I not have any money for food, but the master was quite poor too. It was really tough. But one thing was clear: the strike had to be won at any price. After six stubborn weeks of battle, it was won.

After the strike, I had a name in my trade. The workers chatted with me amiably and treated me with great warmth. After all, I was the organizer and commander of the "night work." They were well aware that it was largely thanks to me that victory was ours. I was deeply moved by this warm relationship to my co-workers. Yet I was not one of those who had come from outside; I too had borne what was the bitter lot of the Jewish proletarian in those days. I had experienced my father's tragedy and my mother's misery. In my mind the matter was clear: this solidarity would never end; I had embarked on the road of struggle for the cause of the Jewish proletariat. But it would be long and hard.

Soon after the strike was over—that was the end of July—I was elected to the trade-union board and made treasurer of the union.

Being elected treasurer of the trade union was particularly significant for me—it meant freeing myself from the last traces of my company with the underworld. To be sure, one would have to say that this was not peculiar to me alone, for all workers conducted themselves the same way at that time. What I am talking about is card playing.

During the lean years of 1907 and 1908 my older brother Shlomo often came over to visit. Hardly would it dawn on him that I had a few groschen in my pocket than he would talk me into playing cards with him. He naturally won each and every time, then jumped up as fast as he had come and ran out to buy a little bread for his children. Later, I would win it all back from my other brother, who was still a child. I always won a few groschen from him.

What a plague it became. Despite everything, despite all I had gone through, I could not free myself from it. Even during the years I have just sketched, I always continued to gamble.

One Friday afternoon, we workers were sitting around waiting for the master to come back and give us our pay. To pass the time we were playing cards. And there I was with the union treasury. All of a sudden, I was called to a board meeting. Of course, I was to account for the trade-union monies which I had on me. Though the treasury was in order at the time, the mere thought that I could have played away the money which had been scratched together from the workers delivered me such a blow that I decided on the spot: no more card playing. This was more than a decision, it was an oath. And indeed, since then—it's been over 45 years—I have never held cards in my hand again. Nor could I tolerate it when others played.

The fact that I became treasurer of the trade union meant that I was immediately thrown into a situation of semilegality. The stamp of the association bearing the name of the Bund was in my possession, for I had to stamp the membership books whenever I cashed in pledges.

Soon, however, the leaders of the union were scattered to the four winds. Avremel was conscripted, another fled from police repression, still another went to work in the province. I then became the de facto leader of the association. After we had won our six-week strike I not only won recognition from the workers of my union, but also attracted attention in the party circles of the Bund as well. Leyzer Levin continually invited me to tea while Bernard Goldstein invited me to the barbershop where he worked. Both of them conversed with me at length. I knew perfectly well what this was all about and was ready to do it too. But I did not want to take the first step. I felt bashful; I had the feeling that I was not yet worthy of it. In the end, it happened as it had to. I became a Bundist.

PART 2

I Become a Bundist

*W*hen I became a socialist my feelings, moods and thoughts were a web of complications. At first glance, one might think that this event in my life ought to have shaken me up. Had I not waited my whole life for it, had I not wandered the streets in search of socialists, had I not cried when I read the story of the martyrdom of the Russian revolutionaries and regretted that I had been unable to participate in their joys and sufferings? And yet, when the moment I had hoped for arrived, when I joined the battle ranks, it did not shake me up. No, I took it as something natural, something self-evident, just as the parched soil awaits the rain and absorbs it. And just as this appears normal and legitimate and surprises nobody, so it was with me in the year 1911 when I joined the Bund. This step was the natural consummation of my earlier life. I rendered an account of all the dangers which would be awaiting me. It is certainly true that being at the frontline in a civil war never entered my mind at the time. I had never read anything anywhere about such things, nor had anybody spoken to me about them. But none of the difficulties I could visualize were able to perturb me; all the more was I consciously prepared to take them upon myself. This was the natural price which every revolutionary has to pay for his socialist idea.

At the end of 1911 I was invited to my first illegal conference of the Bund, where I met for the first time the well-known Bundist leader Moshe Rafes. The conference dealt with the approaching elections to the Warsaw city council. Moshe Rafes impressed me tremendously, an impression which has never been erased by time. I met with him very frequently, both when he was a leader of the Bund as well as later, when as a Communist he came out against the Yiddish language and for complete assimilation. Even when I disagreed with him I always admired him for his iron logic. He belonged to that Seven Sisters of the Bundist leadership, which was to play a great role outside, as well as inside, the Jewish workers movement.

Even though my first illegal conference was not to leave behind any strong traces in my memory—perhaps because the activity around the elections did not amount to much and because I had nothing to do with it anyway—this conference still played a great role in my life. For my part, I drew the necessary conclusions from the proceedings: it dawned on me that good will was not enough to make a revolutionary. Much more than this, one has to come to grips with the problems of society and be able to orient oneself appropriately. It is not sufficient to *want* socialism, one has to *know* which path leads to it. I therefore made a resolution to read and study.

Today, 45 years later, I find it hard to comprehend how I accomplished this, how I finally overcame all the difficulties. I divided my time like this: after spending the entire day at work, I went home to get a bite to eat; then I went to the hiring hall and after that I generally wound up at the consumer cooperative. The consumer cooperative was my home away from home. It was impossible for me to keep out of there even one day. That's where we got the party work done, and I came to know a wonderful group of comrades who are dear to me to this day. Droves of workers came to the cooperative, activists from the various parties. But also something of a natural selection took place: comrades who were ready to sacrifice their lives for one another closed ranks together there.

When the work was done we walked each other home, for we had no desire to go our separate ways. As far as I can remember, we never spoke about personal matters, even though we were all youths and even though each of us had our own dreams. The group of comrades who forged closer ties to one another included Avremel Shtricker, Yuzhek Metalovitz, Black Katz, White Max, Asher Meir, Mendel Kamashenmacher, Itshele Kamashenmacher, Avremel Prikastshik and I.

Arriving home to our little cellar abode on Smocza Street, I would begin to read. Our apartment in the cellar consisted of one room and a kitchen. The whole family slept in this one room; the small bed in the kitchen belonged to me. Whenever I came home late at night, I lit a candle and read.

Often my father would open the door and see how deeply engrossed in my reading I was. He would stand there and mutter to himself. It was hard to understand what he was muttering, but from the isolated words which were audible, I heard the voice of fear and despair. No doubt, he instinctively sensed that my reading was no innocuous pastime, but rather that there was something inherently dangerous about it. His murmurs sounded something like this: "You'll ruin yourself and nobody will lift a finger for you." Then he would shut the door again. Later I would hear him pacing back and forth, unable to fall asleep. The next morning, my eyes would be red and swollen because I hadn't slept, and in the street I would bump my head on the street lamps.

I read a great deal of belletristic and scientific literature at the time. The writers whom I loved most of all were those who placed their talents at the service of the struggle for freedom, above all the Russian writers. Of all of them my favorites were Andreev, Gorky, Tolstoy; of all the French writers, Hugo, Zola, Mirbeau; among the Germans, Heine and Hoffmann; from Polish literature, Żeromski and Konopnicka; of all the Yiddish storytellers and dramatists, Peretz. Peretz was one man I idolized.

It was through the writings of the anarchists that I was first introduced to the scientific literature dealing with social problems. Indeed, they only exercised a certain influence over me in later years, during the period of my emigration and after the collapse of the Second International. But even in the earlier days I read Kropotkin with delight. His deep sense of humanity, his faith in the good-temperedness of human nature, his revolutionary idealism, his beautiful and sensitive style—even when he wrote about scientific problems—had to leave its mark on every young man, even if he did not go on to become an anarchist. Bakunin, on the other hand, had no effect on me. I sensed in him a kind of bombastic rebelliousness, something which is alien to the worker. His famous dictum, "The spirit of destruction is in itself the spirit of creation," did not satisfy me. I needed to know beforehand why I was fighting and what I was seeking to build so that I could get down to work and destroy what had to be destroyed. As for Stirner, I hated the man. His new society, it seemed to me, would turn the world into a jungle in which men would devour one another like wild animals. It seemed to me as if the man who had written those things had returned to the wild, as if he were abnormal.

The Marxist literature, therefore, had a great effect on me from the start. Possibly, this was due to my new environment, which was thoroughly Marxist. Of all the Marxist authors whom I read at the time, Plekhanov and Kautsky—and later Engels—made the greatest impression on me. There could still be no talk of Marx. I liked Kautsky for two reasons: first, he knew well how to present Marx in popular fashion and to spur one on to study Marxism on his own. Second, I liked him because of his struggle against the revisionists and because of his defense of the historical necessity of the social revolution. (In those days all of us in the Bundist circle were filled with faith in the social revolution.)

Even closer to me than Kautsky was Plekhanov because it was he who spoke concretely about the Russian revolution. We belonged to the same family so to speak, and besides, one felt in him more enthusiasm. There was a depth and a richness in Plekhanov's works which were lacking in Kautsky. I still had no idea that even Lenin, Plekhanov's political opponent at the time, acknowledged Plekhanov as one of the greatest of the Marxist philosophers, at least on the terrain of theory. I was well aware though that Plekhanov was more helpful than Kautsky in bringing me to a theoretical understanding of historical materialism.

I read a great deal and had discussions with comrades—and with opponents as well (for they too existed). After a year had passed I had developed into a relatively conscious representative of historical materialism and was already capable of discussing it publicly.

It is generally the case that young people first join the youth movement and only from there go on to become members of the party. It was exactly the opposite with me. After I had already been a member of the party for a time, I was invited to a conference of the youth organization, the Tsukunft. [1] In those days, the Tsukunft was not as yet a purely Bundist organization; people from other tendencies within the socialist movement also belonged to it. In 1913, when I did time in prison with Shaffran, who later became a noted Bundist, he was still one of the Bund's opponents. He made a point of saying that he would either join the PPS-Left or the Social Democratic Party of Poland after his release from jail. [2] He gave absolutely no thought to working inside the Bund. Yet he was one of the leaders of the youth organization, the Tsukunft. Most of the leaders of the Tsukunft, however, were Bundists at the time.

When one Tsukunft conference went up in smoke some time later—

---

[1] the Future (trans.)

[2] The reference here is to the Polish Socialist Party-Left (PPS-Left) and the Social Democratic Party of the Kingdom of Poland and Lithuania (SDKPiL), the party of Rosa Luxemburg, Leo Jogiches, Julian Marchlewski, Adolf Warski and Felix Dzerzhinsky. (trans.)

with all of its leaders—it was such a severe blow for the organization that it had to be completely rebuilt anew. The leader of the organization at the time was Asher Meir, a convinced Bundist. He took the opportunity to propose reconstructing the Tsukunft as a purely Bundist organization. Following this, an extraordinary conference was held in the apartment of a comrade who lived on Karmelicka Street. (We took advantage of the hours during which her father was away at the *shul*.) It was at this conference that we decided to rebuild the Tsukunft as the youth organization of the Bund.

If I'm not mistaken, this took place on Yom Kippur in the year 1911. That day, Asher (whose party name was Alek) came to me with a request. Following the arrest of the Tsukunft activists, a large archive had been left behind. Its present location, however, presented a security risk. Now it was my job to take charge of the archive, for there was a suitable place for it at my home.

We were living at Smocza Street 28 at the time. This apartment house had two courtyards. In the right-hand corner of the second courtyard there was an entranceway. Our home was located in the cellar just below that. The cellar was long and dark, and our apartment was situated at the end of the corridor. Nobody besides us lived down there. The whole cellar corridor was lined with compartments where the occupants of the apartment stored old junk and coal for the winter. Our little shed stood just opposite our room and was just right for hiding away lots of different things.

Late one night I went out to the communal WC and fetched the long piece of heavy iron which the caretaker used in winter to hack away the ice from the street. With this length of iron I hollowed out a pit and placed the archive inside. I did not take a look at everything it contained. Among other things, two flags and some rubber stamps and notebooks for recording members' pledges caught my eye. Since pledges were paid weekly instead of monthly, as was customarily the case, I laid the books and stamps right on top so that they would be easy to get to each week. I also took this opportunity to hide the trade-union stamp there. In addition, Alter Shuster asked me to hide a revolver someplace. As comrades reported to me much later, after my return to Poland in 1919, Alter Shuster turned out to be an informer.

In any case, there wasn't one thing legal about my archive. Should it be discovered, there was no doubt what would happen: a few years at hard labor. As we shall see, it was precisely this which I faced some time later, and it was only an accidental coincidence which saved my neck.

Digging away late one night—I was probably there to take out the pledge books—I heard someone coming down to the cellar. Convinced that it was the cops, I knew that it was already too late to cover up the pit again. As the steps drew nearer, I recognized my younger brother. I figured that he had already noticed something and that if I were to keep my secret from him now, he would go back on his own, take a look and cause nothing but trouble. So I called him into the shed, told him the whole story and showed him where everything was. If he wanted to see me end up in jail, I said, all he had to do was to spread it around. But since that was the last thing he wanted, he was not to let so much as one word fall from his lips. Later, my considerations proved correct. As long as it was unnecessary, he never uttered a peep to anyone. But when I was arrested in connection with the May Day demonstration in 1912, the fact that he knew my secret kept me from certain hard labor.

My First May Day Demonstration

The First of May 1912 arrived. I awaited this day with bated breath, for after all, this was to be my first participation in the great proletarian holiday. Until then I had only read about the First of May in the newspapers or heard about it through word-of-mouth. Now I was going to be an active participant.

There was still another reason why not only I, but all the comrades, were in high spirits. All of us sensed that after the long period of reaction, a new epoch lay before us. We were certain that Stolypin's executioners had lost their power to terrify. We already heard the first stirrings of the approaching revolution.

The events in the Lena gold mines at the time sent the country into a flurry of excitement. The answer of the then minister of justice Shcheglovitov to the inquiry by the Social Democratic Party fraction in the Duma, "So it was and so it will be," touched off a storm from one end of the land to the other. The workers in the factories in Petersburg reacted with a variety of mass actions. We, the youth members of the Bund in those days, welcomed each and every roll of thunder which announced the approaching storm, and walked straight into the tempest with outstretched hands. It was with joy that we awaited the First of May, the day for mobilizing the fighting camp.

There were also mass strikes in Warsaw at the beginning of 1912 which, more than anything, had an economic character. We had a strong feeling, however, that the political struggle would not be long in coming. We wanted to give the First of May a revolutionary imprint and conduct a general strike. This was our greatest dream.

What actually took place was more than a general strike. In April, an appeal by the Central Committee of the Bund appeared which called for a general strike on the First of May. We distributed the appeal in every small Jewish workshop, called on the hiring halls to strike and assembled groups of workers in the streets to explain to them the meaning of the day.

When the First of May arrived we, the Bund activists, arranged to gather on Nalewki Street, to march from there and to fetch the workers from their workbenches along the way. To this day, I do not know why this practice had caught on. I think that the workers were afraid to drop the work on their own, but when we showed up to get them they then had an alibi in the event that the police should mix in. I am not certain, however, that this was the sole reason. Those workers who laid down their tools were told to go home. It hardly occurred to any of us to report them to the hiring hall on May Day. By ten o'clock in the morning the strike in the Jewish quarter's working-class streets and alleys had become a general strike.

And there we were in the consumer cooperative growing more and more nervous by the second. Everyone asked himself: "What now?" We had no desire to go home, but hanging around in the cooperative was dangerous. The police could storm the place any minute. Walking the streets the day of a general strike, however, was no less a security risk. On top of it was that feeling of restless unease: had something perhaps transpired in Petersburg or Moscow? Had the workers fought in the streets at demonstrations there? And we were supposed to sit around on a day like this, boring ourselves and not doing a thing! From the party side no directives for us were forthcoming.

Yet we wanted to do something. Avremel Drucker, a warm comrade whom everybody liked, made a proposal. We should take to the street, toss leaflets in the air, shout out a few slogans, then change over to another street in a flash and start again. In a word: a flying demonstration. But nobody was satisfied with this. We wanted something more; we wanted to do something which would find an echo. If the following day's papers should carry the news that demonstrations and street fighting with the police had broken out in Petersburg, then they had better have the same thing to print about us Jewish workers. We had no intention of lagging behind Petersburg. White Max suggested that we organize a proper demonstration. But at first, none of us knew just how to manage such a thing. The workers were sitting behind their four walls and we didn't have a banner. To be sure, I had hidden away some red flags at home, but these flags belonged to the youth organization and not the party. And even if we did want to use them, it would have been impossible to unearth them in the middle of the day without attracting the attention of the caretaker or my family.

But whenever you want something badly enough, you'll find a way to get it. We had a comrade named Toybele, whom we called the "Bundist nurse." She took care of all the comrades. If somebody needed to have a button sewed on or a shirt washed, she did it. If someone got arrested, she showed up the next day with a care package. We asked her to go home and get her red pillow case. Then we had somebody paint the banner. This person wasn't a genuine Bundist, but he dashed off to his apartment and painted a few slogans. (I am no longer able to remember what the slogans were.) I ran out to the street and bought a pole for twelve Russian kopecks, and then we decided to begin the demonstration on narrow Miła Street. A small group had assembled at the consumer cooperative, hardly twenty people at the most. But we believed that at the commencement of the demonstration people from the street would join in. And in fact, we were not mistaken.

We had intentionally chosen Miła Street because it was small and narrow. It ran from Dzika Street to Muranów Square. The Fourth Commissariat was located there and we intended to press forward to provoke the police, for it was only then that the newspapers would write something and let the whole country know that the Bund had carried out a demonstration. Once we had assembled, the banner painter and I found a gateway where we could hoist our flag. The caretaker there thought otherwise, however, and tried to slam the door in our faces. But after taking one look at my companion, a tall, broad-shouldered man, and after seeing that I too had no intention of letting anyone upset our plan, he concluded that the game he was playing was a dangerous one which would cost him his legs. He in fact scurried off and we prepared our banner.

Accompanied by the strains of the *Internationale* and the Bundist *Shvue*, we marched off in the direction of the police commissariat. Then something thoroughly bewildering occurred: there were no police units at Muranów Square to confront us. Not having prepared for a demonstration, they were quite simply caught off guard. Nor had it occurred to them that we too were so few in numbers. So they telephoned the chief of police for reinforcements. But until the police reinforcements and their cossack auxiliaries arrived, the cops at the Fourth Commissariat were afraid to budge from their seats.

We only heard about this later, however. In the meanwhile, we had no way of knowing what was up. We turned around and headed the demonstration back toward Dzika Street. On the way back we were already some few hundreds strong. Scores of people stood at their windows and greeted us. Gates and shops were closed and our enthusiasm knew no bounds. We reached Dzika Street again but still no police. So we headed back toward Muranów Square. And that's when we ran into the cops and the cossacks.

Before the cossacks launched into battle, we attempted to counter the blows of the police. But when the cossacks finally went to town with their billy clubs, we were forced to disperse. I was carrying the banner and stuck it in my pocket. Managing to reach the courtyard at Nalewki 39, I ran out the other way toward Kupiecka Street. We called this "Krul's courtyard." I succeeded in getting home and hiding the banner away in the cellar. It later turned out that others had had less luck than I: the police had quickly barricaded the courtyard with its two entrances and arrested many comrades.

Meanwhile, there I was at home. My mother and brother brought me news about what was happening outside. There were patrols on every street arresting people for the simple reason that there had been a demonstration. I threw myself down on my bed. Nobody had the slightest inkling that I had done anything. My mother begged me to stay home, and I promised her that I would.

But that was easier said than done. What were they saying on the street? Which of the comrades had been arrested? These and other questions tormented me and lured me away from the house. And when my mother left the apartment, I took off to see what was going on in the street. Approaching the corner of Gesia and Nalewki Streets, I ran into a patrol and was ordered to show my papers. The cop shoved them in his pocket and demanded that I come along to the commissariat. I couldn't understand what he was doing. The events had transpired several hours earlier and my papers were in order. Perhaps my black shirt and black hat, the uniform of all socialists, rubbed him the wrong way.

Whoever remembers the police commissariats in Poland in those days knows that they consisted of two parts: the office and all other facilities on the ground floor, and a large room in the cellar containing a barred window. This was known as the *Koza*[3] and was the holding pen where prisoners were kept before their protocols were drawn up. I was taken to the Fourth Commissariat, that is, to the very same station whose personnel we had had the nerve to challenge so rudely earlier that day.

They brought me straight down to the *Koza*, where I ran into a good many comrades and not a few people who had been seized by accident. It soon dawned on us that we had two important problems to solve. The first involved the archive which I had concealed at home. There was absolutely no doubt that the police would find everything by searching my house and that I would be slapped with nothing less than hard labor. Upon

---

[3] Koza, "goat" in Polish, also means "jail." (trans.)

hearing about it, my dear friend Yuzhek Metalovitz began to kiss me, insisting that I draw him into the trial which undoubtedly awaited me. I was still young, he exclaimed, and forced labor would be exceedingly hard for me; it would be easier if the two of us were in it together. It didn't do any good explaining to him that although his companionship would naturally make things easier for me, denouncing him was something else again. Informing on someone was a violation of our revolutionary morality. But he stuck to his guns. Then the other comrades proposed a compromise: we ought to wait and see which way the trial went, and then decide.

The other matter was a tough nut to crack: it had to do with saving a comrade from certain forced labor. This comrade, a metal worker, was no Bundist. He was a Socialist Revolutionary whom we called Josef Metalovitz. A peculiar man, he often came into the consumer cooperative.

When he had gotten wind of the fact that we were about to pull off a demonstration, he had rushed home to fetch his party's flag. God only knows where he got it. We hadn't a clue what his plans were. But when we unfurled the banner of the Bund during the demonstration, he did the same with his flag—although he was only a Socialist Revolutionary. We were quite happy to see that he had had the courage to do it.

The problem was, he had still had the flag on him when he was brought to the *Koza,* and was afraid that simply tossing it to the ground might implicate others. If he kept it in his pocket, however, who knows how many years of hard labor he might be slapped with. The situation was difficult and we had to act quickly. Laying our cards on the table, we warned the mixed bag of people present that there had better be no snitching—or else. By then we were already so strong that we knew our warning would stick. Then the question was: what now?

Knowing that one could only be convicted according to the tsarist legal code when contraband was found on his person, not however when it was found beside him or even directly at his feet, we simply decided to drop the flag on the ground. White Max then suggested hanging it on the bars outside the window (Max was a master when it came to such clever tricks), a suggestion which was to everybody's liking. It was clear that nobody would be put on trial for it, that in the worst case we would all get a good hiding. And that, we reasoned, was no great price to pay just to pull off our little game.

So dare it we did. Even today, I cannot think about it without getting worked up. In the middle of the night on the First of May, following a demonstration of the Bund, Bundists hung a flag of the Socialist Revolutionaries out the window of the police commissariat—and the red flag fluttered in the nighttime darkness. Certainly, it didn't flutter there for long, but that short wink of the eye sent us soaring.

When the police noticed what we had done, they began to race around, to whistle and to curse in that genuinely Russian way. We anxiously awaited what was going to happen to us. But they took the flag down without laying a hand on us. We just could not figure it out.

The interrogations only began late that night. One by one we were summoned to the offices where drunk informers and policemen were waiting. The beatings began. I have to admit though that we were beaten quite moderately. One got the impression from their lethargy that they simply beat us for the sake of appearances. There was more storming than thrashing. By morning, we were all free again. A few days later a report appeared in the radical newspaper *der Fraynd*[4] stating that the Bolshevik's *Pravda* in Petersburg had been excited about our demonstration and that the action, in their opinion, vindicated the Bolshevik proposition that we were entering a new epoch of revolutionary struggle.

When I got home I learned why I had been set free.

A few comrades, seeing me being arrested and taken to the commissariat, raced over to my apartment to clean the place up. My brother was home. He dug out the pit in the cellar and removed its entire contents. They had to bring everything but quick to another location, but with the big roundups taking place in the streets, the comrades were afraid to carry such things away. So my mother hid one part of it beneath her blouse and carried the other part in a basket, and after several trips the lot of it had been brought to safe quarters. This was an excellent idea. It would never have occurred to any cop to search a Jewish woman wearing a wig which covered her entire face.

When I got home and the comrades waiting there told me all about it, my mother was standing to the side, her face beaming with joy. It was as if she was standing beneath some godly ray of light.

From that time on, my mother was often in demand for such things. She was a mama to all illegal Bundists. Whoever was hungry or homeless always found a bite to eat and a place to sleep in her little cellar apartment. Sometime later, when I read *The Mother* by Maxim Gorky, I got the feeling he was describing her. I was proud of the fact that she had become a Bundist mother.

---

4   the *Friend* (trans.)

My Second Strike

Our elation over the May Day demonstration did not last long. That same month a second strike broke out in our trade. We had accomplished a great deal in our first strike in 1911, but we still had not won back the gains which had been wrested from the bosses in 1905. This was the task we now set for ourselves in the second strike. But we suffered a defeat. Our branch of industry was probably in the thralls of a great crisis. The tradesmen took advantage of the situation; they wanted to destroy the trade union. After the first two weeks of the strike, one part of the trade-union commission called an end to it and the work resumed under the old conditions. Nobody said so much as a word to me about the decision, even though I was secretary of the union. It was only when I took to the street that the workers informed me that the strike had been terminated and lost. I was furious about it and suspected a betrayal. Losing the strike meant losing what we had fought for in 1911. I was strongly in favor of continuing it. In the street I ran into two workers who had one foot in the working class and the other in the underworld. When the working conditions were good, they worked; when things took a turn for the worse, they lived by stealing.

I appealed to the two of them by telling them about the betrayal and by asking them to help out in winning the strike. The three of us set off for one of the shops where the master had already started up the work again. Packing up the wares, we loaded them into a droshky and brought them back to the tradesman, a man who was known as Meir Parekh.[5] When we brought the goods back to him, he had some customers waiting in his office. Deliberately, we asked loudly: "Does Meir Parekh live here?" Then we threw everything on the floor. It seemed as if the workers had simply been waiting for this signal, for that same day the strike was won. But it was not a particularly satisfying occasion. The economic crisis in our branch of industry had destroyed everything; the trade union was stuck in a difficult rut all the way up to the First World War.

---

[5] *Parekh*, literally "head covered with scabs," is an unpleasant, sly low-grade person in the words of *The Joys of Yiddish* by Leo Rosten. (trans.)

Naturally, I lost my job. On top of it, there were none too few masters in my trade whose roots were in the underworld. They organized themselves to lie in wait for me in front of my apartment. I had gotten wind of the fact that they were eager to settle scores with me. But even though I was no longer afraid of them, the matter was nonetheless unpleasant. What did scare me was getting into a scrape with these people and providing the police with an opportunity to learn about my work in the Bund. I therefore thought it best to avoid getting mixed up in a personal feud with them.

Enduring a new round of unemployment was not difficult, for my father had just received something of an inheritance from my grandfather. Half of it went to my brother and sister but the remaining share, 1,000 rubels, allowed us to hang on during my days out of work. Without this money we would have gone hungry.

I spent those days studying political economy and familiarizing myself with the Bund's theory on the national question. I had not yet taken on Marx's *Capital*, but I already understood Kautsky's economic teachings and knew them by heart. Later, during my years in prison, these readings turned out to be quite useful, for it was this introduction which made it possible for me to study *Capital* by Marx. And in prison I became one of the best teachers in this field. The dry formulas of economics were richly and poetically fascinating to me. Nowhere in the revolutionary literature, not even in the works of the anarchist theoreticians, did I feel such revolutionary passion as in Marx's *Capital*. Each and every dry mathematical formula transformed itself before my eyes into a necessary historical law which led to the destruction of capitalism.

I also knew the brochure *The National Question and the Social Democracy* by heart, in which Medem grounded the theory of national-cultural autonomy. It seemed to me that here the synthesis between international socialism and the Jewish national question had been found, and I was deeply thankful to the Bund for having made me a proud Jew and a passionate socialist. Indeed, this question was already under discussion in those days. The Zionist-Socialists attempted to prove that the Bund had taken over this theory from Otto Bauer. The Bund replied that Medem had written his brochure even before the Austrian Social Democracy had included national-cultural autonomy in its program. But none of this was important to me; the only important thing was that in the Bund I was able to unite socialism with the fact that I belonged to the Jewish people. Years later, after I had become a Communist and read

Lenin's critique of the national program of the Austrian Social Democracy—a critique which seemed right to me—I still continued to draw a distinction between the program of the Austrians and that of the Bund. The Austrian Social Democrats counterposed the theory of national-cultural autonomy to the aspirations of the peoples for complete separation from Austria and for the creation of their own state independence. But the Jews in Russia could not dream of territorial independence. The theory of national-cultural autonomy, therefore, was very progressive and, as it seemed to me at the time, the only possibility from the standpoint of socialism.

Today, we know that national-cultural autonomy was far from being able to safeguard the Jews' national existence. One proof of this can be seen in national-cultural autonomy during the rule of the Ukrainian Rada. In those days, however, I knew one thing: I was a proud Jew and a proud Social Democrat.

I also took advantage of being out of work to participate more actively in the work of the party. I was already involved in the work of leading the Tsukunft group and intimately took part in the party life of the Warsaw Bund. When any sort of political action was in the works I was always pulled in for consultation, and thus became better acquainted with the Warsaw Bundist leaders. The leadership consisted of three comrades: Leyzer Levin, Henekh-Bainish and Maxim. I had already known Leyzer Levin earlier, but now we became close friends. It was quite an ordeal for me when the Central Committee of the Bund suspected him of being a provocateur and sent him to Argentina. It later turned out that he was innocent. He had been a victim of Henekh-Bainish's cop work. But until the party rehabilitated him, he was forced to endure a great deal of torment.

The second one, Henekh-Bainish, was not yet an informer in those days: this only transpired later, in August 1912. But even then, the impression he made on me was not a good one. There was something cynical and vulgar in the way he acted, and he treated our women comrades with particular coarseness. But he was smart. Theoretically, I was no less knowledgeable than he; but politically, I was a child in comparison. He was in fact *the* illegal functionary of the Bund in Warsaw. Working closely with him helped me considerably in the process of politically coming into my own.

The third was Maxim. There were numerous legends in circulation in the Bund about him. He was considered a saint, and indeed, with his youthful face and his long, broad, black beard he did have the look of a saint about him. But his theoretical and political level proved to be very low. This was a mystery to me: here was a man whom everybody deified and considered to be a great leader, and yet he turned out be a big nothing. In later years, I met him in the Soviet Union after he had become a Combundist. I was curious to find out whether my first impression had been correct. To my regret, I was forced to conclude that I had been right. All of the complicated problems which the Russian Revolution had raised only landed him into ever more confusion. He proved to be an obtuse man.

One complicated issue of the time was the Bund's organizational structure. The Bund had already overcome the Bolshevistic infantile disorder which had seriously plagued it in the days of the first Russian revolution in the year 1905. Now, in 1912, it stood in formation beside the Mensheviks and actively participated in the organizing of the August Bloc of all Social-Democratic groups which opposed the Bolshevik Party. Yet in terms of organization, the Bund still remained deeply embedded in Bolshevik principles. That is, it still only recognized party trade unions and its Central Committee determined the composition of the local committees. In the cities, to be sure, leadership collectives were elected at conferences of the Bund's activists, but these collectives led the movement in name only. Beside the collectives, party committees existed which were appointed by the Central Committee. As a result, the following situation arose: the comrades from the collectives were continually being arrested because they were known. I cannot recall, however, having ever heard that members of the Warsaw Committee of the Bund had been arrested. That a two-tier system of authority existed was clear to me, for I participated in elections to the party collectives as well. In 1913 I myself was elected. But all party proclamations, aside from those of the Central Committee, were signed by the Warsaw Committee of the Bund, a committee which I never elected.

In this way, the Bund had created a complicated apparatus: a strictly centralized apparatus modeled after the Bolshevik blueprint, but supplemented by an elected body which was supposed to express the right of the party masses to democratic self-administration.

The Warsaw Conference of the Bund in July 1912

On the first Saturday in July 1912 an activists' conference took place. Moshe Rafes, who seemed to work the Polish region of the Bund, attended as the representative of the party. I had already become well acquainted with the questions on the agenda in advance, and the agenda was extremely comprehensive: a report on the situation in the country, the relationship of the Bund to the newly-founded Bolshevik Party, the elections to the Duma and the elections to the conference of the Bund which was to take place in Vienna. I cannot remember whether or not the question of participation in the August Bloc was also taken up. What I can well remember, however, was that Rafes did not have a conference majority behind him on all points.

He suffered a defeat on the first agenda point, that is, in appraising the political situation in the country. Everybody already felt at the time that the workers movement had sprung to life again and that this revival was no accidental phenomenon, that it would change the face of the land. On the question of what was to be the next goal of the newly-reinvigorated workers movement, three tendencies crystallized (aside from the group around Trotsky with whom we were but little acquainted and whose theory we never discussed). The Bolsheviks were of the opinion that the Duma had not solved a single one of the problems which had been posed by the Revolution of 1905, and that it was therefore necessary, just as in 1905, to prepare for the armed uprising. They also argued that the Duma could, under certain conditions, bring Russia along the path of capitalist economic development and introduce a series of constitutional reforms. But because it was uncertain which direction Russia would go if these two paths were to cross one another, it was necessary for a proletarian-revolutionary party to steer a revolutionary course. Inasmuch as Stolypin's Duma could bring about a peace treaty between tsarism and capitalism in order to crush the workers movement with one big fist, it was therefore most desirable to prepare for the armed uprising and fulfill the three main demands of the revolution in a single stroke: first, a democratic republic; second, the eight-hour day; third, agrarian reform. As in 1905, the Bolsheviks maintained, merely preaching the armed uprising was not sufficient; it was

necessary to make preparations for it here and now. They took as their
precedent Marx's policy in the German revolution. He too conceded
at the time that Bismarck could lead Germany along the road of capitalism by checking the reactionary regime of the Prussian monarchy. Yet
Marx stood for the development of capitalism in a revolutionary way,
that is, not along Bismarck's lines, but rather in the manner of the
Americans.

Lenin knew that the Mensheviks would not go this way. That is why
he carried out a radical split of the party in the summer months of 1912
and founded in Prague an independent Bolshevik party. He also split the
Social-Democratic fraction in the Duma.

The Mensheviks did not officially abandon their old battle slogan of
the "democratic republic." They maintained, however, that one must
not follow the path of preparing for uprisings. They accused the Bolsheviks of pursuing a putschist-Blanquist method. More important at the
present time, they argued, was to struggle for those demands for which
all the workers were already prepared to go into battle. As a matter of
course, the rest would manifest itself later. Within the Mensheviks, however, a right-wing grouping formed which was known as the "Liquidators." The "Liquidators" went a great deal further. They were really
ready to make their peace with a "Bismarck regime" in Russia. A passionate exponent of this tendency in the Bund was Moshe Rafes. This
became clear to me from his report at the conference.

He sparked a real uproar when he pointed out that in Germany, even
though the parliament only possessed limited powers—the decisive power rested with the Kaiser while the Junkers held many privileges—the
German Social Democracy had nevertheless developed into a mighty
force. It would not be half-bad, according to Rafes, if Russia were to go
the same way.

In those days, I was still unfamiliar with the sharp critique which Engels had leveled at the German Social Democrats on account of the fact
that they had abandoned the slogan of the German republic. With us,
the majority of the conference, the uprising against Rafes' report was
more psychological in nature. From our first moment in the Bund, we
had dreamed of the revolution in Russia. And now along came Rafes
and renounced it. We attacked him sharply, but supported his resolution
against Lenin's. In no uncertain terms, we wanted a united Social Democratic Party.

A heated discussion broke out over the question of the elections to the

Duma. The question was posed to us, whom should we back? Rafes proposed going along with the PPS-Left because they had promised to support national-cultural autonomy. The Social Democratic Party, to the contrary, wouldn't hear of it.

The elections to the Duma took a turn which nobody had foreseen. Warsaw, the capital of Poland, had the right to elect two deputies: one Pole and one Russian. The Polish reactionaries had often warned the Jews that it would come to a bloody reckoning if they should rob the Poles of their sole mandate from the capital. In the course of the election for delegates, who in turn were to vote for the deputies (direct elections did not exist), it came out that the Jewish bloc had the largest number of delegates. The situation was serious. Afraid of the Poles, the Jews decided to cast their vote for a Polish socialist. Once again, the Social Democratic Party of Poland refused to be elected with the backing of bourgeois votes. Thus the Jewish bloc voted for the common candidate of the PPS-Left and the Bund. Henekh was appointed mediator between the Bund's election committee and that of the PPS.

The delegate elections to the Bund's Vienna congress were a tragedy, but it was only later that this became apparent. At that time we greeted them with great joy. We elected Alter Shuster, who was already an informer, and Henekh, who turned a few days later.

When I arrived in Russia in 1917 as a political émigré from France, the old Bundist Mattes Shnayder took me to an attorney who, as it turned out, was an active Bundist. His name, if I am not mistaken, was Viniaver. We went through the materials relating to Henekh's cop work, and I was startled to learn how exactly he had told all about what had occurred in the Bund in those days! He also betrayed everything he knew about the PPS-Left, with whom he had worked at the time of the elections. A slavish soul of a provocateur! For his work he received thirty rubels per month. At least that is what was noted in the documents. It is interesting how he became an informer; in the reports of the gendarmerie the story is accurately recounted. After Henekh was elected delegate in Warsaw to the Vienna Congress, he was caught while attempting to cross the Polish-Austrian border illegally. It is possible that the second delegate, who was already an informer, had blown the whistle on him.

Taken into custody and interrogated in a small border town, he became an agent for the Okhrana. That he remained until the shadow of suspicion fell on him and he was pulled out of the work. I only learned this, of course, when I came back to Warsaw in 1919. But even earlier, in Moscow, we had signed a verdict against him which branded him an informer. The co-signers of this document were the attorney Viniaver, Mattes Shnayder and myself.

One thing remains a riddle to me to this day: why had he not denounced a number of comrades whose activities he was thoroughly familiar with and who were constantly being sought by the Okhrana? For example, the Okhrana was continuously on the prowl for Rafes, and each time Rafes came to Warsaw Henekh informed the police about it. He had described Rafes so exactly that even a blindman could have recognized him. But no, Rafes was always able to leave Warsaw unmolested. Henekh also associated closely with me, and when the police were looking for me following the actions around the Beilis trial, I met Henekh every day. When the Warsaw Committee of the Bund decided that it was time for me to disappear for a while, he was at the farewell get-together which comrades threw for me. He knew that the police were looking for me, and yet he did not denounce me. Who can peer into the dark soul of an informer?

There were four informers in the Warsaw organization of the Bund at that time: Henekh or Bainish, Alter Shuster, Blond Mordechai and still another one whose name was Nachumson, a leader of the cooperative movement. I cannot remember anything about him. These four informers had a devastating effect. Practically every month conferences were held, probably with the sole object of setting comrades up for victimization. Arrests took place very frequently in the café of the consumer cooperative, in those days located at Dzika Street 21. The best comrades fell into the net: Avrom Prikastshik, Yuzhek Metalovitz, Shmelke Valker, Asher Meir, Jechiel Neiman and dozens of others. But we continued on our way and pushed our work forward, full of faith in our final victory.

My Father's Strike

Ten weeks passed between the conference and my first arrest. During this time I was heavily preoccupied with party work; I joined the committee organized around the elections to the Duma. There were but few people around in those days to help out, for Henekh's work for the police had taken its toll. I also found work again in my trade. Suddenly, we were hit by a thoroughly unexpected disaster, or better said, by a double disaster in one.

Among the people who came into the consumer cooperative was one group of pessimistic individuals whose sole program consisted of committing suicide. And indeed, they called themselves the "Suicides" plain and simple. Their leader was named Bashe and they met in her apartment. Night and day, her windows stayed shut; during the night a candle was lit. Bashe always went around with disheveled hair and looked like a witch. On one occasion, my close friend Black Katz—we called him Ketzl—took me over to her place. To my great astonishment and grief, he too was a member of this group, despite the fact that he was a good party comrade. We treated the whole thing with levity and refused to take it seriously. But one day two of its members, two young workers, jumped out of a window and lay dead on the pavement. Now something had to give. We discussed the problem in our circles and forbade the party comrades to belong to the group.

In 1912 a group of anarchists split off from the Bund. They called themselves the Red Hand. In fact, this bunch had absolutely nothing to do with ideological anarchism; they simply turned themselves into a gang which murdered and robbed and had a grand old time. They became a real danger to us because the police, aware of the fact that their members frequented the consumer cooperative, stepped up their surveillance of the party. We were also worried that even more comrades might get sucked in and held special classes on anarchism and Marxism, my favorite subject. I already felt quite at home in theoretically distinguishing between the two movements. We boycotted this anarchist group and forbade comrades to make contact with them. But they, the anarchists, wanted to maintain good relations with us at all costs. I remember that I was once with White Max (or Maxl as we called him) on Dzika

Street and they came up to us to offer their support. They either wanted to support the party or one of us in particular, for they knew perfectly well that some of our comrades were always hungry. We rejected the offer out of hand and told them not to set foot on our turf any more. The thought of having any sort of relations with them whatsoever simply disgusted us. Day in and day out the press reported shootings and robberies which had been carried out by the anarchists of the Red Hand. Their racket worked like this: first they would write a letter to a shopkeeper or craftsman telling him to show up at some particular location with such and such amount of money, and at the same time inform him that he was a dead man if he didn't. At the prearranged time, the group would sniff out the scene to see whether or not the victim had come and whether or not he had brought the police along. Many people were in fact too afraid not to pay, and those who refused were shot.

On one occasion, I found myself in an unpleasant and uncomfortable spot. I have already mentioned that Alter Shuster, the informer, had given me a revolver to hide. Following the conference at which he was elected delegate to the Bund's congress in Vienna, he gave me a packet of bullets to go along with it. I took it for safe keeping and placed it under my pillow that night. When I left for work the next morning, I forgot to dispose of it the right way. My younger brother, who generally left for work somewhat later than I, noticed the packet filled with bullets; and, afraid to leave it in the apartment, he stuck it in his coat pocket and went off to work.

Even in the intense heat of summer, a fire had to be kept burning in the factory where we worked so that the leather dried quickly. When my brother showed up, he was anxious about taking off his heavy overcoat and, coat and all, he got down to work. The workers asked themselves just what this was supposed to mean; it really was impossible to work in such heat wearing an overcoat! But my brother kept mum. Nor was it clear to me what was up either, for I had completely forgotten about the bullets. It dawned on our co-workers that he must have hidden something in his pocket. The master walked up to him, patted him down and the whole thing came out. I knew that it could fare badly for my brother should word of the matter spread. So I explained to the workers that the bullets belonged to me, whereupon everybody quieted down and nobody said another word about it.

But a few days later we heard a shot. Everybody ran to the window and saw someone running by with a revolver in each hand; he was shooting at some policemen who were in hot pursuit. Many of the workers had often seen me walking with this fellow—in the days before he had become an anarchist. People began to suspect me as well. My worker colleagues were certain that the bullets which had been found on my brother were connected with the attacks. I felt so ashamed and morally downtrodden that I had to tell them the whole truth.

During those same months, another event took place, a deeply moving incident which I reflected a great deal about in later years—in the difficult days of my stay in prison. Every revolutionary has his days in prison which are hard to endure, and it was at such times that I often recalled this event. It warmed my heart, sparked my courage anew and gave me a fresh burst of strength.

It happened in July or August 1912. While at work, I received a message from my father asking me to come at once. That by itself was a surprise, for my father had never sent for me before. (Incidentally, I cannot even remember him ever talking to me. Though I later realized that he dearly loved me, he never spoke of it. Upon discovering that I had become a revolutionary, he merely murmured a few anxious words. When he once saw me reading something by Peretz, who was an employee of the local administration in the Jewish quarter, my father said: "Yes, Peretz is a fine Jew, but he would be better off not making a fool of himself by writing books." This was the one and only time my father ever expressed his opinion.)

When I heard that he was waiting for me, it was obvious that something must have happened. My heart racing, I was off. I found him with tears in his eyes; he looked terribly crushed. I felt my legs give way, for never before had I seen him cry. No more and no less, he told me that his boss had accused him of stealing.

There were lots of masters in those days who operated in the following way: instead of paying the workers their full wages every week, they would part with only a portion of the money. The final tally was made when the season came to an end. (I believe that this was even practiced in postwar Poland.) But my father's boss came up with something original: in order to get out of paying the workers the money she owed, she insisted at season's end that they had been stealing.

With tears in his eyes, my father explained to me: "It isn't at all a question of money, but you see, at my old age she's making me out to be a thief. I'm ashamed of my grey beard." He was unable to speak another word. Despite all my grief, I was full of joy too. Did this mean that my father had grasped what made me go the way I did? Had he understood that the insulted and disadvantaged have to go over to the socialists, that the socialists take up the cause of all the tormented? I was determined to do everything possible to fight the injustice heaped on my father. I was even ready, in the worst of cases, to turn to the anarchist group. But it didn't come to that.

I went back to my shop and announced that I was taking the day off. Then I shot over to the consumer cooperative to dig up a handful of comrades. One of the comrades I met was Viktor Shuster, an old Bundist who had once been exiled to Siberia. He always told the same stories, but they came out differently each time. Whenever we were looking for a good time, we asked him to tell us the story of his exile. I grabbed this Viktor and a few more comrades and we went to pay my father's boss a visit. Inasmuch as she was unprepared for our arrival, her door had been left standing open. We grabbed the finished goods and exclaimed that she would get them back when she paid up. Suddenly, I saw Viktor open up her desk drawer. When I asked him what he was doing, he said, "Looking for strikebreakers." I broke out in wild laughter. That was Viktor all over again with his pranks. After that, we came by several times a day every day to make sure that strikebreakers were not being used. As the strike dragged on, we posted some comrades in the office to prevent anybody from making any purchases.

It went on for some two weeks like this. Seven o'clock one morning, as I still lay in bed, the boss showed up and declared that she had come by to arrest me. Clearly she was lying, for if she really had wanted to arrest me she could have sent the police without being there in person. I knew that she had come to settle the matter peacefully, and was poking a little fun at herself.

I asked her to go outside a minute so I could get dressed for work. But she refused to budge from my bed. With no other choice, I got dressed in front of her. That softened her up a bit and she proposed paying out part of the money. As I reached for the doorknob she said that she was ready to pay up the whole sum—but only to my father. I asked my father not to accept the money until she had paid all the other workers as well.

And he did not accept it either. As it turned out, she paid all the workers their money that same day and published an apology in the newspaper. With that, the matter was closed. I don't believe she ever tried to pull such clever tricks again.

That day was a genuine *yontev*[6] for us at home. All at once everybody began to act differently toward me. I was happy for having saved my father's honor and the honor of all the others with whom he worked.

---

[6] holiday (trans.)

The Saxony Garden

The Saxony Garden played a great roll in our lives in the early days. After the consumer cooperative it was our second home and we went there every evening. There were various reasons for this. First, we met all those people who either did not want to or were unable to come to the consumer cooperative; and second, it was also the one place where we could live it up a bit. Black Katz used to sing his heartwrenching songs there, which we so loved to hear. He was a masterful singer of short songs. I met him years later in Moscow, and during our night-long walks on Mount Vorobyevo (Leonid Andreev's place to dream), he sang equally heartrending Russian songs which echoed so much with the sound of longing. When we used to go for walks in the Saxony Garden I often asked him to sing a little something. The very first notes always made me feel that it was just his singing which formed such a substantial part of our friendship.

I particularly loved the garden on autumn days, when the Polish skies are grey and foggy and when the leaves fall from the trees. I would sit down on a bench and a deep sense of longing would hauntingly ring my heart. What did I long for at the time? For summer days gone by? Or for a better and more beautiful life? Or perhaps for life in general, which I was ready to sacrifice on the altar of the revolution? All of this together generated a strong longing in me, and it was a mood I was very fond of.

There were two paths in the garden which ran parallel to each other: the "proletarian" and the "literary." Of course, these were not their real names, but that's what we called them, for the one was frequented by the Jewish writers and the other by the Jewish workers—or better, the Jewish socialists.

Peretz came to the garden every Saturday, and that was reason enough for us to spend our time there as well. He was not one to take to the literary path right off, for he knew that we were waiting for him. First things first, he strolled our way. He would greet us with a warm and friendly smile. Yes, Peretz loved us. And he was wont to say so openly and frequently. He, the poet of great dreams, was able to appraise our fighting character correctly. We liked him no less than he liked us; it was a great mutual love, even if it was full of polemic and dissension. The polemics often took on a dramatic character, but even in the middle of the sharpest disputes we still felt that Peretz had won our minds and our souls.

Peretz was attacking Marxism particularly sharply at the time. He called it contraband which had been smuggled in from outside. We were ready to fight to the bitter end for this contraband, for Marxism to us was the light in the great darkness. Marxist theory had become ours through hunger and want and in hard combat, and we were ready to defend it against anyone out to do it battle. And in his way, Peretz did battle with Marxism.

I remember how Peretz once gave a talk on his drama *Bay Nacht oyfn alten Mark.* [7] He said relatively little about the play itself (we were already accustomed to that). Instead, he developed his favorite philosophy about lofty mountains and barren plains. The plains, he said, are occupied by the sick and infirm, who grow dizzy and confounded at high altitudes. Only men of healthy body and spirit, however, only those who are fearless and bold, scale to the top. He called on us not to follow the example of the sick and infirm, but to climb the highest peaks. Up to this point, we were enraptured by his talk. But soon Peretz jumped to another subject—Marxism. It's foreign to Jewish life, he fulminated, an idea smuggled in from Germany. We began to steam and threw back a loud barrage of catcalls. Then when he shouted that every word of Marxism preached to the Jewish workers had to be spit back in the preachers faces, a tremendous uproar ensued. It even came to blows. White Maxl slugged it out with his brother's Zionist friend. Peretz' speech was interrupted. Then he spoke again, but to an empty hall—we had all taken off. The next day one of the journalists for *der Fraynd* wrote: "Jewish workers, don't take Peretz' spittle to heart. All the more will it purify you."

Our dispute sharpened when Peretz wrote his famous article on the eve of Yom Kippur 1913 in which he called on the Jewish workers to go to the synagogue and pray. Our protest was a highly original one, and later it became a constant topic of conversation in the literary circles. The whole affair had grieved Peretz deeply, we heard; the Jewish workers, he maintained, had misinterpreted him. The story went like this:

[7] At night in the Old Marketplace (trans.)

When we read Peretz' article—I believe it appeared in the newspaper *der Moment*—we, a group of comrades, wanted to let him know what our opinion about it was. We therefore decided that we would present him with a prayer book when he made his customary stroll down the workers' path on Yom Kippur. This was supposed to symbolize that we were returning the gift to him which he gave us in the form of his article. There were four of us: Black Katz, White Max, Josele Baytlmacher and I.

Early in the morning we awaited Peretz' arrival. Down the path he came and White Max, handing him the book, explained that it was a present from the Jewish workers in answer to his call to return to the synagogue. Peretz accepted the book, went somewhat pale and replied with the two words, "Many thanks." We hadn't any idea at the time that this incident had so affected him that he often mentioned it again in days to come. But despite everything, our love for him never waned. In the future too we would wait for him every Saturday in the garden.

We also used the Saxony Garden for revolutionary drill practice, something the police were also well aware of. Our workers' path was normally crawling with informers whom we all knew, and by the same token they knew us as well. Whenever we went for walks in the garden and they strolled our way, we would greet each other with a smile and meander on.

Our revolutionary drills consisted of carrying out demonstrations in the garden before the onset of mass actions. At eight o'clock in the evening, when the bells tolled announcing that the gates to the garden were to be closed for the night, we would form ourselves into groups at each gate to meet the droves of people as they streamed out. We would then lose ourselves among the throngs, throw leaflets in the air and shout out slogans pertaining to the action at hand.

It was White Max who particularly distinguished himself in the course of these demonstrations. He had a way of holding hundreds of leaflets between his fingers so that when he tossed them in the air every single one landed in a different spot. He had something of the adventurer in him too, and this came out at the same time. He knew that the cops could not lay a hand on him as long as they were unable to find anything on his person, so he waited until the last minute, until some cop approached him, then threw the leaflets over his head. The informer had no other choice but to act as if he hadn't seen a thing.

I cannot remember that the tsarist police ever surrounded the Saxony

Garden and closed the gates in order to carry out mass arrests (as the Polish police were later to do), despite the fact that there were provocateurs there who were undoubtedly in the know about every one of the actions that we planned.

My First Arrest

The day before Yom Kippur was an extraordinarily peculiar one for us Jewish workers. The mentality of begging and praying was repugnant to us; we were full of the spirit of fighting. But all around us preparations for the *yontev* proceeded apace and the whole atmosphere was different. The master of the shop where I worked would be particularly well-disposed that day. The whole year round he would curse like a crook, manhandle the workers he employed and even his own wife too. But come Yom Kippur, he would transform himself into a wholly different human being. He was gentle and good to one and all, particularly to his workers. My parents too would be most particularly tender. All of this produced a queer sort of atmosphere—not a Yom Kippur mood, but a *yontev* mood.

On Kol Nidre [8] in the year 1912 we, a group of comrades, had plans to go to the opera. We had already reserved ourselves a table in a Polish restaurant for the following day. The owners of the Polish inn were so accustomed to the fact that Jews frequented their restaurant on Yom Kippur that they even used to ask in anticipation, "Actually, when does that day roll around again when the Jews eat so much?"

We only worked half days on Yom Kippur eve. After work I went home, washed up and grabbed a little something to eat to tide me over until our last meal. Meanwhile, I did what I always did and headed off for the Saxony Garden.

As I have already said, I loved the mood of autumn, and this particular day was just one of those somber autumn days. The leaves were falling from the trees like rain. It was chilly and foggy. The other comrades had not shown up, so I sat there alone and dreamed. Such a somber autumn day is the best time to give oneself over to one's thoughts and feelings. It is at times like this that you feel every twinge of your soul and every beat of your heart. I lapsed into my world of dreams and totally forgot that I was carrying illegal election proclamations in my pocket,

---

[8] the evening before Yom Kippur, the day of atonement and fasting (trans.)

which had been signed by both the Central Committee of the Bund and the Central Committee of the PPS-Left. Since comrades had not come, I decided to drop in at the consumer cooperative before going home to our last meal before Yom Kippur.

When I arrived at the consumer cooperative, there were hordes of people there. I have aleady mentioned that the fellow who ran the cooperative later turned out to be an informer. At that time, however, we were unaware of this. (When they took us away to the Okhrana headquarters, some comrades commented that he had been seen leaving before the police arrived, but we did not take this seriously.)

Each of us had our pockets filled to the brim with materials for the election campaign. Suddenly, in came the police. Everybody emptied their pockets and threw everything to the ground; I was the only one who did not manage it. Quite possibly, the cops already had me in their sights; perhaps it was my clothes, the typical attire of a revolutionary— broad-brimmed hat and black shirt. Whatever the case may be, they went right for me, held me fast by the collar of my coat, searched me and of course found the leaflets. Everybody else was clean. Then they walked me over to a corner of the room and kept me there.

I sank into a dismal mood, but not because I faced going to trial and the absolutely certain prospect of conviction. I was prepared for that. Something else was making me feel gloomy. The informers holding me fast by the collar of my coat were wearing boots and leather-visored caps. I remembered that the men of the fighting units of the PPS in 1905 had been dressed the same way. Many of them, in fact, became provocateurs. Now they had arrested me. With a stifling ring around my heart, I was cut to the quick. The informers noticed it and most certainly interpreted it in their own way.

They tried to confuse me. Unceasingly, one of them called to another: "Him there, he's the one!" Then eventually they brought in the commissar of the Third Police Commissariat to take a look at me. Later, when the police president arrived, the whole game started up again. I felt my confusion grow and began tying my shoelaces in knots in order to avoid looking at them. And I continued to do so until they were finished with their search. Then they lined us all up in rank and file and took us away to the commissariat. We had an arrangement going at the time: when a group of comrades was arrested and taken away to jail, they were to sing revolutionary songs along the way. So it was that instead of going to the opera, we were led by the police through the streets on a rainy autumn evening, while the clangor of our revolutionary songs resounded in the nighttime darkness.

We were led to the *Koza* in the circle courtyard. The moment we arrived we had a run-in with some underworldniks who were sitting on the wooden bunks. The comrade Eli Becker was wearing a stiff hat and one of these men delivered him one well-placed blow to the head, something to be expected from these cutthroats and hoodlums. But our comrades went for them, and it wasn't long before we had them lying under the wooden bunks. Then we sat ourselves down and turned over in our minds what we ought to say during the interrogation.

For everybody else the matter was straightforward and simple, for they had been clean. They merely had to say that they didn't know anything. But in my case the thing was complicated, for the cops had found a bundle of leaflets on me which had been wrapped in a newspaper. I had to come up with an alibi. We decided that I would defend myself like this: "I went to the Saxony Garden. Then some comrade walked up to me and I gave him something to read while he gave me the newspaper. Since it was dark, I stuffed the newspaper in my pocket without looking to see what was wrapped inside." Yes, it was a weak defense, but we didn't come up with anything better.

Early the next morning, Yom Kippur that is, we were taken to the Okhrana headquarters. I saw my parents through the bars of the small prison van as we drove by. Earlier, we had decided that if we should be transported by van, we would sing the *Internationale* along the way. And that's just what we did. We went through the revolutionary songs with verve, though I doubt that my parents were in such high spirits. I understood their misery only too well, but I went out of my way not to think about it.

Once in the Okhrana jail, we washed up and put on clean clothes. Each of us received a bowl and a spoon. We were all put in one cell, a large and bright one. There were forty of us comrades, but we did not feel cramped. Nor can one say that we felt particularly frightened either. First of all, a few good friends were along—Avremel Shtricker, Eli Becker and others. And the rest? They too were all acquaintances and close party comrades. The food wasn't too bad, and as early as the next day we received small packages from outside.

One thing disturbed me: what should I say to my parents? It was terribly tormenting to me that I, who loved my mother so and who trembled with worry at the very thought of her, should cause her so much misery.

I was terrified of the moment when she would come to see me. Then she came, but instead of me comforting her, she was there comforting me. She also brought a girlfriend of mine along, whom she knew I wanted to see. My father was there too—and as usual, he did not utter a single word. When my mother came the second time by herself and I asked her why my father had not come along, she replied that he was afraid that she would break out in tears. And he felt ashamed. How warm and good my parents were!

As for me, I did them a terrible injustice. My parents still had a little money left over from the inheritance, which they wanted to set aside to make their old age somewhat easier. Because of my arrest they lost the little smattering of money they had. I was unable to forgive myself for several years, and even today, as I write these lines, it still hurts a great deal.

Everything in our cell went quite smoothly, even though there too we were unable to avoid a conflict with the gentlemen from the underworld. It happened once when we were let out to wash up: they jumped a few of our comrades and beat them bloody. The next day we got even with them. The jail administration thereupon decided to completely isolate our two groups from one another, and it was a good thing.

Meanwhile, nothing happened to spoil our good spirits, and that's how it stayed for one entire month. What took place when the month ran out, however, shook all of us.

H., an old party comrade, told us plain and simple that he was prepared to become an informer if we did not find a way to get him released. Before I mention something about the scheme he had in mind, I would first like to say a few words about the tsarist laws which were in force in those days.

There were two methods of punishment for political offences: first, administrative banishment; second, a judicial sentence. One could only be held in detention for three months; following this period, one of these two forms of punishment had to be imposed or the prisoner was released. One was seldom kept in detention for three entire months. Those who faced trial were transferred to the prison where interrogations took place. In Warsaw this was Pawiak prison. Those who were not to be exiled as well as those whom the authorities were unable to try in court were set free after the first month was up. The Okhrana, therefore, was a form of detention.

There were forty of us comrades when we were arrested. By the end of the month 23 had been released. There were only 17 of us left. This gave everybody the impression that a trial would be prepared against us 17, an impression reinforced by the fact that all those who had been set free were not party comrades. Among the 17 who stayed behind were the party activists, Avremel Shtricker included. Avremel Shtricker, beloved by all of us, was a member of the Warsaw leadership of the Bund. We were all certain that we would be subjected to a judicial interrogation. Comrade H. now informed us that he had a fiancée outside whom he wanted to marry and that he would not endure a jail term. He therefore wanted us to do something to get him released. But this would only work if one of us 17 comrades were to take full responsibility for the entire affair upon himself. He proposed that either I assume the role, for I was going to go up for trial anyway, or Avremel Shtricker, who was a member of the Warsaw leadership. (This very same H., by the way, later became a Combundist and then joined the Communist Party. During the war he was involved in speculation, and today he is one of the most active Stalinist functionaries in Paris.) Should we refuse to buy his proposal, he exclaimed, he would denounce us all.

We were all extremely agitated by this—it came completely unexpectedly. We boycotted the man and none too few of us wanted to beat him up. We demanded that he be removed from our cell, but even from solitary confinement he informed us daily: freedom or else.

We really did not know what to do. During my first interrogation, the Polish officer who questioned me did not say anything about a trial. He simply commented that although he did not believe a single word I was saying, he would jot down everything just as I said it because he had no other choice. As the thing began to be unsettling, Avremel and I came up with the idea of jumping into the fray by ourselves. We hoped to accomplish two things: first, rid ourselves of the ignominy of having a provocateur in our midst; and second, save the active comrades so that they could go forward with the work.

But something else continued to plague me. It seemed to me that Avremel Shtricker had the intention of bearing the entire guilt alone. That would have meant his certain death. He was consumptive, spit up blood continuously, and every day in prison was a threat to his life. Aside from this, he was a dear, personal friend of mine. The child of poor parents, he had acquired a great deal of knowledge. He was a passionate revolutionary and a good man. No way was I going to allow him to lay down his life. I therefore decided to accept the guilt myself.

It meant Siberia. I wanted to write home to ask my parents to send me a warm cotton jacket and warm wool socks. It crossed my mind to put in a request for a transfer to the Tenth Pavilion.[9] And I was also playing with the thought of forgoing visits from my mother. I knew she would never survive it, but I no longer had the courage to see her again. Even today, the thought makes me shudder. Why was I prepared to risk my mother's life? Nevertheless, that's what I had decided to do at the time.

When I told the comrades what I intended to do they put up bitter resistance and forbade me to carry it out. Avremel Shtricker in particular was opposed. He spent days on end speaking with me. He told me his life story and refused to leave me alone for a minute. I knew what he was up to: he was seeking to dissuade me and playing for time. In the end, we worked out a compromise. For the time being, I was not to do a thing. But if it turned out that my case should go to trial, the comrades would allow me to go it alone.

At the end of the second month the gendarmerie *pulkavnik*[10] came, summoned me to an interrogation and presented me with Paragraph 132 of the penal code, the mildest in respect to political proceedings. He informed me that I would be sent to Pawiak prison the next day. Since nobody else had been called in, it was clear that the others were to be released. And so it was. At the end of the second month everybody except for me was free. The comrades, however, were despondent; the outcome left them feeling ill-at-ease. After all, I was the youngest in years and the youngster of the movement as well.

I was in good spirits, however. In the course of being interrogated by the *pulkavnik* I wrested the right to speak Yiddish, something I saw as a victory for national-cultural autonomy.

The last time he appeared I was supposed to sign the protocol, but I refused. I had heard that the statements which the police write up often differ from those which they read aloud, and that defendants who sign such protocols might run into a whole string of difficulties later on. I hardly understood a word of the Russian language at the time and the gendarme was unable to speak Polish. It occurred to me to demand that the protocol be translated into Yiddish. I knew that he would have to seek the assistance of one or another of the political prisoners. And that's exactly what I wanted.

---

[9] Tenth Pavilion, prison complex in the Warsaw Citadel. (trans.)
[10] colonel (trans.)

At first, he refused in no uncertain terms to hear of it. I wasn't in Palestine, he exclaimed, and if I chose to remain obstinate they would simply let me rot in detention. He didn't understand a word of Yiddish, he added, and this was the first time that anybody had ever confronted him with such a demand. I told him that I did not understand Russian and that I would not sign the protocol. At that, I stood up to go back to my cell. The gendarme then softened up and called in a comrade. I can't remember the comrade's name, although I met him again years later on the Don. He always remained a Menshevik and in the end died in one of the camps.

The gendarme read the protocol aloud, and in the meantime the comrade and I conversed. By the time the gendarme was finished, I had learned everything I needed to know. Even though I had not heard a single word of it, I signed the statement.

Early the next morning I took leave of my comrades. I was transferred to Pawiak and the others were released the following day. That was the last time I ever saw Avremel Shtricker, for by the time I was set free he had already been arrested again. As for the others, I met many of them once again, years later, in Russia.

In Pawiak Prison

The moment I arrived at Pawiak the difference was obvious to me. The detention jail had been bright and roomy, and I had spent the entire time with my own comrades and close friends. It was totally different here. The prison, which had long, dark corridors, threw me into a state of melancholy. The conduct of the authorities toward me here was stricter and the methods of examining individuals more brutal.

Worse yet was the cell itself—five paces in length and somewhat more than three paces in width. But it was consoling to think that the whole nightmare would soon be over, that I would be together with comrades, for political prisoners were grouped together in separate cells. Pawiak already had lots of them in those days, among them a small number of Social Democrats and an even smaller group of PPS members—from the Pilsudski tendency that is. A group of the Uniteds, with Mordechai Kastenmacher at the head, was also under lock and key there. In terms of numbers, the Bund outdid them all many times over. The politicals had already wrested certain rights from the authorities. The leader of the political prisoners was one of the leaders of the Tsukunft, a Bundist named Shpinak-Josefovich. Later, in Russia, he became a close associate of Lozovsky in the Profintern.[11] Even outside the prison walls we were aware of the important cultural work being performed in prison. That's why I really wanted to be together with my own comrades. My disappointment was correspondingly great when I was stuck in a cell together with two common criminals. I can still remember these two today. One of them went about barefoot, ran to and fro in the cell with disheveled hair and whistled a tune to himself. He was in for raping a young girl. The second one, a large man, wore boots and went around with some kind of sly-looking little hat on his head. He was a petty thief. They were happy about my arrival because they knew that politicals received food from outside, and above all ciga-

---

[11] Red International of Labor Unions. Hersh Mendel erroneously writes "Cominform" in place of "Profintern." (trans.)

rettes. And they were not mistaken. In no time I got a pack and shared it with them. From the first moment of my prison life I held fast to the principle: whoever I may be in with, our living arrangements must be communal. And I conducted myself accordingly with my first two cellmates as well. They were pleased, but I felt miserable.

I knew that behind these same bars were a group of good and sincere comrades. They had their own exercise yard, published a prison newspaper, learned a lot—and I had to sit it out with two lousy and lowly criminals. When I was led outside to the courtyard I discovered that the situation was even worse. There were only four politicals in the entire wing, and we were forced to take our walks side by side with a bunch of convicts, while in other wings there were many, many politicals. It was clear to me that there was no avoiding an altercation.

I shared the cell with these two common criminals for over a month. I do not know why, but I was transferred to another cell where a certain Zussman from the Uniteds was kept. Then came Mendel Kamashenmacher, or Mendel Prager as he was known.

By the time there were three of us it was a cosier situation, but even then we were still isolated from the rest of the comrades. Aside from that, Zussman raised our hackles. In general he was a warm and good comrade. It was through him, by the way, that I first became acquainted with the program of the United Workers Party. But he had a terrible mania. He caught mice—there was more than enough of them in Pawiak's cells—and hung them by their heads. Whenever they began to quiver and squeal, a shudder ran up and down my spine. Nobody could persuade him to give up this particular pastime of his. We breathed easier when he was finally transferred.

So that left the two of us—Mendel Prager and I. It got a bit lonelier. We hit on the idea of going on a hunger strike in order to press the demand that we be transferred to another wing. The plan, however, only came to fruition a few weeks later.

I have already described the struggle between the Jewish workers and the underworld, but in the Polish quarters of the city the battle raged on even more vehemently. In those parts of town the fighting units of the PPS actually slaughtered the people from the underworld in droves, and the hatred between the two was horrible. The Jewish politicals in prison were spared, but whenever Polish comrades arrived, they were terribly beaten and sometimes even beaten to death by the Polish underworldniks.

One day a Polish comrade arrived. They didn't put him in our cell, but we met him during our walk. Overjoyed, we got him everything he needed. We also noticed, however, that the Polish cons were whispering among themselves.

We knew exactly what was up: namely, they were preparing an assault on the Polish comrade. The next day in the courtyard we split away from the others and, just in case, placed the Polish comrade between us in order to defend him. Everything went peacefully during our walk, but on the way back through Pawiak's tight, narrow, dark corridors they attacked us. A real bashing ensued and we of course got the worst of it, for we were only four while they were a pack of professional thugs. Covered with blood, we went back to our cell and I deliberated with Mendel Prager about what to do. There was no doubt in our minds that all of the political prisoners would support us if we were to undertake some sort of action. Next door to us was a Polish comrade, a Social Democrat. We discussed the matter with him but he refused to hear any talk of a hunger strike. When we had defended the new Polish comrade, this one had stood to the side and refused to soil his hands. His cellmate was a Bundist comrade, a limping worker from one of the tailor shops. He was ready to join in. So we, the three Bundists and the newly arrived Polish comrade, decided to declare a hunger strike with the sole demand that we be transferred to another wing.

This was my first hunger strike. I cannot say that it came easily for me. The prison administration attempted to break the strike with all the means at its disposal. Again and again, food was shoved into our cell. And since our comrade next door was likewise on strike, a peculiar war ensued. Whenever the administration placed the food into our cell and then proceeded down the corridor, we tossed the food outside again. And when they shoved it back in our cell, our next-door neighbor disposed of his in the same manner. This game continued until the *klutshniks*[12] got tired of it and capitulated.

The hunger strike had already lasted five days. We had a bowl of water in our cell which we used for washing up. It had already been standing there for four days. As time went on, a layer of dust had collected on the surface. By the fifth day of the strike I was burning with thirst, and threw myself, practically unconsciously, at the bowl. I felt some sort of clump go down my throat, and before long was feverish.

---

[12] stewards (trans.)

That same day the strike ended and I was transferred to the other wing, where I shared a cell with the Tsukunft leader comrade Shaffran. A Bundist today, he lives in America.

This was just the cell I needed. First, strict discipline was the rule. There were definite hours during which you were able to talk and discuss, and others for reading and learning. Shaffran instructed us in the Polish language and Polish literature. His pupils were a comrade named Chatzkele and I. It was in those days that I became acquainted with Polish literature: Mickiewicz, Słowacki, Orzeszkowa and Żeromski came to be my favorite writers. I disliked Krasiński because of the reactionary character of his works. Side by side with my preoccupation with this beautiful literature I continued my study of Marxism. The time passed by very productively.

In that same period my mother came to visit me and brought along the joyful news that the candidate from the Bund-PPS list, Jagiełło, had won. This was the sensation of the day, a *yontev* for all the political prisoners, especially the Bundists.

Meanwhile, I fell ill. A boil had developed underneath my right arm and grew larger and larger by the day. When I went into the hospital the prison doctor was away on vacation. The medic told me that the boil must be removed, otherwise the danger existed that the pus would continue to spread down my side, necessitating an operation. I wanted to wait for the doctor's return before the excision was made, but the medic disagreed. So I had no other choice but to assent.

The comrades Yuzhek and Josefovich were present; they held down my hands while the medic made a cross incision with his knife. Blood shot like mad from the wound. This man was more akin to a shoemaker than a medic; so poorly had he made the cut.

Following the operation, my illness grew worse. And as ever more pus accumulated underneath my arm and the thing grew terribly agonizing, it became necessary for me to go into the hospital.

But in the hospital my condition simply degenerated. The medic attempted the most varied means, but it became worse and worse. He made repeated incisions into the wound in order to drain out the pus. It was so debilitating that I had to be carried out for bandaging.

The *klutshnik* at the hospital insisted that I couldn't possibly be Jewish, for a Jew would have been altogether incapable of enduring such agony. A Jew would have howled with pain, he said, whereas I had borne it in silence. He gave me no peace and demanded to know what the word "*Lecho Dodi*" means. I tried to explain to him that this is a song which Jews sing to greet the Sabbath. He refused to believe me however. "*Lecho Dodi*," he maintained, was a special sort of jargon used by Jewish criminals which contained a hidden meaning.

In the bed next to me lay a thief—a very intelligent man, the son of a banker. He loved to philosophize about the "meaning of human life." He sought to convince me that every man is a born criminal, something which simply finds expression in various ways: the one commits common crimes, the other political. But they all stem from the same source—human nature. He was a very good man, for as I lay there unable to move he fed me food and liquids as if I were a small child. He loved to sing—the prison hospital had no objections as long as it was done quietly. And the songs which he sang so beautifully were hardly those which one customarily heard among criminals.

One of the comrades from the trial of the Uniteds was also there. He had gone crazy. His madness manifested itself in the fact that he ran back and forth through the ward, throwing whatever he could get his hands on at anyone in sight. On one occasion he took his cup of hot tea and splashed it in the guard's face. The guard went for him and gave him a real beating. It was clear to me that the guard had reacted in a moment of excitement and I preferred keeping my mouth shut about the whole story. But I feared that he might report it and land the sick man in an asylum for the rest of his life. With no other choice but to scandalize the guard, I accused him of having provoked the whole scene.

I demanded to see the *natshalnik*[13] and make up a story. I told him that the guard had assaulted and beaten a man who is mentally deranged. That the lunatic had showered the guard with hot tea was my secret. If the guard was not punished, I said, I would break off the treatment and go on a hunger strike. This was the only possible way to save the *meshugener*.[14] The guard was unable to muster up a successful defense, and in genuinely Russian gutter talk the *natshalnik* cursed: "Your mother is a so-and-so and you're a son of a bitch." The guard stood at attention, his hand raised in salute, and replied: "So it is, sir..." I was terribly sorry about the whole thing.[15]

---

[13] head of a department; in this case, warden (trans.)

[14] madman (trans.)

[15] The full impact of the *natshalnik's* remarks cannot be rendered in English, for he addresses the guard with the second-person singular "du." This informal form of address is either used between acquaintances, with children or animals or as an expression of insult and degradation. (trans.)

There was also a big terrorist from the PPS there. He had been condemned to death, but due to his illness the sentence could not be carried out. He was suffering from galloping consumption; with no strength left to speak, every word he uttered came out like a hoarse squeak. They fed him dog fat. He was extraordinarily nervous and was unwilling to speak to anybody about his sentence. I gave it a few tries, seeking to divert him from his sad thoughts—but with hardly much success. He had no understanding for us Jewish socialists; the independence of Poland was the be-all and end-all of his every waking thought. He hated the Bund because in respect to Polish independence the Bund shared the standpoint of the Polish Social Democrats. Yet he paid compliments to me, perhaps because I was still very young and because everyone believed that it would turn out badly for me, sick as I was. The symptoms were in fact enough to leave one with a totally negative picture, and that's why he had sympathy for me.

He died a short time later. That was a horrible day for me. It was the first time that I saw a political prisoner die behind bars and it affected me as if an old and good friend had died. Perhaps I took his death so hard because I believed that time was running out for me as well.

There was no letting up—I became weaker and weaker. Whenever I had to go anywhere, someone had to carry me. For days on end I neither ate nor drank a thing. I felt my powers dwindling and lay in bed on the verge of unconsciousness.

One night two medics came to my bed, the Polish fellow who had been treating me all along and another, a Russian. The doctor was still away. They discussed my illness and decided that I required surgery. This meant either amputating my arm or cutting open my side to drain out the pus. It made no difference to me whatsoever which operation they performed. I was absolutely certain that given my condition I would not survive any sort of operation. This was the first time that I wept in prison. It was no ordinary cry; the tears simply streamed from my eyes. I was not afraid for myself. When I became a socialist, I was prepared for everything. Later in my life, I found myself in many situations in which I was certain that my time had come. Yet I faced them without tears and without even feeling sad. This time I was thinking about my mother: what would she do when she came to visit me and somebody told her that I had passed away? I was certain that she would never endure it. And it made me so weak that I simply broke down. I later remembered that I had actually been prepared to bear the whole weight of the trial by myself, although this would certainly have put my mother in her grave. Why had I been so ready before, whereas now it was so painful? This was one question I was unable to answer.

Meanwhile, the doctor came back from vacation and saved me. He violently berated the medics for treating me the way they did. Nobody was permitted to so much as touch my arm, he declared. Aside from light poultices, the word was: hands off! A few days later, my condition had so improved that I was able to go back to my cell.

But before returning to my cellblock I witnessed still another atrocity. I was standing by the window and looking down on the courtyard. It was the time of day when packages were delivered to the prison from outside. As the *klutshnik* opened the gate and my mother tried to worm her way through with her package, he dealt her a sharp blow to the chest to force her back. I called for the warden and demanded that he punish the brute, and he promised he would.

It was during this period that I became acquainted with a group of anarchists who were doing time in Pawiak. They too called themselves the Red Hand and they too spilled no small amount of innocent blood in the course of carrying out their expropriations. Yet they were a very different lot from the anarchists of the Red Hand whom I described earlier. The others only robbed and murdered, while this group carried out political actions as well. They attacked policemen who had mistreated political prisoners and terrorized *natshalniks* who were known to be torturers. In a word, their methodology was a combination of both political as well as criminal activities.

The leader of the group was Hershel Blashke. I will sketch his story below. I only wish to argue here that in his own way he remained a revolutionary. The prison administration was terrified of him. When Hershel's wife—a fellow prisoner—informed him that the administration had mistreated her, he informed the *natshalnik* that it had better stop or else. Indeed, the *natshalnik* had good reason to be afraid, for Hershel Blashke had already made an attempt on his life. Though the *natshalnik* knew that Hershel was the one who had tried to kill him, he did not inform the public prosecutor's office. Another member of the group, Laypziger, was kept in strict isolation because he refused to submit to interrogation. When the public prosecutor came to his cell, Laypziger turned his back on him. All the anarchists spoke of him with the highest esteem.

They also had an informer among them, a man who had turned after his arrest. He grew himself a long, blond beard and went around praying all day long wrapped in a tallith. In later days, I was to meet lots of similar types in prison, men who sought to win their release by resorting to such means.

Returning from my walk one day, I saw this informer go into the administration office. Hershel ran up to him, grabbed him by the neck and began to choke him. It took some time before the guards managed to separate Hershel from his victim. Somebody else in his place would have had to pay dearly for it, but nobody did a thing to Hershel. When I met him again in Nizhni Novgorod in 1918, he explained the whole story to me.

My Trial

Meanwhile, the date for my trial drew near. Others had to sit it out and wait much longer for theirs, but in my case it went quite quickly. Why? Because I was being brought to trial individually and because the paragraph pertaining to the complaint against me carried with it the expectation of a light sentence. According to this paragraph, one could only be slapped with a maximum of three years in a fortress. My interrogation period in fact came very quickly to an end. I awaited the trial with anxious excitement, for this was, after all, my first appearance before the public. For the first time, I would have to speak. A confession, of course, was out of the question; going to trial demanded that I bear myself with honor, as was befitting a young revolutionary.

What's more, I was enticed by the thought of seeing the streets and coming into contact with people again. The three of us—Shaffran, Chatzkele and I—had often lain awake half the night and listened to people as they walked in the street and chatted. We tried to guess what they were talking about. Were they perhaps thinking that there were three young men behind those walls dreaming about freedom? Did they even have the slightest inkling that there were revolutionaries there, each of whom had his near and dear friends whom he yearned to be with, and that they had taken prison life upon themselves "freely" in order to fight for freedom for all? This was how we used to *schmooze*, [16] especially late at night when Chazkele's feet bothered him and he was unable to sleep. We lay on the small prison mattresses and longed for the world outside. That's why one prepared himself for the opportunity to drive about in freedom—if only in a paddy wagon—as if it were a big *yontev*. And the trip to court really turned out to be a holiday.

There was one more reason, however, why the trip to court set one's spirits soaring. I do not believe that anybody who has never before been in prison can grasp this, for it is intricately bound up with the psychology of the prisoner.

Before his trial a prisoner never knows when it will all be over, when

---

[16] chat (trans.)

he can hope to go free. But even when he has a stiff sentence to reckon with, he knows that after that sentence is passed he can begin to count the days: first a week goes by, then another. And prisoners are masters in the art of counting the weeks so that they pass by more quickly. The prisoner's countdown goes like this: today is Sunday, tomorrow Monday—now, one needn't take them into the reckoning. What you're left with then is Tuesday, Wednesday and Thursday. Friday? Well, Friday is the day before Sabbath, so it doesn't count either. The week therefore has only three days.

My trial took place in March 1912.[17] When the big day came I had two things on my mind. The first was a good, close shave. The prison administration in fact sent in a barber every week, but it always happened that he failed to show at the proper time. If we wanted to be shaved for our visitors, we had to do it ourselves. The clasp of a vest, a fountain pen which we sharpened ourselves—these were the implements we used for shaving. Others simply used a piece of glass from a windowpane. It goes without saying how badly we lacerated ourselves with such razors. Whenever we dragged one of these things across our faces it left behind a string of wounds which we dabbed over with toilet paper. During evening rollcall, the *natshalnik* or an inspector couldn't help laughing. Come morning we would rip the paper away and our visitors would never notice a thing. We stood too far away from them. But going to trial with a face like that was out of the question. The second thing was dressing up in a collar and tie. Until then I had never worn such things. Before I became a socialist the matter was perfectly simple: the shirt which I wore to work was the same which I wore when work was over, and at night I wore it to bed. Such a shirt was collarless. When I became a socialist, I went around wearing a black shirt with a high collar, but such a shirt was worn without a tie. But now, for my trial, I had to wear a collar with a tie for the first time. Comrades naturally lent me a helping hand.

I went to court in a prison van. When I emerged from it and saw the many comrades waiting for me in front of the building, I took off my hat and shouted: "Long live the Bund!" "Long live the Bund!" they shouted in reply. Grabbing me under the arms, the policemen carried me into the courtroom. I still managed to see my mother clutching her head.

---

[17] Hersh Mendel means to say "March 1913." (trans)

She was positive that they were going to beat me to death on the spot. Once in the courtroom, I clashed with my attorney.

My parents had become as poor as beggars again; nothing was left over from their inheritance. I was given a public defender, a Polish reactionary as I later learned. He tried to talk me into making a confession and coming away with a milder sentence. Should I refuse, he argued, he would have to wash his hands of the whole thing. I rejected his demand and he assured me that I could expect the worst. But I stuck to my guns, for this was our general attitude toward the tsarist courts: deny everything.

Before the judges entered, it seems, I must have been in the best of spirits, for my mother signaled to me to pull a long face; even my comrades looked sad. The trial did not last long; it was obviously of little significance. After the completion of the formalities the informers made their statements. The public prosecutor and the defense attorney as well gave short speeches, and then I had the last word. Since I did not admit that I belonged to the Bund, my speech was also short. I simply said that I was unable to understand how people could be so unscrupulous, for every word they said was false. It was very sad, I continued, that one man's freedom was dependent on the oaths of such people.

When the judges withdrew for consultation, I noticed that even the comrades had grown uneasy. It is possible that not the content of my speech, but rather its tone had alarmed them. My father sat there thoroughly stunned. He was probably unable to conceive of the fact that I would so much as dare to contradict such big people.

Truthfully, the sentence was a mild one—a year in a fortress. And since I was a youth, four months were knocked off the top there and then. The attorney turned up his nose and I was really quite pleased that I had not followed his advice.

Hardly had I climbed back into the prison van when I began to sing the *Shvue* and the *Internationale*. I sang the entire way back to Pawiak.

Once in Pawiak again I faced a new problem. I had been sentenced to imprisonment in a fortress and was therefore entitled to a whole series of privileges. I could take walks the entire day or lie in bed from dawn to dusk. In Pawiak, however, this was impossible. Pawiak was merely an interrogation jail and the authorities could not make any exceptions for me. As a political prisoner, I was also entitled to more than double the amount of food which common prisoners received. While they were given nine kopecks, I had 20 kopecks per day at my disposal. For me, it was not a question of better food; in our cell we ate very well in any case. Chatzkl and I received fine packages, and Shaffran even better. He received his food each day from outside. So improved rations were not the motivating factor. The only thing which annoyed me was the fact that the *natshalnik* was to earn eleven kopecks per day off me. I therefore demanded to be transferred to a fortress.

The *natshalnik*, a good man in fact, attempted to talk me into staying at Pawiak. He said that it really went quite well for me there, that I even had a newspaper of my own. This little hint was his way of showing that he knew perfectly well that we published a prison newspaper. Nonetheless, he was unable to convince me—I stuck to my demand. It seemed immoral to me as a revolutionary to sit back and permit a tsarist *chinovnik*[18] to enrich himself at my expense.

My comrades as well sought to dissuade me from changing prisons—in short, with horror stories. Their apprehensions were based on the following: the state did not ordinarily transfer somebody directly from one prison to another, but rather special transfer jails existed from which prisoners were finally delivered to their proper destinations. One such institution was in Praga. Since a prisoner only remained there a few days, relations both between the prison administration and the prisoners as well as between the prisoners themselves were arbitrary. One could not take action against another, for before a complaint could be processed, the prisoner was already on his way.

Comrades told me that there were many *katorzhniks*[19] in this jail who robbed their fellow cell mates and raped young boys. Quite understandably, these dreadful tales impressed me and depressed me. But it was already too late and I felt awkward about withdrawing my request. I decided to muster all the means at my disposal in order to pass the test with honor.

To be sure, I was now able to fend for myself, but it was grisly spending even as little as two days in that environment. The prison in Praga is something I have never forgotten.

---

[18] official (trans.)
[19] hard-labor convicts (trans.)

Off to the Prison in Łomża

I had to live through the experience myself to see that the reports about the horrors of this prison had not been exaggerated. The prison grounds were steeped in concentrated barbarism. At any given time, some few hundred men were incarcerated there who had either just been brought in or who were in transit. Even though it was March and the days were still cold, everybody was stripped naked. I was already accustomed to the fact that prisoners were undressed during searches, but here I was completely alone in a sea of hundreds of strange men and felt ashamed and degraded. There was a terrible accumulation of filth in the courtyard and one was hardly able to breathe. The administration addressed everybody with the familiar "you" and I noticed that many prisoners did not find this the slightest bit astonishing. It seemed as if they had already gotten used to it.

The cell itself presented an even more horrible picture, the likes of which I had never seen before and I would never see again. The bunks were occupied by men from the privileged layers: old *katorzhniks*. The others lay on the floor where there was not even enough room to put one's feet. Those occupying the bunks picked their shirts clean with such devotion that they seemed to be performing some religious ritual. They flung the filth down upon those who were lying on the floor. Nobody protested. It appeared as if these people had reconciled themselves to the fact that those on the bunks were the strong and privileged, who had rights to everything.

There was a large oven in the cell. This oven was hot and beside it stood a big barrel which served as the receptacle in which the prisoners relieved their bodily functions. One can well imagine what a frightful stench emanated from it. When I first entered the cell, I doubled over and vomited. I felt close to passing out and tears came to my eyes.

I noticed, however, that the criminals had interpreted my weakness in their own peculiar way: that is, they saw that I was still a greenhorn. And with greenhorns they went at it mercilessly. I observed them as they whispered about me. Indeed, before long two of them walked over to the little sack of food I had brought along and started to poke around inside. It dawned on me that I was a goner if I stood for this. First they would rob me of everything I had and then go to town on me. For a split second, I hesitated to start a brawl. Then I decided that it would pay, for otherwise everything would turn out even worse. I went for the two lads, flinging the one to the right and the other to the left. They consequently left me in peace for the time being. But they had not abandoned their game; no, they were preparing to pull something again. In the meantime, I opened up the package myself and invited some of the strongest of the lot to join me. This was my winning stroke. It appealed to the *katorzhniks* too. I was not about to let anybody walk off with anything on his own, but I shared what I had voluntarily. That impressed them, and from that moment on nobody dared to make any advances on my food. When it grew dark they suggested that I join them on the bunks. This was an expression of recognition. I refused, however, for it simply disgusted me to lie next to them. I spent that entire night together with two old men, one Jew and one Pole. It was obvious to me that in this inhuman environment they were the weakest, and I therefore asked them to join me for supper. The old Pole had absolutely no idea how to thank me. His daughter, he told me, was a maid in some house which was frequented by high society. I merely had to give him my name, he went on, and he would have me free in a few day's time. The Jew was a simple beggar but he felt some kind of kinship to me. Although he was unable to understand a single word the Pole was saying, he kept whispering in my ear: "Let them talk until they burst, but we Jews know what we have to do." I found the conversation great fun and spent an evening of pleasure with these two old-timers. And so it went for three days. During the daytime hours I cultivated a friendship with the bandits, and when night fell with the two old men.

When the administration summoned me to send me on my way, even the likes of the dirty courtyard looked to me like the Garden of Eden. I was happy to be rid of the society of those bandits.

It took one entire day to travel from Praga to Łomża. From the railroad line to the prison was a several-hour walk.

The moment I set foot in the Łomża prison I began to breathe somewhat freer. The prison was large and clean; it stood in a field behind the city and inside it was bright all over. The way prisoners were treated by the administration was also better and more humane. The corridors were clean and orderly, the cells almost twice as large as those in Pawiak; and each cell was occupied by just one person. The floors were made from wooden boards. In short, it looked half like a prison, half like the world outside.

During my processing in the office, the *natshalnik* asked me if I would be receiving food from outside or if I wanted to eat prison rations. I was figuring on food worth the 20 kopecks which were coming to me and was therefore agreeable to prison rations. I felt good even though I very soon noticed that I was receiving the same food which all the other prisoners were given. My cell had a window which was large enough so that I could sit on the sill and gaze out into the field. Across the way there was a peasant cottage. When it rained the peasant stood before it and looked over his field to see how the grain was maturing and growing. I was deeply envious of him, but I wasn't sure just why. Perhaps because until then I had never seen a peasant at work; or perhaps because he was a free man, able to move about freely without being observed with every step he took. I leaned my face against the iron bars and the wind blew gently in my face.

That was my first time away from Warsaw, and what Warsaw meant to me was that little hovel in the cellar on Smocza Street. Here in the field it was airy and light. A new world was opened up for me, peculiarly enough, through the window of a prison cell.

Something, however, drove me away from my window for a few days. There was one spot in the courtyard where tall grass grew and where cats were wont to hide. In order to lure birds, one of my cell neighbors would throw little pieces of bread out the window. Down swooped the birds and out sprang the cats. I stirred up a row with this neighbor of mine. It turned out that he too was a political prisoner, but I was never able to learn from him just what his political activity consisted of. He was very primitive and was practically incapable of uttering a single coherent sentence.

So it was—the days passed by as peacefully as can be, but I was full of longing. I still had approximately two months to go and waited impatiently for the day when I could see my parents and my comrades again. My parents hadn't a groschen left to come and visit me.

I never discussed the matter of my privileges as a political prisoner with the *natshalnik*. I simply helped myself. My bed remained turned down all day long, and whenever I wanted to I simply made myself comfortable.

While I was lying in bed one day—it was my first Sabbath in Łomża—

112   MEMOIRS OF A JEWISH REVOLUTIONARY

the *klutshnik* called me out. I had no idea what he wanted and went out without putting on my cap. It turned out that he had come by to escort me to the *shul*. It was a principled question among us politicals that we neither went to synagogue nor church, and therefore I wanted to return to my cell at once as soon as I caught sight of men at prayer. However, an anarchist, who had been condemned to ten years in prison, held me back and asked me to stay. I did so as a favor to him but felt terribly embarrassed, for I stood there with my head uncovered. The Jews laid a little piece of cloth on my head and I stayed.

A whole new world revealed itself to me there. The underworld which I had known until then had nothing to do with Jewishness either in manner of dress or behavior. There, however, I met criminals of a new type: Jews with long beards, Jewish hats and long coats. At first I thought that they were innocent men whom the anti-Semites had unjustly condemned. But as I conversed with them, it came out that they really were smugglers and petty thieves. It was extremely peculiar for me whenever a Jew with a long, broad beard and a Jewish hat, a man who had been praying most ardently not a moment before, told me in genuine street talk about the various jobs he had pulled.

I naturally made friends with the anarchist. He had already been there a long time and had practically gone blind. He was a very good and quiet man. What his anarchism consisted of was never clear to me; he had nothing in common with the bandits from the Red Hand. He rather more resembled a Tolstoyan. Later, I heard that he had died two weeks after his release. It was only for his sake that I violated my principles and went praying each Saturday in the *shul*.

Everything went its course normally and peacefully. But all of a sudden something blew.

A new guard arrived, who was not familiar with the situation. He was not aware of the fact that the liberties I was taking on my own were granted to me by law and sought to forbid me to lie in bed during the day. And since he approached me in a not particularly delicate manner, the answer I gave him was short and sweet.

That evening during roll call the *natshalnik* informed me that I was no longer permitted to turn down my bed during the day because I had insulted the guard. I replied that I had the right to leave my bed unmade, to which he responded that Łomża was a prison, not a fortress. I then demanded that he either transfer me to a fortress or grant me my rights there. When he refused, I declared that I would go on a hunger strike, and also said that he would have to make sure that I received my 20 ko-pecks' worth of food from outside, for this is how much was due to me for my subsistence.

The strike lasted six days. This time, I sustained it even better than be-fore, and without liquids either. Don't think for a minute that my politi-cal neighbor did anything to help; he did not even understand what a hunger strike was. Each day the *natshalnik* came in to convince me to start eating. When that failed, he gave in on the seventh day, called all the guards together and told them that they were no longer permitted to so much as give me a little hot water without my paying for it. Each day, I wrote up a list of all the things I wanted to eat amounting to 20 kopecks.

Meanwhile, the day of my release drew near, but I did not have any money for a train ticket to go home. Admittedly, in a situation like this the *natshalnik* could certainly send me home at the government's ex-pense. But it meant traveling from one prison to another and waiting for the corresponding transport to depart. The trip from Łomża to Warsaw took a single day at the time, but step by step—from one prison to another—an entire month. I did not have the audacity to ask my parents for a train ticket. But I came up with an idea: since I had a daily claim to 20 kopecks, I would spend ten and save ten. This way I would be able to accumulate three rubels in the course of a month. A ticket from Łomża to Warsaw cost two rubels and six kopecks.

And that's just how I did it. Each day I ordered a little loaf of bread costing nine kopecks, and each week something to go along with it for the remaining seven. I always ate the small bread as soon as it was brought to me. More than once I resolved to divide it up and stretch it into several meals a day, but never managed it. So I went about hungry the entire day and longed for the moment of my release when I could go to a peasant and buy myself some bread and milk.

The closer I was to freedom the more intensely I yearned to take my parents and my comrades in my arms. Day after day I paced back and forth in my cell with this one thought in mind.

But how does it go? Man proposes and god disposes. Peering out the window three days before my release, I saw my comrade Josef Krayt-man on his way outside to take a walk. He had once been caught with a stack of leaflets I had given him to distribute, spent a year behind bars and then been released. I had his imprisonment on my conscience. When I arrived in Łomża he had just gone free; but what was up now was anybody's guess. He saw me standing at the window and signaled to me that he wanted to smoke. I wrote up an order at once requesting tobacco and food. That afternoon, the guard came in and told me that Kraytman had been arrested by mistake and that he was going to be released again. But he was short one rubel. If I didn't give it to him, the guard continued, Kraytman would have to go back the slow way. I went down to the *natshalnik* and asked him to deduct the full price of a train ticket from my savings and give it to Kraytman. When he said, "But you're going to be released in two days. What are you going to do then?" I replied that this was not his concern. He was insulted and said to me that everything was dependent solely on his good will. If he so wished, he could send Kraytman back with the prison transport. I had gone too far, I thought, and asked him politely to do me a favor and convey my money to Kraytman. The latter would wire it back to me.

On the way back to my cell I walked by Kraytman's door and warned him that he'd better wire the money back to me at once if he didn't want me to have to spend a whole month getting back to Warsaw. In reply, he said that he was wearing prison shoes, and asked me if I would let him take mine. He then promised to send everything back to me immediately. I didn't quite understand just what he had done with his shoes but there was no time to muse about it. This conversation was not allowed. I took my shoes off and threw them through the slot in the door.

Back in my cell, it was the guard's turn to poke fun at me: "First you went on strike, then you saved money for a train ticket and now you're going to go home the long way—and barefoot to boot." I was certain, however, that Kraytman would send everything back to me. He didn't.

My turn came on a Sabbath in July 1913; I was free. Kraytman had been released on Wednesday. Not having received anything by Thursday, I was a bit astonished. I had no desire to spend one entire month going home on the prison transport. When I went out for a walk on Friday, Mendel Prager, who had just arrived, was also being escorted to the courtyard. He did not have a groschen to his name, but I took his shoes from him and then bid him farewell.

I was unable to sleep Friday night. With so many good comrades languishing in the prisons, I thought, I had absolutely no right to be released. In my own eyes I was inferior. Tsarism had tortured so many revolutionaries, so many close friends, and it was setting me free. No matter how strongly I had longed for freedom before, I no longer wanted to be released. I preferred joining all my comrades in Siberia, just as Yuzhek had wanted to join me when he thought that the authorities had the intention of condemning me to hard labor. Taking stock of myself, I thought that it was unbecoming for a revolutionary to think like this. One must strive to be free, to carry on the work and to fill in the shoes of those behind bars. These were the dictates of reason, but my heart was drawn to the imprisoned comrades.

I was released the following morning. I waited impatiently: what will the *natshalnik* do? Will he send me home by prison transport or will he set me free? And if he sets me free, where will I get the money to go back to Warsaw? Finally the moment came and I was summoned down to the office. The *natshalnik* acted as if he was unaware of the fact that I didn't have any money for the trip home. Before I left I thanked him for his cordiality, and he said: "Shtockfish, don't come back. We didn't get along well with each other." I replied: "That doesn't depend on me."

My Release

Now that I was free, I had no idea where to begin. I did not have a groschen in my pocket nor did I have any acquaintances in Łomża. I crossed over to the opposite side of the street and gazed back at the prison building. Funny, I didn't have the slightest feeling that I had spent several months there. It was as if I just happened to be passing by. But I was unable to move on—simply because I did not know where to go. Suddenly, a young man walked up to me and asked if I was Hersh Mendel. I said yes, and he told me that he was a member of the Bund and that Josef Kraytman had informed him that I was to be released that day. The two of us went into town, and awaiting me was a Sabbath meal. Many comrades came to celebrate. I was really glad, for I had been craving to put something warm in my stomach and talk with comrades as a free man. But my joy did not last long, for when we left the house to take a walk, there they were standing in the street: informers. It was clear to us that not only comrades from the Bund had been waiting for me at the prison gates, but agents of the secret police as well.

We tried various methods of shaking them, racing into one courtyard and out the other—but it was no use. Then we jumped into a skiff on the lake in order to row across to the other side, but they were surrounding us on both banks. There was no going back to anyone's apartment, so I stayed on the street until my train departed.

When I arrived in Warsaw, my parents were already waiting for me at the train station. At home, the table was set with a special meal like the one I was supposed to have eaten the night I was arrested.

My mother led me to my bed and assured me that it had not been empty one single night. Every comrade who was homeless and on the run had been able to rest his head there, with a mother's heart to care for him.

Comrades soon arrived. I finished eating and we went outside. Who would have thought that I'd be arrested again that very same evening? Admittedly, this time was a short stint—a single night.

I was standing in front of the consumer cooperative at the corner of

Dzika and Wołynska Streets conversing with White Maxl and my brother. Along came a Jewish woman, and approaching she said: "Run, *kinderlekh*, they're making arrests." Hardly had she gotten her last word out when we found ourselves surrounded by a group of informers, one of whom said in Yiddish, "Too late." We were led off to the Fifth Commissariat. Along the way Max managed to get rid of all the incriminating materials he had had on him. At the commissariat our identification papers were scrutinized and the others were allowed to go. When the commissar demanded to see my identification, I showed him the release papers I had received the day before at the Łomża prison. These papers had only been drawn up the preceding day by the government, I reasoned, and there could be no doubt that everything was in order. But the commissar saw it differently. No sooner am I released, he said, than I begin crawling around again where I shouldn't. You don't let such birds go free. Before I knew it, I was on my way down to the *Koza*, and the commissar made a point of saying that he would be sending me to Daniłowiczowska Street the next morning, that is, to Okhrana headquarters.

Fortunately, my brother and the White Max were quickly able to find a *macher*[20] who got me out early the next morning.

Just about that time, a gathering of the Russian cooperative movement was scheduled to take place. Our consumer cooperative was too destitute to send a delegate, and the bourgeois Jewish cooperative movement proposed that we empower them with our mandate, assuring us that they would defend our principles. Nachumson and the Yellow Mordechai (both were informers) argued that we ought to take them up on their suggestion, but all the party comrades were opposed. The same week I was released a general meeting was held to decide the issue. Comrades put me forward as the main speaker. They were certain that a man who had just gotten out of prison would make a certain impression. And so it was. It was my first appearance before the public. We didn't hand over our mandate to anyone, yet we were too short on cash to make the trip ourselves.

In this period I became popular in the Warsaw Bund. I had just sat out a prison term and distinguished myself in hunger strikes, and the manner in which I had borne myself toward Kraytman in Łomża had

[20] influential person, fixer (trans.)

become a legend. My mother's popularity in particular had grown by leaps and bounds. Moreover, she helped to hide illegal literature and to transport it from one place to another. This boosted my stature in comrades' eyes even more.

Then came the Beilis affair. When it became clear that there really was going to be a trial against Beilis, a mood of uneasiness spread. Meanwhile, signatures on petitions were gathered which were directed at the Social Democratic Party fraction in the Duma. When it came to organizing the petition campaign I played a leading roll. We now stepped up the distribution of proclamations in the Saxony Garden and organized flying demonstrations. We, the Jewish workers, were the sole ones to call for actions against the Beilis trial and the only ones who carried them out.

Historic Days for the Jewish People

In the year 1913 the whole of Russia was jolted by the shameful provocation which tsarism aimed at the Jewish people in the form of a ritual-murder trial.

We had read about the history of medieval ritual-murder trials which had been used to persecute the Jewish people, and it was with a deeply felt sense of pain and anguish that we asked, how can anything on this order have a place in the life of mankind? Even though such trials had recurred in the modern period as well, we were nonetheless certain that they were relapses into the Middle Ages. It was inconceivable to us that such things could also take place in the 20th Century.

Yet a shameful tsarist provocation of this stripe was precisely what happened at the time, and it stirred up Russian society in its entirety. From the moderate liberals to the socialist parties, a common front formed against the Russian reaction, which, by staging the Beilis trial, covered the entire Russian people in shame. It was against the protest of Russian society that the tsarist system arranged to carry through with the trial. When the archives of the Okhrana were opened following the revolution, it became clear that all of this had been orchestrated and organized directly from Petersburg, from the office of the then Russian minister of justice. But we Jewish workers, together with the whole of liberal Russian society, did not have to wait until the revolution opened the Okhrana archives. We knew immediately which way the wind was blowing, what the causes were which had induced tsarism to commit this shameful crime, and we knew what tsarism sought to gain by it.

We have already shown that as early as 1912 tsarist Russia was no longer calm and peaceful. The strike of the political prisoners in the Lena gold mines in Siberia, which the tsarist gendarmerie had drowned in rivers of blood, touched off a storm throughout the whole of the land. Not only the workers parties, but rather the entire liberal public as well protested. Thousands of protest telegrams from workers and intellectuals were addressed to the Social-Democratic fraction in the Duma. In many factories the workers conducted protest strikes and in the high schools mass meetings were organized, exactly as had been the case in the revolutionary years of 1904/05. And when the minister of justice replied to the inquiry of the Social-Democratic fraction, "So has it always been and so will it always be," it was in effect as if he had poured oil on the fire.

We felt that we had entered a new epoch—an epoch of active revolutionary struggle; we felt that the days of reaction and standstill were a thing of the past. And we, the revolutionary Jewish workers, went out to meet the storm. By means of the Beilis trial, tsarism had taken it upon itself to smother the renewed revolutionary upswing in a sea of Jewish blood. For this reason, our will to fight grew, both for the honor and the national rights of the Jewish people on the one hand, and for the victory of socialism on the other. It was clear to us that the Jewish workers must answer the tsarist challenge with a revolutionary action. Just how we were to do this was not even clear to us as yet. We were waiting for instructions from the party.

A few weeks before the Beilis trial, Rafes came to Warsaw. He came to us with the proposal that we organize a conference of the Warsaw activists of the Bund in order to discuss the question of what form the protest action on the opening day of the Beilis trial should take. Those invited included Bundist activists from the trade unions. I was the delegate from my trade. We waited for nightfall and then gathered at a meeting place on Nalewki Street. One by one we were sent to an apartment on Twarda Street, not far from Grzybowski Square. The apartment was completely empty, and even though the conference lasted the whole night, there was nowhere to sit. Candles were lit and placed on the floor next to the wall. The curtains were drawn so that light could not be seen from the street. At eleven o'clock that night, when the gates were closed, the conference began. The empty apartment, the darkness of the room, the candles next to the wall, the curtained windows—all of this corresponded to our mood and to the work which we had to do that night.

First off, Rafes gave a report on the work which had been performed in connection with the Beilis trial. He reported that the Central Committee of the Bund had resolved to carry out a revolutionary mass action on the opening day of the trial. For this reason, the Central Committee had turned to the Russian Social Democracy, the Social Democracy of Poland and the PPS-Left in order to conduct a joint action. With the explanation that the Polish and Russian working masses would not grasp the necessity for such an action and that it would turn out to be a flop, all of these parties declined. They proposed instead that the Social-

Democratic fraction lodge a protest from the tribune of the Duma the day of the trial. This ought to suffice, they maintained. The Bund did not accept this proposal and decided to carry out an action independently. Rafes added that according to the Central Committee's view, the best form of protest would be a general strike of the Jewish working class, but that inasmuch as nobody was certain that all Bundist organizations were capable of carrying out such a strike, the Central Committee concluded that every organization decide on its own the manner in which it would be able to react. After a long discussion it was resolved that the Warsaw organization conduct a general strike embracing all the Jewish workers.

The second question was, to whom should we turn for help in carrying out the action? Rafes argued that despite the intention of the tsarist regime to use the Beilis trial as a truncheon against the entire revolutionary movement in Russia, the full brunt of its attack was first of all directed at the Jewish people. For this reason, he said, the Jewish bourgeoisie must also be included in the action and the bourgeois press utilized. The greater part of those participating in the conference was opposed to Rafes' proposal. The majority defended the stance that if we made use of the bourgeois press, it would be impossible to appeal to the non-Jewish sections of the working class. It was resolved that we publish a call to the Polish workers explaining not only the national, but also the socialist spirit of our action, and calling on them to strike side by side with their Jewish comrades in the name of class solidarity wherever they labored side by side with Jewish workers. The conference concluded with the election of a strike committee consisting of five comrades: Avrom Drucker, White Max, a woman comrade from Lithuania, the noted provocateur Henekh and the writer of these lines.

Soon after the conference a meeting of the committee was held and the work divided up. Each comrade was to take over between four and five different branches of industry, but above all his own trade. Avrom Drucker was the only exception; he worked in a large printing shop and was afraid of losing his job. For this reason, I took over the printing industry myself.

We had no idea whether or not the strike would succeed. But if the newspapers were not to appear, that alone would make a tremendous impression. This appealed to me in particular, and so I took it upon myself to see that the job got done.

The plan was worked out in the following manner: four or five comrades, each of whom were representatives of the various trades, were assigned to the individuals on the strike committee. These comrades were to assume responsibility for their respective shops and factories. A list of the work locations from these five different branches of industry was compiled and it was determined where comrades would have to go. Each comrade from the strike committee, with the assistance of the comrades from the individual trades, was to look up every one of these factories. And it worked like this: walking into the workshop, the leader from the strike committee gave a speech about the meaning of the action, while a comrade from that particular trade distributed leaflets. It is hard for me to judge just what I said and how I spoke at the time. But from the reaction of the comrades, the workers and even the masters, I sensed that my speech had gone to their hearts.

I invested the greatest part of my time and effort in working the newspapers. Three Yiddish dailies appeared in Warsaw in those days: *Moment, Haynt*[21] and *Fraynd. Der Fraynd* was very much a left-radical newspaper; we were positive that they would strike. Things looked worse with *Haynt* and *der Moment*.

The day I paid a visit to *Haynt*, the editorial board promised me that they would strike if *der Moment* went on strike too; the editorial board of *der Moment* assured me that the newspaper would not appear. But when I came into the consumer cooperative the day before the Beilis trial, workers there told me that the following day's edition of *der Moment* was being set. I went over to the printing shop and appealed to the workers to put down their work. They wouldn't hear a word of it, maintaining that they would lay down their tools when the editorial board gave them the go-ahead. One must bear in mind that the newspaper printers were a privileged caste; they earned good money and did not belong to the illegal trade union.

When I saw that nothing good was to be achieved there, I called on some shoemakers, bakers and carpenters from a number of different workshops to come at once to the consumer cooperative. With their assistance I was determined to put a stop to production by destroying the galleys. In the middle of our conversation in walked Henekh the provocateur, and he made what seemed to me a fortuitous proposal. He advised against bursting into the editorial office of *der Moment* with a group of

---

[21] *Today* (trans.)

workers, for the streets were saturated with "informers." We would surely be arrested, something fatal for the strike the following day. He proposed that the two of us, undetected by the cops, steal into the offices of *der Moment* instead in order to appeal to the members of the editorial board to cease working. And this is just what we did.

We were certain that nobody had seen us, but the moment we entered the courtyard to the editorial office the gate slammed shut behind our backs. Inasmuch as our arrest was a sure thing anyway, we decided to go up to the office and accomplish our mission. We were unaware of the fact that we were being followed by a group of workers. As soon as they had seen the gate close, they were determined to force it open again. But the police surrounded the group and hauled them off. Two of the workers, who happened to be carrying leaflets, were tried in the aftermath and sentenced.

But we had no idea what was going on in the street. We went up to the editorial office and ran into some twenty men sitting around a long table. One of them was wearing a Jewish hat and had a blond beard. When Henekh demanded in the name of the Warsaw committee of the Bund that operations come to a halt, the small Jewish fellow with the little beard replied: "Kiss our..." They were responsible for two crimes, I exclaimed: for smashing the protest action of the Jewish workers and for our arrest. Then we walked out. It was not clear to me at the time why Henekh ran out ahead of me so quickly and left me standing on the stairs. Walking out alone, someone by the name of Itshele came up to me. He had quite obviously learned what I was doing there and suggested that I go upstairs to the editorial office. If the police should arrive he would say that I had come on business, and that way avoid arrest. I replied that if he believed he could cover up the crimes of the editorial board in that manner, he was sadly mistaken. I would rather be arrested by the Russian Okhrana, I added, than hide in the editorial office of *der Moment.*

I went down to the courtyard, where I found Henekh running around. Otherwise all was quiet. The gate still barred, we decided that I was to wait at one of the entrances while he waited at another. He wanted to be rid of me, it seems, in order to reach an agreement with the police. That way they might open the gate. After waiting in the entranceway for quite some time, my patience wore thin and I went back to the courtyard. The gate was standing open again and the police were gone. I was astonished that they had not come into the courtyard to nab us, for they knew we were there. It is clear to me today that Henekh had arranged the whole thing. We then set off for a Jewish metal factory on Bonifraterska Street where a few dozen Jewish workers were employed. Henekh spoke there about the meaning of the following day's strike and then we went home.

We had decided that on Thursday morning, the day of the Beilis trial, we would fetch the Jewish workers from their workplaces and, if possible, organize a mass demonstration. I do not know how my mother had learned anything about the action. Naturally, I had not breathed a word of it to her. My mother really was the mama of the Bundists in Warsaw, but I was nevertheless her next of kin and she had no desire to see me arrested again. The night before our strike she hid everything I owned. When I woke up Thursday morning, my clothes were nowhere to be found. Not a soul was home. God only knows how I dug up something to wear and what I looked like. My get-up must have been awfully strange, but I wasn't concerned about the way I was dressed that day.

At seven o'clock the strike committee gathered in the consumer cooperative. We were joined by Bundist activists from all the various trades. There they were given lists in order to snatch the workers away from their benches and to send them to Dzika Street. This was a very favorable location: a street lined by dozens of courtyards with access to Nalewki Street. At ten o'clock the whole length of Dzika Street and all the surrounding streets as well were filled with thousands of workers. When we saw that so large a crowd had turned out, we ordered them at once to form ranks. One of them, a young metal worker (today he lives in Argentina), raised the Bundist flag and, accompanied by the strains of the *Internationale*, we kicked off the demonstration. What was interesting was the attitude of the Jewish propertied class during the demonstration. When we called out the chant "Down with the Beilis trial!" or "Long live the Jewish people!" they all opened their windows and greeted the march. But when we shouted the slogan "Down with tsarism! Long live the socialist revolution!" they shut their windows and disappeared, as if it were the eve of a pogrom.

We managed to make our way as far as Gesia Street. There we were met by the commissar of the Fourth Commissariat together with a group of police, their sabers readied, who were just itching to throw themselves at the demonstration. Just then the call resounded: "Stay where you are, not one step further!" We started up the *Internationale* and the *Shvue* once again. The chorus of voices worked like magic; the masses didn't budge one single inch. The commissar and his police were in complete disarray and drew back until reinforcements arrived from the Third and Fifth Commissariats. Then they launched a joint attack. We led the crowd over to Nalewki Street and there the line of march formed itself anew. When a large demonstration finally became impossible demonstrators were organized into groups of a few dozen men each. And thus we tussled with the police until nightfall. Had we wanted to erect barricades, there is no doubt in my mind that we would have been in the position to erect a forest of them throughout the whole of the Jewish quarter.

When the day was over the strike committee came together for consultation. Some of its members were in favor of continuing the strike. But since the next day was Yom Kippur eve, this was impossible. We therefore decided that the strike be terminated.

How did we react to the shameful conduct of *der Moment*? First we organized a large group of workers, who gathered at the entrance to the editorial office early in the morning. As the newspaper attempted to make its deliveries, we ripped the edition to shreds on the spot. Later we set up a boycott against *der Moment*'s staff. Whenever they attempted to show their faces at literary gatherings, these meetings were immediately broken up. That apparently impressed them. Sending a delegation to the consumer cooperative, they looked up the writer of these lines. I have no idea where they got my name. They offered me 300 rubels to lift our boycott. I gave them no reply whatsoever; I simply showed them the door. Later, the boycott against *der Moment* was joined by all the Jewish cultural organizations.

My First Illegal Trip

Before my trip to Paris I was living illegally with comrade Josef Kraytman. His apartment on Wołynska Street consisted of a small room in the attic. During my days underground, we moved our party meetings to this little apartment. Whenever somebody had a few kopecks we bought a loaf of bread, lit a fire in the oven and prepared tea. This produced such a cloud of smoke that the tiny room became completely shrouded in darkness—so much so that it brought tears to our eyes. Even worse was that the smoke filtered down throughout the entire house, arousing the suspicions of the neighbors. That little attic was home for none too few comrades, and this had probably come to the attention of the landlord.

One day, as a group of us were lounging about the flat, the landlord knocked at the door. And was he astonished when he walked in. Two comrades were asleep in the bed, two more lay beside it and another was asleep on the table—the occupant of the apartment, Josef Kraytman. For the landlord as well as for us the situation was extremely unpleasant. We expected trouble. Suddenly he saw the picture of Karl Marx next to the window. He went pale, stammered a few words and left. It seems that he was afraid of getting into a quarrel with people who had a picture of Karl Marx hanging on the wall.

Even though we knew that he would not denounce us, the apartment was no longer conspirative. We decided that I ought to leave town as soon as possible.

I have to admit that going to Paris was a highly alluring prospect. I once read in Maxim Gorky that every revolutionary must travel to Paris and visit the Bastille, and at that time I had made a resolution to go there someday. Now, however, I regretted leaving, for I did not want to separate from my parents, from the movement and most of all from my comrades. I could not imagine that I would find comrades like these anywhere else.

Before my departure I was tormented afresh by the matter of the collar. To avoid attracting attention, my black shirt really was out of the question. But even then I was still uncertain as to whether I could manage the shirt and tie without help. In Warsaw comrade Katz helped me. But in the border town, where I spent the night lying next to a peasant on top of a heating furnace, I refused to take it off. I wasn't sure I could put it back on by myself.

I had arranged with comrades that nobody was to accompany me to the train station. Similarly, I bid my mother farewell at home. This was the most terrible thing of all, although I was absolutely certain that I would soon return. The only person who came with me to the station was my father. He bought me a ticket to take me to Bendin,[22] and from there I had to cross the border on the sly. How moved I was when I later read the memoirs by the Russian Menshevik leader Abramovich, in which he tells that his father took him by the hand and saw him off to his first revolutionary emigration, and that he himself accompanied his son when the latter set off to fight in the Spanish Civil War. These memoirs reminded me of how my father took me by the hand and elbowed his way through to my compartment in the train. Oh, how difficult indeed it is to forget the scenes of the distant past when they are so deeply buried in the heart and soul! Who would have thought that day that he was to suffer a terrible death from starvation two years later!

I was already settled in my compartment when my comrades appeared. In double file, arm in arm, they marched past my car without looking at me. This silent demonstration of friendship by these wonderful comrades is something I will never forget, even though I was to experience many displays of comradely devotion in times to come.

After I had smuggled myself across the border and reached Myslowitz,[23] a town which belonged to Germany in those days, I encountered new difficulties. The agent who brought me over the German border was probably an agent for a German shipping firm as well, and this company had its connections to the German police. He brought me to the firm's office and there somebody told me that I would either have to buy a boat ticket or they would send me back. It was no use whatsoever explaining to them that I did not need a boat ticket, for I was on my way to Paris and hardly had enough money for the train. They refused to believe me and threatened to ship me back.

I saw only one way out: fleeing. But running to the train and trav-

---

[22] Bedzin (trans.)

[23] Mysowice (trans.)

eling on was dangerous, for I could be seized along the way to Berlin and deported. So I went into town and looked around for a place to hide. The agent followed me but I pretended not to see him. Meanwhile, I found a Jewish inn and that's where I planned to wait it out until the agent had lost my trail. I was able to steal into the restaurant undetected and lay up there for two whole days. Then I went to the train station, bought myself a ticket and continued on my way to Paris.

During the trip through Belgium I made the acquaintance of a young man who was also heading for Paris illegally. So we traveled together.

It was a cold, dark evening when we reached the Belgian-French border. We were ordered to leave the car. Accustomed as I was to tsarist practices, I was expecting to be arrested. It turned out to be customs control, however. When I opened my suitcase and showed the official everything I owned—two pieces of underwear and my black shirt—he looked dumbfounded. He wanted to see my belongings, he repeated. When I finally convinced him that these were my belongings, he gave me a strange look—whether from pity or astonishment I don't know.

Late that night we arrived in Paris. The streets were empty. I had half a franc left from the trip and my traveling companion another half a franc. We decided to use our remaining cash to put ourselves up in a hotel room for the night. After a long search we found a hotel. Did I sleep that night? I can't remember, but I definitely spent the night with a heavy heart. What would I do the next day?

So that night we stayed in a hotel and then we hit the street. We were neither able to speak a word of French nor understand it. The young man accompanying me only knew the name of one street: Rue des Rosiers. Each time we ran into anybody who looked Jewish we asked where Rue des Rosiers was located. And though everyone gave us some sort of answer, we understood but little. Evidently, however, we were approaching our destination, for the last time we inquired somebody led us right to the street. That's when I lost my traveling companion.

Rue des Rosiers was indeed a bit more like home. The only faces there were Jewish faces, people whom you could ask a question. But I didn't have much to ask. I neither had any addresses nor the names of acquaintances, nor did I have any money for a bite to eat. But I began schmoozing anyway. It wasn't hard to see that I was a greenhorn.

At lunchtime, when the workers began to stream into the street, I unexpectedly met two acquaintances of mine: Ari Shuster and Paulus from the Red Hand.

Ari Shuster was a peculiar man: an old Bundist, and yet no close friend. He was a sufficiently intelligent man, but his intelligence exhausted itself in empty chatter. He considered himself something special but he hadn't any close friends in our ranks; he was respected but nobody took him seriously. None of us in Warsaw knew that he had gone away, for he never told anyone. He was glad to see me and invited me to join him for lunch. Figuring that I didn't have a place to sleep, he arranged to meet me in the same restaurant that night. But he didn't show.

That evening at the same place I met Paulus. I would have preferred to be together with Ari Shuster, but now I had no other choice and was forced to stick with Paulus. We ate dinner together and then went out for a walk along the boulevards. I was enamored of the lights, the luster, the gaiety of the Parisian boulevards. It was this life which later helped me to drive away the sadness I experienced in a period of great loneliness and want.

After our walk he brought me back to his hotel. I could have stayed with him for a while, in any case until I found different accommodations. But when I asked him how he supported himself he admitted that he was a petty thief. That being so, I didn't want to have anything more to do with him.

My situation was desperate. I knew that there was a branch of the Red Cross in Paris which supported political émigrés. I went to the Bundist club located on a small side street near Rue des Rosiers, Rue Ferdinand Duval, and they gave me the address of the Bundist representative in the Red Cross, Lazar. Receiving me in a not particularly polite manner, Lazar gave me some money and requested that I produce proof that I really was a political refugee. Otherwise, he said, no more money. Perhaps he was right; after all, is it not the case that none too few people take advantage of such institutions and defraud them? But I was affronted by his mistrust for me. The fact that he called into question my membership in the Bund struck me as something so inhuman that I decided not to go back to him again.

What I got for the money which this Lazar gave me was a hotel room for two weeks—paid in advance. When these two weeks were over, my life took a desperate turn for the worse. Until Paris, I never could have imagined how one can endure a period filled with so much worry and want.

In Paris without a Home

I began to search for work, but without success. The situation I had grown accustomed to back home was that the master employed workers who were sent to him by the trade union. It was a different story in Paris. You had to find work on your own, and it was only after you found a job that you were able to become a member of the syndicate.

I collected addresses and searched for work. Every employer examined me from head to toe, sort of how one assesses horses in the marketplace. This naturally annoyed me and my answers were not as fit and proper as they ought to have been. Nobody took me on and I quickly got fed up with the search. In the end, I went as far as the doorstep, addresses in hand, and turned around again without even having knocked. I found it painful and offensive: can it be that the small, illegal Jewish trade unions in Warsaw have more muscle than the trade unions in free France? I came down with a terrible case of homesickness.

I was out of work and was ashamed to tell anyone about it. I simply went without eating for weeks on end and slept on the street outside the Metro station together with all the *clochards*. I can still remember how I wandered the streets on winter nights, the rain lashing at me. It was as if the raindrops were made of stone. I had read somewhere that one method by which the Chinese carried out the death sentence consisted of trickling water, drop by drop by drop, on the condemned man's head. The drops falling on my head, I thought, may not kill me, but they'll surely drive me mad. Whenever I walked past a bakery, I stopped in my tracks just to savor the aroma of the baked bread.

I once managed to slip into a park and fall asleep on a bench. This is forbidden in France. You were permitted to walk the streets all night long—but not to sleep. And in fact, a policeman soon walked by, woke me up and in sign language gave me the word that I could be arrested. Afraid that I might fall asleep again, I took to the boulevard leading from the Bastille to the zoo. There I ran into a comrade, an anarchist, who looked even grislier than I did. When I asked him what he was so worked up about, he told me that while walking along the boulevard, a wealthy lady had approached him and offered him a franc. He neither accepted the money nor treated the woman exactly tenderly, but her gesture had nonetheless hurt him to the quick. This comrade was an anarchist, a rebel; because of this one franc, he was prepared to get his hands on some dynamite and blow Paris to smithereens.

Meanwhile, I found an amphitheater on Rue Monge, a relic from the days of the Roman empire, where I was able to spend my nights sleeping on a bench. The theater made a frightening impression— people avoided going there. The stone benches, the stone stage, the emptiness—all of this sent shivers up and down one's spine. It seemed as if the souls of the murdered and tortured slaves, who had been ripped to shreds there for the amusement of the Roman dictators, still inhabited the place.

During this period, I often went to the anarchist library, from which I was able to check out three books per day. Where I got the energy and the patience to read so much is a mystery to me. But I think that the source of my strength lay in the fact that in the course of reading Marxist and anarchist literature, my conviction was fortified that the capitalist world was in decline and did not have long to go.

In the meantime, the March days arrived—the time of year when the French proletariat celebrates the anniversary of the uprising of the Parisian Communards. I got hold of a Metro ticket and went to Père Lachaise.[24] When I got there, however, I had no idea where to find the socialist groups. I must have looked lost, for a French worker walked up to me, laid his hand on my shoulder and beckoned to me to follow him. He led me right to the demonstration. That French worker's hand on my shoulder filled me with joy; he understood me without a word being spoken. It seems to me that I can still feel his hand to this day. And perhaps the impact of this experience propelled me along the road of international socialism even more than the theories of Marx and Kropotkin.

How had my mother learned of the straits I was in? In any case, she sent me money so that I could go to London to stay with my older brother Shlomo. The money was just enough for a ticket.

I departed at the end of March, but never made it to London. Free access to England was something which only second-class passengers enjoyed. Those traveling third class were subjected to an interrogation.

---

[24] Cemetery in Paris where the last battle of the Paris Commune was fought and where many of the Communards are buried, along with other leaders of the international workers movement. (trans.)

Obviously I did not please the officials, for they sent me back to Dieppe, to the harbor that is. From Dieppe to Paris I was on my own, but without a franc to my name. I stayed in Dieppe and kept my head down. Then I decided to go to Paris by foot. Had I known the French language I may well have succeeded. But I was unable to speak French and even less capable of understanding it. So I took to wandering. Whenever I set out for Paris, I always found my way back, after a long march, to the Dieppe city limits. After many such attempts I abandoned the idea, but I still didn't know where to begin. I decided to stop musing about it, for it doesn't do any good when you know in advance that you've run out of brainstorms. I went back to town and put my trust in chance: "Something has just got to happen. I won't be stuck in a strange city forever without a groschen in my pocket."

I went to the fish market and looked on as the freshly caught fish was sold. After I had had enough of this sight, I went back to the train station. By chance, a worker emerged from the depot, a Bulgarian, who understood a little Russian. I told him about the scrape I was in and he advised me to go to the Russian consulate in Dieppe. When I replied that I was a socialist and a political émigré, he told me to wait. A few minutes later an old French worker came outside and arranged to meet me when the working day was over—at four o'clock.

Cheerfully, I went back to town. I considered it a good sign that whenever I was in a bind, workers walked up to me and, though I didn't understand their language, lent me a hand. This fact alone did more to lift my spirits than anything they did for me. Even my gnawing hunger vanished. At four o'clock sharp I was ready and waiting. The worker showed up and we were off. Along the way, we stopped in a café. More workers arrived and each of them chipped in to buy me a glass of wine. I was drunk before we got home. What joyful days I spent in the home of this French worker.

This was no mere proletarian, but rather a real socialist family. After I had washed up and had a bite to eat, their son-in-law dropped by. He was a Rumanian who had spent some time in Russia, where he became a socialist. Overjoyed, he engaged me in comradely conversation.

Dinner was served and then we wound up the gramophone and played the *Internationale*. The old worker and his wife, their daughter and son-in-law all sang along in unison. During those cheerful hours I came to envy these people. For the first time in my life I heard somebody sing the *Internationale* at home. How terribly different it was in my family, on my old home turf! Our parents were afraid of this song, it was something incomprehensible to them. Here I felt the strength of a people which had undergone four revolutions in the course of a century, and it was here that the socialist ideal united grandparents and grandchildren.

After we had finished eating and singing various revolutionary songs, they suggested that I try to find work in Dieppe. As long as I was out of work, they said, I could stay with them. In Dieppe, as in every port city, there are many hotels. They gave me addresses so that I knew where I was going. I admit that I deceived them: I knew that I was not fit for this kind of work, that I would not be able to serve anybody. But it was unpleasant for me to refuse their suggestion. So I roamed the streets for a time and acted as if I were in search of a job. After three days, they bought me a train ticket and I returned to Paris.

In Paris, the old misery started up again. I ran into one comrade, however, whose example made it clear to me that my sufferings were mere child's play in comparison to what he was going through.

One evening, when I was crossing Rue de Rivoli, who was walking toward me but Leyzer Levin, the man whom the party had suspected of being an informer. He had received an order from the party to go to Argentina until the matter had been cleared up. All of us were certain that that's where he was and now I saw him, of all people, in Paris! I wasn't sure whether I ought to extend him my hand, but his appearance sparked such compassion in me that I went up to him. He told me that he had been on the run in Argentina and that somebody had been out to murder him. That's why he had fled to Paris.

It was a short walk from Rue de Rivoli to the Bund's club, so I took Leyzer there. A discussion evening was in progress dealing with the Polish economic boycott against the Jews, an act of revenge for the fact that the Jews had helped the socialist Jagiełło win his mandate in the elections. We listened to the discussion but the political level of those participating left us with a bad impression. There was no shortage of intelligent men there, but they were clearly unfamiliar with the circumstances and talked like people who were far away from the country in question. The two of us spoke. Leyzer was no mean speaker and the audience was pleased with our contributions. Esther Ivinska, Viktor Alter's sister, reproached me for not coming to the club and participating in the work. When a commission was elected to work out a resolution against the boycott, she proposed both Leyzer and I. I saw that

Leyzer was going to ignore the fact that he had been accused of working for the police and it irritated me immensely. True, his guilt had not been proven; he was only suspected. But it was his responsibility to report this himself. I called Ivinska aside and told her the story, noting truthfully that it was merely a suspicion and asking her to keep the matter under her hat as much as possible. But the news got around, and it wreaked havoc on Leyzer. I can say with a free conscience, however, that I took no part in that dirty business, and Leyzer knew this and judged accordingly. He expressed his thanks to me more than once, not only in Paris, but later in Warsaw as well when he again became a member of the party.

In May I got a job in a factory specially built by Rothschild. You could only work there three months, that is, until you had mastered one or another trade. I learned carpentry. The pay was three francs per day, not much, but for me it was a real mint. I was able to eat very modestly and pay for my hotel. The organization of the factory exhibited all of the defects of a philanthropic institution, and the relations between workers and management were extremely bad. We sensed that we were looked down upon the way the poor, whom one helps in distress, are looked down upon, and the administration wanted us to bear this in mind and thank them for it at all times. Worst of all were the delegations which came to watch us with their pitying looks, viewing their labors with a bountiful sense of pride. I didn't work badly and would have perhaps mastered the trade had something unforeseen not intervened which forced me to quit.

A new worker from the Ukraine, a political emigrant, showed up for work. He was fond of talking politics and also sang beautiful Russian songs. Later, I learned that he had been forced to leave his wife behind at home, and his songs echoed with his intense longing. He also gave one the impression that he was not a healthy man. Perhaps his numerous personal difficulties had impaired his ability to work as diligently as was expected, and he got into one conflict after another with the administration. On one occasion, when the administrator insulted him and told him to leave, I flew into a rage. I was well aware that it is a crime not to perform one's work diligently—even in a philanthropic institution; but on the other hand, I also knew what was tormenting my co-worker. He was a Russian Social Democrat, an adherent of Plekhanov, and he longed for the workers movement which he had had to leave behind. I was certain that firing him was tantamount to sentencing him to death.

I informed the administrator that if my comrade went, I was going too. Such conduct in a philanthropic institution was probably a novelty.

The administrator looked at me with wild eyes, even insulted me, but counseled me to stay nevertheless because I was a good worker and had the makings of becoming a professional. It may well be that he meant it in earnest, but I felt so closely bound up with this comrade that I found it impossible to stay on without him.

The two of us anxiously left the factory with three francs apiece in our pockets, which meant that as early as the following day we would be unable to continue paying for our hotel. We therefore had every prospect of sleeping on the boulevards again.

Comrade David—that was his name—took the thing more to heart than I did; the whole matter was weighing on his conscience. He knew that it was on account of him that I was out of a job and it was no secret to him that by losing my job I had also lost the roof over my head.

Fortunately, he soon found work as a painter. I went by to see him each evening and together we went to a Russian restaurant on Avenue des Gobelins.

I very much enjoyed those evening get-togethers on Avenue des Gobelins, for it was there that I met for the first time the leaders of the Russian revolutionary movement. Plekhanov, Martov, Trotsky, Lunacharsky and the Socialist Revolutionary Avksentiev frequented the place. I became friends with Antonov-Ovseyenko, the famous hero of the Civil War, who was still a Menshevik in those days and a warm and good man. I also befriended one Grisha, a Bolshevik, who later became the chairman of the Moscow Soviet. As with Antonov-Ovseyenko, he too was murdered by Stalin.

It was also there that I became acquainted with the disputes within the Russian Social Democracy and, from the never-ending discussions, acquired a picture of the factional differences between the Bolsheviks and the Mensheviks. I was surprised that the Mensheviks displayed no less revolutionary passion in these discussions than the Bolsheviks. Antonov-Ovseyenko was no less revolutionary than Grisha, and I came to be equally fond of the both of them.

But how long can you live off your comrade's paycheck? Although David and I were close friends, I wanted to try my luck once again and go to London. The comrades who accompanied me to the train station on that occasion live in Israel today. We often recall how my second journey to London worked out and have a good laugh together over it.

It was July 1914. During the month of July, cheap tickets were available for short excursions from France to England. The comrades all chipped in and bought me a ticket. Escorting me to the train, they adamantly expressed their displeasure at the way I was dressed; it wasn't excursion attire. So one of them removed his collar and necktie and gave it to me, the second one traded his shoes for mine, the third stuffed a clean handkerchief in my pocket. In a word, I was newly equipped from head to toe. But none of it did any good. I was still forbidden to travel on to London. The controller who had sent me back the first time recognized me and again refused to let me enter the country. Insisting that I wished to visit my brother for the holidays was of no avail. The controller was of the opinion that whoever had been sent back once before was forever on his list.

This time, my return trip was a sure thing—I had purchased a round-trip ticket. That evening I was back in Paris and was forced to spend the night sleeping on the street.

I made up my mind at the time never to travel to England again. When I calculated how long I could have slept in a hotel for the money which the two tickets to London had cost, the thought of those foolish trips enraged me.

PART 3

On the Eve of the War

*A*fter returning from my second unsuccessful trip to London, my material situation took a sharp turn for the worse. I decided to take on work regardless of what the conditions might be. For one franc per day I worked for a hatmaker. The exploitation was ghastly. In addition to the hours which I put in at the shop, I had to deliver the goods to the stores as well. From that one franc I was just able to survive, but I never ate my fill. I also had to stay at the home of a comrade, one of Max's brothers. On Sundays or holidays, my days off that is, I was simply forced to fast. On 14 July, the French national holiday, I took part in an excursion to Versailles which cost me one franc. But it was my one and only franc, and I would neither be able to eat nor drink anything the entire day. Some of my acquaintances noticed, however, and they invited me to join them.

But my material situation was by no means the most important thing in those days. Storm clouds were gathering in the skies over Europe. Everybody was shaken by the shot at Sarajevo, for everybody sensed that what was at issue here was no accident, no individual act of terrorism. Rather, dark and powerful forces were at work which would take advantage of the assassination in order to lead the peoples into the great human slaughter which would later come to bear the name: "World War I." July was a month of tension and everybody was expecting something to happen.

Our main topic of conversation during that excursion on 14 July 1914 was the war. What will happen if the war breaks out? We were still unable to believe that the ruling classes would risk such immense carnage on a worldwide scale. And if they do it nonetheless? What will the reply of the world proletariat be?

We were certain that the world proletariat would remain true to the resolutions of the Basel Congress of the Second International dealing with the struggle against the war. If a war should break out the International would utilize the crisis to launch into battle against capitalism.

We did not have Lenin's theses calling for the conversion of the war into a civil war. But the Basel resolution was sufficient to instill fear in the ruling class and to strengthen the revolutionary mood among the workers, to enhance their sense of courage and their belief in the forces of the international working class.

There were signs indicating that these hopes would be fulfilled. In 1912, when a conflict broke out between Germany and France over the Morocco question and it already looked as if we were perched on the wave of a catastrophe, the Second International saved both peoples from the battle of destruction with its resolute antiwar stance. We were certain that in the face of the approaching world war, the attitude of the proletarian International would be even more resolute.

My personal faith in proletarian internationalism was very strong. I knew the declaration which Wilhelm Liebknecht and August Bebel had made in the Prussian parliament at the time of the eruption of war between France and Prussia in 1870, pronouncing that their proletarian solidarity with the French workers stood higher than the interests of the German capitalists. Over the din of the cannons, they sent off their greetings to the French working class. It is indeed the case that Marx was against this declaration, but for us young Marxists it became a holy testament, which pointed the way toward how we must act in times of war. For us there was no doubt that the entire German Social Democratic Party would conduct itself accordingly now. This belief of ours was strong—and our disappointment was all the more terrible.

We also believed in the internationalism of the French proletariat, in the tradition of the Paris Commune. It is well known that during the Paris Commune the Communards demonstratively elected German socialists to their leading bodies. This was the splendid reply of the Parisian proletarians to the greetings from Liebknecht and Bebel. I knew that the syndicalist movement in France was anarchist, that is, absolutely against the state, and would never go along with the war; that in accordance with its theory and practice, it had to put out the call for a general strike on the very first day of the mobilization.

The syndicalists spoke out against the war with extreme sharpness; not infrequently they threatened with an uprising. Among the Socialists,

Jaurès surpassed himself. I heard him speak a few times at mass gatherings. Although my understanding of the French language was quite weak, it was sufficient to see Jaurès at the tribune and to hear him speak in order to feel that here stood a great fighter. In the inner-party discussions between Guesde and Jaurès I was on Guesde's side, but I was in love with Jaurès. Even though he was no Marxist, he united in his person the tradition of the Jacobins with a deeply human, moral *Weltanschauung*. Jaurès was somebody you could love even when you were not of one mind with him.

News from Russia reached us as well: a new period of political strikes had begun, and in Petersburg there was occasional barricade fighting. We Russian revolutionaries were certain that the Russian working class, resting on its European comrades, would have the energy to resist the war in the appropriate manner.

I was also unable to conceive that the Austrian Social Democrats would turn into social patriots. In that land, with its patchwork of diverse nations, social patriotism seemed absurd to me. In the event that the ruling classes should launch into a war adventure, all signs indicated that the proletariat would take advantage of the situation to put some muscle into its struggle for socialism.

The entire colony of Russian revolutionaries awaited the events with impatience. Everyone was certain that together with the war there would be a revolution in France. From the conversations which I listened to at the Russian restaurant on Avenue des Gobelins, I learned that the Russian Social Democrats of all tendencies were in close contact with the French Socialist Party.

When Jaurès was murdered it became clear that this was the direct prelude to the world war.

As far as I knew, a decision had been reached instructing us to gather at the meeting places of the Socialist Party and the syndicates on the day of the mobilization and to wait for the order. That the battle order would arrive was clear to everybody, even though we did not know precisely the character which the struggle would assume.

The War

August 4 was the day the general mobilization was proclaimed and the war began. At two o'clock in the afternoon the master in my shop walked up to me, told me to put down my tools and paid me the half a franc he owed me for the half day's work. Noticing that this had not sent me into a flurry, he looked at me, his gaze full of astonishment, and asked me why I was so calm. It may be that I retained my sense of inner calm and that the mobilization made no impression on me because I had already known in advance that the war was on the way. I was preoccupied by other thoughts: what will the Socialist Party do? Will tomorrow really see barricade fighting? But my master replied that it could not be worse for me, for there is nothing worse than terminating a job with half a franc in your pocket.

I went to the Russian restaurant to grab a bite to eat and find out what there was to do.

The restaurant was packed full with people. Everyone was in the same frame of mind as I. Everyone was asking himself: what will the Socialist Party's response be? What will the morrow bring? In order to avoid offering anybody the occasion to stage a provocation, we decided to leave the locale and return very early the next day—that is, 5 August—to wait for instructions.

The following morning at the crack of dawn we assembled to receive our orders. Comrades arrived—I believe Antonov-Ovseyenko was among them—and informed us of the dismal news: the leaders of the Socialist Party had counseled us to disperse peacefully and quietly if we did not wish to provoke repression. Under the pretext that the German Social Democrats had betrayed, the leaders of the party had resolved to defend the country and to support the government.

One can hardly depict in words how this news affected us. Many stood there with tears in their eyes. Nobody was prepared for anything on this order. Defeated, disappointed, morally broken we dispersed.

The next day another bombshell burst: Plekhanov was calling on the Russian socialists to take to the battlefield and to settle accounts with tsarism later. My comrade David, with whom I had worked at Rothschild's, was an avid adherent of Plekhanov; he cried like a baby. When even the likes of Plekhanov had become a turncoat, David lost his faith in socialism. He was contemplating going home to Russia and informing the comrades there of Plekhanov's betrayal. In the end, he joined the French army as a volunteer. When I asked him why, he answered that it was all the same to him now. He fell a few weeks later, a volunteer in a war which he hated with all his heart.

In the same period a gathering also took place at the Bundist club. The question was, what should the position of the Parisian organization of the Bund be toward the war? Comrade Lazar was the speaker. He personally owed France a great deal of thanks, he exclaimed, and his conscience demanded of him that he take to the front. As for everybody else, he demanded free choice: every individual ought to do what he wants. This standpoint did not console me; I came out for a principled antiwar stance. Leyzer Levin as well trained his guns on the war with intense sharpness. The meeting broke up without having reached a decision, even though it was evident that a large majority there was against the war.

As I departed the gathering, one comrade charged toward me, yanked at the lapels of my jacket and cried that he wouldn't permit me to stay home while he reported for service. As it turned out, he never made it to the front. Today he is a Stalinist and lives in Paris. I would prefer not to mention his name.

France was no longer the same. The Socialists exchanged the slogan, "For the struggle against war," with the slogan, "Fight to the finish." The syndicalists wrote in their newspaper that the workers should take part in the war; they would remain good syndicalists nonetheless. The old left Socialist Gustave Hervé, who published his own newspaper called *La Guerre Sociale*, competed with the worst reactionary elements for the mantle of patriotism. Even such acknowledged anarchist leaders as Jean Grave and the great writer Octave Mirbeau became big patriots.

It was all like a terrible nightmare. It seemed as if everything had been destroyed, as if the socialist ideal had been crushed beneath the iron march of the soldier's boot. What a soulwrenching, agonizing time it was.

In the Jewish quarter, Jewish volunteers demonstrated under the slogan, "On to Berlin." I stood there and observed the demonstration. I knew that there were many among them who had only been in Paris a short time and who were without any means of existence. Having reported for military service, however, they were served lunch at Rothschild's. In fact, all of these demonstrations marched in that direction. I crossed over to the other side of the street, my eyes welling with tears. The kitchen administrator, who just happened to be walking by, took notice of this. Misinterpreting the reason for my despondency, he came up to me and offered me a meal coupon. I cursed at him violently. Now, as I write these lines, I am sorry about it because it is quite possible that his attitude had been dictated by noble feelings.

Life became sad and difficult. During the first days it was impossible for a young foreigner to go outside. I didn't even have enough money to survive a single day; finding work in the first days of the mobilization was out of the question. I stood before the choice of either reporting to the front or starving to death. Some third way was not on the cards.

I was living at the time with comrade Felix, Max's brother. Felix had anarchist leanings. Since it was dangerous to take to the street—draft-age men who hadn't gone into the army were assaulted—the two of us decided to stay indoors, even if it meant going hungry.

The days were still hot and it was suffocatingly warm in the attic apartment where we lived. We opened the door a bit and Felix plopped himself down on the bed. There was no room for two, so I slept on the floor. A few days went by and then Felix began to go outside for short stretches. I decided to stay put in the attic however. With the papers I had, it was better not to have to show them to anyone.

So it went for at least a week. All of sudden, our situation mysteriously changed. When I woke up on the sixth or seventh day, I found a small piece of bread lying on the table along with a bunch of grapes; at lunchtime the same thing. This went on for several days. It was anybody's guess who our guardian angel was; who, in a manner so cryptic, so human and noble was supplying our needs. Who could it be? A few days later, having decided to go outside, I met a French woman in the corridor, an old woman with grey hair who lived a few steps away from us. Spotting me, she embraced and kissed me, and said: "Don't report. It's enough that they've taken my son." Now I knew who was giving us bread and grapes each day.

I went down to the street. It had grown quieter. The hunt for foreigners had ceased, life had returned somewhat to normal. I began to think about finding work.

The Germans were advancing toward Paris. The situation was critical and the government removed itself to Bordeaux. They had resolved not to force the political émigrés from tsarist Russia either to go into the army or to go home; rather, they sent us to the provinces where we lived at the expense of the government. Everyone received one franc per day. In the villages where we lived—and we lived in communes—one franc was sufficient. Along with my comrade Felix, I went to a little village in the vicinity of Tours. This was really a relief for me. I ate and drank and had time to reflect; I was able to arrive at certain conclusions. The conclusions which I drew were quite false, but my waywardness was the product of a young man's depressed state of mind; a young man who had lost the ground under his feet, yet who wasn't about to let himself be smashed to pieces.

I Leave Paris

In the autumn of 1914 we were removed from Paris. Whereas my group was composed exclusively of Jews, there were many Russians as well in the other groups. We were settled in the villages around Tours. The mayor of the village which took in our group received us and bid us a hearty welcome. He was a Radical Socialist, that is, a bourgeois radical, who was nevertheless pleased to open the doors of his village to Russian revolutionaries. Certain as he was that we would all be arrested the moment we set foot on Russian soil, he expressed his satisfaction that the government had not sent us back. He placed an entire villa at our disposal and we set up our own commune.

There were approximately twenty of us. I was the sole Bundist; the others were almost all anarchists. Some of them are worth describing.

One man, Selig Aller from Russia, gave you the impression that he was not completely normal. He let his beard grow, wore long hair and long fingernails. His theory was that man must lovingly accept everything which nature gives him. You are not permitted to counter the laws of nature, he said. He was a big bluffer and every one of us knew that there was no believing what he said. It soon turned out that our estimation of him was correct. He fell in love with a girl from one of the other groups and, shortly thereafter, cut off his long hair, shaved his beard and trimmed his fingernails. In a word, he forgot about all the laws of nature.

Another man from our group was a follower of Nietzsche. In one monologue he argued that it is mankind's task to struggle against nature, for nature enslaves man. Man will never become great, he said, as long as he does not take on the causes of his slavery: that is, those traits nurtured in him by nature. One of the means in this struggle must be the renunciation of sleep. Nature, he argued, demands that man rest, that he sleep at definite times. But man must say no—man must resolve to forgo sleep. This is the certain path, he reasoned, to becoming *Übermensch*.

There was also a certain Michael among us, likewise an anarchist, who considered the Marxists to be the world's worst swindlers. In his *Capital*, Michael said, Marx shows how the capitalists enrich themselves, and by reading Marx's work, the Marxists learn the secret of self-enrichment. He thought nothing whatsoever about class struggle, for if the workers were to win anything by striking, the prices of goods would immediately become inflated and nothing would be left over. There is only one means to counter this: sabotage. And as was his way, he conceived of sabotage in the simplest terms: pilfering from his boss.

There was still another anarchist—I cannot remember his name—who was a devotee of Oscar Wilde. He was of the opinion that the workers must be lifted to the heights of aesthetics. The worker who loves art, literature and music will never want to be a slave. Not revolutions, he exclaimed, but beauty—that is the road to deliverance. One Mrs. Buse also lived with us. Embroiled in a family tragedy at home, she packed her bags and went to Paris. There she became a mother to all the workers who suffered on account of their revolutionary ideas. She used to single me out for attention, making sure that I dressed in clean clothes and ate at regular hours.

Shlomo Salmen, the man we named the "Five-Minute Philosopher," was also a member of our group. He spoke passionately about philosophy but, as it turned out, had not read a single one of the philosophers. His sole claim to authority was a history of philosophy which he had read and committed to memory and which he was able to recite beautifully. He wanted to author a philosophical work himself; the preface to it already existed and he went around reading it aloud to everybody.

There was a group of Russian bohemians in the area, or better said, a group of big boozers. They never gave a thought to revolution. What for? Nothing would come of it anyway. Inequality is indeed a bad thing, they said, but it has always existed and it always will. It's a law of nature and there is only one way to relieve the misery: drink. And to be sure, drinking is something they held in particularly high regard. They were a bunch of semi-philosophers and semi-poets. A Jewish painter was one of their number too. He also drank, but when his Russian comrades weren't around he complained that he no longer had the strength to sustain such a life. From time to time he sang Yiddish songs. His favorite was Abraham Reisin's "You ask me, my friend, how old I am." Today he is a famous painter in Paris.

That's what life was like for several months. There were many discussions and many disputes. Boring it wasn't. For me, village life was particularly pleasant; it was the first time that I was at home in the middle of nature. I took lots of walks, most of all in the forest. I often even spent the night there. I loved the stillness of the woods, for there I was able to immerse myself in my own thoughts. And indeed, I had enough to reflect about.

Meanwhile, life in Paris began to stir again. The Germans had been stopped at the Marne. The factories began working and people began to make their way back, above all, those who were able to find work. Many from our group returned as well. Four of us remained behind. Without any skills, I was in no hurry to go anywhere.

Those days represented an ideological watershed in my life. As long as the whole group of us merrily whiled away the time, I took no notice of the changes which were maturing inside me. When the others went on their way, however, and I was left on my own, the doubts began to gnaw at me: how does it look with my socialism? What were the actual causes of the collapse of the Socialist International? No, an event of such consequence could not be an accident, there had to be laws which gave rise to it. What were they? All of these problems tormented me; I had to find an answer to them if I did not want to go under. The answer was not immediately at hand and I spent several backbreaking months trying to find it. I often had the feeling that I shied away from looking the problem squarely in the eyes, fearing as I did that it might drive me away from socialism. But things could not go on for long like this. I was afraid of morally shattering to pieces. I even tried drinking but soon grew tired of it. For whole days at a time, I left the village in order to find peace in the stillness and solitude of the forest. But it was all in vain. I had to find an answer to the question: who was responsible for the collapse? It seemed to me as if the more I reflected about it, the more rapidly I alienated myself from Marxism. I began to think that the bankruptcy of the Second International was not an accident, but rather a consequence of the entire Marxist doctrine. If Marx teaches that socialism can only be realized in a highly developed capitalist society, that capitalist development in each individual country has its own characteristics, that there are different state forms in individual countries and that the development of the capitalist economy is dependent upon the normal functioning of the apparatus of the state, then it is indeed comprehensible that the Social Democrats must have an interest in defending this state machine. This would mean, however, that the Social Democrats had not betrayed, but rather remained true to themselves when they broke the international solidarity of the working class and supported the militarists of their respective lands. Precisely these false conclusions of mine were only confirmed by the declarations of right-wing Socialists of the sort of Renaudel in France, Scheidemann in Germany, Plekhanov in Russia and Adler in Austria. The fundamental motive behind the way they conducted themselves was the same. They simply arrived at counter-posed results.

When I arrived at this point, the question was posed: what now? Where can you go, what can you do? At that time, the thought surfaced in me that anarchism could answer these questions. Admittedly, I was well aware that the most important anarchist leaders had not acted any differently than the leaders of the Second International. But I saw a great difference between the two, a difference, it seemed to me, which consisted of this: by calling for participation in the war the Marxists had remained true to Marxism; the anarchists, on the other hand, the moment they put out the call to go to the front, were no longer anarchists. The anarchist idea itself remained untarnished. Anarchism in its very essence is antimilitarist—it is against the state, against the imposition of external discipline. The starting point for anarchism is not economic development, but rather a purely human-moral conception. In its eyes, every man is important as an individual entity. Military discipline, to the contrary, stands in open antithesis to human worth. We need only stay true to pure anarchism in order to enter the epoch of the social revolution.

Once again I studied the works of Kropotkin, Jean Grave, Reclus and Malatesta. How much love, warmth and human nobility I found there! Besides reading scientific literature, I read—or better said, reread—such artistic literature with an anarchist character as the writings of Tolstoy, Oscar Wilde and Ibsen. All three left their mark in distinctive ways: Tolstoy through his merciless criticism, Oscar Wilde through his striving for beauty. Ibsen, however, had the greatest influence on me. I saw in him a writer and a fighter. His line, "The strongest man is he who remains alone," left me intoxicated in those days. In my solitude, this was the word I needed.

I Return to Paris

Once I had weathered the storms of my ideological struggle, I again felt the ground beneath my feet. I decided to return to Paris; it was the summer of 1915. I went directly to Mrs. Buse.

Once there, I met practically all of the people I had come to know back in the village, and many others besides. Her abode had become the bohemian central, the gathering point for semirevolutionaries and full revolutionaries. I found there a roof over my head and soon got a job hollowing out trenches. Our work was located not too far from the front, and more than once we heard the cries of the combatants as they went over to the attack.

We were provided for from the army kitchen. In the vicinity of the front it was impossible to get anything, so I accumulated a great deal of money in the course of a month and then took off for Paris for a few days and squandered it all.

But I was not able to endure working in the trenches for very long. The cries of battle brought me to my wits' end. One could clearly hear the moans of the wounded, and it seemed to me as if I heard shrapnel ripping through the human body. This so racked my nerves that I was compelled to quit.

Then I rented a room in a bizarre hotel next to the Metro station Saint Paul. In the corridors, and in the rooms as well, it was always dark—day and night. You had to be well acquainted with the way in order to find your room. This hotel, however, had one advantage: it was cheap—two francs per week.

I became good friends in those days with an Estonian. He was an artist, a violin player. We had made each other's acquaintance while digging out trenches. I had noticed how sad he looked and asked him why. He told me that he had a wife and child in Paris and that from the wages he earned he was unable to save anything. His violin, which he otherwise played every evening, was at the pawnbroker's, and it threw him into a real state of despair. He longed for it. I loaned him what he needed—a really paltry sum by the way—so that he could redeem it, and he was very thankful to me. Although he was much, much older than I, we became good friends. His friendship was to my advantage, for he gave me Russian books to read, and he told me a great deal about his experiences in the year 1905. He was a Socialist Revolutionary with a rich past.

Mrs. Buse fixed me up with a job at the factory where she worked and I earned five francs per day. Such a sum of money made it easy to get by, especially when Mrs. Buse was around to make sure that I didn't fritter it away. Later, my situation improved still more. I got a job working for a Lettish Social Democrat, a personal friend of Lozovsky.

I got on splendidly at my new job. Since I was employed at the press and this machine could only provide me with half a day's work, I customarily worked until lunchtime. Then I took off for Vincennes and spent the afternoon reading. When the working day was over at seven o'clock in the evening, I left the woods and returned home. I had already forgotten that I had worked half the day. On account of this, some people reproached me in the course of political discussion for not being a genuine worker, for not leading the life of a proletarian.

It was in this period that I had come to know Paris. This beautiful and surprisingly multicolored city unveiled itself to me. Not just the museums, concerts and theaters, but the Parisian streets as well left their deep imprint on me.

First of all, the diversity. Parisian street scenes change from one to the other as in a film. There are entire city quarters which are inhabited solely by workers. Whenever you visit them, you feel all around you the breath of the proletarian way of life. You are reminded of the march of the worker battalions which stormed the Bastille, of the battles on the barricades during the June days of 1848 and of the extraordinary nature of the Parisian Communards. Go to another quarter, Saint Michel, and a wholly different picture is revealed to you: young people before their books; people of every nationality and color; the Sorbonne, that symbol of France's spiritual greatness. Not far from there is the Boulevard du Montparnasse, the home of bohemians from all the world—painters, poets and politicians. In Montmartre, on the other hand, you find nighttime gaiety as is possible in Paris alone. On the "great boulevards" you see the world of the speculators and the rich of every sort, great extravagance and refined debauchery. But it is beautiful there, fantastically beautiful. All of these city quarters have one quality in common: gaiety and warm-heartedness, as is singularly the way of the French.

I fell in love with the streets of Paris and could see why the French so dearly cling to them, often so that they forget about their own homes.

The year 1916 arrived, and with it all its horrors. Truthfully, one did not sense the terrible times in Paris. To the contrary, it was downright pleasant. It is incomprehensible to me why Trotsky wrote that it was oppressive and sad in Paris during the war. Schmoozing among ourselves, we often noted how the government had done everything it could to retain and to strengthen Paris' festive air, how it had endeavored to drive away the cares and worries so that one thought less about the front. All was gayness in Paris. But when we heard the news from Russia that the Jews had been driven from the cities and towns which lay in the vicinity of the front, we grew immensely uneasy. We knew what that meant, we knew the brutality of the tsarist militarists and the savagery of the Cossacks only too well. Each of us had family or friends who lived in these border environs—in many cases, next of kin. It therefore goes without saying that my mood of joviality died away when I got wind of the tsarist atrocities. I was ill-at-ease over the fate of those affected, and gave some consideration to the question, how should I react?

In Paris, committees sprang into being to help the Jews who were being persecuted at the Russian front. Mass meetings were held in order to raise money. Shlomo Salmen brought me along to one of these meetings, where he was scheduled to speak. He scandalized himself. Apparently thinking that it was unbecoming for him as a philosopher to speak in plain language, he began speaking in the manner of the prophets, not by imitating their words of consolation, however, only their invectives. His opening line was, "You will be assailed by curses!" People began to walk out. But it was no easy thing for him to alter the tone and content of his speech. After ten minutes there was nobody left in the hall. Out in front, people complained that they had responded to the appeal to donate money, yet had ended up being insulted.

In general, however, a great deal of money was raised. Everyone was employed and earned well. Businesses were thriving. It is difficult to comprehend today how it was possible for one to live so peacefully and sated in the French capital, with the front located only a few dozen kilometers away.

I was non-party at the time. I had only come to anarchism ideologically; working with anarchists organizationally did not appeal to me. On the street, however, I was looked upon as a hair-raising anarchist, one who always packed a revolver in his pocket. The fact is, I did not carry a revolver in my pocket nor did I shoot anybody. But I often thought about taking revenge on tsarism, or on one or another of its satraps.

It soon turned out that I wasn't alone. There were other anarchists who harbored this wish, and we found each other.

At first there were four of us: Meirke, Shlomo, a third one who was a carpenter and I. Whether they had already discussed their idea before speaking to me about it, I do not know. The fact of the matter is, they came to me with a worked-out plan to blow up the home of Isvolsky, the tsarist ambassador in Paris.

When we came together for the second time, we decided to include Russian and French anarchists in the plan in order to prevent exposing the Jewish population of France to special persecution. Meanwhile, everything had to remain strictly secret. Still, people got wind of it. A number of individuals came to the restaurant which I frequented and, to my astonishment, I heard them whispering among themselves about our plan.

Then I got to know another comrade, an odd fellow named Israel Shtern. He was an old Bundist from Łódź. A man with a heroic past, there were even songs about him. But in Paris he had changed. He had not broken from Bundism, but at the same time he had become a Buddhist. I do not know whether he was concretely aware of the business I was mixed up in, but perhaps he had stumbled onto it somehow. In order to work on me, he visited me every day at my job and recounted Indian stories containing a Buddhist moral. What an altogether peculiar man he was. He came up with various and sundry original ideas to help the poor, one of which was the following: he wanted to buy up old things from people who, as a rule, were cheated whenever desperate straits drove them to the pawnbroker. Paying such needy people the full price for their belongings, he would then go into the trading business and donate a part of the proceeds for a workers' library. After we had scraped together a certain sum of money for him and he had bought up a few old things, it turned out that he had paid his customers far too much. The money quickly dried up but nobody was any better off for it. Nor did he save my soul. We were dead set on pulling off the bombing. An event intervened, however, which destroyed our plan and rendered it unnecessary: the March Revolution in Russia.

PART 4

The March Revolution

*T*hose were great days at the beginning of March 1917. It appeared as if the dreams of generations of Russian revolutionaries could now be realized, as if the victory in the hundred-year struggle of the Russian people for freedom was near. The newspapers in France published contradictory news about the struggle and mutiny in Russia. More than once they announced that the revolutionaries had triumphed, only to establish the following day that this was not the case. When definitive news of the victory of the revolution came, we did not initially believe it. On the evening of 11 March, however, the news was confirmed. That evening a gigantic demonstration took place. The Rue des Rosiers was not to be recognized again.

We went to our favorite restaurant, hung out red flags and covered the tables with red cloth. Whoever came in treated us to wine. The sound of Russian revolutionary songs reverberated in the streets. There were many such restaurants on the same street. We marched from one to the other with red ribbons on our lapels. The streets and cafés were filled with incessant singing. Comrades embraced and kissed one another. The great transformation which the Russian Revolution brought to our lives as émigrés was already visible. We knew that our lives in exile were coming to an end, that we would soon be in the land of our dreams.

Late that evening, as the cafés shut down, we took the red flags and set off for the hatmakers syndicate, a trade union composed almost solely of Jewish workers. Lozovsky, the future head of the Profintern, was its leader. There we hung our red flags out the windows, gave speeches throughout the night and recited and sang revolutionary songs.

But our great joy was momentarily spoiled by the whining Leyzer Levin. It was only out of pity, he maintained, that we didn't throw him out. His wails gave us the impression that he was innocent, but we were unable to help him. As long as the Bund had not rehabilitated him we could not allow him to get to close to our circle.

We formed a committee consisting of all the parties and organizations active among the Russian revolutionaries. This committee preoccupied itself with completing the formalities for our return home. Each party or organization put its comrades to work. I enlisted along with the anarchists.

Meanwhile, the situation in France had also become more favorable because, as a consequence of the Russian Revolution, an oppositional group arose in the French Socialist Party. When the socialist parties of Russia altered their course and spoke out for summoning the Socialist International to Stockholm, the leadership of the French party opposed the decision. Subsequently, a strong opposition arose in France which demanded participation at the Stockholm conference.

We celebrated May Day in the revolutionary manner, although but few French workers joined us. A rally was held in a hall on Grande Chaboul, the initiators of which were all adherents of Lenin's "April Theses." Rappoport, Lozovsky and Lurie, defenders of Lenin's theses, spoke. It was Lenin, dealing with the essence of the Russian Revolution, who argued that the revolution in Russia must be turned into a socialist revolution. In fact, all three speakers soon became Communists.

When the rally came to an end, the speakers requested that we leave quietly and separately in order not to make it possible for the police to stage a bloodbath. But as the people streamed into the street, a demonstration composed of Russians, Jews and a few Frenchmen spontaneously formed. Until we reached the "great boulevards" everything went peacefully. At the boulevards, however, we were met by the police. The police had their own strategy; they did not attack the demonstration at the first encounter, but rather positioned themselves in two rows on the sidewalks. After surrounding the demonstration in this manner, they attacked from all sides and clubbed away. The gutters on both sides of the street ran with blood. The free-for-all with the police lasted several hours. Whenever they grabbed somebody, other demonstrators set him free again. Not only in the streets was it open season, but in the courtyards as well, where the police seized anybody whom they suspected had participated in the demonstration. It is worth emphasizing that the Jewish workers got the worst of it. They fought in the front ranks, for they expected more from the revolution than other workers. The next day, the entire bourgeois press wrote that all those arrested and beaten had been foreigners, and this time they were right.

Meanwhile, more news, highly disquieting news, came from revolutionary Russia. It dealt with the split of the revolutionary democracy into two enemy camps. To be sure, the press gave a false picture of the events. In any case, we felt that the revolution was passing through a crisis. News arrived about Kerensky's June offensive, which came to so fatal an end, and, shortly thereafter, we read of the Bolshevik demonstrations during the July days. The Bolsheviks were declared illegal and the reaction, which had had a wait-and-see attitude toward the Russian Revolution, now began to praise it. We sensed that danger was approaching and wanted to be at the scene of the events as soon as possible.

The time finally arrived. In the second half of July we departed Paris. At the train station, Antonov-Ovseyenko read aloud a declaration to the people of France thanking them for the asylum they had granted us in our hour of need. From Paris we went to London. There we were put up in a hotel where we were to wait for a ship bound for Norway.

I sought out my brother and his family, who were very glad to see me. My brother took me around to the trade unions and introduced me to comrades. He was anarchistically inclined at the time and boasted of the fact that I was off to participate in the revolution. He asked me, however, if I wanted to stay with him.

We stayed in London for about a week. As we went to board the ship, we "Parisians" were detained, led into a large hall and interrogated. The officers did not question us individually, but rather as a group. Asked why we were going home, Antonov-Ovseyenko replied, "We are going home to finish the revolution." After that, the officers treated us with extraordinary animosity and we assumed that we would suffer the same fate as Trotsky.[1] But it turned out differently. We departed that same day for Norway.

A diplomatic mission was also on board. For the duration of the trip, therefore, we were accompanied by two warships in order to ward off a possible attack.

We stayed one day in Oslo. After bright and festive Paris, Oslo seemed foggy and oppressive.

---

[1]   On 3 April Trotsky was removed from a Norwegian steamer by English officers in Halifax and imprisoned in a concentration camp. (GE)

Continuing by train, we faced a difficult problem: what happens at the Russian-Finnish border when we are asked which parties we belong to? What will we say? Rumors were circulating at the time that Bolsheviks and anarchists would be arrested and imprisoned. Our discussion had its tragic aspect: already underway, we were split into two enemy camps. We knew that we were not going home to make the revolution side by side, but rather to fight against one another. Yet we all decided that nobody was to say which party he belonged to. This way, the interrogators would be unable to determine who the Bolsheviks and anarchists were. Only one of us was unwilling to bow to the decision, a Jewish emigrant from England, a Menshevik. He maintained that the Bolsheviks were German spies and that it was a *mitzvah*[2] to surrender them over to the police. And it was just this man who was the first to convert to Bolshevism after the victory of the October Revolution. He was an exception though. Aside from him, all of us decided to act in solidarity, and this decision was carried out.

Meanwhile, we arrived in Stockholm. The impression which this city made on us was opposite that of Oslo. Stockholm is beautiful, clean and sunny; it lightens and gladdens the heart. The museum, the water and the forest give the city a character which seems created to fill the human heart with joy.

One incident in the beautiful Swedish capital though saddened me. There were buffets in Sweden with all sorts of good things to eat. You had to buy a ticket at the entrance and were then free to serve yourself. One cannot say that the owners of these buffets earned anything from their Russian customers. To the contrary, they most certainly suffered losses. Within a few minutes the buffets had been picked clean. The owners stood there and smiled sadly at the wild appetites of the Russians, a premonition, it seemed, of the hungry times awaiting them. Perhaps, many of these Russian emigrants had never been able to glut themselves in Paris. They now had the opportunity to do so and took advantage of it to their heart's content. I felt ashamed in the presence of the Swedes. It seemed to me as if it would have been better to leave something on the tables.

We reached Helsinki, and from there left for the Finnish-Russian border. The interrogations began but, as agreed upon, all of us refused to

---

[2] commandment, good deed (trans.)

reply to the question about our party affiliations. Even the Menshevik—the future convert—lacked the courage to break the unity of the revolutionary camp. We were detained an entire day and threatened with every conceivable form of punishment, but in the end we were permitted to travel on to Petrograd.

We were elated. We felt that our opponents—the Mensheviks and Socialist Revolutionaries—had survived a severe test and emerged from it with honor. That filled us with joy. Life, however, is a brutal factionalist. Before we knew it—only three months later—we found ourselves face to face in bloody struggle along antagonistic fronts.

In Russia

Arriving in Petrograd, we were taken to a house for political émigrés. The mood was depressed. The Bolsheviks were not alone in feeling a sense of resignation; the other socialists as well found themselves in
bad straits. We sensed that the revolution was going downhill. Only the
bourgeois camp was cheerful. The reactionary propertied classes, it
seemed, were certain that their time had come.

A group of anarchists who also lived in the house remained confident.
They dressed in soldiers's uniforms and went into the barracks to make
propaganda. It was depressing to see. As a city, Petrograd also made
an unfavorable impression on me. It looked to me like a bad imitation
of Paris.

I still had time to visit a comrade of mine from Warsaw, Zissman, in
the hospital. He had lost both legs after being run over by a streetcar
and ever since was possessed by thoughts of suicide. Laying eyes on me,
however, he broke out in wild laughter. "What's so funny," I asked. He
answered that all he could do was laugh whenever he remembered how I
had been dressed the day of the Beilis trial. If I'm not mistaken, my
comrade Avrom Aronovich was also present (today he is a Bundist in
Paris). I took warm leave of comrade Zissman and departed for Moscow the next day.

Moscow made the opposite impression on me as Petrograd. The city
seemed warm, familiar, typically Russian. I knew just how near this city
was to me thanks to the Russian literature which I so loved. Through it,
I had come to know the feel of Russian Moscow. I found accommodations in a communal apartment for political émigrés. There I met such
old comrades from Warsaw as Max and Black Katz, Mattes Shnayder
and Josef Baytlmacher. I also met many other Bundists.

That house for emigrants on Spiridanova Street became my second
home. It was as though I were back in Warsaw in our little apartment.
Many of the comrades I met in Moscow used to visit me as well in
Warsaw.

Once I had split away from comrades, I began to take a hard look
at the situation in the country. Politically speaking, I had separated from

the comrades of the Bund. I hoped for the Bolshevik revolution because I was certain that we anarchists would be next, just as the Bolsheviks were preparing to take over the place of the Mensheviks. I tried to decipher which stage of the revolution we were now in and which rolls the existing parties were playing in it.

It soon became clear that the Russian bourgeoisie found itself in a tragic situation. At least in the beginning stage, the bourgeoisies of the West European countries had led the democratic revolution. They had prepared it intellectually, organized it and armed the workers. It was only as the workers began to put forward their own demands, later in the course of the struggle, that the bourgeoisie became reactionary. Not so in the case of the Russian bourgeoisie. They feared the working class more than they feared the Old Regime. They did not want the revolution. From the first minute they were counterrevolutionary. After the outbreak of the revolution they took up sides with the tsarist dynasty and wanted to check the revolutionary development—even before the masses of the people had accomplished anything. They praised the revolution and waited for its defeat.

The Socialist Revolutionaries were in no better condition. They had continually maintained that Russia could pass over directly from the tsarist order to the socialist; they had virtually stamped the Russian Marxists as agents of the liberal bourgeoisie. When the peasants, however, sought to realize in a revolutionary way the agrarian program which the SRs had once preached, the SR government dispatched punitive expeditions to the villages. The Mensheviks abandoned the class struggle precisely at that moment when the misery of the working masses rose in direct proportion to the sabotage of the industrialists. They, the Mensheviks and Socialist Revolutionaries, postponed all reforms until the Constituent Assembly, while constantly postponing the date for its convocation. Moreover, the most important problem was posed: peace. This was the burning question of the day, for it had become impossible to continue the war. All of this produced a kind of political and economic chaos which everybody understood. Things could not stay this way.

If one thinks back on those times, one may get something of the impression that the Russian Democracy had missed its chance. Just as the tsar had been able to save his crown at the price of renouncing personal rule in 1905, the Russian Democracy may have been able to save the democratic regime had it in fact granted the workers and peasants all the necessary reforms and had it gone the way of peace. It is open to question whether the Bolsheviks could have prepared the October Revolution had the government convened the Constituent Assembly earlier.

The Kerensky government was simply afraid to tackle all of this. It became clear that this government was leading the country toward a catastrophe. But the Bolsheviks took up these problems and explained that they were ready to solve them. To counter sabotage by the industrialists they posed the slogan of workers control. They demanded that the peasants seize the land at once as well as immediate peace. And they explained that the soviet power would carry out all of these demands. They were the only ones, moreover, who conducted mass working-class strikes. It soon became clear that the Bolsheviks had conquered the hearts and minds of the popular masses and that the moment of decision was near: either the bourgeoisie or the Bolsheviks. Both sides prepared themselves for the final struggle.

From all this, I concluded: first the Bolsheviks, and then us—the anarchists. This was confirmed by the course of events. In July the State Conference took place and the Bolsheviks were against it. The streetcars were struck and the delegates had to go by foot. This alone was a political defeat for the State Conference. Despite Tseretelli's urgent appeal to the bourgeoisie and the latter's declaration that they were prepared to collaborate, everybody sensed that the Kornilov putsch was hanging over the Russian Revolution like a black cloud. A few days later, after the putsch had been crushed and the army had returned from the front, the soldiers marched passed the Moscow Soviet chanting Bolshevik slogans. The leaders of the Moscow Soviet, coming outside to greet the soldiers, had rapidly to disappear again, shutting the soviet's windows behind them.

I stood there looking at the masses of soldiers and the then leaders of the Soviet, and knew that all of the threads between them had been cut. This Soviet was politically dead; I was convinced of the weakness of its policies on the first Sunday after Kornilov's defeat.

Up until now, the Bolshevik Party had not been legalized again by anybody. But the Bolshevik organization in Moscow legalized itself. They put out a call for a large rally in a theater. I was there, saw the enthusiasm and confidence of the people, and understood that this is how men feel when they are sure of victory.

Following the rally money was collected for *Pravda* and the masses then streamed into the street to demonstrate. Nobody bothered themselves about the fact that they were illegal. I followed the demonstration, for I wanted to see how it would turn out. It ended peacefully, for there was nobody to disrupt it.

The job is half done, I thought, they are nearly the masters of the house. The fact was, state power was not yet theirs, but there was not a soul alive who could stop them on the road to power.

What should I do? I was no Bolshevik. And as for the anarchists, there was nothing there to lure me. I was repelled by the fact that at the moment of a great popular revolution they were working in their narrow circles. I made the not particularly anarchistic decision to go into the army. The army, I thought, would decide the revolution, it would be the center of events. I was not mistaken.

Following Trotsky's declaration to the Pre-Parliament in the name of the Bolshevik fraction that the Kerensky government was a government of national betrayal, and following the fraction's subsequent walkout, it was clear that there was no time to lose. The twelfth hour had struck. I joined the 56th Regiment, which was known to be the best Bolshevik unit.

I don't know where it had gotten this reputation, for there was not a single Bolshevik in the regiment. The secretary of the regiment committee was the sole Bolshevik, and a pretty imperfect one at that. In any case, he did not understand much of anything. He was, however, an extremely honest man.

We did not engage in military exercises at all. Meetings were held continuously, everybody coming and going as he chose. Many came because those were lean times, and belonging to the regiment held the promise of a square meal.

As the last days of October drew near, I felt decidedly uneasy. I knew that it would soon come to open conflict but I was still unable to so much as load a rifle. I approached the secretary of the regiment committee and he sent me to someone who was supposed to teach me to shoot. This man began by telling me under which tsar the production of firearms had begun, how many parts a rifle has and so on. That lasted two entire nights, and I realized that I couldn't learn a thing from him. Instead of teaching me to shoot, he gave me the same instruction which he had enjoyed in the tsarist army, accompanying each word in his good-natured way with a Russian invective. The whole thing became utterly tiresome, so I dropped it there and then. And that's how I prepared to go to the barricades—without having the slightest notion how one holds a rifle in his hands. It cost me dearly, especially during the first night of the uprising. My comrade Avrom Aronovich helped me at one point.

He served in the same barracks as I, but if I recall correctly, he belonged to a different regiment. I only wish to emphasize here that the great majority of the combatants were specialists just like me. That's how we prepared to make a revolution.

The October Revolution

In the last days before the October Revolution the most varied sorts of rumors were flying around. It was said, for example, that the leaders of the Moscow Bolsheviks were against the uprising. Later it was confirmed that this had been true; Nogin and his group really wanted to avoid the uprising. But when news arrived on the morning of the 25th that the Bolsheviks had seized power in Petrograd, it was clear that Moscow would go the same way. By accident, I was on regiment duty that very same evening. I had to bring the regiment report to staff headquarters. This was of course completely absurd, but everything still took place according to the law of inertia.

When I went into the street a bizarre scene was unfolding. Everybody who did not think of participating in the civil war hurried themselves home. Their faces were full of fear. The shop windows were closed, the streets became more and more deserted by the minute. From time to time, groups were to be seen going to specific locations for arms. The difference between the Whites and the Reds instantly caught the eye. If men were dressed like workers or wore soldiers' greatcoats, you knew that they were Reds. If they wore officers' uniforms or dressed like students, however, it was certain that they were Whites. Even the Red officers wore soldiers' greatcoats. I doubt that there were soldiers or workers among the Whites. In any case, I never encountered any at the time.

How peculiar the contrast was between the fighters on both sides and everyone else who happened to be outside. Scared to death, the latter rushed home to hide. Reds and Whites, on the other hand, were arming themselves—calmly, all too calmly. Both sides knew what they had resolved to do and were preparing themselves for the struggle.

When I arrived at staff headquarters with my regiment report, complete bedlam reigned. Papers lay strewn on the floor, doors stood wide open. The officers were in a hurry. Where they were hurrying off to was clear: in the City Council building, all the Whites were assembling.

The officer who took the report from me was also on his way out. He asked me which regiment I had come from and I replied that I belonged to the 56th. "Are you a Bolshevik?" he continued. "Yes," I said tersely;

I had no desire to give long-winded explanations. He then informed me that I was under arrest. But I told him that he had better not try it. I knew that the soldiers there were Bolsheviks and that they, just as he, were about to leave for their assembly point: the Soviet. He ripped the packet out of my hand and threw it to the floor. For my part, I wasn't going to stand around and wait for his signature. Instead, I headed back to my barracks.

It was high time. I had still been able to take the streetcar from the barracks to staff headquarters, but now they were no longer running. The streets were still and empty. It made my blood run cold. I crossed Pushkin Boulevard, sat down on a bench beside the Pushkin monument and reflected—or, better said, dreamt.

Writing these lines 40 years later, I am awestruck: can one man really have experienced all that? I sat on the bench and drew the balance of my six years of socialist work. Six years before I had joined the Bund and gotten my first lessons in the social revolution. The revolution became the meaning and content of our lives, but nobody could have imagined when the day would come and what it would look like, or if we would even live to see it. And now it had arrived. I, a Jewish worker from Smocza Street, would go to the barricades tonight.

Who knows how long I would have sat there reflecting had my thoughts not been interrupted by the powerful strains of the *Internationale*. A shudder ran up and down my spine and I set off in the direction of the voices. They led me to Skobolevsky Square, to the seat of the Soviet.

What a moving scene it was. I thought that only during the storming of the Bastille or in the days of the Paris Commune had it been possible to see anything similar. In all the streets leading to the Soviet stood workers in their workclothes with small bowls of food in their hands. They were waiting to be armed. Among them were invalids and war cripples demanding that they not be disgraced; they too wanted to fight. Many of them cried when they were refused weapons. Every few minutes a group of armed workers came outside and loaded onto trucks. A representative of the Soviet gave a speech, and amidst the strains of the *Internationale* they set out for the City Council, where the Whites had assembled. Ashamed that I was still walking around unarmed, I went back to my barracks.

When I arrived at the gate to the barracks—we called it the Pokrovky barracks—I was met by an officer, a left Socialist Revolutionary. Agitated, he asked me if I was a Bolshevik. I'm a Bolshevik, I replied, and exasperated, he added, "At a time like this you go running around without weapons?" I ran up to the barracks, grabbed my rifle (which I was unable to shoot) and rushed into the street. We began to erect barricades surrounding the barracks because a sudden assault was to be expected. After we finished, we ate once more and then took up our positions. That evening, in fact, the Whites attempted to take our barracks, but our return fire drove them quickly away.

What a tragic state I was in: I was unable to load my rifle and I had no idea how to shoot it. I observed how the others did it and imitated them mechanically, but I doubt that I hit anybody that night.

Halfway through the night I was fetched from the barricades and led into a corridor where the office of a brigade was located. I was ordered to guard the door and prevent the *natshalnik* from dispatching anything. Sitting there, I heard him dictate a letter to his secretary requesting aid from the front against the Bolsheviks, who were seeking to block the Constituent Assembly by staging a coup d'état. I didn't know what to do. I was afraid to go inside, for if there were many people there they would finish me off. If I didn't, I thought, the telegram would make its way to the front. I decided to wait for my relief so that the two of us could settle the matter. To be sure, should anyone try to leave the office, I would have to act on my own. Luck would have it that I was not relieved that whole night, but none of the officers inside attempted to leave. Early the next morning, when my relief arrived, I told the comrade what was up. We entered together. The telegram lay on the table. We let the secretary go but arrested the *natshalnik*.

That morning we occupied the post office in our district. It was an easy job because there were no armed forces there. The telegraph station was more difficult. We fought the entire day and conquered the building that evening.

The second day went badly for us. News arrived that the Whites had taken the Kremlin—through deception. This was a severe blow for us. At the very outset they shot down a large number of Reds with machine guns, and during the following three days occupied all the post and telegraph offices, the telephone central, the military school and the depots. We were crammed together in the center of town. The mood in our barracks was depressed. We were not overtaken by panic, but were prepared for the worst.

On the fifth day of the struggle the situation shifted in our favor. This is explained by the fact that we had artillery and they didn't. In those few days I learned the art of handling weapons. No reinforcements came from outside, and when they finally arrived they were no longer needed.

The uprising lasted seven days. We feared that the underworld would take advantage of the events for pogroms and plundering. So we went to the Sukharev market, arrested a group of suspects and brought them back to our barracks. They were a strange and colorful society. Some of them wore furs and went barefoot, others wore winter caps with summer shoes. Before too long it was obvious that they were not particularly fastidious about their clothing. Many of them were without nose or ears. As I led one of the bunch to the toilet, he complained to me that we had allowed people to go free who had shown us false passports, whereas men like he, who had not falsified their papers, were being detained. How, he asked, are you any better than the old government? I had to admit that he was right. They ate the same food as the rest of us and we wanted to prepare a place for them to sleep. Suddenly, however, the Whites opened fire on our barracks and we decided to bring our prisoners to safer quarters, where their lives would not be in danger.

During the last three days of the uprising our group—along with artillery—was stationed at the Pushkin monument. Interestingly, a military group of the French military attaché placed their truck at our disposal. I was overjoyed—they were the grandsons of Communards!

Our fighting group's task was to defend the besieged Soviet on two sides: against assaults launched from the Kremlin and the City Council as well as from the office of the city *natshalnik* on Pushkin Boulevard. We were situated between these two centers and the Whites, using armored cars, came after us time and time again. We had to beat them back.

There was an extraordinary chill in the air and despite the fact that we kept ovens burning in the street, the last three days were miserably cold. It was impossible to be posted outside for more than six hours. Then came the relief. I went up to the Soviet during my first break, but it was filthy there. Soldiers were sleeping on the ground with their rifles in their hands. A terrible disorganization dominated the whole place. After being relieved the following day, I committed a horrible blunder. I had six hours off and decided to spend them together with my friends at our apartment on Spiridanova Street. To get there I had to cross Pushkin Boulevard. The office of the city *natshalnik* and, I gathered, the staff headquarters of the Whites as well, were located right in the middle of the block.

As I reached the boulevard from Tversky Street with rifle in hand, the Whites opened a ferocious barrage of fire. It was too late to pull back and besides, the way home was shorter. Crouching, I began to run. From the gateways, people were watching with horrified looks on their faces. It was a wonder that I was able to save myself. I made it to the corner and started to the left when I heard the cry: "Who goes there?" "A comrade"—this was our password. As I approached, a Red Army man standing inside an empty shop asked me whether I was Jewish. I answered yes and he demanded to see my *propusk* (permit).[3] Grabbing my rifle and challenging him with the bayonet, I called him a counter-revolutionary and an anti-Semite. Although he had a Browning revolver in his hand and was therefore better armed than I, he retreated into the shop. I approached him, my bayonet readied, and sensed that he felt ashamed about what he had said. Perhaps my reaction had stunned him. Who knows how the thing would have turned out had a car filled with Whites not driven up. We both opened fire. He then shook my hand and I went on my way.

I reached Spiridanova Street. Not far from me, three Whites wearing students' caps were patrolling the block and demanding that people shut their windows. I could tell by the way they were holding their rifles that they understood even less of the trade than I. The question was disarming them. In front of our courtyard I met the Poale Zionist Luzer Stoliar and asked him to help me carry out my plan. He went to his apartment and fetched his gun. We ran up to the students and demanded that they throw down their rifles. Even before we got the words out, their rifles were lying at our feet.

Back home I ran into my good friends Katz and Aronovich. We spent a few hours together and then I returned to my post—by a different route.

The last days of fighting in my vicinity became more and more stubborn. With each successive defeat, it seemed, the Whites were all the more hellbent on revenge, all the more determined to seize the Soviet and deliver us the death blow. But despite the fierceness of the struggle in our district, our joy grew by leaps and bounds. The shooting had already stopped at many points, a sign that the Whites had given up.

On the evening of the seventh day, the battle in our district as well all but came to an end. We were astonished. Precisely at the stroke of mid-

---

[3] In tsarist Russia Jews who resided in Moscow had to carry residence permits. (GE)

night a car flying the red flag approached. A comrade informed us that the Kremlin, the last bastion of the Whites, had capitulated and added that we were to cease fire. The Junkers had given their word of honor that they would not continue the fight. A mere eight days later they were at the Don organizing Kornilov's death battalions.

With the order to cease fire, we were told to go home. Although it was bitter cold, nobody wanted to leave. In all of Moscow's streets and alleys revolutionary songs were heard; comrades embraced one another and many cried from joy. Not only revolutionary songs, but cheers for Lenin and Trotsky, and from time to time for Kamenev and Zinoviev as well, echoed in the streets.

After the struggle was over I decided not to go back to the barracks. I hung up my uniform, for it was not to my anarchistic taste. A few days later, of course, I began to get terribly hungry, and had it not been for my good friend Aronovich, who worked in a cooperative, I don't know how I would have survived.

Before the struggle had begun there was a man living with us who belonged either to the PPS or the Mensheviks—I'm not sure which. In any case, he had vilified the Bolsheviks as spies and bandits. How great was my astonishment when I saw him wearing a red armband at the funeral for fallen comrades. He was now a Bolshevik commissar. I came to the funeral in civilian clothes only to have him malign me and threaten me in the name of the new government...

Against Kornilov

Doffing my military uniform was not long granted me. Two weeks after the October Revolution I was called back to my regiment and informed that Kornilov had organized his death battalions, taken Kharkov and was preparing to march on Moscow. My regiment was about to be dispatched to the front and I was asked whether I wanted to join up. It was not to my taste, but I said yes.

I went home in order to take leave of my comrades. They were saddened at the idea of my going and sought to persuade me to stay, arguing that with a Jewish face like mine the cossacks would murder me at the first opportunity. Despite the fact that their words of concern were dictated by friendship, such presentiments nevertheless made me nervous. I bid them all a warm farewell, especially the two who were dearest to me—Katz and Aronovich—and set off for the front.

At the end of November we left Moscow for Kharkov. It was the middle of the night when we arrived in Belgorod, the last station before Kharkov, where the secretary of the Military Revolutionary Committee informed us that the 17,000-strong Polish Legion, with artillery and machine guns at its disposal, was quartered in the city. The day before, he said, the Poles had had a meeting at which it was decided to link up with Kornilov. If we traveled on, they would encircle and destroy us. Therefore, he suggested, we ought to enter the city and disarm them. Easily said, but how? While the Poles numbered 17,000 men and had stocks of machine guns, we were 600 and were armed with mere rifles. It looked as if the results were determined in advance. But it happened otherwise.

It was still dark as we entered the city. Surrounding the barracks, we disarmed the Poles. It took only an hour and then we were the masters of the situation. We let the soldiers go free and sent the officers to Moscow. Only one commander was shot while trying to escape.

That same evening I was on street patrol. Spotting the signboard of a Warsaw literary circle named after I.L. Peretz, I was overjoyed. I rang the bell to go inside. The owner of the apartment, however, who looked to be a man of means, refused to let me in and simply told me to go. Depressed and miserable, I left with a heavy heart.

As it turned out, Kornilov had not gathered his forces in Kharkov after all, so early the next morning we moved on toward Kuban instead. For one entire month we combed the countryside looking for the Whites, but we were unable to encounter them anywhere.

As long as we were in the Ukraine we were in high spirits. Everywhere we went, people carrying red flags came out to meet us. Welcoming us, they explained that the population itself had driven out the Whites and handed the power over to the Soviets. As we crossed the Kuban border, however, the situation changed. The fact is, we didn't see any combat there either, but the population displayed a hostile neutrality toward us. We felt as if we were in enemy territory.

Meanwhile, a mood of demoralization spread. The soldiers began to complain that they had already done their bit in Belgorod and that everybody really ought to contribute their share to the struggle. "Why do we have to put our lives on the line for others," they asked. One must realize that these soldiers were from the old, not yet demobilized tsarist army. It was depressing to listen to it, and I therefore pointed out to them in my miserable Russian that whereas I, a Jewish worker who would not be receiving land, had joined the struggle, they were unwilling to fight, even though they were going to be taking possession of the countryside. My reproaches had a certain effect.

My relationship to them expressed itself in a most original way. Whenever the situation at the front was good, they lifted me on their shoulders. Should it take a turn for the worse, they gave me dirty looks. I was certain that if the Whites were to win, my fellow soldiers would impale me on their bayonets and deliver me to the enemy as a gift in atonement for their sins.

Life was poisoned by drunkenness. At each station soldiers exchanged their shirts, field jackets and often even their boots for *samogonka*.[4] In one town there was a tavern where people got so drunk that the situation was catastrophic. Ten armed Whites would have sufficed to slaughter us all. After the spirits had been poured into a pond, the soldiers dived in fully clothed to drink it all up—in the middle of winter. What a pain it was to make good the chaos.

The mood among the Red Guards who traveled with us to the front was altogether different. Day in and day out, discussions took place. I

[4] home-distilled vodka (trans.)

remember one such discussion in regard to the question, what are we fighting for? Some argued for land; others, for peace; a third group, so that the workers could take possession of the factories. All of these explanations, however, were unsatisfactory. Suddenly, someone stood up and said that he knew why—for the brotherhood of peoples. Faces beaming, this answer pleased everybody.

An odd folk, these Russians. They had made two revolutions in one year and taken to the front in a civil war for nothing less than the brotherhood of peoples. How could you not love such a people? I was happy that I had gone along with them to fight for that great ideal. I only regretted that I was not in the same groups as they were. Among us in the old tsarist regiment, everything was different and worse.

On one occasion, however, a Russian from my regiment surprised me. Calling me aside, he explained that he was the son of a priest and had studied at a clerical seminary. Running away, he had taken up work in a bakery and then run away again. Then he had become a vagabond. He had always hated Jews, for throughout his life he had never heard a good word said about them. That hatred, he said, was in his blood. But ever since he had been traveling together with me and heard me speak, he had changed his opinion about Jews. His only request was that if we should return from the front I had to introduce him to Trotsky. Trotsky was Jewish, after all, and the enemy definitely wanted to kill him. This man would protect Trotsky. Nobody, he said, was going to lay a hand on him as long as he was around. As he spoke, his big eyes shone. I had the impression that I could rely on him in a tight spot. He would be ready to die with me.

But such moments of reflection lasted only until we reached the actual front. On New Year's Day 1918 we hit the border of the Don. That evening we set up camp on the tall hills overlooking the Don Steppe. It was beautiful. Although late in winter, the fields were overgrown with tall grass which swayed in the wind. A still ruled the fields, the sky was blue, the heart filled with calm and joy. This idyll, however, lasted only a few hours. Early the next morning we descended on the Don and pushed on toward Lugansk,[5] the heart of the Don Basin.

We never reached Lugansk though, for the Red Guards from Leningrad had already arrived there before us. They had armed 600 mine

---

[5] formerly Voroshilovgrad (trans.)

workers and sent them to the front. But these miners, it seems, had hardly been frontline men, for the Whites had encircled and massacred them all. Later, as we arrived at the front, we saw them lying in the fields, some without hands, others without ears. This frightful infamy aroused us all to a fury and agitation which the Whites were very soon to experience.

Following this crime Trotsky delivered the order: not to yield and not to take prisoners! We filed down the tips of our bullets, for when such a bullet enters the body it lodges itself upward and rips the flesh to shreds. We called them dumdum bullets. The struggle took on the bloodiest forms.

On the night of 2 February, we pulled into a small train station not far from Lugansk. The station was in a valley. Our detachment received the order to launch a machine-gun assault, establish a position in the field behind a hill and attack the enemy early the next morning. The situation looked like this: the Red Guards occupied the valley and blew up an enemy bridge located nearby. Approximately two kilometers beyond the bridge, on top of a hill, was an Orthodox church; the Whites had positioned themselves inside the bell tower and were shooting down the Reds with machine-gun fire. According to the battle plan, when the detachment in the valley began its assault, we were to attack from the right. It worked out somewhat differently.

When we reached the hill, we sent out a reconnaissance team whose task it was to sneak up on the enemy position, proceed along the railroad tracks, then report back to Staff and return to our detachment.

The moment we reached the railroad tracks a group of Whites thrust forward into our front line. Attacking from behind, they damaged the rails, thereby cutting off our echelon and preventing it from retreating. They had figured out our password, tricked the guard and killed him. Once across the bridge, they opened up with their artillery. We were certain that this was the beginning of an attack and sought out the chief of staff. He was nowhere to be found, however. The Reds Guards lost their heads.

A wild panic broke out, but the old frontniks in our reconnaissance squad ordered us into position in rows on top of a hill and readied us to thwart the coming attack. Early the next morning the Whites made their move. When our detachment saw that we had not returned, they too advanced toward the railroad tracks.

That morning, the Whites launched their attack by sending their storm units forward. The only piece of artillery in our possession failed on us, so we had to retreat. This was our first, but also our last defeat at that front. Pulling back a few kilometers, we were joined by two detachments, one composed of Austrian prisoners of war and a second of workers from Yaroslavl. Our counteroffensive began. The Yaroslavists marched to the left of us, the Austrians to the right and we in the middle. Reaching the bridge again, we saw a Red armored train bearing the name "Kerensky" which it had received while in production. Antonov-Ovseyenko was now in command of it. The train bombarded the Whites' position in the church on top of the hill. We were quickly able to smash their troops and then through smaller actions push on toward Rostov.

We experienced still another moment of crisis. One evening we went to a village for a little peace and quiet. None of the villagers, it seemed, had as yet the slightest idea just what a Bolshevik was. I went with the first reconnaissance team, in all five large men. One peasant woman called out to another: "You see, I told you that the Bolsheviks are big people!" That evening three Tatars, all artillery men, and I went to a peasant cottage. The peasant lit a fire in the oven and served us roasted fish. Peace and quiet it was.

A communication suddenly arrived: we were to return to the front at once—the Whites had surrounded the Petrograders and driven them back in panic. It was already pitch dark by the time we got back to our posts. The Petrograders withdrew from their positions and we stepped in to take their place. Climbing down into a gully, we patrolled the area for some distance until we observed men above us on either side. When we asked them who they were, they sarcastically repeated the Red password and then opened fire. We scrambled out of the gully, hit the ground and took up combat position. It really looked as if it was all over for us.

All of a sudden we were startled by singing. Looking around, we saw an approaching mass of soldiers carrying red flags, and as they marched nearer we could see that they were Hungarian prisoners of war.

We embraced and kissed one another and cried for joy. The red flags; the *Internationale*; prisoners the day before, comrades in struggle today—what a jolt of inspiration it was.

Together we launched our counteroffensive, charging into the Whites like a whirlwind. Nobody tried to stop us and nobody could have stopped us. From Taganrog to within seven kilometers of Rostov, along the banks of the Sea of Azov, we held our victory march, driving on with elation and sure of victory.

I felt cheerless and sad however. It isn't easy facing up to the fact that you neither allow yourself to be captured nor take any prisoners; it isn't easy shooting with dumdum bullets, which mean certain death. It is hard to go over to the attack and, accompanied by cries of "hurrah," to bayonet your enemy in the heat of battle. Incomparably more difficult, however, is seeing unarmed people shot, above all when women are among them. At such times I backed into a corner, for I was conscious of the fact that I could not remain at the front if I had to witness it.

We prepared for our assault on Rostov in the first days of February but, as it turned out, the Whites had already evacuated the city. We were able to enter with our red flags flying.

Our regiment, the 56th, proved to be the best, and thereby received the name, "First Revolutionary Moscow Regiment." Afraid that plundering might accompany our entry into the city, we were ordered to take up the vanguard and maintain order.

Our reception early the next morning was a jubilant one, though not unmarred by sporadic, grating catcalls. One man who came out to greet us roared, "Brothers! The Whites have lied to us! They've talked us into believing that you're all a bunch of Germans and Yids—but what do you know, Pravoslavs!" Spotting me, he gagged.

We went straight to Kornilov's staff headquarters. Aside from rifles, we found there whole cases filled with clothing and jewelry which had been wrapped in paper. The soldiers packed away such "small trifles" as gold rings and diamonds into their pockets. Anyone would do the same thing, they argued, and it's preferable that the loot belong to us. I stood there leaning on my rifle; how disgraceful it was to see our day of victory befouled by stealing gold. A number of Red Guards asked me why I had not taken anything. I tried to find some excuse but saw that it was impossible. They felt insulted, and as hurt turned into hatred, I thought that they might impale me on their bayonets any minute. Bending down, I selected a general's order with the inscription, "For 35 Years of Service." They cooled off and continued to stuff their pockets full. That night at the Hotel Moscow they spent their time playing cards, and on the table lay enormous piles of money.

The next morning started off on a sad note. We went into the hospitals and gathered the wounded officers from Kornilov's army. It was presumed that the war was over, and we were ordered to dispatch them to Moscow. But the Red Cossacks butchered them in the middle of the street. I felt my knees give way. It was a disgraceful murder.

With the foodstuffs which we had confiscated we set up a kitchen in our barracks, where everybody could receive a free lunch. Long lines of people formed in every street.

We patrolled the city and made house to house searches. Officers who had gone into hiding resisted with guns in hand whenever we arrived to arrest them. Each Red Guard was ordered to carry a revolver along with him. Not having a revolver, I was given an address and a written directive to confiscate one. A Ukrainian accompanied me. Once in the street, we were suddenly fired upon from all sides. The shots, coming from Whites on the rooftops, were the signal to launch an uprising. We didn't know what to do. Having two Red Guards in the middle of the street, cut off from their regiment, was playing with fire. Suddenly, I saw an acquaintance of mine, a friend of Aronovich. He told me that the War Committee was located in his father's neighborhood and that if I wanted to, he could take me there. I was certain that the Whites would first attack the headquarters of the War Committee, but arriving there, I saw that everything was quiet. Our artillery had silenced them.

I asked the chairman of the War Committee that I be permitted to visit my acquaintance. His family warmly received my companion and me and served us tea and blintzes. Unexpectedly, Red Guards came by to search the house. One of them said to the other, "You see, Jews always defend Jews!" I reached for my rifle (the Ukrainian did likewise) and declared that there would be no house search there, for pogromists could not be revolutionaries. They showed me a warrant from the War Committee but I nonetheless demanded that they come with me. I reported the incident to the chairman and he forbade them under any circumstances to carry on with the searches.

We stayed on a few more days in Rostov and then received the order to come to the defense of Petrograd which, following the collapse of the peace negotiations at Brest-Litovsk, was threatened by the Germans.

Underway, I experienced difficult moments. Many of the members of my regiment who had heroically distinguished themselves on the battlefield were now playing cards for high stakes. In reply to my question, where had they gotten so much money, they said that they were not such fools as to have gone into battle to fight for ideals. This was a harsh disappointment for me and I yearned to be back with my own comrades.

By time we reached Petrograd on 23 February the Brest-Litovsk peace had already been signed. I then headed for Moscow.

Back in Moscow

I arrived in Moscow on 26 February. My friends were astonished to see me. On one occasion, as we were closed in by Cossacks, I had written a farewell letter to them, and later, as the battles became sharper, I stopped writing altogether. Believing I had been killed, they divided my things among themselves. After my return they gave everything back piece by piece, but it was as unpleasant for them as it was for me.

The following day I went to my regiment to pick up my discharge papers and to get a certificate verifying that I had been at the front. The secretary of the regiment committee strongly advised me to go to a military school, for I had borne myself with distinction on the battlefield. The very idea, however, struck me as something fantastic: an anarchist with a military career! On my way out I was given a sack filled with some of the provisions which our regiment had requisitioned in Rostov. And what a treasure it was in those days: sugar, rice, coffee, tea, cocoa and flour. I brought it all back to Spiridanova Street and divided it up. When Aronovich came home he flew into a rage, assuring me that I would go hungry and that those same comrades would not so much as give me a little tea to drink. Unfortunately, he was right. For me, it was the beginning of a period of terrible hunger.

Aronovich was always there to save me. He worked in a cooperative and often brought home something to eat. Whenever the both of us went hungry we traveled out to Bugorosk, where our comrade Katz was the manager of a Bundist club. This club also ran a restaurant, and we stuffed ourselves.

But in this little shtetl Bugorosk, located all of 20 versts from Moscow, there was talk of pogroms. The atmosphere was frightful and Katz was forced to go elsewhere.

I began to live on pickles and tea. That is, I bought a dozen pickles and drank down a kettle of tea without sugar. Those were the two things which were still available in Moscow.

One cold day, while I was on my way to the tea shop to buy hot water and pickles, I saw a car drive past and stop at the entrance to the Commissariat of Foreign Affairs, which was located behind my apartment.

With a briefcase under his arm, out stepped none other than the man who, during our journey from London to Russia, had slandered the Bolsheviks and accused them of being spies for Germany.

The hunger in Moscow was frightful. My comrade Katz managed to find work for me in a factory in Ufa, the manager of which was a Bundist. On the wages which I earned there, it was just barely possible for Katz, who had come along, and me to get by. A few days before our departure, Left Socialist Revolutionaries murdered the German ambassador in Moscow in order to provoke war between Russia and Germany. The mood was extraordinarily tense. Underway, we heard talk to the effect that the Czechs had rebelled and that their soldiers had occupied the railroad line from Samara[6] to Siberia. Only that section of track between Samara and Chelyabinsk was still in the hands of the Bolsheviks. Passengers were whispering among themselves that the rebels were exterminating Bolsheviks and Jews. We were unsure as to whether the mutinous Czechs would seize our train or not. And it made us feel miserable; we had absolutely no desire to lose our lives in such a foolish way.

We arrived in Ufa unharmed, however, and I was able to put in several weeks of work. As the Whites neared the town, the Socialist Revolutionaries put out a call to make preparations to overthrow the Soviet government. Rumors were also circulating that the Black Hundreds were arming for a pogrom. I had originally resolved not to return to the front, but rather to stick to self-defense actions. It worked out differently however.

I was at my workplace as the Czechs began to bombard the city with artillery fire, and at the same time I overheard several Russian workers murmuring: "Our people are coming back; now it'll go badly for the Bolsheviks and the Jews." That was the last straw. I went to the War Committee, got out of my work clothes, put on a soldier's uniform and joined up with the First Ufa Communist Regiment. Off to the front again. Before our departure, however, something happened in Ufa itself.

It was still morning when the secret White organization began shooting up the streets, and as afternoon approached the attacks intensified. If a lone Red Guard emerged in the street, he was murdered. We spent the entire day searching the houses. As darkness fell the shooting grew even stronger, and I faced a difficult problem.

---

[6] today, Kuibyshev (GE)

My friend Katz, a Bundist and opponent of the October Revolution, was together with me the whole time in the barracks. He wanted to sign up as a volunteer, though it was obvious to me that his desire to do so was not motivated by conviction; rather, he wanted to stay with me. I could never accept such a sacrifice from him. Before I was able to change his mind, however, it was already dark. There could be no talk whatsoever that he go home alone, so I requested that I be allowed to accompany him. The leadership hesitated because it was dangerous, but in the end they granted me permission. With my loaded revolver in hand I walked with Katz through the streets. People peered at us from doorways and windows and were mortified to think that I was leading him off to shoot him. It was a terrible moment for both of us; tears streamed from our eyes as we walked along. Reaching his door, we embraced cheek to cheek and parted ways without a word. Both of us were certain that we had seen one another for the last time.

Returning to my regiment, I found myself in the middle of a great uproar: the *pulkavnik* had disappeared. Some believed that he had deserted out of fear, others that he was a White agent. Late that night we set out for the port; the land route cut off, we were forced to withdraw by water. We were aware that the Whites would fire on us from behind, so we carried sacks filled with wet sand across our backs.

At the port, large quantities of bread destined for Moscow and Petrograd were piled up. We decided to hold out until the bread had been shipped, but the military command declared that we were in danger, that we must withdraw immediately. At our regiment meeting (the regiment committee was almost entirely composed of Jews), we resolved to fight from house to house and to hold our position until the bread had been shipped off to the two revolutionary capitals. Only the following morning, after an order from Trotsky arrived commanding us to withdraw at once or face a revolutionary tribunal, did we set off.

It was really high time. The Whites had forced their way into the city that night, and hardly had we shoved off when they began to fire at us from both riverbanks. The Belaya River is quite narrow and it was therefore easy for them to attack us from both sides.

They pursued us the entire day. We shot back and fled. As darkness fell and the danger subsided, we stopped in a small village which lay at the junction of four gubernias: Ufa, Kazan, Vyatka and Perm.

Entering the town so suddenly in the dead of night, we were a fantastic sight to see, for we looked more like a pursued band than the military detachment of a great army. We called a meeting of the villagers, told them that our retreat was only temporary and demanded that they not submit to the orders of the Whites. To get our message across we then plastered the town with wall posters.

Back on board, we called a meeting and read an order from Trotsky stipulating that all anarchists and Socialist Revolutionaries connected with the assassination of the German ambassador Count Mirbach be disarmed. After the order was read aloud and everybody got up to leave, I requested to speak. "I'm an anarchist," I announced, "and if I were in Moscow I would help to organize such assassinations. I therefore find it impossible to agree with such an order and must also be disarmed." There were two other anarchists present, one who solidarized with me and one who did not.

The next morning the secretary of the Regiment Committee regretfully informed me that although he considered me to be a good soldier, the present moment demanded that unity in all political matters had to hold sway in the regiment. There were anarchist units on some fronts, he said. I would receive papers and money to take me to Moscow, and from there I could proceed to another front and join one of these units. I consulted with the other comrade, and the two of us decided to accept the offer.

Once we had received our documents and money, we departed on a ship headed for Nizhni Novgorod.[7] Within the hour, my money, papers and ticket as well were stolen. The captain said that he was unable to help me, but he allowed me to continue on my way without a ticket.

It was a cool, rainy day when we reached Nizhni Novgorod. My comrade brought me to the apartment of the anarchist federation, where I met Blashke, the anarchist whom I had come to know in Warsaw's Pawiak prison in 1912.

I got a place to sleep, a few days of work in my trade and lots of good food—even a bit too much, for it made me sick.

A peculiar kind of order prevailed in this anarchist federation. Funny how the coats which we hung up in the corridor were always disappearing. But, as Blashke explained to me, there was nothing you could do about it, for nobody had the right to forbid the next man from wearing the clothing which belonged to another...as long as he liked it. This anarchist society was positively unappealing to me. Most of its adherents

---

[7]   today, Gorky (GE)

were old terrorists who had returned from exile only to sit around all day long cleaning their guns and planning expropriations. Its theorist was a blind man who read with his fingers. I heard him give a speech in which he expounded on the origins of anarchism: the first two people, he said, Adam and Eve, had already broken discipline.

It was too confining there for me. I convinced Blashke that expropriations in the Soviet republic were a crime, for Russia was a land in revolution at last. If he was dead set on carrying out expropriations, I argued, he ought to do it in the Ukraine, where Skoropadsky was at the helm. [8] Under German occupation, one could do such things with a free conscience.

Blashke was on good terms with the Soviet and it wasn't difficult for him to obtain letters of recommendation addressed to the War Committee in Kursk. At the end of September we were on our way.

---

[8] Skoropadsky was hetman of the Ukraine during the German occupation in 1918. Later he became a leader of monarchist Ukrainian émigrés. (GE)

My Trip to the Ukraine

The recommendations had probably been excellent, for we were very well received in Kursk. The Kursk War Committee fulfilled our every wish. Then we were told that we should help out the next day in transporting literature and weapons to Kharkov. In those days, both Bolsheviks and anarchists together smuggled literature and weapons into the Ukraine. The anarchists were the smugglers and the Bolsheviks facilitated the border crossing.

In the anarchist central I met a Jewish couple who looked like a pair of rabbis' children. They introduced us to the people who would be transporting the gun shipments and ordered us to leave all our papers and photographs behind. Should we end up in the hands of the Whites, they warned, we would be shot without further ado. They admonished us not to wait before opening fire should anyone stop us. One way or the other, we were as good as dead. We were to completely empty our weapons and save the last bullets for ourselves. Handing over our papers, each of us received two revolvers. We left that night, and by time we reached the border, the driver and his shipment were already waiting for us.

We worked out a series of signals: one whistle meant hit the ground, two meant on your feet. The driver took the lead, for he knew the way. Meanwhile, the three of us walked some distance apart from one another while keeping within sight. Should anybody stop us, we were to open fire, and shoot ourselves with our last bullet.

Everything went smoothly that night, but early the next morning we encountered a group of Austrian gendarmes before the gates of Kharkov. One of them ordered us to halt, yet we didn't open fire. I can't remember what we were waiting for. But the three of us stood there with our backs to the transport, ready to reach for our revolvers at the slightest warning that the Austrians intended to detain us.

Investigating the parcels which lay on top, the gendarme found that they contained tea, flour and potatoes. He was simply too lazy to lift up one of the sacks to see what was underneath. We were permitted to move on.

Early that morning we entered Kharkov. After depositing the illegal goods in a cellar, we ate, washed up and got some sleep. Then we considered what was next on the agenda.

My two comrades' number-one priority, I noticed, revolved around their expropriation plans. They were absolutely uninterested in any other work. Unappealing as that was to me, I decided to go to Odessa and pay a visit to many of my old Parisian comrades.

I packed all my things in a bundle, including the two revolvers, and bought a train ticket to Odessa. Finding my way to a *tieplushke* (sleeping car), I laid myself down on the upper bunk and put the satchel under my head.

Several days went by and I didn't budge from my sack. But when the train made a stop at a large station, Zhmerinka I believe, I asked the conductor how long a delay we had, and understood him to say thirteen minutes. I got out to buy some bread, but when I returned, the train was gone. It had only had a three-minute stopover.

I had left the bundle with all my belongings, including my cap, behind in the train. What a severe blow for me it was, and at first I was totally at my wits' end. I walked over to the station *natshalnik* and asked that he call ahead to the next station to request that somebody fetch my things from the train. Only after he called did it occur to me what a foolish thing I had done. There were two revolvers in my satchel, and if anybody should poke around inside, it was all over for me. I therefore skipped the next train, spent that night in the station and took the afternoon train the following day to Odessa.

The train, however, never made it all the way. The Bolsheviks had blown up a large munitions dump and bullets were flying in all directions that entire day. The train stopped and waited until the explosions had ceased.

When things had cooled down I went into the city. I didn't have any addresses with me and walked the streets in the hopes of finding somebody I knew. Fortunately, I came upon a small hat factory in which one of my comrades from Paris, an anarchist, was working. He called me into the workshop and made me a cap. Another comrade brought me clean clothes. To my great joy, Mrs. Buse was also in Odessa, and I had a place to spend the first night.

It was impossible, however, to stay with her for any length of time. Whoever was caught lodging unregistered persons was subject to the death penalty; that went for the guest too. The only way out was to sleep on the street—for me, no terrible prospect.

Mrs. Buse supplied me with bread each day, which she got from an acquaintance of hers. Although it was already October, Odessa was still warm. Together with other comrades who were out of work, I went to the beach and lay in the sand all day long. In the heat of the day, it wasn't at all bad swimming in the Black Sea. When Mrs. Buse came home from work in the evening, we went to her house, ate something warm, then grabbed some blankets and went to wait in line all night for sugar. Lots of people were accustomed to spending the night on the street until the shop opened in the morning. At daybreak I went back to the beach.

An Austrian garrison was located in Odessa. It was already apparent that the army, bearing the consequences of its defeats at the front, was falling apart. Thereupon, the anarchists and Bolsheviks, on the one side, and the pogromists, on the other, were preparing for the events.

I began to consider establishing connections with the Bolsheviks. I did not trust the Odessa anarchists, a small Jewish group. But as things got underway and I began in earnest to try to make contact with the Bolsheviks, I got an offer which altogether changed my plans. I met a comrade from the anarchist group which I had known from Pawiak in 1912. A tired man, he wanted to retire to his father's pension in Otwock,[9] get married and live in peace. A woman comrade from the Bund was with him. When they suggested that I come along and offered to pay my way, I jumped at the chance. It had really been a long time since I thought about my parents. And besides, I planned to set up an anarcho-syndicalist movement in Poland along the lines of the groups which I had come to know in pre-war France.

We left at the end of November. In Kiev, I was overjoyed at being able to see my old and good friend Chana Frayman (who lives in Los Angeles today) during a literature evening at the Culture League. We spent an entire day together and reminisced about some of the old dreams of ours which had never been fulfilled.

All was well until we reached Rovno; from that point on, however, our way was barred. A Polish government had come into being in Lublin. At Chełm, the Poles were battling the Ukrainians. Impossible as it was to travel beyond Rovno, my two comrades decided to stay put and wait it out. Their cash reserves were running out, however, and I no

---

[9]   one of several resort towns near Warsaw (trans.)

longer wished to live at their expense. I therefore set out by foot for Chełm. It was dangerous going, for civilians stood a good chance of being robbed by Ukrainians who had escaped from Austrian captivity. But they trusted me. Seeing the way I was dressed and obviously taking me to be one of them, they greeted me with the Russian *"zdrav molodietz."*[10] To keep warm, they set an abandoned cottage on fire; the whole field was ablaze with warmth and light. Trains were running again from Chełm to Warsaw, but traveling was sheer hell for a Jew. Anti-Semitism had escalated again sharply. I heard people talking about throwing the Jews from the train. Indeed, surrounded as I was by piercing and hostile eyes, I was truly afraid that it might come to that. We finally reached Lublin, and as Polish soldiers appeared the passengers greeted them with great enthusiasm. But I felt cheerless. It seemed to me that I was among enemies. How irksome it was to see that a people, so recently freed from generations of slavery, could turn its hatred so quickly against another people.

---

[10] "How y' doin', kid."

In Warsaw

When I arrived in Warsaw in the first half of January 1919, I hadn't any addresses with me; I had no idea where to find my parents. On Wołynska Street I ran into the wife of my former master Chaim Voler and asked her about my mother. Not a word fell from her lips—she simply hung her head. At the mention of my father's name, tears welled up in her eyes. I already sensed the catastrophe but refused to face the thought of something so horrible. When I finally asked about my sister and her children, she began to cry in earnest. I felt my feet give way. She brought me home with her and only then did she tell me the whole story.

Hunger and edema had been my father's lot, and in 1915 he died of starvation. My mother and sister as well starved to death, although the both of them were still alive as late as 1918. They had been living on Gesia Street in a small room near the entrance of a particular apartment building. One day, the neighbors noticed a terrible smell emanating from the room. Breaking open the door, they found my mother and sister, their bodies already decomposed. They had died in each other's arms. My sister's children had disappeared. Two of them were found some time later, but the third one never turned up.

The woman told me the story and I cried. I think it was the first time in my life, and perhaps the only time, that I cried in the presence of strangers. I felt guilty for their deaths: had I not squandered my father's inheritance by ending up in prison and had I not left the family in 1914, certainly they would not have died of hunger. I was so deeply affected that I contemplated suicide. With a frightened look in her eyes, the woman stood there staring at me. Perhaps she sensed what was up. Suddenly, she tore me away from my thoughts and told me that my younger brother had just returned from Hungary and was on his way over. And before long, there he was. It would be better not to describe this scene; even today, 37 years later, I haven't the strength to do so.

My brother and I went over to the leather trade union. There I met my old comrades Chanina Kamashenmacher, Shia Kamashenmacher and above all Jechiel Neiman, a truly good friend who knew how to help me in my moment of great distress. Full of despair, tears were streaming from my eyes. I went into a small room to cry to my heart's content while Jechiel made sure that nobody entered to disturb me.

I had come to Warsaw without a groschen. Before long, my comrades got me a job, at which I earned good money. I was also able to support my brother, for he was temporarily out of work.

The terrible news of the deaths of my father, mother and sister was certainly the reason why I gave up political activity for a time and concentrated solely on trade-union work. My comrades attributed my intensive preoccupation with the trade union to my political inactivity. They were unaware of the real reason: I plugged into the work of the union because I had to drive out those dismal thoughts which gave me no peace.

In the winter of 1919 a conference of the Jewish leather trade unions took place. Three parties were represented: the Bund, the Uniteds and the Poale Zion. The overwhelming majority of the delegates were Bundists, and as the only non-party delegate, I was included on the list of the Bund in the central administration.

This new central administration was photographed by Alter Kacyzne. Later, this caused us nothing but trouble, for after I became a Communist the police frequently showed up at the trade union with photo in hand to inquire about me.

Besides union work, I was also interested in the Warsaw Workers Council and often attended its meetings. The Council's activities left me with the discouraging impression that it was terribly impotent. There was a colossal difference between the Russian soviets under Kerensky and the Polish workers councils. The Russian soviets had been full of fight; the whole power was in fact in their hands. The very composition of the government was subject to their will and they published laws of a governmental character. They also put up resistance to the reaction, something which was particularly evident during the Kornilov putsch. All parties had been equally interested in the existence of the soviets, but the Bolsheviks had wanted to assign different tasks to them than the Mensheviks.

This was not the case in Poland. One felt that the PPS wanted to get rid of the workers councils, that it had only contributed to creating them because they were very popular at the time. The PPS, however, had no intention of turning the workers councils into organs of struggle. When Moraczewski handed the power over to Paderewski under pressure from abroad, the workers councils in no way reacted. The PPS was afraid of action by the workers councils and instigated a split. Its role in this split and its role in the process leading to the dissolution of the workers councils was so clear that the Bund remained in the councils along with the Communists. The Communists, on the other hand, wanted to turn the councils at once into organs of state power. This was utopian. The Russian soviets had been able to take over the power because they were supported by the soldiers soviets. In Poland, however, the new army was patriotically inclined. There could not have been any talk of creating soldiers councils, for they would have become one of the props of the reaction, as had been the case in Germany. Nobody gave any thought to peasants soviets.

In this situation, the meetings of the workers councils became cheap mass assemblies at which the rivalry between the PPS and the Communists was fought out. Whenever the meetings came to an end, PPS adherents sang their patriotic workers' songs while the Communists sang their new hymn, the song of the Warsaw Red Regiment, which had originated in Moscow. I always left these meetings with a heavy heart.

During those months I was still non-party; I vacillated continuously back and forth. There was still something of the anarchist in me and I was still wedded to the theory of national-cultural autonomy, which I saw as a guaranty for the national existence of the Jewish people. At that time, I still gave no thought to Zionism; I was strongly drawn to the world socialist revolution, which the Communist movement was striving for. Some kind of impulse had to come from outside in order for me to face the moment of decision. And that impulse came.

The well-known Karolski—the first Communist activist in the Jewish quarter—had just returned from his trip to Soviet Russia. Later, after we became very close friends, he confided to me that he had gone to Soviet Russia out of love for a woman. But in those days everybody was certain that he had undertaken the trip for political reasons.

Karolski was an interesting guy: an intellectual and a glowing revolutionary, he had something of the actor in him at the same time. It was often hard tell which side of him was speaking at any given moment, the revolutionary or the actor. He very much loved to put on a show whenever he spoke and let out with positively frightful phrases. Yet he was ready to sacrifice his life for the revolutionary workers movement.

Poser that he was, he convinced himself that he had artistic talent and hit on the idea of composing a poem after Blok's *The Twelve*—adapted, of course, to the environment of the Jewish quarter. He confided to me that I was supposed to be the hero of his poem.

When he got back from Soviet Russia he looked me up, discussed his plan with me and invited me to a talk of his on Blok's *The Twelve*. I had no idea what sort of *meshugene shtik*[11] he was capable of. But as he spoke about Blok's hero, he pointed to me. Hundreds of faces turned in my direction. How embarrassing the thing was!

Karolski never wrote his poem, but after I met together with him a few times I joined the Communist Party of Poland. That's what it was called: not the "Polish Communist Party," but the "Communist Party of Poland." This way, its international character was emphasized.

---

[11] crazy pranks (trans.)

Russians, Poles, Jews: Russian and Polish Social Democrats together with Bund demonstrate in honor of fallen comrades shot during pogrom in Vilna, 1905.

Suffrage demonstration in November 1905 in Przemyśl. The banner reads: "We demand justice."

Adolf Warski

Wera Kostrzewa

Julian Leński

Alfred Lampe

Literature of Polish Left Opposition. Above: Bolszewik No.5, 1934 of the Łódź organisation of Communist-Internationalists. Right: Oppositionists' first newspaper, published in Brussels in May 1932, with open letter by Trotsky on his being deprived of Soviet citizenship.

I. Artuski

Viktor Alter

Demonstration on Karmelicka Street in Cracow during the general strike, 28 November 1905

Workers strike in Warsaw, 1906

Workers demonstration in Moscow, October 1905. The banners from left to right read: "Proletarians of all countries, unite!"; "Russian Social Democratic Workers Party"; "We demand the Constituent Assembly."

*Above, Bundist BO
(Boevi Otriadi—
fighting division)
in Pinsk, 1905.
Left, Avremel Shtricker.
Right, Jechiel Neiman
speaking at the
graves of fallen
Bundist comrades in
Paris, April 1945.*

Georgi Plekhanov   *Peter Kropotkin*

Eighth Congress of the Bund, Petrograd, December 1917. Front row: Henryk Ehrlich (third from left), Rafael Abramovich (fourth from left), Moshe Rafes (second from right) and A. Litvak (right).

Isaac Loeb Peretz, poet of great dreams

Above, defense battery at the Moscow Soviet during the October Revolution. Below, funeral march in Moscow following the October insurrection, 10 (23) November 1917. More than 1,000 fell in battle against the Whites.

Hersh Mendel at the front during the Civil War in Russia, Ufa, 1918

Revolutionary fraternization and internationalism: former German, Austrian and Serbian prisoners of war join up with Bolsheviks, Nikolaev, beginning 1918.

First victims of the Petlyura pogroms, in which over 60,000 Ukrainian Jews died

First conference of Polish leather workers, 12, 13 and 14 October 1919. Inset of fourth person from left in second row: Hersh Mendel?

Henryk Ehrlich speaking at May Day rally in Warsaw, 1933

Rosa Luxemburg, heart and mind of the Polish and German left Marxists

V.1. Lenin as member of the presidium of the First Congress of the Communist International, Moscow, 2-6 March 1919. Left, Hugo Eberlein from Germany; right, Fritz Platten from Switzerland.

Legendary War Commissar Leon Trotsky addressing troops during revolutionary war against Poland, 1920

Provisional Revolutionary War Committee of Poland in Białystok during Polish-Russian War of 1920. In the middle row, second from left to right: Felix Dzerzhinsky, Julian Marchlewski, Felix Kon.

Miriam Shumik and Hersh Mendel following their release from Siedlce prison, 1928

Alexander Minc

Isaac Deutscher

PART 5

I Become a Member of the Communist Party

*M*y joining the Communist Party was not prompted by the conversations which I had with Karolski. Given his sparse theoretical knowledge and his propensity toward empty phrases, he could not have any influence on me. That influence came from an entirely different direction. I had just read Lenin's *State and Revolution* at the time, and it was this short booklet of his which made so colossal an impression on me. I can well imagine that the *Communist Manifesto* by Marx made a similar impression on the first socialists. Ever since I had joined the revolutionary movement, my dream was the struggle for the human personality, for human freedom and dignity. Wherever I saw a man who, in my eyes, was degraded, I instinctively took flight. It was on these grounds that I drew close to anarchism in 1915. It seemed to me that Marxism sacrificed humanity on the altar of state interests.

In Lenin's little book, I found what I was looking for: the state would whither away, laws would disappear, force would cease to exist. The relations between individuals, as well as between the individual and society, would be regulated by a morality that would be both raised to a higher level and purified by free men in the communist society. Engels had spoken in the same language in his important work *The Origin of the Family, Private Property and the State*. Through the prism of these ideas I saw Marxism in a new light. I had a warm feeling in my heart, for I had finally found the correct path: toward the dictatorship of the proletariat through proletarian class struggle, and from there to a world without the state, without laws and without force. Full of joy and with deepest faith, I entered the Communist ranks.

At that time, two important events occurred within the Communist movement in Poland, although they were of unequal weight.

First, Toybnshlak and the brothers Shmayun and Avrom Zachariash joined the Communist Party together with a small group which had split off from the Poale Zion. That they came to us was of great significance. It was of particular importance to us that we won over a small group from the Uniteds under the leadership of Blond Noah and Israel Gayst. They brought along a few trade unions, and it was thanks to them that we became a mass party. It goes without saying, however, that we only became the greatest force in the Jewish workers quarter when the Combund merged with the Communist Party.

Of far greater significance was the union of both large Polish workers parties, the Social Democrats and the PPS-Left. These two parties really represented the cream of the Polish workers movement; they were the parties which had educated the Polish workers over the years in the spirit of Marxism. They had trained splendid revolutionary cadres. The leading comrades of these two parties created a revolutionary staff of the Polish proletariat the likes of which no party in any other land had. Although I in fact intend to confine myself here to writing my memoirs and wish to avoid polemicizing, I do want to say a few words about a subject which departs a bit from the task at hand.

Many people these days present the history of the Communist movement in the manner of a detective or spy novel. Those who joined the Communist movement—so they say—very soon became Lenin's lackeys and spies for the Soviet Union. There is no greater falsification than such history writing. From the history of the Communist movement in each country, it can be proven that the founders of the Communist Parties either left the Comintern at the appropriate time or, in the case of those who were forced to stay, were murdered by Stalin. I wish to confine my remarks, however, to a few lines about the leader of the Polish party.

Rosa Luxemburg, the heart and mind of the Polish and German left Marxists—those men and women who founded the Communist Parties in their respective countries—was an opponent of the basic principles of Leninism her whole life long. We will enumerate just a few of her differences here.

First, Rosa Luxemburg opposed Lenin's theory of the roll of the party in the workers movement. While Lenin said that the party must determine the forms of the struggle and even fix the calendar of the social revolution, Rosa Luxemburg maintained that the revolution will be spontaneous and that the party must confine its roll to propagating the ideas of the social revolution. The rest must be left to the proletariat itself; the course of the revolution must be determined by the workers alone.

Second, Lenin declared that the slogan of the right of nations to national self-determination was a component of the socialist revolution. Rosa Luxemburg, to the contrary, considered this position dangerous. She believed that this slogan would throw the workers into the arms of the bourgeoisie, and that in the absence of an imperialist war it was an unachievable goal. Of necessity, the slogan meant gearing up for imperialist wars. In the socialist society, on the other hand, the slogan of the right of nations to self-determination would be superfluous, for the oppression of one people by another would in any case be a thing of the past.

Third, Rosa Luxemburg criticized Lenin's approach to the agrarian question. For Poland, she proposed that the land not be divided up, but rather nationalized.

Fourth, Lenin wrote that imperialism in the capitalist epoch only began in 1894, the year when Germany became imperialist, when the world's colonies had already been carved out and when the question of carving them up anew through war was on the agenda. With this as his starting point, Lenin described the imperialist epoch as capitalism's final stage, a stage of decay distinguished by permanent wars and social revolutions. Rosa Luxemburg, on the other hand, identified capitalism with imperialism. From its inception, she argued, capitalism would not have developed without the conquest of colonies, for colonial possessions supplied it with raw materials for its industries and markets for its products. She argued that if capitalism should find itself without the possibility of snatching up foreign colonies, it would collapse on its own, just as it had spontaneously arisen. The social revolution would then break out spontaneously, she maintained. The masses will not make the revolution at the call of a party, but rather as a reaction to the spontaneous collapse of capitalism.

Rosa Luxemburg was able to develop all of these theories at the First Congress of the German Communist Party a few days before her tragic death. That is to say, she remained true to herself to the last days of her life. Yet if she and all of her followers hailed the Russian Revolution, it was because she, together with Trotsky, had already held that the coming revolution in Russia would be socialist in the days when Lenin had still believed that it would be bourgeois-democratic. To depict these people as spies for the Soviet Union means to act dishonorably toward one's own past.

The Polish Communist Party was really the only mass party which spoke out for the October Revolution in its first days, and the only one which wanted to carry the revolution over to Polish territory.

Upon joining the Communist Party of Poland, I became a member of the Jewish Central Bureau (a department of the Central Committee). The Central Bureau in those days had the unlimited right to shape the work in the Jewish quarter according to its own discretion. Its members included Karolski; Israel Gayst, who was added on later; Zambrowski (brother of the present-day Zambrowski), a man of weak character who worked according to his moods and was a wreck for weeks on end; and myself.

One proof of our successful work was our May Day demonstration in 1919. In order to demonstrate our strength among the Jewish population, we had decided to call out the Jewish workers to a separate mass rally, hold a demonstration in the streets of the Jewish quarter and then join up with the general demonstration organized by the party. The results surpassed all of our expectations.

As we marched onto Gesia Street, the well-known writer Alter Kacyzne approached our ranks, fell into line and marched beside us under the party flag. He was quite close to us at the time. More than anything else, he was a friend of Karolski's.

Then along came my younger brother. I told him to leave, for I knew that he was far removed from political affairs. But refusing to budge, he said: "Have no fear. The police aren't going to lay a hand on you." It was obvious that he had come to protect me. He really was a strong man.

The mood of the demonstration, however, was somewhat wrecked by Karolski. I have no idea what possessed him to do himself up the way he did. Was he posing or acting conspiratorially? In any case, he had come to our May Day rally wearing a false beard and moustache. And he was the only speaker there who also had the capacity to serve as translator. Right in the middle of his speech his disguise fell off and he took pains to paste everything back on again. He used up his entire speaking time doing battle with his beard and moustache.

The year 1919 as a whole was a year of successful work. I traveled around the provinces. In Łódź and Tomaszów I came to know the great misery of the weavers employed as cottage laborers. Constructing party groups came easily, for everywhere we went people seemed to have been waiting for our arrival.

And then came the imbroglio of the Polish-Russian war. It was beyond all doubt that Pilsudski was the aggressor. Lenin proposed to meet Pilsudski in the small town of Borisov and was prepared to give the latter much more than he was later to receive through the Riga treaty. But Pilsudski replied that he would beat the Bolsheviks whenever and wherever he wanted. Even the Second International called for actions against Poland, including sabotaging shipments of weapons. They also decided to call a general day of protest. It is paradoxical indeed that while the PPS rejected the proposal of their own International, the Communists solidarized with it.

Poland found itself at the time in a difficult situation. The amalgamation of the three Polish provinces, each of which had undergone a distinct economic development, into one unified state and one common economic organism demanded a great deal of time and energy. The war made this impossible. Tens of thousands of workers emigrated to France. All of this produced favorable conditions for the growth of Communist influence. The battle for the soul of the Polish workers had begun. The railroad workers, the workers of the largest metal plants, the streetcar operators, construction workers and shoemakers all came under Communist influence, not to mention the coal miners. In Łódź, to the contrary, our efforts produced more uneven results. Given this state of affairs, the question was posed: what must be the strategic orientation of the Communist Party of Poland? The answer was: in Poland everything is still unstable and there are two possible roads, capitalism or socialism. The party, therefore, must orient itself toward the goal of socialism and pursue corresponding tactics. This meant sharpening all conflicts to the utmost and driving forward toward socialist revolution.

My personal situation, meanwhile, took a turn for the worse. Across the way from Pawiak prison on Dzielna Street we had a semilegal club. Sometime toward the end of 1919 I became acquainted with a German there who, greeting me with a warm embrace and a kiss, left me from the start with a bad impression. Ripping open his overcoat, he pulled out some papers, declared that the Polish government was intending to mobilize in Posen and that the party wanted to reply with a general strike. His reason for coming, he said, was to consult with the Central Committee. I sent his papers over to the Central Committee and received confirmation that everything was in order. Then I found him a place to sleep at the home of a comrade and gave him some money. It turned out, however, that he was a provocateur. The comrade who put him up was turned over to the police and slapped with a three-year prison sentence. The ringleader, according to this informer's testimony in court, was missing. To be sure, he did not know my name, but he was able to describe my appearance. The search for me began and I was forced to go into hiding. Thus it became more difficult for me to move about freely.

I Become a Member of the Revolutionary War Committee

In the summer of 1920, hard times befell Poland. Pilsudski had decided to realize the dream of generations of Polish chauvinists by attempting to recreate Poland's glorious past through the establishment of a federation embracing Poland, White Russia and the Ukraine. His plan naturally entailed severing White Russia and the Ukraine from Soviet Russia. Pilsudski simply altered the scheme somewhat: White Russia in its entirety was to enter this federation, but the Ukraine was to be partitioned. The western portion of the Ukraine was to be united with Poland while Petlyura was to rule in the south. In thanks, Petlyura was supposed to cede to Poland a corridor to the Black Sea. "From the Baltic to the Black Sea, from Danzig to Odessa" became the slogan of the Polish militarists. This was the background to Pilsudski's march on Kiev.

Pilsudski's march to Kiev was such an irresponsible adventure that every fraction in the Sejm,[1] except for Pilsudski's adherents, protested. This aggression evoked great bitterness within every tendency of the workers movement in all parts of the world. Even among the Polish working masses, who had been patriotically inclined during the early phase of the birth of Poland, the offensive against Kiev produced a big uproar. Nobody was able to comprehend what this move was all about. The popular masses of Poland demanded not Kiev, but peace.

The mood in the Jewish quarter was best expressed by Henryk Ehrlich in the Warsaw Community Council. His appearance was both courageous and daring and, as we later learned from his wife Sofia Dubnov-Ehrlich, could have cost him his life.

It was clear to us Communists that Pilsudski's adventure would end in defeat. We knew this from Soviet sources, who were preparing to launch their counteroffensive.

We too began to prepare. Under the command of the famous workers' leader Królikowski (who was later murdered in the Soviet Union), a

---

[1] the Polish parliament (trans.)

revolutionary war committee was created. The task of this revolutionary war committee was not to seize power—it had a more limited assignment to fulfill. Since it had become known that the PPS was setting up battle units to be used against the Red Army should the latter march on Warsaw, it was necessary for the Revolutionary War Committee to organize Red units to fight the PPS units, and to enable the Red Army to march rapidly to the German border to guage the pulse of the revolution in Germany, as Lenin expressed it.

The first to represent the Jewish workers on the Revolutionary War Committee was Israel Gayst. After he was arrested, I stepped in to take his place.

I faced certain personal difficulties at the time in connection with the fact that my brother was a deserter from the Polish army. Desertion was punishable by no less than the death penalty. Each day, posters bearing the names of deserters who had been shot the night before were pasted up. I was ridden with anxiety over the fate of my brother. My own age group had not yet been called up for mobilization, but within a few weeks I would be pulled into military service as well. Inasmuch as I was a member of the Revolutionary War Committee, the party forbade me to go into the military and was supposed to produce a passport for me stating that I was a few years older than I really was. In the meantime, I took my own passport and affixed my brother's picture to it so that he could move about in the streets. I had two days to go before my false papers were to come back from the factory, but just then our technical apparatus fell into the hands of the police. No passport. Aware of the fact that I was to be called up for military duty within a few days, my brother joined Haller's army as a volunteer under my name. A few days later, he fell during the defense of Brest.

At the same time, Israel Gayst smuggled a clandestine note out of prison stating that the authorities were feverishly busy collecting information about me and that they were already aware of my activities. He recommended that I crop my hair off, grow a beard and disappear from Warsaw. The comrades on the War Committee resolved that I go to Otwock in order to mobilize battle units. With the trains now being searched from end to end, I decided to take the *kolieke*, the local train that is, which supplemented the Warsaw-Otwock run.

Once beyond Falenica, the Jews in my car began whispering among themselves that "they" had come. The gendarmerie, it occurred to me, had arrived in order to search the train. What should I do? I was being sought as a member of the Revolutionary War Committee. I was also a deserter and I had no passport. Jumping from the train was senseless, for a whole group of gendarmes had already entered the car and were heading my way.

Perhaps, I thought, there is a way out: buy them off. As they approached my bench, however, I saw that these gendarmes were the precious little sons of aristocrats—idealists and patriots. It was obvious to me at once that bribing them was impossible. I then grabbed a Polish newspaper—and a reactionary one at that—and acted as if I were reading.

Sitting on the bench next to me were Jews wearing gabardines and Jewish hats. When the gendarmes even demanded to see the papers of a Jew with a long, greying beard, I was seized by sharp bitterness. I pretended to be engulfed in my reading and, to my great astonishment, they passed me by and demanded to see the papers of the person sitting directly beside me. My western-style clothing, it seems, together with the reactionary Polish newspaper had saved me.

I was unable to remain in Otwock. It was too close to the front and the police were making many arrests. In a peasant wagon, hidden between bundles of straw, I made my way back to Warsaw.

Crossing the bridge, an idea suddenly occurred to me which I communicated to the War Committee. They simply laughed at me, but to this day I still believe that I was right—right, that is, given my standpoint in those days.

I confided my plan to Królikowski personally because we did not hold meetings. Our work was of a purely technical nature; we simply received instructions informing us what to do.

My plan looked like this: given that the Red Army was pinned down before the gates of Warsaw and given that it was impossible to organize an uprising—although we were carrying out large-scale strikes—we had to do something spectacular. I knew that for an army, particularly a demoralized army, there is nothing worse than being attacked from the rear. And the Polish army was indeed on the verge of demoralization. I proposed, therefore, that I fasten dynamite to my body in order to blow the bridge, and myself with it, sky high. I was certain that the Polish army would be driven into a panic and that the Red Army would be sparked to a new offensive. I have already mentioned that Królikowski rejected my plan. Afterwards, I also spoke to Karolski about it, but to no avail.

The Death Sentence

Meanwhile, Soviet planes took to the skies over Warsaw and the capital itself began to resemble a ghost town. The civil militia provisionally assumed the role of maintaining order. Roundups took place in the streets. Parks were surrounded and everybody searched. We in the party spread the word around to one and all that the parks were off-limits, and yet even I fell into the trap.

One Saturday morning I went for a walk in the Saxony Garden. I refused to believe that the militia would raid the place so early in the day. Then I met Huberman, a Bundist at the time, and, sitting down on a bench, we schmoozed about the situation. He praised Ehrlich's speech. Suddenly, a Jewish woman who had been sitting next to us and listening to our conversation said, "*Kinder*, the garden is surrounded!" Running from one gate to another, I met patrols everywhere. "Go to the public bathroom," I thought, but there too I encountered soldiers. I attempted to walk away but a gendarme, already spotting me, demanded that I hand over my papers. I had left them with my landlord, I explained, in order to have him register me with the police. Bewildered, the gendarme stood there and said, "You walk the streets at a time like this without papers?"

They brought me to the barracks on Ciepła Street where the headquarters of the military gendarmerie were located. What to do? The death sentence was a sure thing; there was no chance whatsoever of an appeal. Perhaps I was too weak to conjure up any more courage and patience, for I decided to speed things along. I was a deserter, I said short and sweet. The World War had killed my entire family and I had had enough of wars. So as not to complicate the matter, I kept quiet about my political views. I was also well aware that as a deserter I would be tried within a few hours, and therefore decided to tell the gendarmes my real name.

I was led into a hall where five men wearing military uniforms were seated. It was the last Saturday in the month of July. Following a brief interrogation and the prosecutor's speech, the verdict of death was read.

After the sentence was passed, they put me in another room. It positively crushed me to think how carelessly I had acted. And it shamed me to think that my comrades might come to learn of the manner in which I had conducted myself. I had only one wish, that it all end as soon as possible.

That evening, I and several others were taken to the citadel. Together with us was a group of men who were on their way to the Fifth Commissariat.

The gendarmes lined us up four abreast and stuck me right in the middle. All in all there were some forty of us; the gendarmes numbered eight. Along the way I held a dialog with myself: "What can I do?" I asked. "Absolutely nothing. All is lost." That was my one and only question and my one and only answer. Then we approached the corner of Dzielna and Karmelicka Streets where the Bundist club was located. Both streets provided access to the courtyard there, and as we neared the corner I decided to make a run for it. Not for a minute did I believe it would work. I only wanted to be shot while escaping, for that was easier than waiting in some isolation cell for the firing squad.

Not far from the courtyard I asked my neighbor to trade places with me so that I could be next to the sidewalk. At the corner, I instinctively pulled up the collar of my jacket to shield myself from who knows what and dashed into the courtyard on the Dzielna Street side. Shooting out onto Karmelicka Street and not hearing any shots, I stopped in my tracks, let down my collar and then continued on my way. I had things to do, and that same evening, I believe, had a conversation with Itshe Sokolnik. (Today, he is a Bundist who lives in Paris.) He was in charge of one of the battle units.

What saved me? The darkness for one thing, as it was already quite late. And the conduct of the gendarmes themselves, a bunch of real *shlimazls*. [ne'er-do-wells (trans.)]

Party work finished, I went home. I was living with an old friend of mine, Toybele, well to the rear of the courtyard of a tall, four-story apartment house at Gesia Street 49. At the entrance there was no more than a fence. Late in the evening I would go upstairs to the attic, which was specially used for storing coal, and make myself a place to sleep. From there I was able to keep an eye on the gate. Whenever the bell rang and the police walked in, I closed up the opening with coal so that nothing was discernible. These were my nighttime quarters for several months.

One evening—it was still rather early—I was lying on a small bed in the kitchen. Suddenly, the door opened and two women entered. Crying, they told Toybele that they had a package for me and had been looking for me high and low. I was nowhere to be found, they said, a sign that I had been shot. First I, and then Toybele, broke out in wild laughter. The comrades were overjoyed but I reprimanded them just the same for running around with packages at a time like that. One could wind up paying for it with a stint behind bars. But we threw ourselves a party anyway and devoured all the good things a man eats when he is believed to be dead. In the end, the whole episode turned out to be an amusing one. Had various and sundry legal documents not been lost in the course of time, I would have figured both as a great patriot, a volunteer who had fallen in battle against the Bolsheviks, and also as a deserter and member of the Bolshevik Revolutionary War Committee!

For several weeks we lived in great suspense, until we finally received a communication from the staff of the Sixteenth Red Army directing us to discontinue operations. What a pity for those who sacrificed their lives. In about two days, the Red Army would have been in Warsaw.

We had worked up a plan for the first day of Soviet rule. We had decided to take the barracks on Gesia Street as well as the Fourth and Fifth Commissariats. While the printing plant belonging to *der Moment* was to be seized in order to put out a party newspaper, the government newspaper was to be printed at the facilities belonging to *Haynt*. We had decided to leave *di Folkstsaytung*[2] to the Bund.

At the same meeting we also discussed the turn of the Bund, that is, its readiness to work together with the new regime. The Bund had demanded the portfolio of the Ministry of Jewish Affairs, and the Central Committee wanted to know what our opinion about the issue was. We decided to leave the question open until the Red Army entered Warsaw.

But the Red Army did not take Warsaw. Instead, the Polish counteroffensive began, which was to end with the Riga peace treaty. A few weeks after the retreat of the Red Army the party finally procured a passport for me. A woman comrade brought it to me at the factory where I worked.

---

[2] *People's Newspaper* (trans.)

At precisely the moment when the courts-martial against deserters were working day and night, I committed a great breach of security. Certain that nobody had spotted me, I went into the master's office to sign my new passport. But I was wrong: my master had been watching me.

I was not yet a party functionary at the time; I still worked in a factory and was still the leader of my trade union. With the Red Army before the gates of Warsaw and the thought in everybody's mind that they might march in any day, all the tradesmen in my branch of industry did their best to get on my good side. It seemed as though they had begun to love and cherish me. With the Red Army gone, however, one of them said to me as I arrived to settle a work dispute, "Your name is Hersh Mendel? I'm not sure. Let me see your passport." It was clear that my master had betrayed me and that the tradesmen knew something they weren't supposed to know. I decided to disappear from Poland for a time and go to France. I was yearning to visit France again, but it worked out differently. I headed instead for Soviet Russia.

Off to Soviet Russia

From Warsaw I traveled to Berlin via Katowitz.[3] Once in the German capital, I was short on money to continue on my way. Karolski, who had already been in Berlin for quite some time, was supposed to help me out. But when I showed up at his doorstep, I learned that he had been arrested some days earlier while addressing a Communist gathering along with Brandler. It was a bitter blow for me. And where could I find Karolski's wife? I asked the apartment owner to send her to me should she show up and, indeed, the next day that's just what happened. She brought me to the MOPR,[4] which set me up with some money and a place to sleep.

Meanwhile, Karolski was released and we were invited to celebrate the 7th of November at the Soviet embassy.[5] The celebration, though a rather lean one, was heartening. There were no diplomats there. Groups of foreign Communists who happened to be in Berlin as well as Red Army men from prisoner-of-war camps had been invited. We ate an extremely modest meal, but to make up for it we sang Soviet and revolutionary songs throughout the night.

I decided to go to Soviet Russia together with Karolski. We had to wait until our papers were prepared. The sole possibility was to go as Russian prisoners of war.

In the intervening time I had an opportunity to participate in a semi-legal demonstration in Berlin. The Communist Party of Germany called a large mass rally to mark the anniversary of the murders of Rosa Luxemburg and Karl Liebknecht. A great many workers attended. Nevertheless, the speaker's insistence that everybody join in the subsequent demonstration was of little avail. Very few people came along. As it turned out, the speaker himself—the parliamentary deputy Kaufmann—did not participate in the demonstration either.

Some few hundreds of us, therefore, formed the line of march. At a

---

[3] Katowice (trans.)
[4] Mezhdunarodnaya Organizatsiya Pomoshchi Revolutionerom, International Red Aid (trans.)
[5] anniversary of the October Revolution (trans.)

particular point the police barred our way. I learned once the demonstration was over that its organizers belonged to the party's left wing, which later split from the organization. In any case, I was astonished by their tactics. The police were not stopping us from marching to the cemetery, they only demanded that we follow another route. In response to this, those in charge of the demonstration gave us the word to ignore the police directive and break through their lines. The police opened fire and a sizable section of the demonstration scattered. There were no casualties, however, for the police had simply been firing into the air. In the end, only a few dozen people, mainly Polish and Russian comrades, made it to the graves of Luxemburg and Liebknecht. Among them, the Jewish element predominated.

What a depressing finale it was. And how different indeed things were in Poland! There the parliamentary deputy would have marched at the head of the demonstration and the shots would not have caused anybody to bat an eyelid.

Soon after the demonstration, I took off for the prisoner of war camp at Altdamm in order from there to travel to Soviet Russia. In the camp I ran into Alexander Minc, who was still a Bundist in those days. I had already met him in Berlin, but it was in Altdamm that his friendship came in handy. He took down letters from prisoners to their next of kin and received various things to eat in return. He also had a number of other original ideas up his sleeve to avoid going hungry, and in the interim the two of us managed to survive.

The ship on which we sailed was probably only a simple freighter, for our sleeping quarters consisted of planks without mattresses. The three of us—Karolski, Alexander and I—found ourselves a corner. Another man, a stranger, also joined us. We soon found out that he had previously been an officer in Bela Kuns' general staff. He described to us a number of episodes from the revolution and counterrevolution in Hungary. There was something bitter in the way he spoke, and I asked him what the cause of it was. He told us how, in the wake of Horthy's victory, the counterrevolution settled accounts with the adherents of the soviet government. Women were raped in the presence of their husbands and men were shamefully mutilated. He was possessed by one thought: revenge.

On one occasion a misunderstanding erupted between the two of us. He suddenly began calling me "the dashing Jew." That word "Jew" in the mouth of a non-Jew rubbed me a certain way; that is, it smacked to me of anti-Semitism. When I confronted him about it, he began to laugh. In Bela Kun's general staff, he said, there had been a liaison officer who was known as "the dashing Jew." I simply looked like him.

Immersed in such friendly conversations, we approached the Estonian port city of Revel. [6] An Estonian officer came aboard and declared in good Russian that Kronstadt had rebelled and that the sailors were bombarding Petrograd. By time we reach Petrograd, he added, it may already be over for the Soviet government. The news threw us into a minor panic. What now? Some of the Polish comrades were in favor of waiting out the fight instead of going on. In the end, however, we decided to tell the captain to make haste; should it be necessary, we wanted to be able to participate in the defense of Petrograd.

The uprising had already been crushed by the time we arrived. A congress of the Communist Party was taking place at the time and one third of the congress participants had taken up arms in order to assist in defeating the insurgents.

I ended up in Moscow again, and this time I lived at the home of an old friend, a Bundist. I soon had to move out, however, for Litvak, a leader of the Bund, was a frequent visitor. One day, I found a proclamation which Litvak and my friend had left lying on the table, which concluded with the slogan: "The Bund is dead. Long live the Bund!" I decided to move out and act as if I hadn't seen a thing.

This was the period of the Third Congress of the Communist International. Despite the fact that the war was already over, conditions were tragic and the mood bad. The famine which had broken out, due to the destruction of grain fields by locusts, was so extensive that the situation came to cannibalism. The misery was indescribable. Kronstadt had also signaled a political crisis. Nobody as yet knew what the NEP [7] would bring. Many were disquieted and even disappointed. I met a Polish poet (whose name I cannot remember) in the Polish section of the Comintern who had ceased writing because the NEP, as he put it, had killed his Muse.

Under these conditions, the Third Congress of the Comintern was a historic event. It was at this congress that the program for the individual parties was worked out. I did not attend the congress itself, only the reception which was held in honor of the delegates. Bukharin spoke. He

---

[6] Tallinn (trans.)
[7] the New Economic Policy (trans.)

said that the delegates were now in Moscow for the third time and that with each successive visit the situation had grown worse. Things would only be able to improve when the international proletariat comes to the aid of Soviet Russia by making revolutions in their own countries. A storm of rapture greeted his remarks.

I developed another boil beneath my arm and went into the hospital to have an operation. The mood there was frightful. Red Army men with amputated hands and fcet vehemently cursed the Soviet government. The ward supervisor as well was an enemy of the Bolsheviks. It goes without saying that above all else the Jews were blamed.

Tremendous hunger was the patients' lot. Whenever comrades brought me a few roasted potatoes I was looked upon as a rich man. This atmosphere made me feel miserable and, sick as I was, I left the hospital. I decided to return to Poland and did everything in my power to make it possible. A few months had already passed and I hoped that the authorities had forgotten about me. Perhaps, I thought, there had even been an amnesty. At any price, I wanted to go home.

The evening before my departure I had time to hear a speech by Rafes. This time I found his remarks embarrassing; now he was preaching the renunciation of the Yiddish language and Jewish culture, and calling for assimilation into Russian culture. He received a sharp reply, however, from Esther and Litvak.

On my return trip to Poland I stopped in Minsk, where, at the apartment of a Polish comrade, Skolski was waiting. Skolski too was a member of the Polish party. A notoriously immoral man, his personal record had become legendary. One case in point is the following. When his consumptive wife went into the hospital, he never even visited her. Instead, he took up with another woman. Called to account for it, he replied that his wife was a goner anyway and would soon die.

I traveled with him in a peasant wagon as far as the border. Both my arms were still bandaged and it was impossible for me to maneuver about freely. As the cart ascended a hill, I fell off into the snow and was unable to budge. Skolski took me in his arms and laid me back on the wagon like a sack of potatoes. By the time we reached the frontier, the smugglers, who were to bring us clandestinely over the border, were ready and waiting at the home of a Jew. In exchange for their services, they were permitted to smuggle anything they wanted to and from Poland. We had a few hours to kill before leaving, and in the meantime they stuffed themselves full with food and liquor.

After bringing us over the border, they bought the two of us train tickets to Vilna. There I took leave of Skolski, for he stayed in Vilna. And on New Year's Day 1922 I was back in Warsaw.

My Imprisonment in Brest

Late that night I arrived in Warsaw. The address which I had was not particularly accurate. But, dressed as I was in a Russian coat sewed from a colored sack and not terribly certain that my passport would stand up to an inspection, I did not want to check into a hotel. Instead, I wandered the cold streets the whole night.

Meeting with comrades the following day, I was surprised by two changes which had taken place in the Jewish workers quarter. Everything was geared to what was going on inside the Bund. While the Combund was still formally in the Bund at the time, it was in fact working wholly and completely in collaboration with the Communist Party. During this period, if I am not mistaken, Rafes spent the entire time in Warsaw. He led the Combund or, in any case, was in close contact with it. We on the Central Bureau saw little of him; he had practically nothing to do with us. We worked under the direct leadership of the Central Committee. I can remember Rafes once complaining to me that he met many Ukrainian Whites in Warsaw who greeted him affectionately. They believed that he too belonged to the White emigration, for they had known him during the period when he was fighting the Bolsheviks together with them. The man was deathly afraid of falling into their clutches.

I traveled often in the provinces. On one occasion in Częstochowa I just barely avoided ending up in the hands of the police. It all happened because I had not studied my brand-new passport as thoroughly as I ought to have. Checking into a hotel one night, I had to hand it over to the owner in order to register for a room. But when he asked me the name of my father, I broke into a cold sweat. He stood there with a pen in his hand and waited for my reply. What a scrape I had gotten myself into. I then began storming that the asking price for a room was too high and demanded my passport back. Luckily, I escaped from the jaws of disaster.

It was around this time that we scored a big victory over the Bund in Łódź. One Saturday at the end of January or the beginning of February, meetings were scheduled to take place in a series of Jewish trade unions along with elections for new executive boards. We came out victorious everywhere. In each trade union, we had gone in together with the Combund. Alexander Minc and I were to speak at the most important and largest trade union, the textile workers. Henryk Ehrlich made a special trip from Warsaw just to attend this meeting, and the struggle was really hot. After Ehrlich's speech, Alexander spoke in the name of the Combund and I in the name of the Communist Party. Our list received the majority; we won one more mandate in the executive board election than the Bund did. Some time later, one Combundist bailed out and joined the Bund, thereby handing it back its majority. Meanwhile, we threw a victory celebration which lasted the whole night.

One incident is worth noting here. It was a deeply stirring moment. In the middle of my speech, a number of informers entered the hall. Although I didn't notice them, I was in any case quite certain that they were there. Henryk Ehrlich went pale, whispered in my ear that I had better be careful and suggested that we leave the hall together as soon as the meeting came to an end. I cannot remember whether I followed his suggestion or not; I do not believe so. But the way he conducted himself filled me with respect for him.

On 22 February, a Saturday, I went to Brest to attend a party conference. At that time, there was still no separate Communist Party of West White Russia. Thanks to a provocateur I was arrested at the meeting. One of the members of the party organization in Kobrin was a policeman. The comrades there believed that this policeman would protect them from the police. In reality, however, he blew the whistle on the conference.

Sixteen comrades had gathered at the apartment of Esther Gam. She was so young and so small that she looked like a child. After everyone had arrived, an informer with the look of a murderer about him, followed by a handful of policemen, barged in. He was positively elated, this informer, and made sure everyone knew how proud he was that he had had such good luck.

We were taken to the office of the secret police and the interrogations began. One after another they roughed up the comrades a bit. It only went particularly badly for two of us, above all little Esther Gam (who lives in Argentina today). The police believed that they could get everything out of a child, but they were wrong. To her honor, she came through it intrepidly. They also went after me with a vengeance, for the provocateur had informed them that I had come from the Center. To this day I still have big, beautiful marks on my body from that night. I did not tell the comrades about it, for I was uncertain as to whether they would hold out—and they already had enough to worry about. Among the sixteen people who had been arrested, only one was a worker. The others were children of bourgeois parents. I was never able to determine what their parents did for a living. The young worker happened to be there by accident. He was a brother of the little Esther and a Poale Zionist at the time.

The next morning we were transferred to a small, dirty jail illuminated by oil lamps. The administration, however, was good. If one had money, one could do anything. I was thrown into a cell with a bunch of common criminals but never even managed to size up the situation. Dead tired, I stretched myself out on a bunk and passed out. When I woke up the next morning, I walked over to the window directly facing the prison gate, leaned my head on the bars and began to turn over in my mind the question: what now?

I wanted to instill the comrades with courage and steadfastness. When I heard my cellmates, all Jews incidentally, mumbling among themselves, "a real jailbird," it was clear to me that in their world this was the highest expression of recognition. I asked them to put me in contact with my comrades, and before I knew it the job was done. Before our first day was out, I had managed to speak to each and every one of them, and, as it turned out, they were all holding up just fine.

Life with my fellow prisoners worked out well and we shared everything we had in common. In difficult moments, whenever they got drunk, they poured out their bitter hearts to me. They told me how miserable it was that they were forced to climb through strangers' windows in the dead of night while everybody was asleep. And whenever they ended up in jail, they would tell me, their wives slept with other men. But there was one question in which we did not see eye to eye: the belief in ghosts. One *ganef*[8] assured me that he had once stolen a horse and ridden in the night into the forest. It suddenly became light, he told me, and men wrapped in talliths emerged. They were ghosts.

On 1 May all the criminals in my cell put on red armbands and then went outside for their walk in the yard.

Yet there were also bad days in prison. It was particularly painful to

---

[8] thief (trans.)

be with these men the night before their execution. Losing themselves, they would cry and cry and cry. An equally horrible moment was the night a prison breakout by a group of criminals miscarried. They were so terribly beaten that I thought I could hear their bones breaking under the blows.

Our interrogations dragged on. I had been carrying a false passport under the name of Bellman and knew that this would soon come out, but I did not want to give them my real name. In those days, the Russian law according to which vagrancy was punishable by four years in prison was still in effect in Poland, and I believed that by keeping quiet about my identity I would be sentenced as a vagrant. This was in any case preferable to betraying my real name, for even if my death sentence had lapsed, I still faced life imprisonment. The examining magistrate, however, refused to conclude the proceedings until he knew my real name, and the thing therefore dragged on for a whole year without budging an inch.

Meanwhile, under the pressure of their families outside, the comrades had begun to get edgy. I had no other choice but to tell them why I was unwilling to reveal my true identity. Then we decided that I ought to tell the authorities who I really was. But after I did so, new complications arose. Whereas the examining magistrate had previously refused to buy my false name, he now refused to believe my real one and demanded that I summon witnesses to confirm my identity. But whom? I had no idea where to locate the families of my mother or father, and in any case, they were all wealthy businessmen whom I had never had anything to do with. Naturally, calling on comrades was out of the question.

When the examining magistrate finally got around to reading the protocol to me, I discovered that he had not written down what I had told him. He flew into a rage when I refused to sign it. If he had the power, he roared, he would shoot every Communist without trial, just as they shoot the bourgeoisie in the Soviet Union. I told him that I was not interested in his political opinion and that he should simply take down my statement without falsifying it. Then he cried, "*Zhidovska Morda!*"[9] In reply, I said, "I share a cell with criminals more intelligent than you." I had nothing more to say to him; I simply requested another examining magistrate.

---

[9] "Jew face!" (trans.)

He continued to question me but I didn't say another word. Finally, I had had enough of this game and, standing up, told him that I was going back to my cell. "Stay where you are," he roared. "You're not going anywhere until I tell you to." I was standing at the door and that's where I stayed. Now, whipped into a frenzy, he came at me with clenched fists. As he approached, I exclaimed quietly but sharply that he did not scare me. That disarmed him.

His arms sunk and he went back to his seat. Calling the *klutshnik*, he said that I was about to strike him over the head with an oil lamp. And indeed, only then did I realize what had happened. As he charged at me, his fists clenched, I had instinctively glanced over at the oil lamp. Had he laid a hand on me, I surely would have thrown it at him, and that's what he had apparently sensed. Maybe that's why he did not touch me. I stood there for some time, and then he ordered me to go back to my cell.

The next day I filed a complaint with the public prosecutor demanding another examining magistrate. Although my request was turned down, I was assured that things would be different from now on. But I had had enough of this man and refused to say another word to him. Then he summoned a few of my comrades and asked them to work on me to sign the protocol. And under their pressure that's how it finally ended.

Meanwhile, we proceeded with the work of political education. Practically every week I prepared political talks. My favorite classes were "Marxism and Anarchism" and "Peretz and his Roll in Jewish Literature."

The day of our trial finally arrived. The families of my comrades were not exactly poor and had hired the famous Polish attorneys Paschalski and Szmiarowski. For my defense the party had appointed Duracz.

This was the first big political trial in Brest and the judges and the public prosecutor were simply terrified of such attorneys. The informers muddled themselves in contradictions and the court only got us for illegal assembly. The charge of communism was dropped. The whole group of us were sentenced to sixteen months in prison apiece, but since the period between our arrest and trial had already exceeded the sentence itself, we were all set free at once.

The comrades were able to go right home, but I had no money for a train ticket. Eydl, one of my co-defendants, scraped together some money for me and the next day I returned to Warsaw. But the Brest trial did not end there. Our case was to end up in the appeals court, and the sentence finally turned out to be far heavier.

One More Arrest

After finally divulging my real name during the Brest investigation, I waited each day for all my sins to come to light. But nothing happened. The examining magistrate had certainly gone over my past with a fine-tooth comb. Yet he had not believed me for a minute when I told him my real name. It is of course possible for somebody to forget a single fact, but nobody could forget three facts all at once: my sentence for desertion, my work in the Revolutionary War Committee and the fact that I had fallen as a volunteer in Haller's army. (My brother had indeed enlisted in the army under my name.) In addition, I still had another trial. But even after further probings, my long criminal record had not yet surfaced. When I was mistakenly released from prison in 1928, I still had two years and eight months to go. And years later, in 1938, this finally dawned on the authorities, who proceeded to go after me. That is to say, they remembered me. If all my sins had not been uncovered in Brest, I would argue that this was the case because the official documents had gotten lost in the year 1920 during the evacuation of Warsaw.

Returning to Warsaw at the end of August, I noticed great changes in the Jewish workers quarter. With the entry of the Combund into the ranks of the Communist Party, we became the strongest force in the Jewish workers movement. The trade unions of the textile and leather workers, retail trade employees and even half of the tailors' association came under our influence—not to mention other, smaller trade unions. A significant change had also taken place in the leadership of the Jewish Central Bureau. New, excellent activists had been added on, the likes of which any central committee would have been happy to have welded together.

Three leaders from the Combund joined: Alexander Minc, Aba Flug and the White Aba. The last two were leaders of the textile union. All three, former Bundists, were excellent activists with a history of mass work under their belts. Their coming to us therefore lent the work a particular seriousness. From the Uniteds we got Itzhak Gordin—an empty man, a windbag, a bluffer. Better than he was Israel Gayst. A good organizer, Israel Gayst nevertheless had all the vices associated with being a braggart. I

remember hearing from Maiski (today, a culture leader in Poland) that
he had once gone to visit Gayst at his home and found him standing beside the oven, his face stricken with grief. Asking him what the matter
was, Gayst replied: "How sad. Lenin has died, Dzerzhinsky is no more,
and I feel miserable." We also won over three leaders from the Poale
Zion. Józef Lewartowski was a calm man of solid character and a good
organizer. Although he was no journalist, he had the ability to edit what
others had written. Everybody was particularly fond of him because of
his seriousness and honesty. Gershon Dua also made a good impression.
A glowing revolutionary, a real firebrand, he was able to write an article
on any subject. What he wrote, it's true, was shallow and chock-full of
phraseology, but was not without a certain luster. The most intelligent of all
of them was Amsterdam. He combined great intelligence with good political training and distinguished himself by his clear comprehension of
things. The man was a born political leader. He was also the representative of the Jewish Bureau on the Central Committee and very quickly
became one of the central leading figures of the party. He participated in
all the gatherings of the Comintern.

In this period, two important political events took place. For one
thing, the Fourth Congress of the Comintern condemned the rightist
policy of Radek and Brandler in respect to the 1923 events in Germany.
They were both accused of having falsely interpreted the policy of the
united front. Zinoviev at the time coined his unfortunate formula according to which the united front was no more than a maneuver to win
over the Social Democratic workers. One must commend the leaders of
the Polish Communist Party, who decided to defend Radek. But Zinoviev's pronouncement about maneuvering had sad consequences; it im-
peded the united-front movement in every country.

The other important event was the Second Congress of the Communist Party of Poland. This congress undertook the revision of Rosa
Luxemburg's theories on the agrarian and national questions and came
over to Lenin's standpoint. That is, it came out for dividing up the land
among the peasants and for granting the Ukrainians and White Russians
the possibility of seceding from Poland. At the same time, it committed
itself to defending Poland's national independence. The formulation on
Polish independence was substantiated as follows: the October Revolution had brought independence to Poland; German imperialism threatened Poland; therefore, the slogan of the defense of Poland's national
independence was objectively a revolutionary slogan.

The new slogans contributed without a doubt to the growth of the Communist Party. They strengthened her influence among the workers and peasants, above all among the White Russian and Ukrainian peoples. In September 1923 I was sent to work in White Russia as secretary of the Jewish Central Bureau and a member of the West White Russian Central Committee. It was at that time that we made our first inroads into the White Russian village; the recent resolutions regarding White Russia and the Ukraine had opened up fertile territory for our work. I traveled to Grodno, Baranovichi, Pinsk and Volkovysk in order to get the Jewish workers on their feet. We supplied the Jewish comrades with literature and sent them into the villages in order to forge party organizations.

The Central Committee in West White Russia consisted of three Jewish comrades: the first was Shlomo, a former anarchist and a good activist, whose character was never entirely clear to me. At times he seemed to be a sincere comrade, and at other times an unscrupulous man. In the end he was morally spent and applauded every one of Stalin's murders. Later, he too was murdered. The second comrade was a textile worker from Białystok, a man without a trace of culture. The third was I. We were guided from Warsaw by the infamous Skolski.

Two White Russian comrades were also members of the Central Committee. One of them was known as "Stari"[10] and was indeed an old and politically antiquated man. He only performed the technical work. The other was a poet who had translated Gandhi into White Russian. He was hardly much of a politician.

I lived in Białystok but was often preoccupied with the work in Grodno. Party gatherings were held on top of a hill near the Neman River. In the middle of a huge forest, it was very well suited for illegal work. After such party gatherings we bought a batch of sour milk, bread and radishes and threw a banquet. I did this intentionally because I knew that many of those who participated were unemployed. I felt ashamed to eat in a restaurant and allow a bunch of comrades, who sacrificed everything for the party, to go hungry.

At the beginning of 1924 we received a directive from the Comintern stipulating that we were to prepare an uprising in order to sever West White Russia from Poland and to unite it with the Soviet Union. We got

---

[10] "Old Man" (trans.)

down to work and appointed a revolutionary war committee composed of four comrades: Shlomo, myself, the poet and the new recruit Miron, a former left Poale Zionist who had come over to us along with Amsterdam.

We committee members divided up the districts between ourselves and I was put in charge of Grodno. While we were engaged in preparations in all the cities, two deputies from the White Russian Hromada, a peasant party under the direct leadership of the Communist Party, worked the villages.

In the course of a few weeks we actually prepared the region for an uprising. In the meantime, however, I ran into yet another mishap which almost cost me an arm and a leg. And once again, I came through it—by accident—unscathed.

I had to go to a regional conference in Volkovysk, a district which was also included in my area of responsibility. This was—or better said, was supposed to be—among our final preparations. It was agreed upon in advance that nobody was to carry addresses around in his pockets. Everything was to be committed to memory. I had arranged to meet the comrades on a particular street and they were supposed to wait there for me. But the lads overslept and failed to show. Meanwhile, the neighborhood's Jews were on the lookout for *goyim*[11] to come in and light their ovens for them.[12] As they opened their windows and looked at me, a stranger, as if I were an evil spirit, I got the feeling that something was about to blow. I was also aware of the fact that the public prosecutor from Brest had filed an appeal against the Brest verdict demanding a stiffer sentence. All of my party co-defendants had already been forced to flee.

Nobody came, so I walked to the train depot in order to return to Białystok. There I learned that the next train would be leaving at four o'clock in the afternoon. It was only nine o'clock in the morning, however, and I decided to go back to town. Perhaps, I thought, somebody had shown up after all.

As I excitedly walked to the train station and back, I took the opportunity to size up the neighborhood courtyards for a possible escape route. And sure enough, I found one which led directly out to the railroad tracks, one I would use in case of emergency.

---

[11] non-Jews (trans.)

[12] According to the Jewish orthodoxy, all physical labor is forbidden on Saturdays (trans.)

I was well aware of the particularly savage manner in which political prisoners were tortured in those parts. Imprisoned women comrades had been brutalized in such a way that after two weeks in custody they came home thoroughly deranged. Thus I decided under all circumstances to make a run for it.

All of a sudden I was approached by two policemen, who demanded to see my papers. That very week, a shop in the same street had been robbed, and the policemen, it seems, took me to be the thief. I was certain, however, that the conference had been busted and that someone had betrayed me.

Although I attempted to foist my false papers on them, they said, "Come along peacefully. You can say what you have to say at the commissariat." Reluctantly, I went with them. Once at the commissariat, I was interrogated by some cop who refused to believe the rather wild stories I was telling him. Finally he said, "Cut out the games and let's talk seriously." He then called in four more cops, who surrounded me right and left. I knew that the worst blows possible are those delivered just below the shoulders and therefore stood with my back to the wall. Then I waited. Suddenly, they came up with what they thought was a clever trick. But it was just this little trick of theirs which saved me. They sent me out to the corridor on my own. Nobody was there, but I sensed nonetheless that this was not the moment to cut and run. Eventually, they called me in again, gave me back enough of the money they had confiscated from me so that I could buy lunch and told me to return in the afternoon to pick up my passport and the rest of my money. Followed by two cops, I went back outside. Meanwhile, the comrades whom I had been waiting for arrived, and as they saw me leaving the commissariat, they took me to be an informer. For my part, I noticed the way they were looking at me and thought they were spies. In a word, what a mess! I turned around and made sure the cops were in plain view. Finally, after wandering around awhile, the opportune moment arrived. I shot through the courtyard, cleared the train tracks and ran off.

The way was already deeply covered with snow. I knew that the train from Volkovysk to Białystok stopped in Svisloch', and that's where I intended to catch it. After two or three kilometers on foot, however, and with another five or so to go, the train sped past. Then something incomprehensible happened to me. Hardly had the train passed me by when I was suddenly unable to move. It was as if I had become paralyzed. In the valley below the train tracks there was a peasant cottage. Seeing that I was unable to move, a peasant who happened to be looking out the window came outside. I wanted to ask him to take me in so that I could warm up, but I was unable to turn and face him. In order to do just that, I had to stoop down and put my hands in the snow as supports. Then I thought up the story that I was unemployed and had tried to flee to the Soviet Union. Seized at the border, I managed to escape again. Now I needed to settle down a bit.

Maybe he believed me and maybe he didn't. In any case, he took me back to his hut and offered me a small piece of bread and sweet black coffee. He refused to take money from me. When darkness fell, he asked me to go, but added that there was a Jew living near the train station who would surely help me. His son saw me out and I gave him my scarf as a present. Sensing that he was one of us, I told him that I was a Communist fleeing from custody.

I found the Jew, but he refused to listen to a word I was saying. That area, he said, was full of bandits, and he didn't want to take any risks. But he did me a favor and showed me a shortcut to town. I had no idea what to do once I got there, but had no other choice than to go.

I made my way into town through a field of snow. During the trek, I landed myself in a stream which had been covered over by snow. At first, it only seemed to be a small pool, but the further I went, the deeper it got. Before I knew it, I was up to my neck in water. A Pole, who happened to see what was happening, let out a cry. "Turn back or else," he shouted. I propped myself up with my hands and crawled out of the water on all fours. The Pole then brought me to a Jew and I repeated the same old story. The Jew looked at me and declared that he didn't believe a word I was saying. But since I didn't look much like a bandit either, he added, he would allow me to spend the night with him.

The next afternoon, a Sunday, I caught the train and returned to Białystok. It was International Women's Day and I was supposed to speak in honor of the event at a meeting scheduled to be held at the central office of the trade unions.

Hardly had I begun my speech when the police burst in. I sprang out one of the first-storey windows and found myself in an enclosed courtyard without any exits. God only knows how I scrambled up a fence and made my way to another courtyard. Those who had jumped out the window after me were fired upon from behind and caught.

After all of these adventures I went home and slept. It was a well-deserved moment of peace and quiet.

But the story didn't end there. The passport which the police in Vol-kovysk had confiscated from me was one of a particular sort of party passport. We feared that others carrying similar papers would be arrest-ed. To prevent this, we sent a *macher* to Volkovysk to fetch it back for a price. From him we also learned that the police, once they had gotten wind of the fact that I was a Communist, deeply regretted having al-lowed me to slip through their fingers.

I had my dreams as well in those days. This should not amaze anyone, for every revolutionary must have his moments of fantasy. It is at such times that he can breath easier, and it is this which makes it possible for him to bear all the difficulties. In Grodno, I often used to lie in a wood-ed riverbank in view of the castle on the Neman River. This castle had once belonged to the Russian governor-general and later became the residence of the *Woyevoda*. [13] I dreamed of conquering the place and mak-it my home. I saw it as an act of justice that none other than I, a Jewish worker from that cellar hovel on Smocza Street, would become the master of this castle.

But this was no time to while away too many hours fantasizing. Fol-lowing the aborted putsch in Estonia in the year 1924, the Comintern called off the uprising in West White Russia. We submitted to the Com-intern directives, although the White Russian regiment stationed in Bara-novichi was ready to give the signal to commence with the general uprising.

At the meeting of the Revolutionary War Committee where we decid-ed to put a stop to the uprising, the poet, the sole White Russian com-rade, declared that he would not submit to the decision, that the inter-ests of the White Russians were foreign to us Jews. He subsequently founded an independent White Russian revolutionary party. After his arrest, he decided that above all else his party must liberate the White Russians from the Soviet Union and decided to collaborate with the sec-ond department of the Polish general staff. He was released from prison and, soon thereafter, was shot by White Russian partisans.

We shifted back to "peaceful" Communist work and the former Combundist Avrom Slushni came from Grodno to take on a post in the trade union. But the meeting where this question was discussed was raid-ed by the police and we were all arrested. For me, this began a term of imprisonment which was to last five years.

---

[13] local representative of the Polish government (trans.)

My Prison Wanderings

Five of us were arrested: Kaptsevich, Slushni, Josef Epshteyn, a fourth man who was a member of the party committee in Grodno (today he lives in Paris) and I.

That was in either February or March 1924. The morning following our arrest I was taken to a long, dark cellar, which was but weakly illuminated by petroleum or gas lamps. There was no electrical lighting. Grodno's chief police agent interrogated me. I didn't know his name, but I knew him as well as he knew me. He had spied on me continuously during my stay in Grodno, and I often saw him at our hilltop meeting place in the forest after we had finished our work, feasted on bread and radishes and sung our spirited songs. At such times, this sideburned fellow with the face of a bandit would bore through me with his piercing eyes as he walked by. Perhaps he conducted his interrogations in that dark cellar as a way of emphasizing his bandit character, for in the nighttime darkness of that subterranean chamber, he could demonstrate that he was lord and master over the lives and deaths of political prisoners.

As he took down a record of the interrogation, his pen scratched on the paper in such a way that it made my head spin. No doubt, he did it intentionally in order to throw me off keel. I had never in my life heard anyone write so loudly.

The agent commenced the interrogation by addressing me with "*du*."[14] I refused to answer him. When he asked me what I was waiting for, I replied—also with "*du*"—that he wouldn't be getting any answers out of me as long as he addressed me informally. That brought him to a white heat and he picked up the ink pot and smashed it to pieces. He did not lay a hand on me however. The interrogation dragged on. He asked me questions and I refused to talk. I was not to think, he opined, that Thugutt, the leader of the radical peasants, who was touring the prisons in order to determine whether or not political prisoners were being beaten, would be able to help me. He, the interrogator, could see to it that I never got out of there alive. And he was right too. But I was determined

---

[14] familiar form of address meaning "thou" (trans.)

not to answer him as long as he persisted in addressing me with *"du."* One thing, however, was clear to me from his remark: Thugutt's tour would soon indeed put a stop to the raging of the White terror inside Poland's prisons.

I would like to mention here that people such as Herriot and Briand in France signed a protest declaration against the White terror in Poland. Given that Poland was dependent on France and that Briand was the French foreign minister, the government was forced to permit Thugutt to visit the prisons. I suffered a deep moral depression at the time after reading a letter in the newspaper from the great writer Żeromski, in which he contested the fact of the terror—the terror which I had seen with my own eyes. I was very fond of Żeromski and therefore found his letter particularly demoralizing.

When it finally dawned on the interrogator that he was not going to get anywhere with me, he shifted to the third person. For example: "The accused might explain..." I replied in the same manner and everything went smoothly. The interrogation took place at the office of the secret police. When it was over I was transferred to Grodno's prison and put in a one-man cell. I wasn't exactly in the highest of spirits, for it was obvious to me that I wouldn't come out of it with one year in prison—as was the case at my first trial—or with a year and a half—as it turned out with my second. I was prepared for a long term of imprisonment, and was not mistaken.

In Poland at the time an old tsarist law was in force which stipulated that in instances of multiple convictions, the longest sentence canceled out the others. If, for example, somebody had been sentenced to six years in prison at one trial and to four years apiece at two others, he would only have to spend six years behind bars. This was only applicable, however, if all of the offenses had been committed prior to the trial covering the last offense. Had your trial just taken place, following which you committed another crime, then your longest sentence would not cancel out the other; rather, the first sentence would be added to the second.

I had come away from my first trial in Brest with a light sentence. In the meantime, however, I had been released. And while the public prosecutor initiated appeal proceedings, I went ahead and committed another offense. In other words, that old tsarist law did not apply in my case.

Now I had to think about conserving my powers, building myself up morally and arming myself with iron patience in order to survive the coming days as a political *katorzhnik.*

Alone in my cell, I had only one wish: to rest up as long as possible, to sleep it all off and not to reflect about what lay before me. And that's just what I did, for it was as if the one-man cells in Grodno had been especially designed for peace and quiet. My small room had a high ceiling, a large window, a wooden floor—and above all, it was clean and warm. Seldom had I had such an apartment on the outside.

Slowly but surely I became my old self again. Now it was time to put some thought into the business at hand. Priority Number One was transferring over to one of the communal cells. Many good comrades were there, after all, and through them I wanted to get into contact with the comrades involved in my upcoming trial. Although things were not as involved this time as in Brest, it was nonetheless incumbent on us to make sure that comrades did not contradict one another. I had once again been arrested under an assumed name. In my new passport my name was Katz. In Brest I had been known as Bellman. One thing was clear to me: I would have to betray my real name in Grodno and talk about my previous trial in Brest. I wanted to consult with comrades first and together with them establish our tactics for the upcoming interrogations. I demanded to be transferred to the communal cells, and before long my demand was met.

Once my transfer had come through, I found that life was both better and, at the same time, worse than in my one-man cell. I had no more peace and quiet, cleanliness was a thing of the past, water trickled from the walls. We slept on the floor on small, dirty mattresses. The kitchen was located in the cellar directly beneath our window and whenever fat was fried, a horrible stench permeated the place. The flies gave us no rest. It was law among us that everybody had to catch one hundred flies per day. Had a stranger entered and seen fifteen men running around the room catching flies, he would have thought that we were a band of *meshugenes*.

White Russians and Poles were there, but we Jews formed the largest group of all. Koszczewnik, the Communist candidate in the elections to the Polish Sejm, was there as well. A typical intellectual and a nervous man, he kept somewhat to himself. But all in all, he was a thoroughly good comrade.

We were all on very friendly terms with one another. Besides catching flies, we spent the entire day reading or playing chess. Following evening roll call we talked politics. After turning in for the night, each comrade—one after another down the line—told about his past. We did this intentionally to bring comrades closer together. Many bragged and bluffed their way through, but we acted as if we hadn't noticed a thing. Whenever somebody overdid it, however, we gave him a towel and a jug of water so that before continuing with his fairy tale of lies, he could wash his hands.[15]

Once each month we elected a cell elder, who was to conduct business on our behalf with the administration. On one occasion we elected a White Russian comrade, who immediately wrote to his wife that he had become an important man, the spokesman for more than twenty people. We learned of this from the inspector during one of our roll calls and had ourselves a hearty and affectionate laugh over it. From that day on, we decided, the comrade was to remain permanently at his "post."

In the early summer of 1924 the appeal proceedings relating to my Brest trial were set to take place in Pinsk. I received a communication from the party notifying me that I was to be freed on my way to court. According to the Polish laws then in force, a defendant did not have to be present during appeal proceedings but could file a request stating that he wished to travel to the trial at his own expense. In that case, he had to cover the expenses of the two policemen who were to accompany him. Just such a sum of money was sent to me in prison.

I brought absolutely nothing along with me on my journey to Pinsk, for I did not want to be encumbered by anything during my escape. Before departing, I bid my comrades a warm farewell. After all, who knew how long it would be before I would see them all again.

But a long time it wasn't. As I was led to the train, I looked all around me...to no avail. Underway, I kept an eye out for familiar faces at each and every station. Now's the time, I thought. But nothing, absolutely nothing, happened.

It was at the prison in Pinsk that I suffered my first moral crisis behind bars. Political prisoners were brutally tortured in that part of the country. Most people, many good old party comrades included, were unable to come through it without spilling the beans. The prison itself was sheer hell, although the conditions there were good. Conflicts broke out continually; one prisoner accused the other. The whole environment was hard to bear, and I wanted to get back to Grodno as soon as possible. But I had a few days to go before my trial.

---

[15] Hand-washing is a Jewish religious and cult ritual. (GE)

Once again, Duracz was appointed to represent me in court. Two days before the trial, however, he sent a telegram to Pinsk stating that he was unable to come on account of illness and requested that the court appoint a lawyer in his stead. In the courtroom, a Polish attorney walked up to me and asked whether I was amenable to having him defend me. "But how?" I asked. How could he defend me without being in any way familiar with the materials pertaining to the charges against me? He told me that he would orient his case around the statement of charges and the public prosecutor's speech. I was left with no other choice but to assent.

Following the completion of the formalities, the public prosecutor presented his case. His speech was logical. First, he proved that I had been roaming around the border environs with false papers, invariably, he went on, with the same old excuse that I had been looking for work. Yet money had been found in my possession each and every time I was arrested. Following him, my attorney took the floor and carried the case against me one step further. Keeping his remarks good and short, he simply requested that the court confirm my old sentence. Then he took his seat again. Clearly, he solidarized with the public prosecutor's case.

The court sentenced me to four years in prison along with the loss of my civil rights. Truthfully, I had been expecting a stiffer sentence. Four years behind bars did not surprise me. But I was enraged about the lawyer who had been appointed to defend me. "You're a vulgar and base man," I shouted at him.

The time had come for my return trip to Grodno. Now, I thought, comrades would spring me along the way. But as before, this proved to be a pipe dream. I returned to Grodno a little disappointed and tired. Luckily, I was placed in a one-man cell, where I could revive my energies. Later, I received greetings from the party along with an apology explaining that due to the great number of arrests, they had been unable to keep their word about freeing me along the way to Pinsk.

Hardly had I gotten back on my feet again when a hunger strike broke out. Until that time, political prisoners had been forced to take their walks one by one, that is, five paces apart from one another with their hands behind their backs. We demanded the right to stroll together in groups, the right to move our hands about freely and the right to talk to one another during our walks around the yard. On the fourth day of the strike the *natshalnik* came to my cell to inform me that he was prepared to give in to our demands. The other comrades, however, were unwilling to call off the strike without my concurrence. I told him that I was unable to take action to terminate the strike as long as I remained in isolation. He then permitted me to meet with my comrades, following which the strike came to an end.

For my part, I liked being alone in my cell. (I spent the greater part of my prison years in solitary). Comrades, however, demanded that I come back to the communal cells and I had to submit to their decision.

Before long, a new hunger strike broke out, this time initiated by Grodno's criminal elements in response to the fact that some of their number had been beaten. We considered it our moral duty to solidarize with them but set no demands of our own. After two days the criminals abandoned their own action and left the field to us. We found ourselves in a bind. What in the world were we to do with a strike which had lost any meaning? It was the *natshalnik* himself who got us out of the dilemma. Calling me to his office, he asked me why we were on strike. I replied that all of us were nervous enough from sitting around in our cells all day without having to hear the screams of the cons whenever the guards beat them. What we needed was peace and quiet, and their cries of pain made us sick. (All of this was true.) Our request: no more beatings. The *natshalnik* pledged to put a stop to the practice, and we broke off the hunger strike.

I had the impression that Grodno's *natshalnik* was a man with a human heart, a man who avoided useless conflicts. Something humorous happened in the middle of the strike. I received a bill for the court costs from my trial in Brest. (Whoever lost a case had to cover the legal costs himself.) While the bill was made out in the name of Bellman, I was known in Grodno as Katz. What's more, I had also divulged my real name. The warden summoned me to his office and asked me whether I knew one Bellman. He, the warden, had been looking for him high and low and couldn't find him anywhere. When I told him that I was Bellman, he asked, "How many names do you have, anyway?"

He handed me the bill and added that if I was short of means, I could file a petition with the government and have them settle the payment. I then went out to the secretary and told him to forward the following reply to the government: I refuse on principle to pay the trial costs on the grounds that I do not recognize the bourgeois courts.

The anniversary of the October Revolution was just around the corner, and a few days prior to the occasion I was transferred to Białystok. The prison there was an enormously large, barrack-like place. It was commonly said that the facility was located beyond the town in order to prevent people from hearing what took place there. Discipline was strict; the floors had to sparkle like mirrors, and if you missed a spot you were punished. Bowls, coffee cups and tin spoons were to gleam at all times so that the *natshalnik* could verify that everything was spick-and-span. The *natshalnik*, in general, was a brutal man and his head guard a hangman. He himself lived at the prison, for he was afraid to take to the streets.

The day I arrived I was placed in a one-man cell and was unaware that directly across the corridor from me was Avrom Zachariash. Having been tortured following his arrest, he was in a downtrodden mood. He wrote me a short, forlorn note, which was unworthy of a Communist, and I told him so. He then wrote me another note in which he apologized for his conduct and thanked me for having brought him back to his senses.

It was in this period that another hunger strike broke out. This time it lasted five days, and this time I began to lose my hair. So rapidly was it falling out, in fact, that I felt just as if I were taking off a wig.

But I was not to be staying in Białystok, for my trial in Grodno was drawing near. It was a great relief to get out of there, but I also knew perfectly well that I had left behind a group of good comrades. The inmates' *starosta*, [16] Lampe, was beloved by comrades one and all. A very intelligent man with sharp political insight, he had come from the left Poale Zion and experienced a rapid ascent as a party activist. He was elected to the Central Committee and later became a leader of the minority faction. Two years before the outbreak of the Second World War he was arrested in Danzig and sentenced to fifteen years in prison. Once behind bars, he was accused of being an informer. But when the war broke out and he was freed from jail, he fled to Moscow and prepared the program of the Union of Polish Patriots. A very sick man, however, he died a short time later. When the Stalinists needed Lampe, they forgot that he had been accused of being an agent provocateur; but they were nevertheless his hangmen. Neither he nor anybody else could have endured the anguish which they caused him.

---

[16] elected head, elder (trans.)

My Trial in Grodno

In the spring of 1925 my trial in Grodno took place. The famous attorney Honigwil, a Bundist who lives in America today, defended Kaptsevich and me. Because both of us had been as clean as could be—absolutely nothing had been found on us—the public prosecutor was pushing for stiff sentences. This sounds paradoxical, but it only demonstrates the depths to which Polish justice had sunk in those days. His case against us was simple: the fact that nothing had been found on us proved that we were good Communists; we had managed to hide everything. Four comrades, I among them, received four years in prison apiece. Kaptsevich alone was slapped with a six-year sentence. Why was anyone's guess.

After reading the verdict, I asked my attorney what I could do to combine my two sentences into one. Such a thing was impossible, however, and it really crushed me. Up until the time of my trial, I had already spent three years behind bars. And now I had eight more to go. I had the feeling that I would never survive it. There was also no doubt in my mind that my attorney was absolutely unable to help me. In the end, I went back to prison a thoroughly defeated man. I kept quiet about my emotional state, of course. Besides, it burnt itself out before too long.

Meanwhile, prison conditions took a turn for the worse. The majority of my fellow inmates were poor White Russian peasants, whose families back home were too destitute to send them anything. What's more, the MOPR suspended its activities because the government had begun to arrest MOPR workers. In addition to the great hunger which was rampant among us, we were also agonized by the moral torment of the terror in White Russia. In all its terrible savagery, the terror there had begun to lift its head. We once had occasion to talk with some inmates from Białystok who had been brought to Grodno. They told us that the Białystok police had tried to force them to rape their own women comrades, who had been stripped naked and chained to the ground. These very same women comrades, in fact, soon arrived as well and were in the depths of depression. And as we soon learned from the women's cellblocks, it was impossible to lift them out of it.

The imprisoned White Russian comrades, almost all of whom were poor peasants, fared no better. Among the police in White Russia, two favorite methods of torture were in vogue: forcing water up one's nose or beating him over the head. Those who had had water forced up their noses arrived in Grodno with pallid faces and swollen eyes. The others, victims of beatings, were quiet and pensive; one heard hardly a peep from them. By and by they stopped eating and finally lost their senses entirely. We knew at once how our fellow prisoners had been tortured simply by looking at them.

I became ill at that time. The grounds for this illness were threefold. First, I had a foreboding that I would never make it out alive. As poor as our conditions of life were, I sensed that I would never muster the strength to see it through. Second, it was sheer agony for me to witness the anguished lot of my tortured comrades. As I have already said, they were in the main extremely simple peasants, who were neither politically nor morally prepared to withstand such torment. And they did not hold up; they told everything.

During all my years in prison I very rarely cried. I warded off the urge to do so for the simple reason that I did not want the enemy to see my tears. I was well aware that such a display of emotion would trigger his thirst for sadistic pleasure. That was just what he was waiting for, and I did not want to spur him on.

There was yet another reason why I had fallen ill: the food. I have already mentioned that the kitchen was located just beneath our window and that a terrible stench—something akin to the odor of melted tallow—filtered through our cell whenever fat was fried. But that's not all. The stocks of rice and kasha, which were stored in the cellar, had become infested with worms. Come mealtimes, food was poured into our bowls and we were clearly able to see tiny worms' eggs in the clumps of coagulated fat. One usually pushed them aside with the spoon. I too ate around them for the longest time but found it so disgusting that I eventually stopped eating the soup. Things were no better in respect to bread. While every prisoner's bread ration was officially set at 400 grams, it was common knowledge that the members of the prison staff supplemented their meager salaries by stealing from the prisoners. Then the administration hit upon a scheme whereby they weighed out the official 400 grams of bread with one hand and kept on stealing with the other. Instead of baking bread all the way through, they merely browned it on the outside. Past the surface it was a lump of raw dough. And what was it like to eat? While the crust on top was like a piece of coal, the bottom was the consistency of sand. It ground between your teeth when you bit into it. And as for the soft inner portion, it stuck to your fingers like clay. Although I ate this bread for the longest time just as everyone else, it had come to be so repulsive to me that I gave it up. And without any aid from the outside world, I simply started to starve.

So it was that I went hungry for months on end. In the mornings I merely drank what went by the name of black coffee. But it was impossible to sustain myself for long on such a diet. I became seriously ill.

Such was my illness that I began finding it difficult to breathe. I had to support myself with my hands on a table while attempting to take in gulps of air in short breaths. But even that was a painful and barely successful procedure. I was unable to wear a coat, even the lightest one imaginable, for it cut into my shoulders. I was certain that my last days were approaching. Several comrades had died around that time, and, as was always the case, comrades' deaths left a deep imprint on us prisoners. Each of us saw ourselves as the next candidate.

For the longest time I did not complain to my comrades. It seemed to me that my days were numbered and I did not want them to experience the tragedy first hand; I knew how badly it would affect them. I therefore requested their permission to transfer to a one-man cell for a short time. This took place at the end of 1925.

Alone in my cell, I began philosophizing in precisely the same manner as I had philosophized that night back in 1920, when I believed I was going to be shot. True, now it wasn't a question of my last night. But I was certain that this was going to be my last home, that I would never make it out alive. I looked at the door and at the barred window and asked myself: how do you feel when you know you're in your last apartment? I have to admit, however, I was unable to awaken in myself any particular feelings. Death did not terrify me; I had become accustomed to looking it square in the eyes. I had only one wish: that nobody disturb the stillness surrounding me. Everything, come what may, was to take place quietly and peacefully. There were to be no disturbances. I was prepared to face the unavoidable calmly. Yet once again, it worked out altogether differently than I had imagined.

Itzhak Gordin, a functionary in the Jewish Central Bureau at the time, had just stopped over in Grodno for a visit. Hearing that I was sick, he went to a woman comrade who ran a restaurant in town and gave her enough money to cover a month's worth of food. Prisoners who had notified the prison administration that they no longer wished to receive prison rations were entitled to receive food from outside. She brought me something to eat each day. It was only lunch, but it held me over. Before I knew it, I was my old self again.

One day—it was shortly before the commencement of my third year at Grodno—the *natshalnik* came to my cell. He was very friendly and explained that according to the existing laws, I had the right to apply to the ministry of justice to have my sentence reduced by one-third. He would be happy to support my application, he added, although he knew that I was the *starosta* of Grodno's political prisoners. He was certain that my request would be granted.

A strange sight to behold, this guardian of the law, for beneath his uniform one heard the beating of a human heart after all. He simply could not comprehend why I rejected his proposal out of hand. I attempted to explain to him that it was a question of principle among us not to lend credence to bourgeois justice. But he went away insulted, for he knew nothing about the decision of our commune which stipulated that because such applications weakened the militancy of the political prisoners, they were off-limits. At the next opportunity, shortly before May 1, he transferred me to Lukishka.

At Lukishka

The Lukishka prison in Vilna looked like a fortress. It was the largest of all the penitentiaries which I had yet had occasion to see from the inside. Even though it was located well within the city, one felt completely cut off from the world. The administration there was liberal, at least up until a certain time. I had never had occasion to experience a prison in which the politicals enjoyed such rights as in Lukishka.

I was placed in a one-man cell. This prison was so large that each of the politicals could be kept in solitary confinement.

For the first few days I had absolutely no idea which of my acquaintances were serving time there, for I had not yet succeeded in establishing connections with comrades.

Meanwhile, it was May 13, the day of Pilsudski's coup d'état. Through the window of my cell I heard Skolski speaking to another comrade. He was incapable of thinking for himself and had at once accepted the official party line supporting Pilsudski's coup. In truth, Pilsudski's putsch could have appeared to bear a democratic and liberating character. Even the prison guards reassured us consolingly that we would soon be released. For my part, however, I did not share these illusions, for I considered Pilsudski's coup d'état to be fascistic. But I too was wrong.

We were wont to confuse Bonapartism with fascism at the time. (Several years later I had occasion to debate with Trotsky for a few hours on this question.) Despite the fact that both Bonapartism and fascism direct their cutting edge against the workers movement, there is a great difference between the two. Bonapartism does not necessarily have to destroy every party and organization; it contents itself with controlling their activities and penalizes them whenever they overstep the framework of its control. With the exception of the Communist Party, for example, Pilsudski permitted all of the political parties in Poland to exist. The trade unions as well remained legal. This is out of the question under fascism, for in fascist regimes one, and only one, party rules. Party members stand above the law. While fascism props itself up on the raw violence of its adherents, Bonapartism finds its main base of support in the army. Under Bonapartism it is still possible for the proletarian movement to work semilegally, something which is excluded under fascism. I did not know at the time that it was a mistake to consider the toppling of the government by Pilsudski to be fascistic. But even though I was wrong in respect to the essence of the Pilsudski regime, I was right indeed as against both factions of the party, which held that Pilsudski's putsch was an act of liberation and that it would pave the way for proletarian revolution. Later, after being transferred to a communal cell, I wrote a number of papers on this topic.

We carried out an intensive program of political education behind bars and published a monthly journal in both White Russian and Yiddish. I visited all of the cells and gave talks. The climate was excellent, for the Vilnavites were splendid revolutionaries. There were, to be sure, other elements among us, but they too came under the spell of the Vilna comrades.

When I got to Lukishka, the *starosta* of the political prisoners was a White Russian, a very warm and good comrade. In later years, I was to see him once again in the Soviet Union. But now that he was on his way, I stepped in to fill his shoes.

My prison comrades worked out a plan of escape for me. During our walk, I was to slip into a large tower which was located in the courtyard and hide out there until nightfall. To fool the inspector during roll call, comrades were to make up my bed so as to make it look like somebody was sleeping there. They were to tell him that I was sick.

After dark, comrades were then to stage a big tumult and cause all the guards to come running to the prisoners' quarters. Waiting at the prison gate was supposed to be a guard who sympathized with us, a brother-in-law of the parliamentary deputy Taraszkiewicz. He, the guard, was then to open the gate for me, and that same night the both of us were to flee across the Soviet border. But life is spiteful. Before I knew it, that very same guard felt compelled to knock me over the head with his keys.

It was the year 1926 and time for our November celebration. We organized it in such a way that it would be really and truly festive. All of us met together in one great cell. Paper chains in different colors hung from the ceiling and pictures of Lenin and Trotsky decorated the wall. The tables were covered and *yontev* foods were sent in from outside. First there was a speech and then I told comrades stories about the October Revolution. The inspector appeared and we expected him to raise hell. But he simply looked around, wished us good *yontev* and went on his way.

A few days later the trial of one of our comrades took place. We had decided that after the court read his sentence he was to stand up and sing the *Internationale*. When, as planned, he rose to sing, he was beaten to a pulp and brought back to prison in a droshky.

We called a hunger strike and demanded to see the public prosecutor. At the same time, we also took advantage of the situation to raise demands against the prison administration. It was the end of November.

As the second day of the strike rolled around, the strike committee responsible for negotiating with the administration was transferred to another prison in Vilna. The leadership of the strike, for all intents and purposes, was now in my hands. And I led it incognito. That is, only comrades were in the know. We refused to talk with the administration again until the transferred comrades had been brought back.

We were all asleep in our cell on the fourth exhausting night of the hunger strike when the *natshalnik* came in, turned to me—I can't imagine how he found out that I was the strike leader—and in the following words said: "Listen Katz, I know you're a determined revolutionary and you can't make any compromises. But this time I'm asking you to end the strike. It will go badly for all of you if you don't. From my side, I'll do everything in my power to accommodate you." He spoke with great foreboding and I had the impression that he was a decent man who wanted to do us a good turn. But we had decided not to negotiate before our comrades had been brought back. He left looking crushed. We weren't at all clear about what was in store for us.

The next morning—the fifth day of the strike, that is—the kettles containing our rations were waiting in the corridor for us. Meanwhile, we opened the window as usual to sing the *Internationale*. Just then, the door flew open and the inspector, followed by a handful of policemen with their bayonets raised, entered our cell. The inspector pointed to me and said, "Him first." I held fast to the legs of the table. Two policemen grabbed me from behind, threw a blanket over my head and dragged me to the hospital for force-feeding. All hell broke loose in each of the cells as the prisoners barricaded themselves in. The police had to take them by storm.

By time they had carried me to the hospital, the procedure for force-feeding was already in full gear. It looked like this: two convicts held me by my legs, one held down my belly and one my head. The medic's task was to attempt to insert a nozzle-tipped hose into my stomach and discharge a certain liquid substance. Those who refused to open their mouths had their teeth knocked out with the nozzle. The hose was then inserted by force. Those few moments of force-feeding wreaked havoc on my teeth. Even the ones which had not been knocked out wobbled so much that I was later able to remove them from my mouth without difficulty.

During force-feedings the presence of a public prosecutor was required, for lacerated larynxes due to carelessness were not unknown. (In Białystok a number of comrades had died in this manner.) Sitting there waiting for my turn and seeing what these men were doing to my comrades, I was seized by a fit of hysteria. Grabbing a chair, I rushed at the public prosecutor and screamed, "Look at the things you do to us!" Next to me sat a young comrade, one of the lads who was supposed to have waited for me on that street in Volkovysk. Throwing his arms around me, he kissed me and implored me not to precipitate a calamity. The public prosecutor replied softly, "There is no other way to deal with people like you." As I neared him, however, I noticed that there were tears in his eyes. That brought me back to my senses and I calmed down.

They led me back to the cellblocks and put me in solitary. I wanted to communicate to comrades that the strike was not over, and as I heard a group of them on their way to the hospital to be force-fed, I rushed to the window and shouted, "Long live the hunger strike!" The majority of my fellow inmates, however, broke down and began eating. That evening comrade Pietka, a member of the Central Committee of the West White Russian Communist Party, was brought to my cell. I asked myself, "Why isolate him too?" But before long I found out why.

Late that night the two of us were dragged to the cellar, chained hand and foot and brutally beaten. Back in our cell, I said, "That only goes to show you, Pietka, how they hate the White Russians. They didn't lay a hand on me, but they beat you bloody." With tears in his eyes, he responded, "They're anti-Semites with a vengeance; they practically beat you to death." Only then did it dawn on me that the both of us had been bludgeoned to within an inch of our lives. The police, however, had left us in such a state that we didn't feel a thing.

Just as I began to lose consciousness, I wanted to lie down. And with Pietka and I chained hand to hand, I asked him to lie down beside me. Then I blacked out. When I came to a few minutes later, I was no longer able to remember why we had been put in chains. "Pietka," I asked, "why are we here? Why aren't we back in our cell with our comrades?" He looked at me and began to cry. Later he told me what was running through his mind that night: he thought I had gone mad. His suspicions had only intensified when I suddenly burst out laughing. Having returned to my senses and looking back at the methods with which the police had sought to break our strike, I was so amazed that all I could do was laugh. At the same time, my outburst had scared Pietka half to death.

I was already aware of the fact that eighty percent of the comrades had given up. But for my part, I was not morally ready to lose a hunger strike.

The next morning the head guard walked in and demanded that we undress. I thought that he was going to question my right to wear my own clothes and force me to beg for a prison uniform. This, I decided, was not the issue to start a brawl about. But they did not bring us prison trousers. Rather, early that afternoon they came to get us for another round of force-feeding. We refused. Then they threw us to the ground and dragged us along by our feet, our heads trailing behind in the snow. It was one hell of a trek from the cell blocks to the hospital and I now knew what was up: they had deliberately planned to drag us there stark naked so that we might catch pneumonia.

On Day Six of the strike the warden summoned me to come along with him to the bath. This was merely a pretext and I knew it; he wanted to talk to me. So I put my coat on over my underwear and joined him. On the way back, he demanded that I terminate the hunger strike. I replied that I had no right to end the strike and insisted that the comrades from the strike committee be brought back to Lukishka. Threatening me, he responded that it would end badly for us.

Coinciding with our hunger strike were the appeal proceedings relating to my Grodno trial. Inasmuch as the courthouse was located in town, I had to be driven there. I was not the least bit interested in what the public prosecutor had to say, but with the courtroom jam-packed with comrades, I decided to use my final remarks to tell the world that we had been tortured. When it was finally my turn to speak, I opened up with an account of what was going on behind the prison walls. Interrupting me, the chairman demanded that I stick to the trial. But I kept right on going. Just then, two policemen grabbed me under the arms and dragged me from the courtroom.

On the eighth day of the strike, a guard came in to announce that the warden was about to inspect the cells and that we were to greet him at attention. As politicals, we said, we had never stood at attention before, and we were certainly not about to do so now, right in the middle of a hunger strike. Hardly two minutes later the warden, accompanied by a group of guards, appeared in the doorway. Then something inexplicable happened: while I remained seated, comrade Pietka sprang to his feet. The guards began pummeling me with their keys and I started to scream. That was the signal. Suddenly, a terrible clattering din echoed through the corridor as comrades jostled the doors of their cells. The guards stopped cold. Among those bullies was that very same guard who was supposed to have opened the gate for me the night of my planned escape. I couldn't look him in the face, for I understood what was passing through that brain of his.

With the guards gone, Pietka began sobbing loudly. He begged me to believe him when he said that he was a revolutionary, that he was ready to fight on the barricades. But he simply did not have the energy to starve so long for a strike which we had no prospect whatsoever of winning. I saw that logic was on his side and asked him to transfer to one of the cells where comrades had already begun eating again. But I was going to continue striking, I said, until my last ounce of strength was gone. I was simply psychologically unprepared to end a lost strike. Pietka said no. He was for sticking it out side by side with me. That meant having another victim on my conscience, however, a victim who would be dying for a futile cause.

From experience, I had learned that there is always a commotion in the press whenever a hunger strike takes anyone's life. Representatives from the capital appear on the scene, who attempt to work out a compromise. So I decided to commit suicide. In a brief note to my close friend Chana I revealed my plans and told her to pass on to all our friends that I had not acted out of despair. To the contrary, I saw no other way to save the honor of the prison commune.

Even though I had contrived my plan behind comrades' backs, word had probably gotten around anyway. As Pietka and I were transferred to Białystok, for example, he told me that he had known exactly what was up. But night after night, he said, he had kept his eye on me.

The ninth day of the strike saw a new development: we were not dragged off to be force-fed. We later learned that because of the strike a special delegation from the British Independent Labour Party had come to Vilna along with Hallawash, a member of the British Parliament. A large demonstration had taken place in the city and the Britons had negotiated with the public prosecutor. He had sent them away disappointed however.

That night, the inspector, accompanied by one of the White Russian comrades, came to my cell to inform me that the administration had conceded on all points. The whole story sounded fishy to me, for if the administration had really given in, why hadn't they summoned me? Why hadn't they told us to go back to the communal cell? I asked this White Russian comrade whether I was the first one he had come to visit. Had he answered in the affirmative, I would have ordered that the strike continue. He explained to me, however, that I was the last, that all the other comrades had already received their rations of bread and milk. I was almost positive that the whole thing was a trick, but it was no longer possible to insist that the strike go on.

The following morning, the trick was exposed for what it was. We had just left our cells for the exercise yard when the command resounded: "Hands behind your backs, five paces apart, no talking!" With that we all went back to our cells.

Not having eaten for so long, we had all developed stomach troubles. But at Lukishka we were only permitted to use the toilet once a day. All day long we were compelled to relieve ourselves into a pail which had been placed beneath a stool with a little trap door in it. We sat there for days on end. And since we were not going out into the fresh air, it was utter torment for us.

Meanwhile, we prepared for a second strike. Two strike committees were formed this time—just in case—and preparations lasted an entire month. We had planned to fix the precise date for the strike during our exercise period, informing comrades that it was to begin the following day. But there had probably been an informer among us, for that very day the inspector, together with police backup, came to our cell just before daybreak and ordered us to get dressed. They told Pietka that his trial was to take place in Białystok and that he was to be transferred. As for me, they said, I was to find out where I was going as soon as I was ready. I wanted to let comrades know that we were being removed by force. But when I saw that the whole corridor was lined with policemen—their rifle-mounted bayonets flashing in the nighttime darkness—it was clear that they were armed to the teeth for a bloodbath. Given that the strike committees had already been organized anyway, we decided to avoid a slaughter and go.

Once they had led us downstairs to the administration office, they tried to handcuff us. We threw ourselves to the floor, clasped our hands together underneath our chests and exclaimed that if they wanted to put us in handcuffs they would have to carry us. We would not take a single step on our own. It was against the rules, they said, but out of respect for our struggle during the breaking of the hunger strike, they agreed to let us go unshackled. Our fight had been a futile one, they added, for Warsaw had ordered that the strike be smashed at any price.

Both of these two policemen had previously been workers. One of them had just recently returned from America. In truth, they were both sympathetic men. After they had told us about themselves, we proceeded to agitate for the cause of socialism. So it was that we had a pleasant journey to Białystok.

Back in Białystok

It was strict isolation cells for us in Białystok. Undoubtedly, reports of bad behavior had accompanied us from Lukishka. Despite the isolation, however, it wasn't too bad at the beginning. It was like coming out of a nightmare, and we got a chance to settle our nerves. We were only worried about the fate of our comrades back at Lukishka. Would they be able to conduct a second hunger strike? If yes, what would come of it? Rumors reached us some two weeks later that the strike had indeed broken out, but we had no way of finding out whether it had been won or lost.

During our stay in Białystok, a series of passionate discussions flared up between Pietka and myself. He belonged to the younger generation in the party and, along with it, had learned that the party line was a sacred and unquestionable truth. This was the case, that is, until just such a time as one permitted members to think something else. The very idea made my skin crawl. I just could not get used to it. When I formulated my doubts to Pietka, he assured me that I would be expelled from the party as soon as I was released from prison. He never forgot to add, however, that my expulsion would be painful for him; what a pity it would be. Pietka found himself in a moral depression at the time. He was unable to forgive himself for his moment of weakness at the time of the hunger strike in Vilna. He brought it up time and time again. How could I ever forgive him, he would say. But he was wrong. Who knew about all the terrors of hunger strikes better than I?

We were in solitary confinement for approximately five months. Meanwhile, May Day 1927 was just around the corner and the prison commune notified us that we were to mark the occasion by wearing red armbands during our walk. Once outside, we were to break out with the *Internationale* and the White Russian revolutionary hymn. Come what may, we were to sing both songs to the end. Should we be beaten, we were not to resist, just sing.

The day arrived. As we made our way to the courtyard, the strains of the *Internationale* went up. But not for long. Without further ado, we were all herded back to our cells. For us, however, that meant walking up four flights of stairs, and along the way we had time to finish the *Internationale* and break out with the second song. The *natshalnik* and the director entered our cell. We were thrown to the ground and beaten by the guards. The director piped in, "As long as we're in Poland, you won't be setting up a commune." And the warden added, "I was director here under the tsar and served him faithfully. Today I serve the Polish state. When you come to power, then I'll serve you." All the while, we kept singing and the guards kept thrashing us. Had a stranger been there to see us sprawled on the floor, had he seen the guards pummeling us as we sang—or better said, screamed—a song, he would no doubt have thought that he was in an insane asylum.

After May 1 Pietka and I decided to try to get into a communal cell. Little did we know that we would be separated. He ended up in one cell and I in another. We only met again in 1930 in the Soviet Union.

In my new cell I met many old Polish comrades again whom I had come to know while on party assignment in Białystok. They were not like the Polish Communists from Warsaw, however. Białystok was a city of Jewish and Polish textile workers. Almost to a man, the Polish workers there were under the influence of the Christian trade unions, and were strongly anti-Semitic. We knew that individual Polish Communists had also been poisoned by this virus and that certain of them had come to us for material reasons. We would re-educate them, we thought.

But as it turned out, once they found themselves behind bars, they told the police everything they knew. Until that time, I had grown accustomed to the fact that such was the way of primitive White Russian peasants. But Polish comrades spilling the beans—this was a first for me. What's more, once in prison, they revealed their anti-Semitic face.

We also had a group of Ukrainian peasants from Volhynia among us. The Communist Party there had engaged in a big adventure: it had organized itself along military lines, formed armed units and probably prepared for partisan combat. The whole affair blew up in their faces. There is no lack of informers in such organizations, and every one of those arrested wasted no time in singing to the authorities. They were sentenced to long prison terms. And inasmuch as the majority of them were wealthy peasants, they deeply regretted the entire episode. In prison they took out their anger on the ruling "Jewish Commune." They received great quantities of food from home and refused to share any of it with others. It even came to the point that during our walks they cried out the old Black Hundreds slogan: "Down with the Jews! Save the Ukraine."

It was too confining there for me. For the first time in my life, I was forced to sit it out with my enemies. To my great misfortune, however, they still elected me *starosta*.

It was a tough job being leader of the political prisoners in Białystok. The *natshalnik* there had a policy of his own, a brutal policy. He allowed a hunger strike to continue for a few days before giving in. After a brief interregnum, however, he began to roll back the fruits of our victory piece by piece. He knew that it was impossible to organize a new hunger strike each week.

At the same time, I was also suffering continually from headaches. Resting my head on my pillow was like pressing it against a stone. That, in addition to the sufferings brought on by my environment, caused me to fear a repetition of my Grodno experience.

One day I received a letter from Avrom Slushni. He had written to tell me that the conditions at Siedlce prison were good and that I ought to look into getting a transfer. I wrote up a request and it was granted. Who could have known that this was to be my last prison in Poland?

On the Way to My Release

Political prisoners enjoyed many more rights in Siedlce than in other prisons. We were allowed to go from one cell to another and to take two walks per day. A delegate from the commune was able to go into town once a week to go shopping for the rest of us. And each week, all of us behind bars, men and women alike, were permitted to receive visitors. We had a school of our own, which had been placed at comrades' disposal for instruction in the Polish language. But the administration knew perfectly well what was going on in the classroom. We studied political economy and the history of the October Revolution; we organized talks on subjects which were of interest to us.

Here too was a group of Ukrainians from Volhynia, but they did not have any appreciable influence. I shared a cell with my friend Slushni in the first days, but inasmuch as he did not want to belong to the commune, we were forced to part ways.

Once I came to be *starosta*, I had occasion to visit the women's wing. That's where I met Miriam Shumik, my future wife.

It was also her lot in life that fate had spared her nothing. She was the daughter of a poor *heder* instructor and had lived in poverty her whole life long. She joined the Bundist youth organization very early on and together with the Combund joined the Communist Party. Once in the party, she took on the most dangerous assignment possible: directing our propaganda work in the military. After her imprisonment she was hideously tortured. The police commissar locked her alone in a cell with the intention of raping her. In the end, all of this weakened her heart, and by the time she was released she suffered from a heart ailment. At the outbreak of the war, she was afraid to go to the Soviet Union because she feared being tried as an Oppositionist. She finally perished in the Warsaw Ghetto.

In general, I felt very good in Siedlce prison and dreamed of making it my home for the five years which still lay before me. From time to time, conflicts broke out there too—on 1 May 1928, for example. The official word from the administration that year was that demonstrations in prison were forbidden. Should we choose to sing the *Internationale*, they announced, the police would open fire on us through the windows of our cells. May Day arrived, and with it a great many policemen were indeed in position, their rifle barrels aimed point-blank at the cellblocks. With a bloodbath seemingly so unavoidable, it looked as though we were left with no other choice than to forgo the festivities.

At twelve o'clock sharp we opened our windows, unbuttoned our shirts and with our chests bared broke out with a chorus of the *Internationale*. The police did not react.

In the summer of that year there was talk of amnesty in the air. Pilsudski was up for election to the Sejm and for the occasion had prepared an amnesty plan. It was July or August. What an amnesty meant for me was that my first sentence would come to an end while one-third of my second would be wiped off the boards. I would be left with another two years and eight months to go, a great relief to be sure, but a prison term which I never believed I would survive. I had already made peace with the thought that I would never see the outside world again. In any case, I had never imagined that the amnesty would set me free at once. But that's exactly what happened.

The day of the amnesty, I was sitting by the window with my head resting on the bars. Those who were leaving bid me farewell. My face was unshaven; I didn't even have anything to wear. Suddenly, the door sprang open and a guard walked in. "Pack your things," he said. "You're a free man." It was obvious to me at once that somebody had made a mistake. Turning to a comrade, I said, "You see, I told you they'd let me go unshaved." I didn't have anything to take with me, not even a jacket, so I went down to the administration office empty-handed.

There was a long line at the door and I got into place. As the inspector walked by and saw me standing there, he asked me what I was doing. I told him that I was waiting to be released. He replied that I may as well go back to my cell—it wasn't my turn yet. I knew he was right and started for "home."

When I walked in the door, comrades looked crushed. They had no idea that it was all the same to me; it had to be a deep, personal tragedy, they thought. Many of them had tears in their eyes. At first it raised my hackles. I simply couldn't comprehend why they had taken it more to heart than I. But when I looked into their faces—faces filled with so much goodness, so much nobility, friendship and grief—I was deeply moved.

During our second walk that day, the comrades didn't dare to approach me. They were sensitive enough to leave me to myself. From the bottom of my heart, I was thankful to them.

We returned from the courtyard and ate dinner. Roll call was over; it was already dark. I sat down at the window and leaned up against the bars. Just then the door opened and the guard announced once again that I was free. I was furious. "Haven't you got anything better to do than to make fun of me?" I shouted. "You're wasting your breath," he replied. "You really are free." I knew where the slip-up was: as a result of the amnesty, my first sentence had come to an end.

In the office I met the very same inspector who had sent me back to my cell earlier that day. I assumed that he had discussed the matter with the public prosecutor in the meantime and that the latter had instructed him to release me. The error rested with the public prosecutor; it was he, I thought, who was ultimately responsible for the fact that the prison administration was forced to let me go. As it turned out, my assumptions were right after all.

When the inspector asked me what he was supposed to do with me, I replied that he had shown his true colors earlier in the day. "If it all depended on your good will," I added, "You'd keep me here. But you've probably gotten a directive from the public prosecutor to release me, so cut out the games and do it." In the middle of my reply, the *natshalnik* walked in and said, "You still have two years and eight months to go, but the error is the public prosecutor's. He's responsible. I'm therefore setting you free."

They did not even bring me back to my cell. I was to leave at once. But I insisted on saying goodbye to my comrades and ran back to the cellblock to tell them the news.

It was a farewell the likes of which I will never forget. First, comrades shouted slogans out the windows. Then all at once, masses of them from behind the bars rang out with the *Internationale*. In four different languages, comrades from four nationalities poured out their hearts in song. It was the kind of enthusiasm of which only the most devoted revolutionaries are capable. I couldn't tear myself away. I stood in the courtyard and sang along with them.

Even the warden and the inspector were so impressed by this splendid demonstration that they stood there as if hypnotized. They made no effort to disturb it. As the song finished, they took me by the arms and bid me quietly to go. It was difficult leaving my comrades.

I have no idea how the news had spread to town so quickly. But comrades were waiting for me at the gate. They had even brought along something for me to wear. We spent a joyful evening together and that night I slept in a stable. I was afraid that the public prosecutor might discover his error.

The next morning Miriam Shumik and I were off. We took a droshky to the station two stops beyond Siedlce and from there caught a train to Warsaw. Two days later we learned in Warsaw that the error had been cleared up and that two peasants, who had also been released by mistake, had already been brought back to prison. I was told to be careful and went underground at once.

Who would have known at the time that this was the beginning of my separation from the movement? I did not anticipate the coming break and continued to place myself at the service of the party. Things took a different course, however: I undertook the hard struggle against the Stalinist movement. It did not come easily, but it was a holy struggle.

On the Road

Upon returning to Warsaw in the wake of the amnesty, I had more luck than previously. I didn't have to roam the streets this time, for my nephew, my sister's son that is, made room for me alongside his family in his apartment on Chłodna Street.

It was on account of me, he noted, that he had encountered one difficulty after another. Having dearly loved his mother, he had chosen to register officially under her last name rather than that of his father. What's more, his first name was Mendel. The problem was this: the political police in Poland had adopted the particular practice of rounding up everyone on their suspects list on the eve of all the larger working-class actions. And so it was that every time the workers took to the streets, my nephew with the same first and last name as me found himself under arrest.

Two days after my release from prison I met my girlfriend Miriam Shumik, and together we moved in with my good friend Rudi. It was Rudi who had spent three years in Pawiak after a house guest of his, the German agent provocateur from Posen whom he had taken in at my request, blew the whistle on him. In times of great hardship, when I was on the run from the double enemy—the Polish police and the Stalinist goon squads—Rudi's little home was a warm place for me to rest my head.

Getting together with comrades for the first time, I was startled by the sharpened factional struggle within the party. It was difficult to figure out just what the fight was all about. Both factions praised the line of the Comintern. Even more, the one faction competed against the other in claiming to be the only devoted proponent of the party line. At the time of Pilsudski's coup d'état, however, both had supported Pilsudski. Their factional difference came down to no more than this: the minority faction demonstrated that whereas the majority's backing for Pilsudski had derived from a highly opportunistic policy, its own stance had merely been an accidental error.

It took a sharp eye to spot particular nuances. The majority faction was led by the former comrades and pupils of Rosa Luxemburg. They had retained a certain feeling for dignity and independent thinking and were less inclined to land themselves in adventures. With the exception of Lampe, the leaders of the minority faction, on the other hand, were unscrupulous and wanton individuals, men who were ready for any kind of immoral deed just to please Stalin. And they did in fact accomplish something. The first victims of the Stalin regime were the members of the majority faction. But once they had been murdered, the minorityites were next in line—with Leński at the fore.

To my great regret, I must say that my sympathies were on the side of the minority in the first period. Perhaps this was so because my closest and best friends—Karolski, Amsterdam, Gershon Dua and Itzhak Gordin—were all minorityites. Only one thing speaks well for me: I quickly found my bearings. During my stay in Moscow I drew close to the majority.

The party was of the opinion that I deserved a long period of rest and relaxation and decided to send me to the Caucasus for a month. Prior to my departure, however, I went to Otwock—with a false passport of course—and rented an apartment without even knowing what it looked like. The large garden in the courtyard had appealed to me and I simply forgot that one was also supposed to take a look at the apartment itself. When I told my wife the news and she asked me what the rooms were like, it finally occurred to me that I had never seen them. Embarrassing it was, but humorous too. She assured me that I would never rent another apartment again and was right. The place was miserable, but the garden really was beautiful.

Once my papers were ready, I left for the Caucasus. The trip was a semilegal one. Although I indeed had a passport, it was a fake.

In Minsk I was received by the then premier of White Russia and future chairman of the Comintern, who was liquidated during the first wave of the terror (probably for White Russian nationalism). An intelligent man, he was a warm-hearted comrade with a vast reserve of noble sentiments. His name was Knorin. He knew a lot about me and suggested that I establish myself in the Soviet Union. I had already suffered too much, he reasoned, and it would be a crime to go back to Poland with the police still on my tail. I thanked him for his friendly gesture but replied that I had not been the only one to suffer. I still had enough strength left to hold my own on the battlefield.

At Comintern headquarters I met Furman-Furmanski, the representative of the Polish section in Moscow. A highly intelligent man whose appearance was typically Jewish, he immediately left one with the feeling that he belonged to that special breed of men known as professional revolutionaries. Sochacki was also there when I arrived and the two of them received me warmly. He, Sochacki, had already told Furman-Furmanski something about me. The two of us were old friends; we had both come to the Communist Party around the same time. In the days when I had been taken on as a member of the Jewish Central Bureau, Sochacki had learned to read and write Yiddish and immersed himself in the party's Jewish work. In 1920 he saved me from arrest more than once by coming to my home to warn me that I'd be best to sleep elsewhere. It had been seven years since I had last seen him—seven years had gone by between the time of my first imprisonment as a Communist and my visit that day to the Comintern. We were positively overjoyed to see one another again. As for Furman-Furmanski, his destiny was to be a bitter one in years to come. Both he and Sochacki belonged to a faction which occupied a position between the majority and minority. Following Sochacki's arrest and conviction, Furman committed suicide.

All of that happened five years later. Meanwhile, the three of us chatted away amiably and then bid one another a hearty farewell. Now that I had my train ticket, some money and a place to stay some thirty kilometers outside of Sukhumi, I departed for the Caucasus.

What now served as a pension had once been a convent for the daughters of the gentry. The narrow road leading from the gate to the pension itself was lined with trees and flowers. Inside, sacred frescos from the old days decorated the walls. My nerves, it seems, must have been frayed, for whenever I turned out the lights it looked to me as though the figures on the walls began to move. So terrifying and nightmarish a time it was that I was forced to sleep with the lights on.

I never breathed a word about my nightmares to anyone, however, and paid dearly for it. There were some seven or eight of us Poles in all, and we made frequent excursions into the mountains. It was rough going; there were no footpaths as yet and the way consisted of narrow, rocky trails which often took us over logs. What dizzy spells I had whenever I looked down from the top of a ridge. I was afraid of slipping and falling into the abyss. But at the same time, I was too ashamed to tell anyone about my nervous condition. I went along each time and suffered in silence.

Among us Polish comrades was Kostrzewa—a wonderful woman. Despite the fact that the Stalinist apparatus had already clipped her wings, she was still in possession of her powers in those days—the end of

1928. It was a pleasure to be with her, for her very appearance was enough to spark feelings of warmth and affection in others. She was a tall woman, blond, blue-eyed and delicate, and her mere presence radiated brightness. How had she united in her person so much feminine delicacy and political stubbornness, such inner subtlety and revolutionary valor? Who knows. Rosa Luxemburg had possibly surpassed her in many things. But in the realms of history, culture and art Kostrzewa certainly did not stand behind Rosa.

I shudder to think that the hangmen murdered her in the cellars of the GPU. My blood runs cold and the pen falls from my fingers. Will the guilty ones ever be punished?

I was surrounded by great warmth and kindness during my one-month stay in the Caucasus. Notwithstanding the fact that my comrades belonged to the Kostrzewa faction, while I, quite rightly, was viewed as a sympathizer of the minority, we all felt like one big family. All of us loved the party, its history and the hopes which we had invested in it. All of us had made sacrifices for it in the past, and all of us were ready to put our lives on the line for it in the future.

The month came to an end and we departed friends. Whereas the others stayed for some time in the Soviet Union, I went back to Poland.

I have to admit that it was somewhat painful to think that before long I would again be forced to see the police beating up wretched bagel vendors with their rubber truncheons. And the informers: how I loathed the way they followed my every step with their piercing eyes. I felt a little cheerless and even regretful that I had not allowed Knorin to talk me into staying in the Soviet Union. But the scores of comrades whom I had left behind in the prisons, the horrible misery which had accompanied me during my entire life, the struggle under the banner of the Communist Party, the certainty of our final victory—all of this drew me back to Poland.

When I arrived in Danzig, however, Gershon Dua informed me of a party directive ordering me not to return to Poland. The police were still after me, it stated, and in the meantime I was to go to Moscow and enroll in a three-year course at the Lenin School. Once the authorities had forgotten about me, I could come back to Poland.

Just before my return to the Soviet Union, it suddenly occurred to Gershon Dua to throw me a going-away party. That evening revealed to me how far the party had declined, how morally corrupt the party cadres had become. The champagne flowed like water, the finest chocolates and the finest fruits available anywhere in the country were there for the asking. I was tormented by the thought: by what right? Who had permitted comrades to spend so much money? Who would have the courage to hand over the receipt to the Central Committee? I was still unaware that such extravagant sprees were already a daily occurrence.

At the Lenin School

Upon my arrival in Moscow in 1928 I went to my old comrade Miron, a former left Poale Zionist and a dear, good man. At his home I met a comrade whom I cannot name for specific reasons. His first words were, "You'd better know, Hersh Mendel, Trotsky was not defeated by the party, but rather by the GPU." This declaration of his made a deep impression on me. But what impressed me even more was the dread with which Miron reacted; he pleaded with us to break off the conversation. The look of terror written all over his face was the same expression I had once seen in my father's face when he begged me to stop reading illegal literature.

The following day I went to visit two women comrades from Vilna. Both of them had been exiled to Siberia under the tsar for having belonged to the Bund and later joined the Communist Party along with the Combund. It was already eight years since I had last seen them and I expected a tender reunion. But to my surprise, they sat there silently and ruefully. When I asked, "Why the cold reception after so many years," they burst into tears and whispered, "Hersh Mendel, if you knew what they've done to us, how the GPU has tormented us and driven us from our jobs, you'd cry too." It made me sick at heart to see how fearful they were that I might turn them in. I was unable to tell them, however, that I shared their views, for I had not yet formed a picture of the situation for myself. I kept my mouth shut and left with a broken heart. I positively adored the two of them, two heroines who had frittered away their girlhood years in the wastes of Siberia. Their tears cut me to the bone.

There were two categories of students at the Lenin School during my years there. The first consisted of those who studied for eight months—that is, the course of study for ordinary party activists who were to work in the base at some future time. The White Aba and Aba Flug belonged to this category. The second consisted of those who were to complete a three-year course and then go on to be Comintern functionaries. This school only took on Central Committee members or those who had been responsible for an entire region for no less than four years. I went into the second course.

There were approximately fourteen of us Polish comrades enrolled, including the future Polish president Bierut. The food was very good, notwithstanding the fact that many of the course participants from England and America were dissatisfied with it. I ate well for the first time in my life. Two times per day we were served soup with meat in it along with various sorts of vegetables. We were able to consume as much bread, butter and coffee as we wanted. Our housing quarters consisted of large double rooms. I shared one with Balin, a White Russian parliamentary deputy and a warm-hearted man. For pocket money we received forty rubles per month. The library was rich and abundant and the workrooms good. Our main topics of study were political economy, historical and philosophical materialism, the history of the international revolutionary movement and the history and organizational structure of the Communist Party of the Soviet Union. Instruction was conducted in four languages: Russian, English, German and Polish.

It all looked quite good on the surface. We were provided with everything we needed to enable us to pursue our studies with unburdened minds. Yet the regime was a monstrously offensive one and a disgrace to all the fundamentals which we held sacred and dear. Human dignity and the worth of the human personality were dragged through the mud.

The Stalinist net was already being woven, the Stalinist machinery of murder was already in place. Stalinist morality, founded on the trinity of flattery, denunciation and murder, had already taken shape.

A period of time would elapse before I grasped this gruesome truth, but meanwhile doubts began to gnaw at me. I noticed things which were incomprehensible at first. Beside the entrance to the Lenin School, for example, stood a small gatehouse, which was manned day and night. Against the background of my own experiences, there could be no doubt in my mind that that man inside was an informer, that he was there to keep tabs on us. It was clear to me at once that we were being spied on. And what a wild notion it was—to spy on the staff of the world revolution!

The business manager was a German—a drunkard—who neglected his duties. When we attempted to discuss the matter and to have him removed, comrades went pale: "It's better not to talk about such things. He works for the GPU." He often brought along a bloodhound to school with him which he ran in the courtyard all day long. He took it to our rooms too. It was perfectly obvious to me what he was up to.

Meanwhile, the struggle against the Bukharin faction—whose leaders were Bukharin, Rykov, Tomsky and the chief of the Moscow Party organization Ordzhonikidze-Uglanov—broke out.[17]

It is worthwhile to emphasize that Stalin was frequently in the limelight at the Fifteenth Party Congress in the latter part of 1927, the congress at which the Left Opposition was expelled. But the theoretical brain behind the attacks on the Left Opposition was Bukharin. In his appearances before the party gathering, Stalin still found it necessary to speak in the following manner: "Why listen to what I'm saying? I, Stalin, am an insignificant and simple man. Let's listen to what Lenin has to say instead." And then he drowned everybody in quotations from Lenin. In general, it must also be stressed here that whenever Stalin alluded to Marx, he steadily drew on quoted excerpts from Lenin.

Following the expulsion of the Left Opposition, the Sixth Congress of the Comintern was compelled to confirm it. Once again Bukharin was the main reporter on the political situation. But once the Comintern Congress had confirmed the use of police repression to get the Opposition and thus ushered in the bloody chapter of the murder of the Communist leaders of all countries, Stalin promptly launched into the struggle against Bukharin. It was as if he had already noted it in his calendar.

It was all the same to Stalin that he now buttressed his attack on Bukharin by relying on Bukharin's theses. The latter in fact maintained that these very same theses even bore Stalin's signature. But instead of denying this, Stalin insisted that Bukharin be smashed with redoubled vigor, for now Bukharin was pointing the accusing finger at Stalin.

But what did Stalin accuse Bukharin of? First, at the Sixth Congress of the Comintern Bukharin said that Germany had undergone an economic revolution in the years 1923 to 1928. (It is true that he had not foreseen the coming crisis.) Second, Bukharin, according to Stalin, failed to notice that the Social Democracy had grown over into social fascism.

I am not writing here a critique of the history of the CPSU(B)[18] as it was in the late 1920s nor do I wish to engage in polemics. My task is simply to impart to the reader the impression which the polemics between Stalin and Bukharin made on me. I would nevertheless like to make a number of comments.

---

[17] Hersh Mendel incorrectly alludes here to "Ordzhonikidze-Uglanov." While N.A. Uglanov was indeed chief of the Moscow party organization and an ally of the Bukharin faction during the period in question, Gregory Ordzhonikidze was one of Stalin's top assistants. (trans.)

[18] Communist Party of the Soviet Union (Bolsheviks) (trans.)

Bukharin formulated two theories in his day. In the first of these he attempted to prove that capitalism had entered a new epoch, an epoch in which it was striving to put an end to the process of spontaneity in economic development and endeavoring to introduce a certain order. This is what Bukharin called *organized* capitalism, the *organized character* of capitalism. In each country, however, this process would be accompanied by great conflicts of international scope, he argued, and these conflicts would in turn lead to large-scale world wars.

In his second theory Bukharin argued that the Soviet Union must first of all prop itself up on the kulaks. The kulak, he argued, would peacefully grow over into socialism.

While much of what Bukharin said in his theses was true, many of his ideas were wrong at the same time. But one question kept plaguing me: why didn't Stalin reply to Bukharin's assertion that in the struggle against the Left Opposition Stalin had defended Bukharin's theses; that these theses, for all intents and purposes, were both Bukharin's and Stalin's? Why did Stalin maintain that the capitalist countries were in the midst of an economic crisis at the very moment when capitalism worldwide was in full-bloom? To be sure, the crash came two years later, but this was the product of the upswing of the previous period, a period which Stalin had insisted was already racked by crisis.

Why did Stalin invent the theory of social fascism, despite the fact that the Social Democrats faced the same persecution at the hands of the fascists as the Communists? What's more, even before Mussolini went after the Communists he had already proceeded to exterminate the Social Democracy.

I was looking for answers to all of these questions. It seemed to me that the cook was preparing a dish which would prove hard to digest. And a short time later the whole affair became clear to me: Stalin needed all of these theories in order to enable him to carry out his plan to murder the revolutionary leaders. He also needed them in order to give the seal of approval to that mass slaughter which would come to bear the name "One-hundred percent collectivization."

Meanwhile, the snooping at the Lenin School proceeded apace, and with it a sense of dread among us students intensified as well. One was afraid to utter a word. At that time, I befriended a Polish comrade by the name of Marek. A man of great experience and a member of the majority faction, he was a brother-in-law of the future Polish president Bierut. My sympathies as well were already on the side of the majority. One day, when I ran into Marek on the street, he pretended that he hadn't seen me. I was perplexed at first as he hurriedly rushed passed me, but I soon reasoned that he had been afraid to talk. Nobody knew anymore who might be arrested the following day, and people therefore avoided talking to acquaintances on the street. What should happen if a friend were seized? Everyone went out of their way to make sure that they were not tainted. My worst experience of all, however, was meeting my former prison comrade Pietka on the street. He was too afraid to greet me. Even though he had just recently been freed from a Polish prison through a prisoner exchange, he had already learned how to behave. A few days later I met him at the apartment of another comrade. As we embraced one another, he broke into sobs and begged me to forget about how he had faltered in the days of the hunger strike at Lukishka. This honest revolutionary still continued to torment himself mercilessly on account of a long-past moment of weakness. He was thrilled to see me again and greeted me like a long-lost brother. Yet he had been too afraid to approach me when I had first seen him on the street. That's how this cursed system had begun to look in the year 1929.

Although I have read a great deal about the Stalin regime, nothing I have come across has impressed me. It seems to me that I know something more. I saw how the machinery was set into motion; I grasped how it would function. It was not only dangerous to greet comrades on the street, it was also dangerous to meet with them in our rooms. Whenever one wished to discuss even the most innocent of questions with another, he plugged up the keyhole of his door with a hand towel, stopped up the air duct which fed into the adjoining room and whispered softly in the other comrade's ear. This, I thought, was probably how our grandfathers had whispered to one another in the days of the Inquisition.

The situation grew worse and worse as arrests and shootings began to take place. Not one single week went by without somebody being taken into custody. One of the comrades among us, a White Russian, had served in Denikin's army. The White Russian party was just as aware of this as we in Poland were aware of the fact that the White Aba had worked as a policeman for the Germans during the First World War. But neither the White Aba nor the White Russian comrade had reported these details to anyone as they entered the Lenin School.

In the course of the party purges, the White Russian divulged that he had once fought under Denikin. Before long, the GPU had gotten wind of the story and the following day came to take the comrade away. He broke into a terrible fit of crying the night before his arrest and told us that he had a wife and children back home. One day later he was taken out and shot. No trial, no defense. When I spoke about the case with an Armenian comrade, he found it astonishing that the whole thing had agitated me so. When he explained to me that a Communist's primary duty was to aid the GPU, I felt as if something inside of me had shattered. That the primary duty of a Communist was supposed to consist of abetting the informers in their work of denunciation and human entrapment seemed so fantastic to me, so base and criminal, that I began trembling. I sensed that the situation could not go on like this, that it would have to end in a catastrophe. But more than a year was to pass before all hell broke loose.

If I was well off materially, my wife suffered from terrible hunger. She worked in Moscow's largest electrical works and was quite literally on the verge of starving to death. Once a week, the workers there received rations of impossibly tough horsemeat. I saved my wife from starvation by bringing her bread each day. And what little I brought her she shared with a fellow comrade. It made me shudder to see how ravenously she devoured those few crumbs of bread.

Sometime during this period I was supposed to give two talks on prepared subjects before groups of Russian factory workers. My first talk dealt with the First Five-Year Plan. I was to demonstrate that after the plan had been fulfilled, the Russian workers would be better off than the English workers in London. I gave that talk with a free conscience, for I truly believed what I was saying.

My second talk was an entirely different matter however, and I turned it down by pretending to be ill. I was supposed to assert that the Russian workers ate three times more meat than the French workers. While the Russian workers were served horsemeat—old, tough horsemeat—once a week, I knew only too well that the French workers ate meat two times a day. I still had it in me to suffer in silence. But consciously lying—to my own class at that—struck me as something egregious and criminal. Had it been the case that the police were no longer looking for me in Warsaw, I would have left for home immediately. But even though I did not pack my bags at once, one thing was already clear: I would return to Poland an enemy of the Stalin regime and become an Oppositionist. What's more, I had made another resolution: no secrets. Out with the whole truth about the Soviet Union!

I later carried out my resolution. And bound up with my fight to tell

the truth was the birth of the Trotskyist movement in Poland. It was precisely in this period that I had had a chance to read the Trotskyist literature, for it had been placed at our disposal for the study of party history.
At the same time, I was able to convince myself that Trotsky was right.
People can have different opinions about Trotsky and Trotskyism, but
for anybody who acknowledged the October Revolution, it was impossible not to recognize that Trotsky defended the ideas and principles which
had been formulated during the October days.

The conflict revolved around two issues: socialism in one country and
peaceful coexistence between two different social systems. An analysis
of these two questions would take us beyond the bounds of personal
memoirs. But what really shook me was the fact that Stalin relied on
Lenin in his struggle against Trotsky. There is not so much as a single
word in Lenin which might support Stalin's theses. To the contrary,
what Lenin had written and said, especially in his last report to the Third
Congress of the Comintern, gave the lie to each one of Stalin's positions.
For me, the following question was posed: "Everyone knows that Stalin
lies, that he falsifies Lenin. Yet how is it that they all agree with him?
What this signifies is that people have been forced to raise their hands in
assent; that the infamous terror, the revolver at the temple, compels
people to agree to things which they do not feel in their hearts." Today
we have grown accustomed to this, but in those days my conclusions
were personally and morally catastrophic. I already knew that I was
going to war under Trotsky's banner against a regime which crushed un-
derfoot and besmirched everything human, everything free, everything
for which generations of revolutionaries had sacrificed their lives.

Meanwhile, the moment for me to return to Poland had not yet arrived. I still had to pass through each of the seven circles of hell before
openly joining the struggle.

Forced Collectivization

In the previous chapter, I made particular reference to Stalin's view of the world economic situation. He proclaimed that capitalism was in the midst of a crisis when no such crisis had as yet broken out. To the contrary, in each of the capitalist countries the economy had just undergone a sudden upswing. It was also no accident that Stalin declared the Social Democrats to be social fascists. He had to have a crisis and he had to turn the Social Democrats into social fascists in order to awaken the impression that the time was ripe for the social revolution. Whoever was against the social revolution was a fascist as well. Stalin had to have the social revolution in order to cover up that bloody plan of his which predetermined the slaughter of millions of people.

I can no longer remember whether the slogan "One-hundred percent collectivization" was propagated the day the action began or whether it made its appearance during the course of events. Local reports appeared daily in *Pravda*, and in some parts of the country the level of collectivization had reached 80 percent in the first week. But *Pravda* responded with the call: "Who's going further, who's going the whole way?"

The entire thing was a riddle to us. It was clear to anyone who understood something of the basics of political economy that such a policy would necessarily lead to an economic catastrophe. But there was more to come, and we were only apprised of the details later, at the plenum of the Comintern Executive Committee which convened in the last part of 1929. It was in his report to this meeting that Manuilsky revealed the murder plan which was connected with forced collectivization. Two million kulak families, according to this plan, were to be evacuated. While the half of them, one million families, were expected to adapt to the new circumstances, it was calculated that a million would die along the way, would end up on the scrap heap. One must remember that Manuilsky was speaking about one million families, not one million peasants.

Meanwhile, the process of collectivization had sparked a wave of rural unrest, which began to assume a threatening character. At the order of the Comintern we all interrupted our studies and went out to the villages to propagandize for collectivization.

I know that much has already been written about the bloody collectivization, perhaps far more than anything I am capable of writing. But whoever saw it with his own eyes will never forget it.

I went to a village not far from Moscow where the inhabitants were engaged in cattle breeding rather than land cultivation. It was a sight the likes of which I had never seen before in my life. Men and women, crying, ran about in the streets tearing their hair out. Many peasants were beating their heads against the wall. I walked up to one of them and asked, "What's happened, why are you beating your head against the wall?" Sobbing, he answered: "It'll always go badly for us peasants. First the tsar choked us to death, and now the Bolsheviks."

Consoling him was dishonest and I knew it. There just wasn't any consolation for a man in his shoes. The only thing I was able to say was that the situation might change, that the collectivization was only aimed at the kulaks and not at such poor peasants like him. He then took me by the hand and led me to an enormous stable. It was a dismal scene: every cow in the village had been rounded up and brought there, yet nobody had taken the trouble to feed them. They stood there bellowing so loudly that it was deafening. The peasant walked up to his cow, squeezed her udders and saw that she had no milk. Then he threw himself to the ground once again and began to tear his hair out. This is just what dozens of peasants like him did whenever they raced over to see their cows. It was a picture of inconsolable human misery and grief. With a broken heart, I went to see the party secretary of the village.

I found him lying in bed, a man in anything but a cheerful mood. He himself was probably a peasant, and one could see that the whole thing had left him highly agitated. There could be no mincing words here, I decided. "Why did you allow this to happen?" I asked. "It's an unparalleled crime against the revolution. The cows are dying of hunger; the peasant is filled with hatred for the Soviet power. The basis for order, the alliance of the poor and middle peasants with the working class, is being undermined."

The comrade adamantly justified himself. It was not his fault, he insisted. He had been in uninterrupted telephone contact with the editorial board of *Pravda*, he said, and the editorial board had an open line to Stalin's office. When he, the secretary, had notified the editorial board the previous day that 88 percent had already been collectivized, the latter replied: "Too little." They told him that he was responsible for the entire 100 percent. It was already clear at the time just what personal responsibility meant. I knew that this comrade was the victim of a wicked despot and I knew that he was running scared. Cutting him short, I asked him to come along with me to town to see what was happening. He refused, however, and it was obvious to me that he was afraid to run the risk of showing his face in public.

I returned to town by myself only to find that another unspeakable atrocity had been committed. Someone from the GPU had walked into the village church, tossed the sacred icons into the street and wrote on the wall that the church was to be turned into a culture club. I had the impression that this chap had acted on his own, for it had not yet occurred to anybody at the time to resort to such methods. The townspeople were incensed. Gathering before the church, peasants crossed themselves, fell to their knees and refused to budge from the spot.

I needed to lie down for a while but was unable to sleep. It was clear that the revolution was heading for a catastrophe, that an iron-fisted kulak was plunging it into the abyss. I was seized by enormous pity for the Russian peasants, whom the tsar in his day had oppressed and strangled and who were now under the heel of a wild despot—a wild despot who was eating away like a leech at the body of the October Revolution.

I began to put some thought into my departure. It was best, I decided, to approach the matter carefully, for a hasty move might arouse suspicion. It goes without saying that I had not decided to break with the Communist movement. I simply wanted to cut loose from Stalin's regime and hoped that in Poland—where the party was illegal, where it was still necessary to make great sacrifices—the movement had not yet lost its untarnished idealism. This was my sole consolation.

Sleeping late the next day, I missed what had happened early in the morning. When I went to say goodbye to the secretary, I found him sitting in a chair, sobbing. Stalin had published an article in the previous day's *Pravda* about the dizzying success of the collectivization. The secretary, however, had not known anything about it; even though he had spoken to the editorial board the night before, nobody had mentioned a word about it to him. And it was in precisely this article that Stalin was now calling for a retreat. It was all the party's fault, Stalin wrote. The party had gone too far. No sooner had the peasants gotten ahold of the newspaper than they marched to the secretary's home and staged a demonstration, crying: "Down with the Bolsheviks—long live Stalin, the liberator of the peasants." The comrade was afraid to go into town.

Trotsky and Rakovsky once discussed at length the question of Soviet

Bonapartism, a discussion which is being repeated today in the organ of the Mensheviks. For me, there is absolutely no doubt that Soviet Bonapartism began the day Stalin published his above-mentioned article.

It was obvious by the time I returned to the Lenin School that the situation was extremely critical. A series of uprisings had broken out, and there was a widespread fear that printing accounts of them might set the whole country ablaze. The government was also afraid to send in the military, for nobody could be certain that the soldiers would not go over to the side of the insurgents. We were therefore informed that we would be mobilized to suppress the uprisings. Before we received our arms and marching orders, however, word reached us that the GPU had already quashed the revolt and that tens of thousands of peasants from Turkestan had fled across the border to Persia.

The country was gripped by ever-worsening deprivation. The terror of the collectivization only revealed its true proportions in 1931 in the Ukraine, where nearly seven million people died of hunger. But as early as the end of 1929 a catastrophic famine ruled the land, a famine which was reminiscent of the most difficult days of the Civil War.

I spent one month during that period at a textile factory not far from Moscow and was struck by the fact that the machines stood idle for hours at a time. For days on end there were no workers there. The party secretary of the factory explained that he was unable to do anything about it, for the workers had had nothing to eat and were therefore too weak to work.

Stalin, who was accustomed to scoffing at human suffering and the spilling of innocent blood, found it necessary at precisely this moment—in the midst of mass starvation—to declare that the peasant led a sated and happy life. One and all were compelled to repeat this, even though it was obvious to every Tom, Dick and Harry that it was a shameful lie. I remember reading a letter in *Pravda* at the time in which a peasant thanked Stalin for having opened up his eyes and for having made it clear to him that he led such a happy life. He had never noticed before.

Toadying and denunciation had spread in such measure that every foundation of social morality was undermined. Each comrade in our party cell was secretary for a month. What did his task consist of? He had to go to the administrator, Kirsanova, each week and "innocently" inform her of the mood of the comrades. Those whose mood did not concur with the party line disappeared. Of the more than thirty comrades from Poland, barely seven or eight made the trip back home. The others were arrested and later killed. Even such a worker-leader as Aba Flug, a comrade with a praiseworthy service record, went along with the system. After learning that his factional opponent, the White Aba, was too ashamed to say that he had been a policeman for the Germans, Aba Flug denounced him. White Aba was later killed.

The Decision

Life in the Soviet Union for foreign revolutionaries was unbearable. It seemed as if everything was being done to degrade and dishonor each and every socialist who had not gone through the Russian school. It went badly for any Communist, for example, who praised his own party, who held that it was revolutionary and who, as a member, took pride in it. One could be certain in those days that such sentiments meant big trouble. The Soviet bigwigs even had a name for it: "underestimating the Soviet Union." How could such a man exist: a good Communist abroad who had not learned his communism in the Soviet Union? Such a man was petty bourgeois because he had underestimated the pervasiveness of his petty-bourgeois surroundings back home under capitalism. If he did not practice self-criticism, if he did not heap filth on himself, if he had not ascertained that he was still full of petty-bourgeois tendencies and that he had come to the Soviet Union in order to learn what real communism was—then he could forget about ever returning to his country. This, of course, only pertained to the members of illegal parties. Comrades from democratic countries were not in danger; they were able to rely on the intervention of their consulates to get them out of a scrape.

There were those who found the right tone. One such man declared that the Communist Party in his country was still full of petty-bourgeois prejudices, that it was not Leninist, that only in the Soviet Union could one become a good Communist. And being a good Communist is precisely what he had come to learn. Men like him shot rapidly to the top. Every door and every career stood open to them. The Soviet bureaucracy knew that such "Communists" made good lackeys.

Aside from sycophancy, one was surrounded by the most shameful lies as well. We already know that the Soviet Union was in the throes of a raging famine in those days and that Stalin cynically tried to talk his way into people's hearts by telling them how happy and satisfied they were. Every charlatan echoed this line in the following manner: "Things are getting worse and worse in the capitalist countries. But here its's almost like paradise." Those who talked like this went about sumptuously dressed and complained that the food at the Lenin School was not to their tastes, that it was fit for pigs. These people had mastered Stalin's style; they jeered at the terrible misery of the Russian masses in the crudest manner. But it paid—they were seen as the best Communists.

I once had occasion to do some propagandizing at a factory with an American lady from the Lenin School. So obtuse was she that she went wearing a silk dress. No sooner had she begun to preach in the accustomed manner than a woman walked up to her, fingered her silk dress and said: "People die of hunger in your country wearing dresses like this? In our paradise one doesn't even see such dresses." That lying and cynical palaver left me with a deep feeling of shame.

Lies and falsehoods not only came to dominate the field of propaganda, but science and philosophy as well. My instructor in the history of the Russian workers movement, for example, had written a work dealing with the Revolution of 1905 and devoted his entire class time to telling us about the masses of material on which he had drawn. His book, he kept repeating, would have great significance. The very day he was supposed to bring us the finished work, however, he came to class in shambles. Stalin had pronounced that his book was good for nothing; the historian had merely rummaged through old books like a mouse but had failed to see the blood and guts of life. His book also evinced Trotskyist tendencies, his accusers said, and it underestimated the role which Stalin had played in the party in the early days. They wanted to force him to falsify history.

A second case dealt with Plekhanov. Plekhanov had always been considered the best Marxist philosopher—and that with Lenin's blessing. But with Stalin already on the way to making himself the greatest philosopher, Plekhanov's renown stood in his way. Stalin therefore passed judgment on Plekhanov, labeled him a religious philosopher, a believer, and insisted that he be banned. On what grounds? Because Plekhanov had correctly demonstrated that before worktools began to influence and determine economic relations, man was dependent in his material existence on the workings of nature. According to Stalin, however, nature and god were one and the same. Our professor in historical materialism brought this to our attention and commented that Stalin understood absolutely nothing about philosophy. "But he has a good political nose," the professor added. There were many such cases. Stalin approached philosophy and science with a revolver in his hand. Had that not been so, nobody would have crowned him the greatest philosopher of our time.

At the end of 1930 a plenum of the Comintern Executive Committee took place at which the notorious Manuilsky gave a report on the political situation. I would like to confine my remarks to two of the issues which he touched upon.

One. The Social Democrats covered up their fascist character by spouting democratic phrases. With this, Manuilsky raised the theory of social fascism to a new level. Until then, the argumentation had been that the Social Democrats had grown over into fascism. Now it turned out that the Democracy itself had become fascist and that the worst fascist of all was the left Socialist. We will talk about the criminal character of this infamous theory below. But I was already certain at that conference that when it came to the workers movement the Stalinist bureaucrats were up to no good.

Two. Manuilsky also dealt with the question of the relationship between the Soviet Union and the peoples of Asia. The defeats suffered by the Soviet Union, he argued, were attributable to this fact, that up until then the USSR had striven to buttress itself on the progressive, but still very weak, forces in the region. Manuilsky cited as an example the revolt against Afghanistan's progressive shah. The shah relied on the Soviet Union and attempted to carry out a series of progressive reforms. If the Soviet Union wanted to become influential, however, it would have to seek the support of the real, existing—that is, reactionary—forces. The ambiguous meaning of this thesis was already clear to me at the time. All of us knew until then that we must give national liberation movements a progressive character by struggling for a series of social reforms. Supporting the reactionary forces, however, not only meant betraying the national interests of the popular masses, it meant selling out the social struggle as well. It meant delivering up the masses of the poor to the rule of the landowners and clerical reaction.

Before my return to Poland I visited a Jewish kolkhoz in the gubernia of Kherson. I was interested in seeing how the Jewish peasants lived. A comrade from Bessarabia went with me and the two of us were supposed to do propaganda work.

We arrived just in time for a general meeting of the kolkhoz at the peak of the harvest season. But due to a shortage of rope to bind the stalks of grain and due to the dilapidated state of their wagons, the farmers were unable to reap the crop. I advised my Bessarabian comrade, a blacksmith, not to lecture people who were on the brink of a disaster on account of a little rope, but to repair the wagons instead.

Meanwhile, I went out to the fields to work with the peasants. The situation was terrible. Those who brought along a small piece of bread and a radish were looked upon with envy. And how these people were able to keep going in such heat and to work without food in their stomachs was simply beyond me.

When the month was over and we told the peasants why we had actually come, they were dumbfounded. A year earlier they had been visited by another student from the Lenin School who had insisted that he be driven around in a wagon. He had refused to go anywhere by foot. Upon my return to Moscow I gave a report about our work and was put forward as a model Bolshevik. I naturally kept to myself the fact that I hadn't so much as uttered a single word of propaganda.

With the ensuing purge of the party in December 1930 I finally and definitively decided to return to Poland. We, the Russian language section, were particularly hard hit. The chairman of the purge commission was a Jew by the name of Mickiewicz, the leader of the Lithuanian Communist Party. The first one brought before him was Kirsanova, the administrator of the Lenin School. She had taken over the post from Bukharin. One blushed to hear her talk; she was unable to differentiate between Mensheviks, syndicalists and anarchists. But she had one thing going for her: she was the wife of Yaroslavsky, who was still in his glory at the time for having falsified the history of the party according to Stalin's wishes. She had another asset as well: she was an intriguer who had mastered the art of buying and bribing.

Most of the comrades among us who fell to the purge were members of illegal parties. Although their lives were one long history of blood and heroism, the chairman went to great lengths to turn all of this into small change. He never forgot to remind them that they were not Russians, that they still had much to learn from the Russian comrades. Whenever these Russian Bolsheviks recounted their personal histories, Mickiewicz rose to his feet and adjured everyone to follow in their footsteps. And their biographies? Not one of them had had anything to do with the illegal struggle and none of them had participated in the October Revolution. They were apparachiks, and the stories they told recounted the history of wandering from one post to another. It was so base, so sycophantic that it made one's blood boil.

When it was my turn to talk, a comrade from the minority faction—the faction in power at the time, that is—told me that the party abhorred hearing about the Revolutionary War Committee and that I was not to speak about my participation in it. And why did the party abhor such talk? Because the War Committee had been headed by Królikowski, a comrade from the faction which had been edged out of the leadership. This meant that one was supposed to renounce his own party history so long as the work had been performed under the leadership of a comrade who belonged to an opposing faction.

The cup ran over when another comrade from the Polish party got up and told the story of his life. He too had long years of prison behind him and he too had escaped from the clutches of a death sentence. (Comrades attested that he was emotionally abnormal.) He had already been living in the Soviet Union for quite some time and was a member of the society of Old Bolsheviks. After he had finished recounting his heroic history, Mickiewicz stood up and said that the comrade ought to resign from the society of Old Bolsheviks because he was unworthy of it. I was on the verge of exploding. It was no longer possible to go along with this vulgar game.

The next morning I went over to the Comintern to see my good old friend Sochacki, the representative of the Polish section to the International in those days, and categorically informed him that I wanted to go home at once. I wasn't going to allow my revolutionary honor to be trampled under the jackboot of the new Soviet bureaucracy. I was well aware of the risk I was taking should Sochacki wish me the worst. But I had resolved to speak my peace loud and clear. Sochacki went pale and gazed at me bewilderingly. He had obviously been unprepared for such a declaration.

Calmly but firmly he bid me to stop and added that he had not heard a thing. He promised, however, to fill my request as quickly as possible. Two weeks later I went home.

Back to Warsaw

I returned to Warsaw with mixed feelings, for I was not certain that the police had given up the search for me. Should I be arrested once again for a new offense, it would mean the stiffest sentence possible. In addition to the two years and eight months in prison which I still "owed," I would face so many years behind bars that I might just as well say goodbye to the free world. Nevertheless, I was glad to have left the land of the terror regime. I was still under the illusion that it would all be different in the illegal movement in Poland. But I was quickly disappointed.

The blackest fantasy imaginable could never have painted a worse picture than the one which I found. It is no exaggeration to say that in all the years which I spent participating in social movements, this was the first time that I saw a political movement transforming itself into a criminal one. The Communist Parties of that period had embarked on a new, criminal phase of their history.

Upon my return to Warsaw at the end of 1930 I became secretary of the Jewish Central Bureau. In my first speech, I recounted the experiences I had had in the Soviet Union and warned the comrades in Poland against following the Soviet path. The Central Bureau in those days had five members. Toyber Moshe[19] was one of them. A man who had never read a thing in his life, he had been raised on the Stalinist gutter press and was perfectly cut out to become a leader in that sad period. Comrades said of Toyber Moshe that he constantly nodded his head while schmoozing with people. Whenever he was speaking to somebody with a lesser party function than himself, he would shake his head no. Should he be speaking to one of his superiors, however, he would shake his head yes. He was later murdered in the Soviet Union.

Another member of the Central Bureau was Moshe Batlen,[20] the foremost journalist on the editorial board. It was no easy thing at the time being a party journalist. In order to know what he was not permitted to write, he had to keep a running tally of all the existing parties and remember that each and every one of them was fascistic. He always had to emphasize the great role of the Soviet Union as well. It went

---

[19] *Toyb*, literally "deaf," is a nickname for a yes man.
[20] *Batlen*, a lazy person or someone with intellectual pretensions.

bitterly for him whenever he forgot to throw something into the balance, for this meant that he was underestimating, that he was concealing something, that he had deviations. Moshe Batlen always carried a list around with him with which he kept tabs on things, and he stayed abreast of the latest developments by making additions to it. Everything he wrote had one and the same face. He too perished in the Soviet Union.

The third member of the Central Bureau was Hershel Metalovitz, a devoted worker-leader who lives in Canada today. The fourth was Lazevnik, a current citizen of Poland. His story is better left unwritten in order to spare the paper. The fifth member was I.

Life for me on the Jewish Central Bureau began to get tough. I saw that we had not only gone to the dogs politically, but morally as well. It was a time during which the Communist Party sought to get everything done with the aid of cold steel. It is no simple task to recount each and every crime; one would have to write several books to tell the whole story. I will therefore sketch a picture of these times in rough outline.

During the elections to the steering committee of the Jewish Literary Society, for example, the party called for a boycott on the grounds that the Society was fascistic. The conference of the Jewish *folkshuln*[21] was boycotted because these schools were fascistic. When I attempted to point out that it was a disgrace to stamp the whole of Jewish culture as fascistic and that such a policy could only lead to creating a pogrom atmosphere, I was viewed as a deviator. Matters were even worse in the workers' quarters, where many of the trade unions were split. Until that time the leaders of the different unions used to collaborate with one another in order to organize joint strikes. But if the Bundist trade unions were now declared to be fascistic, there could naturally be no more talk of negotiations. Strikes were decided upon separately and then the organizers approached the workers of the other trade unions with revolver in hand. The result was brother against brother within the ranks of the working class.

The same practices were also attempted in the Polish factories, but there the party was confronted by the watchful eyes of the secret police. While the Communist groups inside the Polish factories were quickly liquidated, the same process took somewhat longer in the Jewish quarter, for the Jewish cottage laborers were afraid to resort to such means.

---

[21] primary schools (trans.)

The incident surrounding the bakery worker Luxemburg was very characteristic. A conflict over whose influence was to prevail in a particular bakery had broken out between our trade union and the trade union of the Bund. Upon learning that our group had decided to resort to the use of terror, I went to a meeting of the party cell in the bakers union and forbade them to solve the dispute with revolvers. But somebody had already been at work behind my back. After all, it was generally known by then that I was a deviator. In broad daylight a member of our bakers cell, Luxemburg, shot a Bundist bakery worker. The trade union was shut down at once and the Bund began to ready their goon squads. We were a breath away from a bloodbath. I spent days on end at the hiring hall to ensure that nobody else be victimized.

The fate of the comrade who had shot the Bundist worker was a terrible one. He was a primitive worker who was unable to read and write. After he pulled the trigger, comrades hid him away for two days inside a WC located in a courtyard on Wołynska Street. Then somebody came to inform me that our own comrades wanted to liquidate him because they had no idea what to do next. It was only with great effort that I succeeded in putting a stop to their criminal plan. They found him a safe house for a time and then sent him to Danzig. From there he was to go to the Soviet Union. Meanwhile, however, he fell into the hands of the police and was dreadfully tortured. Word reached us that he had been cut to ribbons and that he lay unconscious in Pawiak prison. Although he had not betrayed any of his comrades, the party nonetheless labeled him an informer. He naturally went without a stitch of help and died. A double murder had been committed: a Bundist worker had fallen and his assailant had died a terrible death.

The left Poale Zion held regular literature readings each Friday evening at the Workers' Home on Karmelicka Street and our goon squads had decided to disrupt them. But the Poale Zion, it turned out, had a different view of the matter. They gave a handful of the disrupters a good beating on one occasion. Subsequently, the Warsaw Office decided it was time for revenge and intended to send in a team of men once again, this time with knives. As soon as I got wind of the idea, I dashed off to the comrades and told them that I forbade any such actions. With a derisive smile on his face, the head of the Warsaw Office Pinie (a member of the wood workers who lives in Paris today), reproachfully countered that I thought it a pity to spill Poale-Zionist blood. As I write these lines, my hand trembles. How low the movement had sunk!

But the party committed even more atrocious crimes. Practically every week it put out calls for general strikes, which only brought out a tiny smattering of Jewish youths. These strikes had to be organized in order to give grist to Stalin's thesis that every small strike would grow into an armed uprising. Indeed, one had to prove that there were also general strikes in Poland. Inasmuch as nobody struck, however, it was left to the party to attempt to provoke excesses. For example, demonstrations were called almost every other day. But Polish workers refused to attend them. And when even the Jewish workers stopped going, the field was left to an ever-dwindling number of youths. They too decided to stay away in the end, for the police were able to disperse them with ease. Each time, there were casualties. Instead of putting a stop to these shameful adventures, the party sought to cover them up with new crimes. It maintained that the masses did not attend these demonstrations because they wanted to fight with guns in hand. It followed from this that it was necessary to organize armed demonstrations. There was even one strategist who worked up a plan for armed clashes.

According to this plan, armed groups were to position themselves in an area including the site of the demonstration itself as well as the neighboring police commissariats. Their task was to prevent the police from approaching the demonstration. Interestingly, such demonstrations were organized solely and strictly in the Jewish quarter, for, as I have said, Poles had nothing to do with them.

The party once planned to hold an armed demonstration near the appeals court at Krasińskich Square, where Jewish military squads were to battle it out with the police. It was clear to me that besides the victims who would fall on the spot, it could also come to pogroms. Thoroughly flabbergasted, I met with comrade Artuski, at the time a member of both the Warsaw Jewish Bureau and the Warsaw Party Committee, and poured out my bitter heart to him. I didn't have to say too much; like I, Artuski was opposed to such adventures. The two of us arranged to sabotage this adventure, and, in fact, it never took place.

A particularly infamous chapter was the party's efforts to organize the plundering of shops. In order to prove that Poland was in the grips of a great famine, the party found it necessary to see the streets filled with hungry hordes stealing things to eat. The organization of these food heists looked like this: gangs of people would go to the Jewish quarter wearing tattered clothes, smash shop windows and grab whatever they could get their hands on. It often turned out that somebody snatched two shoes for the left foot or two for the right, and in many cases the members of these gangs traded blows with each other in the aftermath as they divided up the booty. On one occasion, after some of them had broken into the sole Polish pork shop in the Jewish quarter, located at the corner of Dzika and Dzielna Streets, the stolen pork was carted off to the textile workers union and left there to rot.

A comrade from the Central Committee once came to a meeting of the Jewish Central Bureau with a project which I rejected out of hand. Inasmuch as bringing out the Polish workers to plunder shops had not met with success, he argued, we ought to wait for nightfall, organize a mass meeting and then steal surreptitiously into the Polish district. There we were to break into Polish businesses and plunder them in the night.

In the days when the Communist Party was organizing the plundering of shops, putting out weekly calls for general strikes and attempting to arrange armed demonstrations, ruffian gangs of anti-Semites had taken to the streets and were launching daily and murderous attacks on Jews. The Bund's military squads often fought out pitched battles with them. But when we turned to the party with the request for at least ten Polish workers to stand side by side with us in the name of working-class solidarity, they told us that they were unable to find so much as a single man who was interested. So we were in the midst of a revolutionary situation in those days and it was high time to experiment with civil war, yet the party was unable to place some ten workers at our disposal for the struggle against pogromists. Even worse: the party demanded of its Jewish comrades that they dress up as Poles in order to rob Polish businesses. And all of this in order for somebody to be able to write that the civil war in Poland had begun.

In order to paint the picture even clearer, I would like to recall two more facts. We already know that between one hundred and two hundred Jewish youths participated in the "revolutionary" mass actions. Yet at the meetings of the Jewish Central Bureau the Central Committee representative persistently demanded that our reports on the actions put the head count at between 20,000 and 30,000. He refused to hear of anything less than 10,000. We were thereby to emphasize that these demonstrations bore an almost Polish character, despite the fact that not one single Polish worker participated.

Another fact. A Polish drunkard and pogromist had gone on a fling beating up Jews on the railway line between Warsaw and Otwock. On one occasion, however, he insulted a Polish officer—under the influence, of course—and ended up with a bullet in his head. A few weeks later a correspondent's report from Poland appeared in the German-language organ of the Comintern stating that military maneuvers had taken place in Otwock. Polish workers had demonstrated against militarism, it continued, in the course of which a fascist officer had shot a revolutionary worker. Honor to his memory!

This is how the party bluffed, so deeply had it sunk. Such was the criminal state it was in.

PART 6

We Found a Faction

*U*ntil this point I had conducted the struggle entirely on my own. I knew, however, that things would have to change, that something would have to happen. And finally, the time for organized battle had come. It was the last attempt to save the party.

I was out visiting an old friend in Żoliborz[1] on one occasion when I ran into Alexander Minc. We were both overjoyed to see one another, for it had been a long time. First we talked about private matters and then in due time Alexander switched the conversation over to the political track. The theory of social fascism, he complained, was false; it was having a devastating effect on the workers movement. He did not need to speak to me at great length on this score. But even though we were old friends, he spoke very guardedly. For my part, I did not take up his objections directly. I merely pointed out to him that one could not blame the Polish Communist Party alone for the wretched state of affairs, for the party was only acting under orders from the Comintern. Fighting the wrongdoings in our party, I argued, required taking up the struggle against the Comintern as a whole. Alexander as well avoided addressing the question head-on, but it was clear that we had established a fine mutual understanding.

We arranged to meet again in the city baths on Leszno Street where, shielded from the eyes of the enemy, we would take a room with a double bath and openly speak our minds. We were more concerned at the time about protecting ourselves from the party than from the secret police.

---

[1] a district in Warsaw (trans.)

It was under such conditions that we met several times and finally decided to organize a faction. We did not speak of founding a Trotskyist faction, although it was my sincere desire to do so. Inasmuch as I was uncertain as to whether such a faction would quickly find its echo, we decided to formulate a three-point program: one, for united fronts with the Social Democrats in the struggle against reaction and fascism; two, for the unity of the trade-union movement; three, against bureaucratic wrongdoing, that is, for party democracy.

Once we had worked out our program, we thought it best to look for a third comrade before getting down to work. And to that end we turned to the Black Aba. Aba, however, declared that the party was preparing to make a revolution in the winter of 1931 and that nobody was to stand in the way. He told us to count him in if the revolution should not take place. Aba Flug was not such a fool as to prattle about revolutions. My impression was that he was stalling for time, that he wanted to talk with Warski and Kostrzewa.

Meanwhile, Alexander and I got down to business by ourselves. It went better than we had imagined and the number of our sympathizers grew rapidly. Aba Flug came to us in the meantime as well and we began to forge such roots that the party was very soon forced to take notice of us. They spread the word about me and slandered me as a right-winger from one end of the country to the other. Comrades began to inform themselves; they turned to the party, of course, but they also came to me. I spent days on end walking around the Gesia cemetery with comrades explaining to them what the fight was all about. Ninety percent of them became Oppositionists.

Once we had won over a large number of adherents, we decided to work out a memorandum to the Central Committee. We enumerated all of the crimes which had been committed and wrote that if the party truly believed in the social revolution, it had to put a stop to its dangerous policies. Continue, we wrote, and the moment the revolution actually broke out, there would no longer be a party capable of leading it. We concluded the memorandum with the three demands from our program.

The memorandum was worked out by a series of comrades—Alexander, Aba and I among them—but it was sent to the Central Committee under my name because I was the sole party functionary among all the Oppositionists. Meanwhile, I carried out two party commissions. First, I organized the Communist writers group, the members of which included such people as Lis, Heller, Knaphais, Shulshteyn, Shlevin, Bergner, Kagan, Mitzmacher, Zaromb, Olei and Vulman. Second, I headed up a group which had split off from the left Poale Zion.

It was in this period that Isaac Deutscher, editor of the Yiddish-language *Literarishe Tribune*, came to us. Another comrade had been assigned to work with him on the newspaper, and in my capacity as secretary of the Central Bureau I was responsible for its political line. My acquaintance with Isaac Deutscher stems from this period. We often used to speak to one another about the sad state of the party. He was too intelligent not to see how catastrophic the situation was.

Some years earlier, when the literary tendency known as Proletcult had come into being in Soviet Russia, Lenin suggested to Trotsky that he write a book on the question. In his work Trotsky naturally fought the theory of proletarian culture. He pointed out that the working class could not produce proletarian culture in the process of the social revolution, for by doing so it would isolate itself from all those layers in society which follow its lead. In times of revolution, he argued, it is the task of culture to promote the struggle of all those who go along with the proletariat. With the advent of socialism, however, the proletariat as such will disappear; what will remain is free, socialist man. It was therefore absurd to create a purely proletarian culture. When, in later years, Stalin became the lord of the manor, he spoke out on this question and accused Trotsky of approaching culture from a military standpoint.

At one of the editorial board meetings of the *Literarishe Tribune* an article dealing with proletarian culture was read aloud. The author of the article defended Stalin's position. It was not my wont to keep my views to myself, but when comrades asked me what I thought about the question at hand, I did just that. Coming out against the article meant breaking at once with the party. We spoke with Deutscher about the issue following the meeting and I succeeded in interesting him in Trotskyism. Before long he became an avowed Trotskyist.

A comrade from Switzerland, whom Trotsky had specially sent to Poland to work with us, arrived in this period. He was a warm, dear man, a glowing revolutionary and an extraordinarily good publicist as well. After Deutscher, he became the second journalist on our press. Even in the Warsaw Ghetto, where he perished, he still brought out a newspaper called *di Royte Fan*. [2]

---

[2] *the Red Flag* (trans.)

In the meanwhile, two things happened which accelerated our expulsion from the party. For one thing, I received an article by Manuilsky which I was supposed to translate into Yiddish. This article maintained that the struggle between the German Communists and the fascists for hegemony over the German peasantry had ended with the complete victory of the Communist Party. And that at a time when Hitler was marching from one victory to the next. Manuilsky's article seemed to me so wild, so criminal, that I refused to translate it. The second case dealt with an article by Deutscher in the *Literarishe Tribune*, which bore the headline, "The Twelfth Hour." In this article, Deutscher wrote that the Communist Party of Germany must immediately form a united front with the Social Democrats in order to prevent Hitler's rise to power.

Trotsky wrote a brochure at the time in which he called on the proletariat to close ranks at once.[3] In this pamphlet he ridiculed the Stalinists, who believed that Hitler would prepare the way for the Communist revolution in Germany. To the contrary, he pointed out, Hitler was gearing up to roll his tanks over the corpses of the workers. Trotsky's brochure exercised so great an influence on us that virtually our entire opposition went Trotskyist. A small group around Aba Flug did not come around, however; they took the path of capitulation.

At the end of May 1931, we received word that the party was about to summon a special conference in Danzig to deal with my case. To this day, I am still unable to comprehend this move. After all, it was already quite in vogue in those days to expel comrades for the slightest deviation without, to be sure, convening party gatherings. Meanwhile, we worked out the program which I was to defend there.

Among other comrades present at the Danzig conference, the participants included Hershel Metalovitz, Maiski, Toyber Moshe, Moshe Batlen, Pinie and I. While Amsterdam was there in the name of the Central Committee, Bronkowski had come as the representative from the Comintern. I must emphasize that I was treated relatively liberally there. The main reporter was Amsterdam. He argued that the Opposition did not understand the period in which we were living. Even a lost strike, he said, tore a brick from the edifice of capitalism and was of revolutionary significance. Whoever preached the united front with the Social Democrats betrayed the revolution. As for me, he said that I was

---

[3] *The Turn in the Communist International and the Situation in Germany*, 26 September 1930 (GE)

a good Marxist. Nevertheless, he feared that with my demand for the united front with the Social Democrats I was about to go over the deep end of renegacy.

I was granted an entire hour for my co-report and used the speaking time to defend the theses of our memorandum. Only the united front of the German proletariat, I pointed out, could block Hitler's rise to power and save the entire world from disaster. I stressed how absurd it was to demand that the united front only be carried out from below—that is, only with the mass base of the Social Democracy. If the Social-Democratic workers were ready to go along with the Communist Party against the will of their leaders, then they would join the Communist Party. Should they not do so, I argued, it was a sign that they still had confidence in their leaders. If we really wanted to go along with them—and yes, they were the decisive force in Germany—then we had to turn to their leadership, that is, to the Social Democratic Party. That was the essence of my report. Hershel Metalovitz did not defend me politically, he simply demanded that I not be expelled. Maiski was of the same opinion. The others maintained that I must be expelled at once. Following a passionate debate it was resolved that I be temporarily pulled out of party work and that I be granted one month to think things over. The conference ended on a depressing note; it was clear that both sides would stick to their guns.

Early the next morning while I was still asleep, Amsterdam, looking morally broken, came to me. He had come to suggest that I pull back. I told him that he ought to be ashamed of himself for proposing such a thing. The two days of discussion at the conference had not turned me around, I said, and he wanted to do the trick in a minute. Who could have known that I would never see him again. He was soon to brand me a renegade. Eventually, he met his death in the Soviet Union.

In the course of the next month there was to be no backsliding on my part. To the contrary, I wrote a letter to the Central Committee in which I sharpened the conflict still more. In the end we received word that we had been expelled from the party.

When the news finally arrived, I stayed awake the whole night with my wife. Unable to go to bed and with tears in our eyes, we didn't so much as say a single word to one another. We were heartbroken. But we knew that it had all been unavoidable.

Our Opposition

Following our expulsion from the party we found ourselves in a tragic contradiction. It was not our fault, for this contradiction was a product of objective conditions. We already knew that we had nothing but the worst to expect from the Stalin regime, that a machine had been created in the Soviet Union which would commit not only the most hideous political atrocities, but criminal atrocities as well. We already knew that the Soviet Union had transformed itself into a giant prison for all those revolutionaries who dared to say that they did not agree. What's more, we knew that the Soviet Union had become a place of execution for Communists who were not considered sufficiently obedient. Whenever the party wanted to get rid of somebody, they sent him to the Soviet Union; and that meant that he may just as well abandon all hope, for the trip was the trip of death. It necessarily followed that one had to break with the movement and wash away the ignominy with which the Soviet Union in those days had already besmirched the October Revolution. Yet we continued to consider ourselves a faction of the Comintern, precisely as if the Comintern were something other than a tool in the hands of the Stalinist bureaucrats!

No, the Comintern was fully dependent on the Soviet Union, without whose material support no single section could have existed. This support demoralized, and both morally and politically laid waste to all the leaders of the Communist Parties. Somebody once told me that the leader of the opposition in the German Communist Party, Brandler, remembered the good old days when the Spartakusbund lived off the nickels and dimes which comrades had scratched together. It had not been possible in those days to buy off and demoralize people, as became customary when great sums of money were there for the asking.

We expected the worst from the Soviet Union, but psychologically we were not prepared to completely break with it. Even comrades who had not personally participated in the October Revolution paid a high price in Poland to defend it. Each had prison and unremitting persecution behind him. But we made every sacrifice in the profound belief that we were thereby inaugurating the epoch of the social revolution the world over. To suddenly make the break meant breaking with a piece of one's own life. Neither we nor Trotsky were able to do that.

I have reflected at great length about the zigzag policy which Trotsky pursued all the way up to the Second World War. Politically this policy was impossible to fathom. He did not cease to appeal to the Comintern, even though he knew all the while—and often repeated—that the Communist movement was controlled and led by the GPU. Better than anyone else, he knew the moment Hitler came to power that Stalin would seek to conclude an alliance with him. Trotsky warned of this danger, and yet he maintained that it was necessary to defend the Soviet Union. While propagating the slogan of a political revolution in the Soviet Union and the emancipation of the Ukrainian people from the Stalinist yoke, he did not renounce his policy of the unconditional defense of the Soviet Union. Even as he condemned the Red Army's aggression in shamefully falling upon little Finland, he nonetheless maintained that it was impermissible to engage the Red Army in combat. When both Stalin and Hitler carried out the third partition of Poland, Trotsky came forward with a sharp condemnation of it. Stalin was like a jackal, he wrote, who had come to devour the carcass of the animal murdered by Hitler. Yet here too Trotsky remained true to his old stance. There is no easy way to untangle the foregoing politically; but psychologically it was all comprehensible. This was a terrible contradiction for which all of us paid dearly.

Until the moment I left the party ranks I had been a functionary. Once we were outside the party, however, I lacked the means to sustain myself materially. I had something, it's true. As a functionary, I had frequently supported comrades who were out of work. Fearful as they were of being compromised in the wake of my expulsion, all of them handed me back the money which I had previously given them. Isaac Deutscher helped me out a great deal. He divided his income into three parts: one for the organization, one for comrades and one for himself. His own share was not always the largest.

I lived in Otwock at the time. My home was the staff and gathering point for the Opposition. Comrades often stayed overnight and slept on the floor. It reminded me of the Moscow Soviet at the time of the October uprising.

I would disappear from home for days at a time, moved by the burning passion to build an organized and strong opposition as rapidly as possible. To that end, I had to stay in the city or travel around the provinces. My wife often complained that I spent so little time at home. She argued that we wouldn't always live in a dacha and that I would do better to stay home more often. But I just did not have the time for that.

Finally, my money reserves were at an end and it became necessary for me to put some thought into looking for work. There were no jobs in my old calling, and so I decided to learn shoemaking. One of the handful of Trotskyists on the trade union's skills committee, Moshe Diner, signed me up and began to train me in the field. Before long, however, the administration decreed that I not be permitted to work, for I was a danger to the union.

News suddenly arrived that the Black Aba and I had been summoned to Moscow. Word of it reached me at work one day by way of Toyber Moshe. Seeking to muster my courage, he assured me that my wife would be put up in the best hotel during my stay abroad and receive a full pension besides. First off, I told him to cut out the lures and enticements if he wished to talk to me. Regarding the matter itself, I said that I would give him my reply after a meeting of our faction leadership. But he threatened me on the spot. If I did not go to the Soviet Union, he warned, the party would initiate a special campaign against me. Refusing to go, he said, was tantamount to saying that I expected to be arrested once I got there. It meant insinuating that Communists were arrested in the Soviet Union; it meant dragging the Soviet Union through the mud. Just from hearing him talk, it was obvious to me how corrupt comrades had become. They simply sought to entice me, arrest me and kill me. To bolster my courage, they promised that my wife would be set up with money and the finest hotel accommodations. At the same time, they tried to blackmail me with a threatening campaign. Toyber Moshe had known me for a long time. How could he say all those things, knowing full well that he was sending me to my death?

We called a meeting of our faction leadership in order to come to grips with the latest turn of events. A hot debate ensued in which Aba Flug came out for going while Shlomo and Alexander said no. I presented a proposal which was accepted. The party had already been issuing proclamations at the time stamping us as agents of the social fascists. My proposal was as follows: if the party publishes a special proclamation in which they withdraw this accusation and in which they declare that we are Communists who are of another opinion on a series of questions than the official leadership, then we will be prepared to go. I had absolutely no doubt that the party could not go for my proposal, for it meant unmasking themselves with the aid of their very own Big Lie. They neither accepted our proposal nor did we go to the Soviet Union.

In connection with our leadership plenum, an incident took place which is worthy of mention here. In the days when the Opposition took shape a certain young chap wanted to join, whom we, for particular reasons, refused to accept. Then in the period following our plenum a pamphlet appeared under the signature of one "X"—the very same lad, that is, who had tried and failed to join our faction. The pamphlet which he put out tells us that Hersh-Mendel was said to have come out against sentimentality and to have called for the use of the secret police in the struggle against the party. Worse things were yet to come, but it was lies like this which could have set the stage for the famous Moscow Trials.

We decided to bring out two publications, one in Yiddish and the other in Polish. Meanwhile, Aba Flug departed from us with a small group of capitulators, whom the party nevertheless turned down cold. Even though they offered to help out in the struggle against the Trotskyists, the party didn't trust them. Perhaps it didn't need them either. The group even stooped so low as to attempt to justify the Moscow Trials. Why did Aba leave us? Alexander was certain that he had gotten a wink from the erstwhile majorityites, who shrank in horror as the Opposition assumed a Trotskyist character. Perhaps he had other motives. In any case, following the exit of the Aba group the Opposition officially became Trotskyist and established connections with the Trotskyist Center.

Both of the publications which we brought out were on a politically high level.[4] They gave vent to the free, critical word, which had been suppressed for so long by the party apparatus. The main publicists were Deutscher, Shlomo and Artel. In Warsaw, our Yiddish-language newspaper had a higher circulation than the party press. I cannot say the same for our Polish edition, however. The Polish component of the Communist movement in general was already thoroughly demoralized and rotten.

The fact that the party lost the best forces it possessed in the Jewish quarter when it expelled the Trotskyists was probably what lay behind its order to clean out the Jews and to remove its Jewish members from the Polish work. Poles were being seized right and left. The entire party became riddled with informers.

The Opposition exercised great influence over the youth as well, for

4   In 1933 the Polish Trotskyists published, among other things, a Yiddish-language journal called *Unzer Gedank (Our Thought)* and a Yiddish-language biweekly called *Shtern (Star)*.

there was indeed a splendid revolutionary youth movement. Our influence also spread in the provinces, especially in Vilna, Lemberg[5] and Łódź. There is absolutely no doubt that we would have become a force in Poland had it been objectively possible and had we had the material resources. When I became acquainted with other Trotskyist organizations in days to come, I continually got the impression that ours was the best and most ideal. The material means to carry out our work stemmed exclusively from comrades' contributions, and our comrades were all proletarians. Deutscher undoubtedly gave away the half of his income. Another one of our comrades, a merchant, was also among our strongest financial supporters.

In the meantime, the party set loose its terror against us. Whenever the Stalinists got wind of the fact that we were holding a meeting, they appeared on the scene in order to provoke us. They used to break into comrades' apartments and search them high and low—just like the cops. We were well aware that they were dead set on provoking incidents in order to brand us as informers. But we were very careful; we had no intentions of obliging them.

I was terrorized from all sides. The notorious Skolski arrived from Moscow and—as we learned—had been invested with extraordinary powers to fight Trotskyism, up to and including our physical extermination. Pinie from the wood workers and Avrom Zachariash made public declarations at workers' gatherings to the effect that they themselves were prepared to shoot me. It was clear which way the wind was blowing: they were planning to do away with me in the dead of night. It was best to play it safe, I thought, so my wife and I decided to disappear from public view for a time.

A sympathizer and personal friend of mine, the well-known artist Chaim Hanft, lived in Otwock. It was in his warm and cozy home that we took refuge. For days on end he told us interesting stories, among them particularly beautiful anecdotes about I.M. Weissenberg. I had a chance to settle my nerves there and it was a good thing too, for I felt that old nervous disorder from my prison days returning. Once again I was unable to fall asleep in the dark.

One evening the three of us went out for a short walk. All of a sudden we stopped in our tracks, turned around and silently went back to

---

[5] Lwów (trans.)

Chaim's apartment. Not one of us said a word that entire night, and just as silently we went to bed. Only the next morning did we confide to one another what had instinctively prompted us to head for home so suddenly: we had the feeling that somebody had been following us. It was clear that our days of peace and quiet in Otwock were over, that the Stalinists were after me step by step. Following the incident, my wife and I decided to return to Warsaw.

We had a standing invitation to stay at the apartment of my dear friend Rudi. His home was our illegal (and only) domicile. Even the caretaker was in on the secret, and whenever the cops lingered at the gate he ran upstairs to warn me. At the same time, the apartment served as headquarters for various Trotskyist activities.

Once I was back in Warsaw, I found that the party made no bones about putting someone on my tail. The man who followed me, Leybunyu, was a famous member of the party's military squad and a well-known lowlife. Curiously enough, he was always in the company of a certain thief who had tried to steal my suitcase upon my return from the Soviet Union. And how symbolic this constellation of men was. A thief and a bandit (who later went over to the fascists) had appeared on the scene to ensure that my communist credentials were kosher. Leybunyu once let me in on a secret: it never would have ruffled his feathers, he said, had I become an anarchist; he could have pardoned such a thing. But to think that the Bund wasn't fascistic was downright unforgivable. So unforgivable, in fact, that it meant a bullet in my head. Then he showed me the revolver in his pocket.

With no intention whatsoever of winning him over, I nevertheless tried to shed some light on the matter. Indeed, I suspected that he might make use of his revolver. But he stuck to his standpoint. As the story dragged on (I was pestered by this man until the very day I left for Paris), I asked myself more than once, "Why hasn't he shot me?" I really had no idea, but there was one possible explanation, I thought: criminal types are filled with respect for men who had spent long years behind bars and come out clean. And my past was known to one and all. Whatever the case may be, Leybunyu always let it go with empty threats.

My wife was working in a tailor shop on Dzielna Street at the time. She was in fact in quite poor health, her old prison malady having left behind strong traces. I used to go shopping for her each day at lunchtime and Rudi's wife, a good friend of mine, cooked up something for us to eat. Meanwhile, a group of porters, the backbone of the party's military squad, always kept an eye out for me. As I walked to my wife's shop, her lunch in hand, they would run along behind me, shouting at the top of their lungs: "There goes the king of the Trotskyists with his little lunchbox."

But the political events of the day made it possible for me to forget about my personal difficulties. No sooner had Manuilsky authored his notorious theses, which claimed that the struggle between Communism and fascism for hegemony over the German peasants had ended with a Communist victory, than it became clear that Hitler was making enormous strides toward power without encountering any resistance from the working class. Thaelmann's and Remmele's stance, that Hitler was the lesser evil for the proletariat, that his coming to power would clear the way for the victory of communism, had so befogged the minds of a part of the working masses that some few weeks before Hitler came to power the Communists led the strike of the Berlin transport workers in a united front with the fascists against the Social-Democratic trade unions. The Communist Party triumphantly proclaimed that it had won a victory, that it had won over masses of fascists. In their criminal state, however, they did not see that this was their last triumph, that this conquest of theirs had accelerated Hitler's takeover.

When Hitler came to power in January 1933 the Social Democrats declared that since he had become chancellor legally, everybody had better get used to it. The Communists, for their part, did not so much as lift a finger. To the contrary, at the plenum of the Executive Committee of the Comintern which took place that same winter, the Comintern declared that it was proud of the fact that the German Communist Party had pulled back without a fight, for now it could save its energies for the suitable moment. And this was following the Reichstag fire. By now it was really and truly clear that Hitler was gearing up his tanks to ride roughshod over the German working class. Under such conditions, the Comintern was proud to have yielded without a fight! I didn't know what was personally more agonizing: Hitler's seizure of power; the formal, legalistic attitude of the Social Democrats; or the "pride" of the German Communists.

Storm clouds were gathering and the darkness closed in on all sides. In all lands the reaction lifted its head. Truthfully, nobody foresaw the great catastrophe which befell the world six years later, but we all sensed that we stood before a catastrophe which was without precedent in hu-

man history. We had reverted to the epoch of barbarism, the workers
movement had been dealt a deadly blow.

It was in this period that Trotsky sounded the call for the necessity of
building a Fourth International. This was the spark for passionate discussions in our ranks. I was later to participate in the founding conference of the Fourth International and can honestly say that our discussion in Poland took place on a higher plain; it went deeper and lasted
some several weeks.

While comrade Shlomo was the main defender of Trotsky's theses
among us, Deutscher and I spoke most vociferously against them. Alexander vacillated between the two camps while the majority of our organization stood with Deutscher and me. Shlomo held that if it had been
necessary to found a new International following the defeat of the Paris
Commune; if the creation of the Third International had been on the order of the day following the collapse of the Second—then the bankruptcy of the Comintern, its shameful capitulation in the face of Hitler and
its incapacity to foresee the march of events, were grounds enough to
found a new, a Fourth International. The opponents of Trotsky's stance
grounded their arguments essentially as follows: negative factors are not
sufficient in order to create a new International. Following the dissolution of the First International Marx did not create a second one at once;
rather, he waited until the conditions for it were ripe—that is, fifteen
years. The Third International was not founded because the Second had
proven to be bankrupt; rather, it had drawn its lifeblood from the October Revolution. Moreover, a new International must have the firm prospect of being able to usher in a new epoch of the workers movement and
this new epoch must be bound up with its name. Side by side the Second
and Third Internationals, what prospects could the Fourth International
have? None—the idea would only be compromised.

Later, at the Congress of the Fourth International, I was able to convince myself how right we had been. There I broadened the scope of my
counterarguments still more and became a principled opponent of creating a special, Trotskyist International.

Meanwhile, my personal situation had taken a turn for the worse. I
was living at the home of my friend Rudi at the time. He had a small
workshop where he employed three workers and his brother—all of
them fiery Stalinists. They incessantly made life miserable for him and
every few days called a strike. Everyone at the trade union knew—and
openly said as much—that the working conditions in Rudi's shop were

better than elsewhere. But if he wanted peace and quiet, they said, he would have to show me the door. As long as I continued to stay with him, there would be strikes without end. I would have moved out at once had I known, but Rudi was too noble a man and too close a friend to let so much as a word about the matter fall from his lips. And it ruined him. His home was destroyed even before Hitler burned it to the ground. Only in Israel did I eventually learn from one of Rudi's sisters that the party had given the order to drive the family of my friend to the grave. Why? Because I had taken refuge under his roof from two types of enemies: the Pilsudskiites and the Stalinists.

With a heavy heart, I decided to take up my walking stick once again and go to France. Getting my hands on travel papers was impossible, and ever since returning to Poland I had been using the passport with which I had left the Soviet Union. It was still good on the street, but using it to register with the police was risky. Nor could there be any talk of applying for travel documents with it. I therefore had no other choice but to smuggle my way from country to country until I finally reached Paris. But things did not go so smoothly. On the contrary, I was forced to spend a four-month vacation in the police jail in Vienna.

My Arrest in Vienna

In the summer of 1933 I departed Warsaw with a heavy heart, for it was difficult separating from my wife, from my near and dear comrades and from the movement which I saw as the sole chance to save the October Revolution.

Along the way from Warsaw to Zakopane my mind was drawn to the one thought: will we live up to the demands of the day? Until now, everything had been clear, the path had lain distinctly before us. We had had the political and moral support of the Soviet Union as well as the guiding hand of the Comintern; we had carried out the tasks assigned to us. Then the situation changed radically and we lost everything. What's more, yesterday's enemies now shared the field with new, stronger and more dogged ones. Would we hold out in the face of temptation, would we pass the test? Would we have the political and moral strength to stand on our own two feet? I had never been an adherent of Kant's philosophy, but I really hoped that each of us might find in his heart the moral strength to shield himself from all the storms on the horizon.

In Zakopane I found my way to a peasant who ran the smuggling trade at the Czech border. We spent the whole day climbing over the mountains. In a hut along the way, we encountered a rather shifty sort of hermit who had posed for far too many photographs in the guise of a saint. He said that he never climbed down from his mountain refuge. But I wasn't so sure. On the other hand, when he mentioned that the peasants from the surrounding environs brought him everything he needed, I believed him at once. There was a coffin there which bore the inscription, "From dust you're born, to dust you'll go." Now I knew the hermit was lying, for he told me that he slept in it.

From there we descended the mountain until we arrived at the border. In order to avoid arousing suspicion I put on all the clothes I had brought with me and limited myself to a single suitcase. I managed to make my way from the Polish border through the heart of Czechoslovakia for several days without anybody so much as glancing at me askance. Once we had reached the border, I hopped on a boat and within the hour found myself in a Slovak village. It was the evening before Sabbath. I stayed in a Jewish inn for two nights and early Sunday morning took the train to Prague.

I had the address of a Trotskyist comrade in Prague whose name I have forgotten. The very evening I arrived I attended a public meeting, which left me with a bad taste in my mouth. The proletarian element was totally lacking; it was a gathering composed exclusively of intellectuals, virtually all of whom were Jewish. They spoke German and I got the impression that they were cut off from the life of the workers. Upon leaving, I was accompanied by a comrade who had recently come from Switzerland. Why he had left Switzerland to wander about in the countries of East Europe in such disquieting times was beyond me. As we walked through the streets of Prague, he told me in his rich Yiddish that he had dreamed of seeing the Prague synagogue his whole life long. The idea delighted me too and so off we went. Jews were praying there when we arrived. But without anything to cover our heads, we lingered outside. For the longest time we stared at the *shul* around which generations of Jews down through the centuries had woven so many fantastic legends.

The next morning I traveled on to Bratislava. Once again, I was to look for the address of a Jewish comrade, or better said, of a Jewish couple. A strange folk, these Jews. They had succeeded in sending their emissaries to all corners of the globe, where they became models of devotion and idealism. These two looked like a pair of saints, like two Essenes.[6] In their small town, they had set up an entire publishing house for Trotskyist literature and translated the works of the Trotskyist movement into the four languages of the region: German, Czech, Hungarian and Slovak. What's more, they distributed everything themselves. Day and night their apartment was a veritable melting pot of comrades who spoke these diverse tongues. I spent a single day with the two and could see that they lived in want. They recommended a Hungarian comrade to me, who brought me over the border to Austria.

At the crack of dawn I arrived in Vienna. It was the first time in my life that I saw such throngs of people going to church. It seemed as though each and every soul in Vienna got up early in the morning to go to church, just as the Jews in the *shtetls* woke up early to go to the synagogue and pray.

---

[6] ascetic Jewish sect, Second Century B.C. to the Second Century A.D. (trans.)

My contact address in Vienna was that of the secretary of the Trotsky-ist organization there. His name was Falder. Although he was a good man and a warm-hearted comrade, staying with him and his Jewish wife was out of the question; they simply had no room for me. I spent the first few days with a comrade who ran a business on Marszałkowska Street in Warsaw. His family lived in Vienna and he went home twice a year. Together with his wife and two sons, he was living a short distance from the Praterstern, a forested park where one could walk for hours and hours and forget that he was in one of Europe's largest capitals.

It was impossible to stay there for long, however, so Falder arranged overnight accommodations for me with various comrades. Before long, my hosts were forced to pay dearly for having put me up. But in the meantime, I had a long stay ahead of me in Vienna, for I had to wait around until a false Austrian passport could be prepared in my name. Then I could continue on my way to France legally.

A German woman with acquaintances in the secret police was supposed to undertake the procurement of my passport. But things turned out alto-gether differently: instead of setting me up with papers, she set me up.

This woman had arranged several meetings between me and her ac-quaintances and we came to an agreement about the price. It hardly pleased me that each time she and I met with them, they kept glancing over their shoulders. An old veteran, I knew what that meant. But there was no pulling out now. I was well aware that if they really were inform-ers, they would be right behind me every step I took; there would be no way out. But I wanted to give it a final try and therefore arranged to meet them once again. No passport this time, no more meetings.

I had arranged to meet my connection in a park, and the day of our meeting I brought along one of our Jewish comrades. No sooner did I approach the bench where my *macher* was sitting than I noticed two men wearing bowler hats standing off to the side. It was obvious at once that they were cops and that they were waiting for me. First things first, I told my comrade to disappear and then walked over to the *macher*. We spoke a few disjointed words to one another and it was clear that the one had read the other's mind. He knew that I had figured out who he was exactly as I knew that his buddies had come to arrest me. Hastily finish-ing up with him, I turned around to go. With the two cops close at my heels, I began to run. Inasmuch as I was a stranger in the area, I raced through a gateway. And with the cops in hot pursuit all the while, that's where they caught me.

Once they had dragged me to the police station, I learned that there were two charges against me: first, that I had sought to acquire a false passport under an assumed name; and second, that I was on my way to a conference of the Fourth International. Both accusations hit home. I really had intended to have a passport prepared for me under the name of Rosenberg and I really had been empowered by my comrades to represent the Polish group at the conference of the Fourth International, which was scheduled to convene in Paris in the near future.

They threw me in a one-man cell. I must have had something of a fever, for I felt unusually warm the moment I climbed into bed and pulled the covers over me. "What in the world do the Viennese do with such warm blankets?" I wondered.

Late that evening I was summoned to an interrogation. I have no idea where it took place, but the drive there was a long one. The examining magistrate was a Jew-turned-Christian, a scoundrel of a man who, as we later heard, continued to perform the duties of his office under Hitler. He demanded to know whom I had come to see in Vienna and whom I knew. I had been out of work in Warsaw for the longest time, I replied, and the Polish government had refused to issue me a passport to enable me to go to France. Once I reached Vienna, I continued, I had no idea where to turn. No names, no addresses. I had only been in town one day and spent the night at the apartment of a stranger. I had simply asked him to put me up for the night. "I can't remember where he lives either," I added, "but I might recognize the street if you drive me around." With that, the first interrogation came to an end and I was glad to go back to my one-man cell.

Meanwhile, another calamity struck. The money which the police had found on me was confiscated and I was unable to buy anything. According to regulations, prisoners received a single piece of bread the first day, two pieces the second and so on. The rationing leveled off on the sixth day, following which prisoners were forced to live with six little pieces of bread per day. I was miserably hungry at first and asked the jailer to give me some salt so that I could dunk my bread in it. With each bite, I drank down a gulp of water and thereby did my best to subdue my gnawing hunger.

The following evening I was once again brought before my interrogator. This time I came face to face with Falder's caretaker. No sooner had I entered the room than she confirmed that I was given to visiting Falder at his apartment. But I disputed her testimony so categorically that she began to vacillate and retract it. She had possibly sensed what it was all about and did not want to get involved. After she left, the examining magistrate flew into a rage. On the table beside him lay a knotted whip. He began waving it around above my head and screamed that although beatings were not permitted in Austria as yet, the time would come. "Then I'll know what to do with people like you," he shouted.

I went back to jail with the sole desire to rest up. The fact that I was suffering from headaches was a sure-fire sign that I had a fever, and it occurred to me that I might let something slip. The next day my fears were confirmed.

The third night of the interrogation the examining magistrate inquired about a certain Hungarian comrade with whom I had indeed spent the night. Replying that I knew no such man, the interrogator then had my suitcase brought in and asked me whether or not it belonged to me. I had left it at the Hungarian's apartment, it's true, and it was clear that the apartment had been searched. But I was certain that the Hungarian would not confess to anything. I stated that the suitcase did not belong to me. Then the examining magistrate asked me whether I waived my claim to it. I replied that it was not necessary for me to waive my claim to an item which did not belong to me in the first place. They then opened it and noticed that the number fifteen, the laundry tag which I had been assigned at the Lenin School, had been printed on my clothes. The examining magistrate ordered one of his agents to track the number down, but the latter was unable to crack the riddle.

The Hungarian comrade was then brought in and he admitted that I had been to his apartment. After he left, the examining magistrate asked me what I had to say now. I replied that I had met the Hungarian by chance and asked him to put me up for the night. He had refused, I continued, but had permitted me to store my suitcase at his home. I had not wanted to repay him good with bad, I added. As the interrogation dragged on I sensed that I was beginning to muddle myself up. Thus I interrupted the conversation, told the examining magistrate that I was not feeling well and requested that I be brought back to jail. A shrewd enough man to figure out what was up, he flew into a wild fury and threatened me with his clenched fist. He did not strike me, however, and ordered me returned to the police station.

The same story repeated itself several nights on end. But while I bluffed my way through one interrogation after another, the comrades who had been summoned to testify all stated that they knew me. It was positively abhorrent, but even worse was the fact that my comrade from Warsaw, the merchant from Marszałkowska Street who went home to Vienna for the holidays, admitted to knowing me as well. For several nights running the police tormented me as to whether I knew him, and for several nights running I denied everything. But the moment they called him in, he admitted to knowing me. In the end, they slapped him with a month in jail for having allowed me to sleep at his apartment illegally.

Only one comrade conducted himself as was fitting, namely the secretary of the Trotskyists. My interrogator tormented me for nights on end about Falder too, but I insisted that I had never heard of him. The examining magistrate then informed me that he was going to call Falder in and put me in a line-up. "So much as budge," he said, "and you'll wind up in a concentration camp." So I stood against the wall and Falder came in. We looked at one another as strangers and he walked out again. But the moment he turned to shut the door behind him, I nodded my head to signal him to play dumb. I was certain that he would notice my gesture and was right. The examining magistrate saw it as well and launched in with his threats once again. But he didn't lay a hand on me.

I went back to the police station somewhat consoled. One comrade, at least, had borne himself honorably. The thing was behind me now, I thought. But I still had one more hair-raising night to go.

The following evening I was summoned before the examining magistrate to sign the protocol. I refused. Even earlier I had sensed that I might foul myself up on account of my weakened condition and therefore decided not to answer any more questions. I told him that I had already said everything there was to say and that I had no strength left. Now it was time to sign and I said no. No signature, no more answers.

The central apparatus for Communist work in the Balkan countries was located in Vienna in those days and, by the same token, the central counterespionage bureaus for each of the Balkan governments as well. Following my refusal to sign the protocol, I found myself surrounded by a gang of cops from the Balkan states, who let out a string of threats against me. One of them screamed that in his homeland they would already have had me climbing the walls with electric shocks. Another, that back home I would have been crawling on all fours. And so on. I made no reply whatsoever and they sent me out into the corridor. Physically I was in such bad shape that I was afraid I might collapse on the floor. A high-ranking police officer, who happened to be walking by, took one look at me, called one of his agents over and asked him why in the world nobody had offered me a chair. "The man's about to fall over," he said. Pointing at me, the second cop replied, "He's the one who refuses to talk." With that, the two of them walked on. I must be known around here, I concluded. Back I went into the office and the examining magistrate informed me that I was wasting my time thinking about a trip to France. He was going to send a notice around to every capital in Europe, he said, making it impossible for me to set foot anywhere. And he stuck to his word.

With that, the examining magistrate gave the word to release me. But the story didn't end there. To the contrary, the worst was yet to come. Back at the police station another examining magistrate summoned me and said that he could not let me go as long as he did not know my real name. I told him what my real name was but he insisted that he had no way of knowing whether I was really Rosenfeld or Shtockfish. He would have to pursue the matter with the Polish police, and in the meantime I would have to stay in jail.

For a short period of time I shared my cell with a Viennese man who introduced himself to me as an organized worker, a Social Democrat. It turned out, however, that he had been sent up for raping a ten-year-old girl. A filthy man, he sat there the entire day picking away at himself. But it was precisely this chap who spoke without end about the purity of the German race, a fact, as he put it, which must be acknowledged by both friend and foe. When I asked him what he intended to do as a Social Democrat should Hitler come to Vienna, he replied that he would look neither right nor left, just straight ahead. Then nothing at all would happen. This filthy rapist believed in the superiority of the German race and had already decided to look "straight ahead." But a miracle happened: he was removed from my cell.

This was the period of the first assassination attempt on Dollfuss, the then chancellor of Austria. In choosing between the two fascist leaders, this dogged reactionary and fanatical Catholic had decided to go with Mussolini. Following the Hitlerites' attempt on Dollfuss' life, the brown shirts were arrested in droves and packed off to jail. There they filled the cells and lived high on the hog. Each day they received food from outside and carried on as if they owned the place. From dawn to dusk they sang fascist songs and chanted Hitlerite slogans. Until then I had grown accustomed to the fact that *we* were supposed to act like this in the prisons. Those fascist songs drove me positively *meshuge*. Each evening, I worked out an agenda of things to think about the following day so as to keep my mind off that infernal fascist merrymaking. And to some degree it worked.

Each morning, when I went out to the corridor to wash up, I found on my return that the walls of my cell had been smeared from top to bottom with the slogan "Heil Hitler." It was the first time in my life that I found myself in so hostile an environment.

Finally, a catastrophic correspondence from the Polish police arrived. It did not take up the question as to whether my name had been registered in Poland, but rather passed on the fact that whoever it was whose finger-prints had been transmitted to them went by the name of Bellman, had stood trial in Brest as a Communist and been sentenced to four years in prison. The cop investigating my case became terribly agitated, for not only was he unable to establish my real name; on top of it, I was a Communist with a prison record. If my name were really Shtockfish, he maintained, there was no doubt that the Polish police would have confirmed it.

I was curious to know what had become of my suitcase, the very same suitcase which I had denied was mine in the first days of my interrogation. I was not at all certain that I would be getting it back. Yet it contained everything I owned. I told the guard that I wished to change my clothes and asked him to bring me to the office. This went on for several days running in fact, but to no avail. Then I took it upon myself to resort to our old and tested tactic—the hunger strike. I climbed out of my dirty clothes, threw them in a heap beside the door and then added to the pile my bowl, spoon and water jug. Then I waited. When the guard opened the door to serve me my lunch, I had decided, I would throw the whole works into the corridor.

When the time finally came, the guard opened my door and told me to go change my clothes. I was in seventh heaven—my belongings had not been lost after all. I was down in the office in a flash and grabbed myself a couple of pairs of clean clothes. Once back in my cell, however, I discovered that instead of a shirt and a pair of long underwear, I had grabbed two pairs of long underwear. It meant going without a shirt for an entire week.

Once again, days and weeks went by and my sense of uneasiness grew. The examining magistrate threatened to throw me into a concentration camp along with the Hitlerites. Finally, a second reply from the Polish police, an even more dreadful communication, arrived. What they had to report this time was that the man with said fingerprints had been tried as a Communist in the year 1925 in Grodno and sentenced to four years. But not one word about my real name. The examining magistrate then declared that he would not be sending off any more inquiries to the Polish police. The whole thing would end badly for me, he threatened. I was certain that he meant it.

On the way back to my cell the jailer asked me whether or not the matter was finished. I told him about my difficult situation and he advised me to write my wife a letter asking her to send me the records held by the municipal government. I told him that I was unable to write German, but he nevertheless advised me to do my best. It only had to be good enough for somebody to read, he said. I took his advice, and when he read my letter he assured me that anybody would be able to understand it.

It wasn't long before I received a certificate from the Warsaw magistrate stating that I was indeed the man I claimed to be, that my name really was Shtockfish. The jailer who had given me the advice was no less overjoyed than I, and even the examining magistrate was glad to have found a way out of the maze. He informed me that inasmuch as there was no common border between Poland and Austria, he was unable to send me back to Poland. Instead, he commented, I was to be sent to Switzerland at my own expense. Moreover, I would have to go in the company of a policeman until reaching the border.

The next morning I was brought to a barbershop to have my three-month-old beard shaved off. It was in no respects inferior to the beard my father used to wear. Together with a policeman, I traveled to Feldkirch through a part of the country which looked like the Swiss Alps. Once we reached the border station, the detective told the watch that they were to write up a pass for me stating that I was an inhabitant of the area who was crossing the border in order to buy tobacco and coffee. If I were a man with an ounce of scruples, they said, I would destroy the slip as soon as I reached the other side. I found the form as well as the content of their remarks insulting and replied that they were hardly the right men to give me lessons in morality. No doubt, I added, they had mastered the art of illegal border crossings no less proficiently than the smugglers. As for their pass, I was most certainly going to rip it up. Quite simply, it could make life difficult for me in Switzerland.

In Zürich I went to the home of a comrade whose address I had committed to memory. She lay sick in bed, but the minute she saw me she burst out laughing. That same day, it seems, a police agent with a bundle of papers under his arm had been by to inquire about me. Then when I remembered that the Viennese police had found her address on me, I feared that I might encounter difficulties in residing in France.

I was therefore forced to stay in Zürich illegally and found a place to sleep at the home of a local Communist, a dear and lovely human being. Staying with her was like staying with my own family. A few days later I set off for Basel, and from there comrades brought me over the French border. After sixteen years, I was in Paris again. Sixteen years earlier, I had been on the run from the tsarist police. This time, it was Stalin's agents.

My Second Trip to Paris

I arrived in Paris in the first days of 1934, and this time I knew where to go. I had many comrades in Paris, among them such good and dear friends as Aronovich and Jechiel Neiman. Neiman did a great deal for me; he supported me and taught me a new skill—ironing in a garment shop. Some good it did me though, for the workers in the industry, who were under Stalinist leadership, refused to let me anywhere near the work. My material situation would have been difficult had it not been for my two comrades.

The political situation in France was extremely shaky and great events were on the horizon. On 6 February 1934 the fascist students took to the streets against the democratic-parliamentary regime, gathered at the Place de la Concorde and intended to storm the Palais Bourbon, the seat of the National Assembly. They were supported by the police prefect Chiappe. The adventure lasted an entire night and sparked a crisis which brought Laval to power.

The following day the Communist Party carried out a counteraction, albeit a weak one. Only on 12 February did Doriot arrive with his workers from St. Denis. They were the masters of the streets all the way from Gare de l'Est to Barbès and fought it out with the cops the whole night through. Eight days later a giant demonstration of both workers parties, together with the trade unions, took place. The fascists were repelled and smashed. At the same time, the legend was born that the People's Front was a consequence of these events.

This joint demonstration proved how abysmally criminal the Stalinist theory of social fascism had been, a theory which prevented the German proletariat from closing ranks in the struggle against Hitler fascism. I am convinced that had both workers parties in Germany converged in the united front, Hitler would never have come to power and mankind would have been spared the terrible calamity which was bound up with the Hitler period. In developing his thoughts about the necessity of the united front and the unity of the trade unions, Doriot apparently felt the same way I did. We know, of course, how shameful a turncoat Doriot ended up being and just how far he went. He betrayed his country, he betrayed socialism and he covered himself with eternal ignominy when he finally turned up as a Hitlerite officer.

But this did not come about all at once. Doriot certainly had an adventurist streak in his character which drove him down this path. Indeed, it was also the adventurer in him which thrust him to the highest rungs of the Stalinist bureaucracy. But if the man had his adventurist side, he also supported a policy at the time which was de facto in the interests of the proletariat. Instead of going the way of the united front the party opened up a campaign against him. "Doriot to Moscow!" was the slogan at every Communist gathering. But Doriot knew full well what awaited him in Moscow and therefóre refused to go. To the Stalinists this was the greatest of all crimes, and their incitement against him took on the most shameful forms imaginable. He often complained to comrades that he felt more and more as if he were suffocating, as if he were unable to breathe. The adventurer in him won the upper hand and in the end he became a fascist. So it was that the criminal policies of the Communist Party of France bred fascist elements in its own ranks.

As I have already mentioned, the events of February 1934 brought Laval to power. This may seem paradoxical, but it is a fact. In those days, of course, Laval was not yet an agent of Hitler's, as in 1941; rather, he was a typical political climber—that is, a careerist and speculator who used his office to get rich. Moreover, he was in his own way a patriot. Once in power, he took pains to strike up a bargain with Mussolini. For his part, Mussolini, a detractor of Hitler's race theory at the time, pointed out that the Italians had already had their Caesars in the days when the forefathers of the Germans were still wildly wandering the forests. A conflict had broken out between Hitler and Mussolini over the question of Austria. Mussolini wanted Austria under Italian influence and threatened Hitler with war should the latter attempt to violate Austria's independence. Dollfuss, the then Austrian chancellor, was so convinced that Mussolini would come to his aid that he bid the latter before his death to care for his children. The agreement between Laval and Mussolini was really directed against Hitler.

Laval's second agreement, this one of a military nature, was with Stalin. When Stalin demanded that Laval strengthen the French army and Laval asked him what ought to be done with the French Communists, the army's opponents, Stalin replied in his typical manner: "Hang them." It was characteristic of Stalin that he did not rush to inform the French Communists about the change. When Laval delivered a report to the

National Assembly in which he demanded that the army be strengthened, the Stalinists resisted vehemently. But Laval then informed them
of Stalin's order. The following day the Stalinists posted placards all
over France with the words, "Stalin is right." Overnight, they had become convinced that it was right to hail the very institution which they
had struggled against for almost two decades. Typically, they plastered
up their new posters in praise of the French army without bothering to
remove the old ones, which stamped it as imperialist. Both posters bu-
colically appeared side by side as a symbol of Stalin's theory of the
peaceful coexistence between two different social systems.

As we can see, it was not the joint demonstration of both workers
parties in the February days which provided the impulse for the People's
Front in the July days of 1936, but rather the Stalin-Laval Pact. While
the Stalinists still firmly continued to tout their theory of social fascism
two years after the united-front demonstration had taken place, they at
the same time supported Laval's militaristic policy. They were already paving the way in those days for the Hitler-Stalin Pact against the
democratic peoples, but unfortunately nobody comprehended this. And
thus it was possible for Stalin to play his cunning game on two fronts:
on the People's Front and on the front with Hitler.

In the summer of 1934 I learned from Lyova Sedov[7] that Trotsky
wanted to meet with me in order to discuss a problem which had generated differences of opinion between himself and the Polish comrades.
The dispute revolved around the question of characterizing the Pilsudski
regime in Poland. Our meeting took place in a photo studio in Versailles. After being led to the first floor and waiting a short while, I
looked out the window and saw Trotsky and two other comrades approaching. Whereas I knew one of them—he was the well-known attorney Rosenblat,[8] today a great friend of Israel—the other was unknown
to me.

My meeting with Trotsky made the deepest impression on me. Imagine how I felt the night before coming together with one of the greatest
Marxist revolutionaries of our time, the legendary War Commissar from
the days of the Civil War in Russia. One sensed all of that at first glance.
But his face told another story as well—that of his whole tragic situa-

---

[7] Leon Sedov, Trotsky's elder son (trans.)
[8] Hersh Mendel obviously means to say Gérard Rosenthal. (GE)

tion. Hunted and pursued by the entire world, he was accompanied everywhere he went by secret agents from a series of countries, who were nevertheless unable—or perhaps unwilling—to protect him from the Stalinist murder gangs. Perhaps he had already had a foreboding of the tragic end which awaited him at the hands of men who were both traitors and murderers. Although his frightful situation had not broken him, it had left its stamp on his appearance and demeanor.

My heart pounding, I awaited our talk. It turned out, however, that we conversed with one another like two near and dear comrades; the one attempted to convince the other. While Trotsky was of the opinion that the Pilsudski regime possessed all of the elements of the fascist form of state, I argued that it was a typical Bonapartist regime. Whereas I pointed out that Pilsudski's regime more resembled Bismarck's than Hitler's, Trotsky countered that Pilsudski and Hitler both propped themselves up on the same classes in society. We talked for two hours and, as often happens, both of us consolidated our own opinions in the course of the discussion. Before we parted company, Trotsky stated that he would examine the matter once again. Then as I stood up to leave, he suddenly asked me whether I had heard any news about the Jewish workers movement in Palestine. Unprepared for such a question, I did not know what to say. He then asked me to gather the appropriate materials especially for him.

I transmitted Trotsky's request at once to the comrades in Poland and quickly forgot about the matter. From the history of the international movement I knew of a whole series of Jewish revolutionaries who occasionally remembered that they belonged to the Jewish people, but who always put it out of their minds again before long. I thought that Trotsky would be the same. But he was not the sort of man who forgot about things which he considered important. And not only did he not forget about the question at hand; as was his wont, he drew the necessary conclusions as well. Although not yet sufficiently consistent, the balance sheet which he drew at the beginning of the Second World War was an extremely radical one—namely, that the Jews were justified in having their own country. What's more, I discovered that his conversation with me in the year 1934 had not been the first time that he reflected about the Jewish question. As early as 1929, when the Jewish Trotskyists in Paris brought out the first number of their journal, Trotsky sent them a letter in which he recommended that they establish contact with the Jewish workers movement in Palestine.

One must bear in mind that the Stalinists defended the Arab pogroms which occurred in Palestine at that time, and insisted that they were revolutionary freedom struggles. Jewish Communists from Palestine were arrested in Moscow on the grounds that Palestine was an Arab country. Jews, according to the Stalinists, had no place there; only Arabs were permitted to lead the movement. It was precisely in this period that Trotsky began to take an interest in the workers movement in Israel—a daring step which was fully in accordance with his character.

When the Trotskyist movement went into decline in later years, I reflected at great length about Trotsky. I saw not only his strong sides, but his weak sides as well. Even Trotsky, it turned out, was no more than a man, a man with human weaknesses.

His analysis of the social forces and their roll in the Russian Revolution proved correct. As early as the year 1905 he was the first—and for a certain period of time the only—person who pointed to the workers councils as a small kernel of the working class in power. While Marx and Lenin argued that the workers must first destroy the old state power in order then to construct a new one in the service of their own class interests, Trotsky pointed out that in the process of the struggle itself and in counterposition to the old state, the workers will construct the new state power. With his revolutionary perspicacity, Trotsky had understood that this was the role which the workers councils would play. When the Stalinists invented the infamous "theory" of social fascism, Trotsky demonstrated how adventuristic it was. He ridiculed as absurd the notion that the Social Democrats were working for their own downfall. Fascism meant the total liquidation of every class movement of the proletariat. While the Stalinists cooked up their damnable theory that Hitler's rule would bring nearer the victory of socialism, Trotsky explained that Hitler's victory would inaugurate an epoch of the renewed struggle for democracy. In comparison to fascism, he argued, democracy will seem like paradise to the workers. And this was confirmed to the letter. Today, even the Stalinists are forced to talk of democracy (with fraudulent intent of course) when seeking to strengthen their influence. During both the uphill as well as the downhill phases of the revolutionary stream, Trotsky's analyses proved to be filled with genius.

But Trotsky also had his weak sides. Even though he knew perfectly well that the Comintern had become a plaything in the hands of the Stalinists, he was unwilling to break with it. And even after the Comintern branded him as a fascist, he continued to make advances toward it, despite the fact that he knew from the outset that it would condemn him. With the intensification of Stalin's fight against the Bukharin faction, Trotsky argued that Stalin must be backed against Bukharin because the former was a "centrist" while the latter was a rightest. He did not see that Stalinism was barbarism plain and simple, that it meant the annihilation of everything human. Even though Trotsky condemned the Red Army's invasion of little Finland, he nevertheless maintained that the Red Army must be supported. When Stalin invaded Poland together with Hitler, Trotsky compared Stalin to a carrion-eating jackal. Yet he believed that the Red Army must be supported. These were errors which could only be explained psychologically. It was difficult for Trotsky to come out against an army which he himself had created and which he believed would be the very last army in the history of mankind.

On the organizational plain, Trotsky committed even greater errors. For the longest time he considered the Left Opposition to be a faction of the Comintern. Had Trotsky gathered together all the elements who were neither in agreement with the Comintern nor with the Second International, he might have been able to create the cadres for a new movement. He wanted to create a new movement with a new International which was to be composed solely of Trotskyists, however, and therefore met with failure. Creating a new International solely by welding together small groups was indeed a shot in the dark.

At the beginning of 1935 the First Conference of the Fourth International took place in the vicinity of Paris at the apartment of Rosmer, the former syndicalist who later joined up with Trotsky.[9] Represented there were delegations from France, Germany, Poland, Holland and, I believe, from Belgium and England. Two delegates were in attendance from the United States, Cannon and Shachtman. Trotsky was supposed to be present to give the political report, but for reasons unknown to me he did not appear. His report was read by a member of the French delegation, Naville. In its political conclusions the report zeroed in on the necessity of creating a Fourth International. If I had already come out against founding a Fourth International while I was still in Poland, this conference only reinforced me in my beliefs. All of the groups associated with the Trotskyist movement, with the exception of the Dutch or-

---

[9]   Hersh Mendel is in error here. The First Conference of the Fourth International convened in the village of Périgny on 3 September 1938, not at the beginning of 1935. The conference coincided with Hersh Mendel's third stay in Paris. (trans.)

ganization, were small circles, none of which had representative spokesmen who were known within the international workers movement. In the course of the discussion I further developed the theses against the founding of a new International which I had put forward in Poland, and found myself in a minority of one. The other comrade from Poland, comrade Stephen (who lives in Canada today), abstained. He was elected to the Secretariat of the Fourth International while I was taken on as a member of the Executive Committee. Teasing me as the conference drew to a close, Shachtman remarked that I was all alone.

Even though I had been elected to the Executive, I was never once called to attend a meeting. There are two conceivable reasons for this: first, I broke with Trotsky for a time; and second, it is possible that the Executive in general never convened, for it had nothing to do.

In the summer of 1935 Trotsky was expelled from France. He was accompanied on the train by some twenty armed comrades. Naville and Gérard drove ahead to the port to make sure that the coast was clear and in fact ran into a Stalinist leader from Paris there, whom they held personally responsible in case anything should happen.

A short time after the conference of the Fourth International, Trotsky began to propagate the view that the Trotskyist groups ought to enter the Socialist Parties as special factions. This confirmed how right I had been in opposing the creation of the Fourth International. For how was a Fourth International to come into existence if we were members of the Social Democratic parties? It was my opinion that we ought to enter the London International, or the 2¾ International as it was dubbed. It was against this background that strong frictions erupted between Lyova and me, which led to a definitive break. For me, it was a particularly painful parting, for Lyova Sedov was a warm, good comrade and a flaming revolutionary. But when I told him that I was going to break off all relations with the movement, he said that he and his father were convinced that I would be back before long. And he was not mistaken.

After my break with Trotsky, a German comrade by the name of Bauer and I looked into establishing contact with the London International. Before long the opportune moment arrived. This was to be my first, as well as my last, encounter with the organization.

In the late winter of 1935 a conference of the London International convened in Paris, to which I was invited as a guest. In contrast to the conference of the Fourth International, the gathering of the London International was made up of a whole series of parties, including the

English Independent Labour Party, the German Independent Party and the Dutch party which had also joined the Fourth International. Kruk represented the Polish Independents, Barbusse the Doriot group. In attendance were also delegations from Sweden and from the Spanish POUM.[10]

Despite the fact that a number of small parties were represented there, the ideological and political level of the conference was utterly wretched. It would be more correct to say that in general the conference was altogether void of ideas. The reports and the discussion were very superficial. But above all, the ship had no rudder. While the English delegation had one foot in the Comintern, the Swedes and the Doriot group had already turned their backs on it. The Dutch were officially Trotskyist, the POUM semi-Trotskyist. The Germans, the movement's self-proclaimed ideologues, avoided posing questions of principle in order to prevent the conference from coming apart at the seams.

The reports and discussion were wishy-washy and the resolutions, which were the product of so many counterposed tendencies, were utterly and completely bland. One could sense that nobody took them seriously, that nobody would breathe life into them and carry them out. I saw that Trotsky had been right when he said that nothing would come of it. Kruk had brought along with him a letter by the left Bundist Chmurner, in which the latter demanded a more consistent attitude toward principles and more activity. At the conference itself, Kruk had nothing but trouble in pressing these demands, for everybody was terrified of a living, breathing movement.

Even though the Dutch had sent Trotsky a report about the conference, Lyova Sedov informed me that Trotsky wanted a report from me as well and requested that for his benefit I write one up. Trotsky praised my report very highly in his letter to the Polish comrade Viktor (that was my pseudonym). But he also utilized his letter to combat the theses on which my report was based. This time he was right.[11]

At this point I decided to join the Bund. But inasmuch as I preferred taking this step in Poland, I headed back. It was the beginning of 1936.

[10] Hersh Mendel is probably referring here to the German Sozialistische Arbeiterpartei (SAP—Socialist Workers Party). The other organizations referred to are the Revolutionary Socialist Party of Holland, the Independent Labor Party of Poland, the Socialist Party of Sweden and the Spanish Partida Obrero de Unificación Marxista (POUM—Workers Party of Marxist Unification). (trans.)

[11] Hersh Mendel's report and Trotsky's reply to it were printed in *International Information Bulletin* Number 1, 1935 of the Workers Party of the United States. Trotsky's letter to comrade V., "Centrist Combinations and Marxist Tactics" (28 February 1935) appears in *Writings of Leon Trotsky (1934-35)*, Pathfinder Press, New York. See Appendix 2. (trans.)

Once Again in Warsaw

When I arrived in Warsaw on 1 January 1936, I had the firm intention of staying put this time. The moment had come, I thought, to settle down. Besides, I was bored to tears of one emigration after another. But how does it go? Man proposes, god disposes. Hardly had I returned than I was forced to take up my walking stick once again and leave Poland—this time forever.

As soon as I got back I went straight to Duracz for consultation. I was afraid of blowing my cover; after all, I was still a "debtor," for I still faced two years and eight months behind bars. I asked Duracz whether it would be better to register with the police under my own or an assumed name. Duracz the attorney advised me to register legally. After so long a time, he reasoned, my case had most certainly been relegated to the archives. If nothing extraordinary should happen, the authorities would leave me in peace. I followed his advice.

It was good to be home. Upon seeing my comrades again I was able to ascertain that they were suffering from a certain fatigue. But all of them to a man were still attached and devoted to the movement. Thanks to Deutscher's generosity I was able to rent an apartment on Gesia Street and register legally. Our material situation was difficult but my wife and I were happy nonetheless. After all, we finally had a roof over our heads. For the first time in my life I had my own apartment and for the first time since I had become a revolutionary I was registered under my real name—if only for a short time.

I turned to the Central Committee of the Bund with the request that they take me in as a member. All of my comrades were already in the Bund at the time, aside from a few intellectuals who had joined the PPS instead. The Bund sent my old friend Bernard, the very same comrade Bernard, that is, who had recruited me to the party in the early days, to talk to me. He explained that the Bund was somewhat hesitant to take me in as a member, for not too long before they had allowed a comrade from the Communist Party to join who about-faced and went back to the CP a short time later. I burst out laughing just at the thought of it. What a peculiar notion it was to think that I might become a Stalinist again. I assured Bernard that he could put his mind entirely to rest. Anything in life was possible, I said, but that I might become a Stalinist was out of the question.

After I joined the Bund, Emanuel Nowogrudski looked me up and laid out the Bund's proposal that I become secretary of a district. He told me I could choose any district outside of Warsaw. The party's attitude toward me was deeply stirring, but I nevertheless turned the offer down. I had worked in other parties for twenty years, I explained. In order to run a district, it was not sufficient to be ideologically familiar with the movement; it was necessary for one to grow into it intimately. For my part, I did not feel up to the task as yet. I emphasized that this would be possible after I had actively worked in the party for some time.

But when I threw out a proposal of my own, that I become a porter, that is, Emanuel practically hit the ceiling. It was my heart's desire to be able to arrange things in such a way that I could earn a living and still have time for independent community work. Since I knew that porters worked half days and earned good money besides, I therefore asked Emanuel to find me such a job. He smiled and said that the Bund could not compromise itself. It was not my opinion that working as a porter would compromise anyone, but I was unable to convince him.

I had to find work at any price because I simply had nothing to live on. Thus I took on a job as a shoemaker. Shoemaking was seasonal work. Eleven hours per day was the norm at peak season and the wages were paltry. It was exactly what I had not been looking for.

In the summer of 1936 the Fifth Plenum of the Central Committee of the Communist Party of Poland took place. I only learned of it when the resolutions made their way to the public printed on thin sheets of paper. Reading them made me shudder.

Before discussing these resolutions, I would like to say a few words about the kind of money it took to convene such a plenum. In those days the members of the Central Committee resided in various countries. While Berlin had been the seat of the Central Committee in the days before Hitler came to power, its members were scattered in Czechoslovakia, Austria, France and the Soviet Union following January 1933. To gather them together illegally in one place required enormous sums of money, not to mention the fact that the party was not exactly modest in its expenditures. Printing illegal literature and transporting it across the border alone consumed hoards of money. And all that just to pass rubbish resolutions.

Those resolutions which stated that Poland was at the threshold of the social revolution also contained a characterization of the various parties which existed in Poland. It read like this: the Bund—Bundist fascism; Poale Zion—Poale-Zionist fascism; the People's Party—people's fascism; Zionism—Zionist fascism. The Polish parties were treated in the selfsame manner. How unscrupulous one had to be to write such things! But now we come to the heart of the matter, for a special resolution was devoted to the Trotskyists. The Trotskyists, we hear, were traitors to the Polish people because they had made a pact with Hitler to deliver Poland into the hands of the Nazis. But this was small change for them, it continued; they also had their sights on Czechoslovakia. And inasmuch as the Polish Trotskyists were for the worldwide victory of fascism, they had also concluded an agreement with the Japanese mikado to deliver up China to Japan. Imagine this: the leaders of the Polish Trotskyists, a group of Jews, were supposed to have closed a series of deals, whereby Poland and Czechoslovakia were to go to Hitler and China to the mikado! How could the darkest fantasies of the world's most diabolical criminologist have equaled the likes of this? Moreover, the resolution also referred to comrades by name. And with the unmistakable intention of delivering them into the hands of the Polish secret police, it also listed their home and work addresses. At bottom these resolutions amounted to nothing more than banditry, provocation and wantonness.

Some time later I gave a talk at the leather workers union on the Spanish Civil War. Hardly had I stepped to the podium when the cry rang out, "Agent of Japanese imperialism!" The odd thing about this meeting was that it remained relatively quiet in the hall when I said that Enemy No. Two after the fascists were the Stalinists, for the Stalinists were wiping out the best fighters of the Spanish proletariat, were turning Spain into a slaughter house and were luring revolutionaries there from all over the world in order to murder them. "You've sold Poland, Czechoslovakia and China down the river," was the Stalinists' sole response. I was naive enough to get myself all worked up over this and thought that Stalinist wantonness had already hit bottom. But it turned out that I had underestimated the matter.

Just after the outbreak of the Spanish Civil War the Stalinists, upon reading an article of mine in the *Arbeter-Vort*,[12] wrote that I was a rene-

---

[12] *Workers Word* (trans.)

gade, a Trotskyist bandit, a warmonger, an anti-Soviet baby eater, a fascist and a cosmopolitan. When I met with the late poet Katsherginsky a few days later, he quipped that I was a lucky man after all, for the Stalinists had already drained their reservoir; they had already maligned me with every conceivable epithet in the book. But he was wrong too. A few weeks later I saw an article in the Warsaw *Folks-Shtimme*[13] which explicitly stated that I was responsible for the murder of Maxim Gorky.

Meanwhile, the famous Moscow Trials had begun. While a great deal has been written on this subject, all too little has been said about the connection between the Moscow Trials and the People's Front. The question, why did Stalin stage these trials precisely at the time of the People's Front, has almost never been posed. But this connection, better than anything else, throws significant light on Stalin's character. He knew that it was precisely in this period that nobody was about to stand in his way, that nobody was about to imperil the "brotherhood" of the People's Front over something so trifling as the Moscow Trials. It was not clear to me then nor is it clear to me today, however, whether Stalin took advantage of the People's Front in order to commit his infamous murders or whether it was his murderous aims which specially compelled him to go with the People's Front.

One must admit that Stalin was a good psychologist. He organized and carried out the carnage splendidly. Even such a man as Leon Blum had no more to say about the trials than this, that every revolution devours its children. Different people may have differences of opinion about Leon Blum, but a banal man he wasn't. Yet in the face of so great a tragedy as the Moscow Trials, he did nothing more than utter a banal platitude. One can be certain, however, that while he said one thing, he was thinking another. He was chained hand and foot by the People's Front. It is important to recognize that those Socialists who were not enraptured by the policy of the People's-Front movement reacted more sharply. I am certain that it was their attitude toward the People's Front which cost Ehrlich and Alter their lives. This, in any case, was one of the reasons why Stalin killed them.

It was during this period that our comrade Shlomo wrote an article about the trials for the Bundist *Folkstsaytung*. Despite the resistance of the Stalinist elements on the editorial board to having it printed, Viktor

---

[13] *People's Voice* (trans.)

Alter, who just happened to be walking by when the dispute erupted, insisted that it was the moral duty of every honest socialist at a time like that to give the Trotskyists the floor. In the end, the article appeared.

We published a pamphlet on the Moscow Trials, an outstanding work which Deutscher wrote.

It was in 1937 that the extermination of the leaders of the Polish Communist Party began. Whereas a series of murders, which started with the trial against Sochacki, had indeed racked the party in earlier years, in 1937 it became clear that the total annihilation of every leader of each of the factions was at hand. Comprehending Stalin's move was easier said than done. We knew, of course, that the axe was poised over the heads of many of the leaders of other illegal parties as well, but such unrestrained fury as befell the Communist Party of Poland had been reserved for the Polish leaders alone. It was difficult to grasp.

The matter became even more embroiled when Stalin dissolved the Polish Communist Party *in toto*. Better than anyone else, he knew that the accusation of espionage against the Polish Communists—against all of them without exception—was a diabolical fabrication. What, after all, was the reason for this? Two years later the matter was clear. When Stalin sealed his agreement with Hitler to partition Poland anew, it was plain as day that every party—even a party which served Stalin—was superfluous. Not one single organization, Stalinist or otherwise, would have been able to assume responsibility for such a crime. The total extirpation of the Polish Communist leadership and, finally, the liquidation of the Communist Party of Poland itself had been planned in advance. Zig and zag as he may, Stalin continually strove in those years to forge a bond with Hitler. And he understood that such a bond would have to be consummated at the expense of Poland.

It was precisely at this time that the Polish Trotskyists decided to leave the Bund. Perhaps their hopes that better conditions had been created for winning over the Communist masses in the wake of the dissolution of the Communist Party played a great role here; perhaps they believed that their work would be facilitated by establishing an independent organization. I, in any case, was not in favor of leaving the Bund. I never believed that the Trotskyists could create their own organization. On the contrary, I was certain that the construction of our own special wing in another party would broaden our horizons immensely. The majority, however, had decided differently. As for me, the problem was finally solved in an entirely unforeseen manner.

At the beginning of 1938 the Polish secret police finally remembered me and intended to collect payment on my outstanding debts: 32 months in prison. The day the summons arrived from Pogochelski, the chief of the Polish secret police, I naturally knew what it was all about and left my apartment at once. My wife went in place of me. Pogochelski re-received her quite kindly, schmoozed with her about philosophical questions (he fancied himself a psycho-philosopher) and finally got down to brass tacks. Showing her a mountain of official documents and numerous photographs, he told her that he wanted to get to know me personally. I had so many names, he maintained, that he had never been able to establish which was my real one. So he wanted to schmooze with me too. When my wife asked him for one of the photographs, he replied that it didn't pay to save them. After all, I had often come out looking like a bandit. He finished up by saying that I would simply have to come down to headquarters on my own. If I should fail to do so, he threatened, he would arrest my wife instead.

I was left with no other choice but to hit the road again. It goes without saying that I had no money to make the trip, not to mention the fact that it cost an arm and a leg to have false papers prepared. Once again, Deutscher helped me out; and another comrade of mine, who lives in Israel today, gave me his last twenty dollars. Emanuel Nowogrudski, the secretary of the Central Committee of the Bund, also contributed a certain sum. Thus I scraped together enough money for the trip.

Before my departure the Trotskyist group asked me to carry out two assignments: first, that I serve as intermediary between the Trotskyist Center in Paris and the comrades in Poland; and second, that I notify Alexander, who was about to join the Bund in Paris, not to do so. I promised to do what they asked but informed them at the same time that for my part I was not going to resign from the Bund upon arriving in Paris.

My Third Stay in Paris

When I reached Paris in August 1938, Lyova Sedov already knew about my arrival.[14] We were close friends, after all, and it was perfectly obvious that I would go to see him first. Comrades told me that he was ill, however, and informed me that I would be able to visit him in the hospital the next day around noontime. Yet when I appeared at the hospital the next afternoon, I learned that he had died during the night. His death was a riddle, for he was in good health and was about to be released. Trotsky was certain that Stalinist agents had murdered him. I was advised not to attend the funeral because doing so could well harm my chances of being granted asylum. It was morally tormenting, but I followed comrades' advice and stayed away.

I met with Alexander and informed him of the decision which the Polish Trotskyists had reached. At the same time, I told him that I considered it wrong and that I had the intention of staying in the Bund. For his part, Alexander said that he was still on his way into the Bund and that he would be joining as an unaffiliated individual, not as a Trotskyist. It was precisely at this time, however, that a substantial group of people resigned from the French Communist Party under the leadership of Shrager and Jechiel Neiman, and together with them Alexander joined the Bund.

Meanwhile, the sad September days, the Munich days, arrived. Two things were clear to me. First, I knew that the European democracies would pay a high price for their criminal conduct in the Spanish Civil War. It was thanks to Franco's victory that Hitler and Mussolini forged their machine-gun brotherhood and that Hitler acquired a free hand to go over to the attack on all fronts. In his Munich Pact with Hitler, Chamberlain as well continued to pursue the policy of the European democracies from the period of the Spanish Civil War: that is, acquiescing to the fascist victory and oppressing the peoples of Europe. And only to avoid an armed clash with Hitler. Hitler took advantage of this situation

---

[14] This date is obviously incorrect, for Lyova Sedov died on 16 February 1938. (trans.)

and, shortly after Franco's victory, proceeded to seize one country after another. The defeat of the Spanish people was the direct prelude to the Second World War.

Second, in France during the Munich days a partial mobilization took place in which certain military units were dispatched to the German border. But the mood of the land was particularly sad—yes, even beaten and resigned. I recalled what France had been like during the First World War and asked myself more than once, what had happened? It was clear, after all, that Hitler was a greater foe of France than Wilhelm II had been. Why then this defeatist mood? The roots of the matter lay in the attitude of the reactionary layers, those sections of society which saw in Hitler a protective rampart against the workers movement. In the fight against Wilhelm the question had been a simpler one; in those days it had been a struggle for national hegemony. The struggle against Hitler, on the other hand, did not merely pose the question of national interests, but rather social interests as well. Hitler's victory would mean the destruction of the workers movement. And this was the determining factor.

Notwithstanding Chamberlain's assurances that he had brought peace to the world for many generations to come, it was clear to all that he had led the world's peoples to the brink of catastrophe, that he had paved the road which Hitler would speedily use to make himself master over Europe. Everybody sensed the approaching catastrophe but there was no force in sight with the courage to go out and check it. It seemed as though all the efforts to develop mankind in the direction of progress and freedom had been lost, as though 100 years of the workers movement had been destroyed. What's more, Chamberlain accomplished exactly what he did not want in respect to the Soviet Union. The Munich Pact quite rightly terrified Stalin and facilitated him in his efforts to seek a rapprochement with Hitler. The latter cleverly exploited the situation and placed the Soviet Union in the service of his gameplan.

Although all of this is comprehensible today, the matter was by no means so clear at the time. The reactionary layers were overjoyed at the Munich Pact and the Stalinists were—or pretended to be—enthusiastic about the Hitler-Stalin Pact. Both were great calamities for mankind. There were Socialist Parties and even liberal groups, it's true, which were against both pacts, but all of them were gripped by a peculiar kind of powerlessness. Once the Munich Pact came to naught, there was not a soul alive who was capable of standing up to the Hitler-Stalin Pact.

For me, the events of the day were truly tragic. The thirty odd years which I had devoted to the struggle for socialism were lost. In the name of that struggle I had given everything of which a man is capable. I had never endeavored to go to the top. If, from time to time, I had climbed to the highest echelons of the movement, it was only because particular historical events had forced me to step outside the ranks. There had never been any effort on my part to do so and it often took place against my will. For me, the struggle for socialism was everything. I had never given a moment's thought to anything else. And now I was witness to a frightful storm which would destroy everything. An entire life full of struggle and hope was lost. This was my tragedy—a personal and social tragedy in one. My heart was heavy and everything around me was enveloped in darkness.

Two months before the outbreak of the Second World War I was destined to experience yet another shocking event.[15] I have already mentioned above that the Polish Trotskyists had requested that I serve as intermediary between themselves and the Trotskyist Center in Paris. In this capacity I used to meet with the secretary of the Fourth International, a comrade from Germany known as Adolf, several times a week. On one occasion another man came along as well. It never occurred to me to ask Adolf how he knew him, but now the latter accompanied us wherever we went. He had introduced himself as the wealthy son of a Jewish banker from Kovno[16] who had come to Paris in order to study at the Sorbonne. A man of means, he insisted each time on picking up the tab for the three of us. And what a relief it was for both Adolf and me—we quite frequently had no money. The new "comrade" repeatedly suggested that we all spend the day together somewhere, at his cost of course. And although we did not take him up on his offer for the longest time, in the end we assented. We made plans to take off one Sunday in July and go to Bois de Boulogne.

I can no longer remember why I did not show up. Adolf and the other man went by themselves. The following day news arrived that the new "comrade" had disappeared and that Adolf had been found in the Seine. His head and hands had been hacked off. Trotsky later explained that his murderers had cut off his hands because even decapitated it would have still been possible to identify him by his distinctively long

---

[15] This date is incorrect. Rudolf Klement, or "Adolf," mysteriously vanished on 13 July 1938, not 1939, and his mutilated corpse was found in the Seine approximately two weeks later. (trans.)

[16] Kaunas (trans.)

fingers. The French comrades advised me to disappear temporarily, at which time I went to stay with the comrade Genia Kenig in L'Hay les Roses, a small village not far from Paris. After staying with her for a month, they informed me that I could return to Paris.

The story about Adolf was a sensation in the French press, for it was clear to all and sundry that the murder had been the work of the GPU. But it quieted down after a few days; France had quite other cares at the time. The French military mission in Moscow was in the process of negotiating the terms of a military pact with the Soviet Union and the French government did not wish to concern itself with such a trifle as investigating a murder in which the victim had been beheaded and mutilated.

Trotsky had already warned at the time that Stalin was cooking up a swindle, that he would not conclude an alliance with France and England, but rather with Hitler. He explained that only in order to squeeze more favorable conditions out of the Nazi dictator was Stalin negotiating with England and France. Two weeks later Trotsky's warning was confirmed. But what was clear to him was not clear to others. People still continued to underestimate Stalin in those days.

I was horribly affected by Adolf's death. To be sure, I was already accustomed to Stalin's murders, for thousands of comrades with whom I had come into contact during my years of Communist activity had been done away with by him. But there was something new behind this latest murder of his: only somebody who had been specially trained could cut off hands and hack off heads. This meant that there was a school under Stalin in which one learned such things. This new discovery sent shudders up and down my spine.

So it was that I went from one catastrophe to another in the course of a single year. It was a year filled with terror; it was a year in which I was personally in constant danger. And it was a year which culminated in the terrible August days of the Hitler-Stalin Pact—that alliance of two world murderers. The Night of the Long Knives, which was organized and led by Hitler and supported and welcomed by Stalin, was descending upon the peoples of Europe.

But if the Night of the Long Knives was poised over the heads of other peoples, our people was haunted by the portent of merciless and total extermination. This question deserves special attention. I merely wish to sketch my impression of the situation of the Jews in France during the period in question, that is, in the period between Munich and the beginning of the Second World War.

During the Munich days incitement against Jews intensified to an extraordinary degree and the fascist elements were active. Even before Hitler handed them the power, the fascists had begun to strike out against Jews and beat them up in the streets. They had singled out none other than Belleville to stage their nightly meetings, for Belleville was the largest Jewish district in the whole of Paris. And each of their meetings ended with rampaging assaults on Jews. I found myself in the middle of one of these gangster attacks on one occasion. And when I returned to my hotel at Boulevard Belleville 64 I saw one of the thugs through the window jotting down my address. I knew that I was in danger and found new accommodations that same week.

Night after night fascist groups from Ménilmontant made up of Frenchmen and Moroccans descended upon the Jewish quarter, threw each and every Jew they encountered to the ground and beat them bloody. The groans and cries of the victims made my blood run cold. I felt as if I were back in tsarist Russia—the land of pogroms—rather than in France. I do not want to say that it was the French people who were carrying on in such a manner. To the contrary, the French people proved to be full of courage and daring—as is well known—in saving Jews during the years of the Hitler occupation. But one did not hear the voice of the French people night after night in Belleville; no, one only heard the cries of society's dregs, of the fascist gangsters.

The stance of the Jewish Stalinists was perfectly typical. Together with their French comrades they greeted the Hitler-Stalin Pact. After the war broke out, I had occasion to read one of my wife's terrifying letters from Warsaw to a handful of Stalinists who had gathered at the apartment of the writer Chlawne Kagan. I was spreading horror stories, they replied. One of their number, a man who later died at the hands of Hitler, said that it would be no great calamity should three million Jews die. Instead of fourteen million, he commented, eleven million would be left behind.

I have asked myself more than once, why did this Jewish Stalinist express himself in such a fashion? After all, he had left me with the impression that he was a delicate and sensitive young man.

The answer became clear to me in days to come. As Hitler's armies approached Paris and I was forced to flee from the capital with a woman comrade of mine, the two of us ran into a French chauffeur—a Stalinist. Conversing with him, my comrade wanted to know what he thought about Hitler's armies. The chauffeur replied that they were no better and no worse than any other. That one could compare other armies to the armies of the Nazi dictator, which were under the command of the SS, was in itself a hallmark of Stalinism. But when a delegation from the French Communist Party later entreated Abetz, Hitler's ambassador in Paris who had been expelled from France for espionage before the war, to permit them to publish *l'Humanité* and agitate against French imperialism, it was clear to me that this move of theirs was a consequence of the frightful theory that Hitler was better than the Social Democracy; it was a result of Thorez' demand that Daladier travel to Moscow at once to be party to Stalin's and Hitler's "progressive" peace pact.

On the other side, the German Social Democrats' opposition to taking up the fight against Hitler on the grounds that he had come to power legally also took its toll. All of this demoralized and split the working class, rendered it incapable of any action against German fascism and consequently paved the way for Hitler's victory.

Nearly all of Europe's peoples were forced to pay a bloody price for these policies in the end, but the highest and bloodiest price of all was paid by us, the Jewish people.

AFTERWORD

*T*he foregoing book contains but one part of my memoirs. My second book, dealing with my path to proletarian Zionism, still remains to be written. Let us hope that it will not be long in coming. Meanwhile, I would like to clarify a number of points.

For a man who had dedicated his entire life to the struggle for socialism and, as a matter of course, for the victory of a socialist Jewish people as well, I experienced the deepest moral crisis when Hitler's armies invaded France. For their part, the French Stalinists took a positive attitude toward Hitler's armies. But I asked myself, as a Jewish worker what must I do? It was soon clear to me that Hitler's victory meant the destruction of Jewry in every country in Europe. And it is clear to everyone who lived under the occupation that had the war continued for one more year, the Jewish people would have been wiped out to the last man. Its physical strength and moral firmness would have been sapped. Hitler's murderous deeds against the Jews in France were particularly horrible precisely in the last days of his great defeat.

After wrestling with this question for a long period of time and after a great deal of consideration, I became convinced that only the Jewish workers in Israel were now capable of struggling for socialism, for it was only in Israel that the Jewish people would gather once again and begin to create a new and free life under the rule of the workers. I resolved to join the ranks of proletarian Zionism.

When I met my old comrades again in 1946 and they expressed their astonishment at the fact that I had become a Zionist, I explained to them that even if I were not a Jew it would have been my duty as a Marxist, as an international socialist, to place myself under the banner of the struggle for Jewish national liberation. Engels once said that no people anywhere in the world can be free as long as a single people is oppressed. He was right; and in respect to the so oppressed and blood-spattered Jewish people, he was a thousand times right. I would have gone the way I had chosen had I not been a Jew; and as a son of the Jewish people there was absolutely no question what I had to do.

They accused me of being sentimental. I admit that one cannot serve a single great idea without great and deep sentiments. We Jews have the right to be sentimental. In the last weeks before the retreat of Hitler's armies from France I experienced an event which shook me to the bones. In Grenoble the Hitlerites went from house to house, dragged the Jews into the street and shot them on the spot. A Jewish child was among them. A large crowd of Frenchmen had gathered and many of them wept. One woman, however, stood to the side without tears in her eyes. The mother of the small Jewish boy, she was afraid to cry, for she was terrified that the Nazis might single her out. I too stood to the side, and as I looked into the face of that Jewish mother, I literally felt her unshed tears.

He who has been witness to such a scene will never forget it. And he will never rest until the conditions have been created in which its recurrence is no longer possible. He will ever and always be ready to devote his body and soul in order to guarantee the existence of the Jewish people in a Jewish land.

Even today one often hears the arguments of people who have learned nothing from and understand nothing of the great calamity. They continue to argue that the reactionary forces were responsible, that following the victory of democracy, holocausts will no longer be possible. We are no less aware of the fact than they that the extermination of Jews has always been the work of the reactionary elements in society. But these people neither answer nor even pose the question, why does the reaction continually choose to victimize the Jewish people, and none other than the Jewish people? Were they so much as to pose this question, they would necessarily come to the conclusion that the secret rests in the fact that we Jews are without a land of our own. They would necessarily come to the conclusion that they must join the ranks of proletarian Zionism.

We are adherents of the dialectical philosophy of Hegel, which Marx adapted to his materialist conception of the world. We know that everything which occurs is real, that historical events have concrete and material roots. This necessarily leads us to the conclusion that if the same conditions come into being once again, the same results can follow. When we consider the situation of the Jews in various countries today, we notice that anti-Semitism has not laid down its weapons. To a greater or lesser extent, the Jews are threatened everywhere.

The survival of mankind is dependent upon the brotherhood of peoples, not national hatred. In practically every country, anti-Jewish excesses have broken out in one form or another. Nobody can foresee which forms these excesses will assume in times of great crisis. But every individual who wants to be honest to himself and to his people must come to the conclusion that in various countries and in various ways the existence of the Jewish people is threatened. In some cases it assumes the form of physical extermination, in others assimilation. The sole hope for the Jewish people remains its own country. The sole hope for the Jewish proletariat in leading the Jewish people along the path to socialism is the construction and defense of this country.

APPENDIX 1:

Exchange Between J.S. Hertz and Hersh Mendel

REMEMBERED OR INVENTED?
by J.S. Hertz

From *Unzer Tsait* No. 11, November 1960

'Memoirs by a Jewish worker" (Hersh Mendel: *Memoirs of a Jewish Revolutionary*, Tel Aviv, 1959)

The author is from Warsaw. He was active in the trade-union and political movement. What is peculiar about him is that he underwent a chain of ideological metamorphoses. From a pious home, he started out as a Bundist, crossed over to anarchism, went the way of Bolshevism, drew close to the Bund once again and then joined the Communist Party of Poland. A period of Trotskyism followed, after which he again found himself in the Bund. Finally, he landed on the runway of Zionism.

From this alone it is plain to see that we have before us a wayward man. It is irrelevant in the case of a wayward man to inquire about where he is going or to look for logic in his course. Nevertheless, such a book ought to be interesting, should the author provide *important* arguments for his zigzagging ideological wanderings. The motives which Hersh Mendel provides to explain his disappointments and passions are entirely superficial. With motives of this sort, he ought to be able to make his way through a new round of the above-mentioned political tendencies and add on a few more besides.

Isaac Deutscher, who accuses Hersh Mendel of "a narrow, emotional anti-Stalinist dogmatism", says in his preface that in certain respects the "memory has led astray" the author of the memoirs. Were it merely a question of this, we would still be faced with half of the problem. What is worse is that reality is to a considerable degree mixed up with fantasy. It is not my task to point out all the fantastic yarns which appear in this book. For the sake of illustration, I will confine myself to three.

On page 204 the memoirist tells us that he was arrested during a police raid in the Saxony Garden "on the last Saturday of July" 1920 due to the fact that he was without papers and that he was brought to the barracks of the military gendarmerie on Ciepła Street. Now we will let him speak:

> What to do? The death sentence was a sure thing; there was no chance whatsoever of an appeal. Perhaps I was too weak to conjure up any more courage and patience, for I decided to speed things along. I was a deserter, I said short and sweet. The World War had killed my entire family and I had had enough of wars. So as not to complicate the matter, I kept quiet about my political views. I was also well aware that as a deserter I would be tried within a few hours, and therefore decided to tell the gendarmes my real name.
>
> I was led into a hall where five men wearing military uniforms were seated. It was the last Saturday in the month of July. Following a brief interrogation and the prosecutor's speech, the verdict of death was read.

How does a man feel after having just been sentenced to death?

> And it shamed me to think that my comrades might come to learn of the manner in which I had conducted myself. I had only one wish, that it all end as soon as possible.

But his wish was ignored. Is this perhaps to say that he was pardoned? Not at all. Instead of shooting him at once or shackling him and taking him to the site of the execution under a strong guard in a paddy wagon, as was customary in such cases, he was even included in a group of forty other prisoners and escorted by eight gendarmes through the streets of Warsaw. The procession first went to the Fifth Commissariat and was then to go to the Citadel. Passing the corner of Dzielna and Karmelicka Streets, where the Bundist club was located, our hero sprang from the ranks and ran into the courtyard. Is this to say that he was trying to save himself? God forbid. Listen to what he says:

> Not for a minute did I believe it would work. I only wanted to be shot while escaping, for that was easier than waiting in some isolation cell for the firing squad.

The armed guards, apparently sensing Hersh Mendel's strong desire to get it all over with, refused to indulge him. The villains did not even open fire.

His whole plan having been squelched, what did Hersh Mendel do?

... not hearing any shots, I stopped in my tracks, let down my collar and then continued on my way. I had things to do [*party work*] ...

These days some authors write with an eye toward Hollywood. But even for Hollywood, the notion of the shirt collar is a too unexpected and nonsensical transition from death to "party work".

In order to weave an even more beautiful yarn, one must add that following these events our hero lived in Poland, that he walked the streets as free as a bird and that the police were on to him. And even though he was arrested in later years for Communist activities and spent years behind bars, nobody reminded him that he was a fugitive from a death sentence.

In 1920 "the last Saturday in the month of July" was 31 July. Eleven days prior to this, on 20 July, the Polish head of state Josef Pilsudski issued a decree stipulating that deserters and persons eligible for the draft who had not initially reported for duty could do so in the course of the next two weeks, until 4 August, *without being penalized in any way whatsoever.* Had Hersh Mendel been a deserter, he could have indeed taken advantage of this decree on 31 July. Given its existence, it would not have been possible to try him that day.

And the most important thing is that Hersh Mendel was not in reality a deserter at the time. He says: "I turned nine years old in 1902..." (page 30). This means that he was born in 1893. It was only in the month of August 1920 that those who had been born in the five years between 1890 and 1894 were conscripted. Conscription for those born in 1893 took place in the three days from 12 August to 14 August. Hersh Mendel was to have reported for duty on the last day, for his family name is Shtockfish and it was only on the last day that those whose names began with the letters from S to Z were to have reported. In that case, why did he have to jump ahead of the others and announce two weeks in advance that he was a deserter, thereby forcing upon himself a "death sentence"?

A second yarn. Listen to this:

At the beginning of 1924 we received a directive from the Comintern stipulating that we were to prepare an uprising in order to sever West White Russia from Poland and to unite it with the Soviet Union. We got down to work and appointed a revolutionary war committee composed of five [*sic* − *trans.*] comrades: Shlomo, myself, the poet and the new recruit Miron, a former left Poale Zionist who had come over to us along with Amsterdam (pages 220−1).

The "revolutionary war committee", the task of which was to sever the White Russian provinces from Poland, is said to have been composed of four Jews and one White Russian ("the poet") or of two former anarchists, two former Poale Zionists (Miron and Amsterdam) and a man who had translated the writings of Gandhi. [1] (If this committee also included one White Russian, he was later shot as a traitor by the White Russian partisans.) We will dispense with the comical side of the matter and return to our Hersh Mendel, who traveled to a regional conference in Volkovysk in order to complete some of "our final preparations".

I had arranged to meet the comrades on a particular street and they were supposed to wait there for me. But the lads overslept and failed to show.

In short, the insurrectionists overslept and their leader, Hersh Mendel, went back to the train station "in order to return to Białystok". But inasmuch as it was nine o'clock in the morning and the train was scheduled to depart at four o'clock in the afternoon, he went back to town. Meanwhile, police agents were on the prowl for a thief and arrested Hersh Mendel. Following an interrogation at the police commissariat, his passport was confiscated and he was told to return later that day. Going back outside, he was shadowed by two police agents. In the meantime, the insurrectionists, the comrades, appeared on the scene. Seeing Hersh Mendel leave the commissariat, they jumped to the conclusion that he was an informer (a police agent). He in turn thought them to be spies.

I turned around and made sure the cops were in plain view. Finally, after wandering around awhile, the opportune moment arrived. I shot through the courtyard, cleared the train tracks and ran off (page 222).

Perhaps he means to say that the two police agents who had been sent outside to spy on him followed in hot pursuit or fired at him. Not at all. He wants to flee; he wants to escape in good health.

It should also be noted that when the sleepyheads who were supposed to be preparing for the uprising left their leader to roam the streets, Jews in the meantime "were on the lookout for *goyim* to come in and light their ovens for them. As they opened their windows and looked at me, a stranger, as if I were an evil spirit, I got the feeling that something was about to blow" (page 221). It was Sabbath and it was wintertime, but in winter people did not in fact open their windows. In order to keep out the cold, double windows were inserted, sand was poured between the panes and the edges were sealed. This is something which the revolutionary "Menachem Mendel" forgot. [2]

Hersh Mendel also tells us that in 1920 he belonged to a war committee of the Communist Party. This committee was supposed to prepare an uprising at the rear of the Polish army and to "organize Red units to fight the PPS units, and to enable the Red Army to march rapidly to the German border..." He says:

> At the same meeting [of the war committee − J.H.] we also discussed the turn of the Bund, that is, its readiness to work together with the new regime. The Bund had demanded the portfolio of the Ministry of Jewish Affairs, and the Central Committee [of the Communist Party − J.H.] wanted to know what our opinion about the issue was. We decided to leave the question open until the Red Army entered Warsaw (page 206).

The entire story of the Bund's turn is a fabrication. Either somebody deceived him or it is a product of his own imagination. The position of the Bund at the time was not to participate in the government organs of the Soviet occupation force. (Incidentally, the chairman of the Central Committee of the Bund, comrade Noah, instructed the writer of these lines to inform the Bundist organizations in the Warsaw region about this decison.) In general, the Central Committee of the Communist Party in Poland had precious little to say regarding the "new regime", for the Red Army "*oboz*" [3] was to run a "Polish government" from Moscow with Felix Dzerzhinsky, the chief of the Cheka, at its head. And it is of course ridiculous to say that the Bund would link its working together with the Communists to the demand that it be entrusted with the "portfolio of the Ministry of Jewish Affairs".

As we have already remarked, these are merely samples. Similar fantastic stories appear in these memoirs in abundance. How has this come about? A key to the riddle is provided by the author himself. He writes:

> I had my dreams as well in those days. This should not amaze anyone, for every revolutionary must have his moments of fantasy. It is at such times that he can breathe easier, and it is this which makes it possible for him to bear all the difficulties. In Grodno, I often used to lie on a wooded riverbank in view of the castle on the Neman River. This castle had once belonged to the Russian governor-general and later became the residence of the *Woyevod*. I dreamed of conquering the place and making

it my home (page 224).

Hersh Mendel has traversed a long, difficult road and now is the time for him to relax. His memory is a jumble of dreams and fantasies which are served to the reader as incontestable truths.

Hersh Mendel's memoirs are also replete with factual errors. Inasmuch as it would take up too much space to draw attention to all of them, we will simply dwell upon a sampling below.

On page 32 the author says that as a result of the war with Japan an "economic upswing" set in throughout the whole of Russia in 1904. He became aware of this in the course of studying the history of the revolutionary movement. If so, then he is a bad student, for exactly the opposite was the case. Because of the war, the country was gripped by a very sharp economic crisis and by mass unemployment in 1904. The press in general and the revolutionary press in particular offered a plethora of facts pertaining to this question. One finds in the newspapers of the time shocking descriptions of the hunger and want which afflicted the victims of the crisis in Warsaw, Łodz, Białystok and in a large number of towns deep in Russia. Additionally, one reads reports of factory closures, of a standstill in trade and of a large number of bankruptcies.

In regard to Medem's pamphlet *The Social Democracy and the National Question*, we read:

> The Zionist-Socialists attempted to prove that the Bund had taken over this theory from Otto Bauer. The Bund replied that Medem had written his brochure even before the Austrian Social Democracy had included national-cultural autonomy in its program (page 74).

Bauer published his work on the nationalities problem three years after Medem had formulated his position. The Zionist-Socialists would have made themselves look ridiculous by "proving" this sort of thing. They maintained that the theory was taken from Rudolf Springer (Karl Renner). And the Bund, of course, could not have said that the pamphlet was written even before the Austrian Social Democracy had included national-cultural autonomy in its program because this pamphlet appeared years later.

Regarding an article by I.L. Peretz on the eve of Yom Kippur, which called on Jews to go to the synagogue, Hersh Mendel tells us: "When we read

Peretz' article — I believe it appeared in the newspaper *der Moment* — we, a group of comrades, wanted to let him know what our opinion about it was" (page 88). I.L. Peretz never collaborated on *der Moment*. The article was printed in *Haynt*.

Regarding Shpinak-Josefovich (a leader of the Social-Democratic youth organization Tsukunft) we read: "Later, in Russia, he became a close associate of Lozovsky in the Cominform" (page 97). It should read "in the Profintern". The Cominform was only created after the Second World War.

Several times the names Uniteds and the United Workers Party are cited (pages 97, 98, 101) in connection with political prisoners in Pawiak on the eve of the First World War. No such party existed at the time. What did exist in those days was the SS.[4] It was only following World War I that the SS began to call itself the Uniteds.

On page 91 Hersh Mendel writes that *on the eve of Yom Kippur 1912* he was arrested at the consumer cooperative. Yet on page 106 we learn from him that he was tried as a result of this very arrest in "March 1912".

In regard to the "purge" in the Comintern's international Lenin School (1930), the author informs us that "The chairman of the purge commission was a Jew by the name of Mickiewicz, the leader of the Lithuanian Communist Party" (page 271).

Vincas Mickiewicz (Kapsukas) was a well-known figure in the Comintern. Hersh Mendel himself went before him during the purge and recounted his personal history. The memoirist may know enough to say that Mickiewicz was a Jew, but the latter was no *"Litvak"*.[5] Rather, he was a genuine Lithuanian from peasant stock and even a former student of a religious seminary (in Sayni, Suavalker Gubernia).

But Mickiewicz is not alone. Persons and facts have been "converted" by Hersh Mendel in abundance. He writes, for example, that when the Trotskyist Shlomo sought to have an article dealing with the Moscow Trials printed in the Bundist *Folkstsaytung*, he met with the "resistance of the Stalinist elements on the editorial board to having it printed". The article appeared only after Viktor Alter intervened (pages 316-17). We need not mention here how often and how sharply the *Folkstsaytung* came out against the Moscow Trials and against Stalinism in general. Hersh Mendel, however, wanted nothing more than to convert the Bundist editorial board to Stalinism. It is perhaps the case that the editorial board had one or another reason for initially not wanting to print the article, but to say that this was due to Stalinist tendencies is absurd.

Our memoirist writes further:

When I reached Paris in August 1938, Lyova Sedov already knew about my arrival. We were close friends, after all, and it was perfectly obvious that I would go to see him first. Comrades told me that he was ill, however, and informed me that I would be able to visit him in the hospital the next day around noontime. Yet when I appeared at the hospital the next afternoon, I learned that he had died during the night (page 319).

Lyova Sedov, Trotsky's son, died on 16 February 1938. (His father, and many others as well, were certain that agents of the GPU had poisoned him.) If Hersh Mendel arrived in Paris in August 1938, his arrival in fact took place half a year after Lyova Sedov's death.

In connection with a second victim of Stalin's murder machine, we read that "Two months before the outbreak of the Second World War" (page 321) our hero once again escaped with his life. Together with comrade Adolf (Rudolf Klement, who had previously been Trotsky's secretary and who was now secretary of the Fourth International), Hersh Mendel planned to take off "one Sunday in July" and go to Bois de Boulogne. He did not go along for some reason and comrade Adolf, who went without him, did not return. "... Adolf had been found in the Seine. His head and hands had been hacked off." This, however, took place one year earlier. Rudolf Klement disappeared on 13 July 1938. And it was not a "Sunday", but merely an ordinary Wednesday.

We still have before us a great number of footpaths to follow through the thick forest of errors, but I already feel tired and wish to end it here.

I first saw Hersh Mendel at a meeting of the Bundist faction of the Warsaw leather trade union in the year 1919. Attending this meeting were members of the Bund and sympathizers. I had come as a representative of the Warsaw committee of the Bund and gave a talk on the nationalities problem. The chairman of the leather union and the Bundist party group, Chanina Kramarsky, told me at the time who Hersh Mendel was and praised him highly. In later years, I heard that in the Communist movement as well people had a good opinion of him as a loyal and devoted worker-leader. I do not wish to question this. I merely want to say that his devotion as a worker-leader is not matched by his honesty as a writer.

Such a man was obliged to make sure that his memoirs can be read with confidence. Unfortunately, he bungled an opportunity to write a book which might be valuable.

Finally, one must ask: why did his friend Isaac Deutscher, a professional writer, fail to point out to the author the above-mentioned errors? And if he failed to do so, why didn't Hersh Mendel demand Deutscher's friendly assistance in order to avoid the mistakes? Or is compromising himself and misleading the reader all the same to him?

Translated by Robert Michaels

Notes

[1] The Yiddish original of Hersh Mendel's book obviously contains a typographical error here, for only *four* names are cited. Amsterdam is not mentioned in this connection as a member of the committee. In this translation the word "five" has been changed to "four". (trans.)

[2] Menachem Mendel, character in a work by Sholom Aleichem, is symbolic of a dreamer. (trans.)

[3] *Oboz*, Russian word meaning column of vehicles. (trans.)

[4] SS, acronym for Zionist-Socialist Workers Party. (trans.)

[5] A Lithuanian Jew. (trans.)

Letter to the Editor
ONCE AGAIN: "REMEMBERED OR INVENTED"
by Hersh Mendel

From *Unzer Tsait* Nos. 1-2, January – February 1961

I request that you provide me with space for a number of clarifications in connection with the article by J. Hertz entitled "Remembered or Invented", which appeared in the November number of *Unzer Tsait*.

1. In regard to three inaccuracies in the dates: these mistakes are truly regrettable. I noticed them earlier, but it was already too late to correct them. When the book is translated, the errors and the dates will be set straight.

2. Why did I write that Mickiewicz was a Jew? Mickiewicz was the chairman of the East-Europe bureau of the Comintern. When I attended the Lenin School we held meetings each month at which the monthly budgets for the various parties were determined. As the meetings came to an end, comrades would jokingly remark that being a Jew did not suit Mickiewicz. He was a very obtuse and politically immature man. But he was cruel; he was a leader who shot to the top during the Stalin epoch. I do not know where comrades got the idea that he was a Jew.

3. When Zhdanov created the Cominform, Lozowsky and Josefovich were no longer alive. Josefovich was Lozowsky's right-hand man in the Profintern. To have written "Cominform" instead of "Profintern" is an annoying blunder, but everyone will understand that this is merely a mistake in words.

4. The waywardness for which Hertz reproaches me was only formal. It was not until 1942 that I really felt wayward.

5. Hertz reproaches me for dreaming. Everybody will understand, however, that a young worker who found himself going from one prison to another, who meanwhile fought on the barricades and at various fronts in a civil war, and who was twice a member of revolutionary war committees cannot do without fantasies.

6. I did not write that the Bund got the theory of national autonomy from Bauer. I merely wrote that the Bund was accused of this, and that is a fact. The SS accused the Bund of this and the Bund replied in the spirit which Hertz describes.

7. Hertz maintains that I err when I write that there was an economic boom in Russia in 1904-1905. I would argue that the error is his. Leaving aside the fact that my own family's situation improved at the time, one can

also conclude that this boom occurred from the polemic which Trotsky engaged in with Stalin. Trotsky demonstrated that it is more opportune to make a revolution in moments of economic revival rather than in the midst of crisis (i.e., in desperation), for it is precisely at such times that the revolution assumes a more conscious character. In the course of this dispute Trotsky referred to the Revolution of 1905.

8. It is amusing when Hertz says that Pilsudski issued an amnesty for deserters at the end of July 1920 and that I had an opportunity to report for military service. Hertz is probably unaware of the fact that the party instructed me not to report for service because I had a responsible assignment to fulfil in preparing the struggle against those forces which were geared up for battle against the Red Army in the event that the latter entered Warsaw. Furthermore, Hertz may also not know that my brother had already joined Haller's army under my name and that the police were on the prowl for me as a member of the Revolutionary War Committee. Moreover, according to this mistake which Hertz has uncovered, I was arrested at the end of August. In general, Hertz does not believe that such an arrest took place. Three comrades who were on trial with me in Brest live in Argentina today. I hope that they will read these lines and be able to set the record straight.

9. Hertz maintains that somebody prompted me to write that the Bund was supposed to have made a turn in favor of taking over the Ministry of Jewish National Affairs. The idea alone that I was prompted is dangerous, for Hertz thereby confirms after all that whoever prompted me was already talking about the matter. But the truth is, nobody prompted me; rather, as a strictly Jewish matter, the question was thrown open for consideration at the last meeting of the Jewish Central Bureau upon the request of the Central Committee of the Communist Party. I do not know if the Bund would have in fact entered the government, for its turn was posed as an ultimatum, and we wanted to reserve the Ministry of Jewish Affairs for ourselves.

I do not know when Noah told Hertz that the Bund did not want to enter such a government. It could have been earlier. But whatever Noah discussed with him in this regard, it indeed shows that this was a topical issue in the Bund.

10. What Hertz writes in regard to White Russia gives one the impression that he was not in Poland at the time. Everybody knows that the slogan calling for severing White Russia from Poland and uniting it with Soviet White Russia was the main slogan of the Polish Communist Party in those days.

In late 1923 the Central Committee in West White Russia transformed itself into a revolutionary war committee. This war committee was composed of four comrades: three Jews and one White Russian — a poet.

It is not worth writing about my flight from Volkovysk, for this is a fact which was known to one and all.

I am certain that you will print my clarifications, and I thank you in advance.

SEVERAL REMARKS by J. Hertz

From *Unzer Tsait* Nos. 1-2, January−February 1961

1. I did not reproach Hersh Mendel for being wayward. I merely established the fact that he was. Nor did I question his right to be so.

2. Mickiewicz was a leader even prior to the "Stalin epoch". A writer and activist in tsarist times as well, he occupied high party-political and state posts. He edited newspapers and journals and was the author of some forty books and pamphlets on literary, historical, philosophical, economic and political subjects. How can one say that he was an "obtuse and politically immature man"?

3. The *Cominform* was created in September 1947. Josefovich (I. Shpinak) was in earlier years a pioneer of the Social Democratic youth organization Tsukunft and a Bundist leader. Later he was a leader of the leather workers trade union in Soviet Russia and a leader of the Profintern. I knew him well, yet I do not know what finally became of him. S. Lozowsky's story, however, is well known. I.B. Zaltsberg, a member of the delegation of Canadian Communists who visited Khrushchev to find out about the destruction of Jewish culture as well as the Jewish cultural leaders, learned from the latter that Lozowsky, although innocent, had been put to death. Zaltsberg says: "According to the information which I have, Lozowsky perished together with the Jewish writers group on 12 August 1952." That is to say that after "Zhdanov created the Cominform", Lozowsky lived nearly five more years. It would certainly be easy to determine the facts of the matter in Tel Aviv, for a short book published there in 1957 entitled *Yidishe Komunistn vegn der Yidn-Frage in Ratnfarband*[1] includes Zaltsberg's report (see page 33).

4. Indeed, Hersh Mendel "did not write that the Bund got the theory of national autonomy from Bauer", nor is this my claim. Yet he did write in his book and repeats in his current letter as well that the SS accused the Bund of this, an assertion which is *not* correct. All the SS maintained is that the Bund got the theory from Rudolf Springer (Karl Renner).

5. There is an abundance of material dealing with the 1904 economic crisis in Russia following the outbreak of the Russo-Japanese War. Just as Hersh Mendel refers to Trotsky, we will take a look at one of Trotsky's works as well. In one of his pamphlets, we read in regard to the year 1904 in Russia: "Just as in every terrible calamity, the war with its attendant woes − crisis,

unemployment, mobilization, hunger and death — evoked in the first stages feeling of depression and despair, but none of conscious protest" (*Do Dyevyatovo Yanvarya,*[2] page 48, Geneva, 1905).

6. In my review, I pointed out that on Saturday, 31 July 1920 Hersh Mendel could not have been a deserter, for he was only to have reported for military service on 14 August. Now he pushes the date of his arrest one month ahead to "the end of August".

In the November number I presented my considerations as to why the tale about the death sentence is not true. I want to add a few points here. It is out of the question that a man detained by accident in the streets, a man without papers, would be placed before a court-martial immediately following his arrest and sentenced to death merely on the basis of his own declaration and without one shred of official inquiry to determine who he is. Had that been the case, it would have been known in Warsaw. In order to terrorize men into not deserting, the government was interested in assuring that word got out about death sentences. It immediately notified the press in such cases and utilized other means to inform the general public of the news. Had a Jew been tried before a court-martial, his case would have immediately come to the attention of the *Kehile*[3] as well as Jewish deputies, counselmen and journalists. Parliamentary deputies would have sought to convince the head of state to pardon the man. This would have had a chance of success because, formally speaking, Hersh Mendel was in no way a deserter. One could only become a deserter after having entered the military and after having taken the oath. Hersh Mendel did not even report for duty. In late 1920 he left for Soviet Russia and in 1921 he returned to Warsaw. It is hard to believe that a man would return to a country where a death sentence had already been handed down against him. As for the possibility of turning to the three Argentinian comrades, they will most certainly not be able to "set the record straight". They were not present at the ostensible court-martial, and the matter was *not* addressed at the Brest trial.

7. In respect to the readiness of the Bund to enter a Communist government should they have been handed over the "Ministry of Jewish National Affairs", I do not maintain that anybody "prompted" Hersh Mendel. I wrote: "Either somebody deceived him or it is a product of his own imagination." And that the Bund did *not* intend to enter such a government and that it did *not* make such a turn was known to me not merely from the instruction which I received from Noah (a fact which I only mentioned "incidentally").

8. I do not doubt that there were instructions from Soviet Russia to carry

out an uprising in order to sever the northeastern provinces from Poland. On many occasions, the Communist Party of Poland called for uprisings and general strikes which never took place. I simply pointed to the lack of seriousness and the comical nature of the preparations. It may well be that the insurrectionist in fact fled from Volkovysk, but it could not have taken place as he describes it in his book. Either the two police agents, who were sent to shadow him, would have fired at him as he fled or they would have caught him. Hersh Mendel was indeed no Nurmi. [Nurmi, a Finnish athlete, was the fastest runner in the world at that time.] While his letter notes that "this war committee was composed of four comrades: three Jews and one White Russian", Hersh Mendel writes in his book (page 221) that there were five comrades in the war committee: four Jews and one White Russian. Even the names are cited. What happened to one of the Jews?

9. I have absolutely nothing against the things which Hersh Mendel fantasized. I do not even have anything against his including these fantasies in his book. After all, this is his private matter. But one condition must be fulfilled. A subtitle ought to appear on the title page stating: *Fantasy and Reality*. (Or take an already used line from Johann Wolfgang von Goethe: *Poverty and Truth*.) It will then be obvious that the material is to be divided into two categories.

Notes
1 Jewish Communists on the Jewish Question in the Soviet Union. (trans.)
2 Until the Ninth of January. (trans.)
3 Jewish local government in Poland. (trans.)

APPENDIX 2:

Exchange Between Hersh Mendel and Leon Trotsky

REPORT OF THE POLISH COMRADE V. [HERSH MENDEL]

From *International Information Bulletin* Number 1, 1935
of the Workers Party of the United States

When I came to the conference[1] and recognized its complete impotence and its inability to make any decision that would really be binding, I asked myself: What is the conference for? In my opinion it was not convoked to get any work done, but rather to prepare a larger conference at which the leaders of the Left wing groups in the Second International were to participate. (Such a conference actually took place on February 17.) The intention was to get a general resolution against war adopted by this conference and to establish an anti-war committee together with the Left wing leaders, in order to create a basis for a mass movement. If this was, indeed, the purpose of the conference, then it must be admitted that it was a failure. But we shall come back to that.

The preparatory conference gave evidence of the disproportion between the organizational growth and the ideological decline of the London Buro. Organizational growth was demonstrated by the adherence of a number of new organizations, such as Doriot's, the Austrian Red Front, the Spanish Federation, the Swedish C.O., Kilbom Party, etc.

Doriot, the Swedish C.O., the Spanish Federation, the SAP, ILP and especially the two Dutch organizations deserve to be taken seriously. Naturally, they cannot as yet be considered mass parties, but their cadres are already large enough to be able to serve as a base for parties of the new International. But that will be possible only if they develop a precise and revolutionary ideology and if they express the will to create the new International. Unfortunately, that is not yet the case. I fear that at the first real step forward, a split will occur. The whole conference made that self-evident. Among the delegates, there were three principal groupings:

1) The Dutch, who more or less clearly viewed all questions from the point of view of the new International.

2) The ILP which combatted the very idea of the new International and

declared that it is impossible to create international unity without the Russians, that is, without the CPSU and the CI. Together with the Swedes and the Polish Independents they proposed a resolution which says that to pose the problem of the new International would be to hinder the work among the masses.

3) All the groups (with the exception of the Austrians who supported the Dutch point of view), led by the SAP, expressed points of view which were not very clear. In principle, they did not reject the new International, but they declared it would have to be created of itself in the course of the process of practical work. It must be said that the SAP gave the impression of really wanting the new International, but it has neither the courage nor the strength to say so clearly. Of the other organizations, it is hard to tell whether they want the new International or whether they want to go to the Second by way of the London Buro. It is necessary to analyze the character of these groups.

In the discussions and in the reports, the SAP took a more or less correct position, in general agreement with our principles. But in the voting, it accepted every compromise without even putting up a fight. It must be admitted, of course, that the resolutions voted are what really count, because they furnish the directives for action. The SAP's behavior was typically centrist.

The ILP, which regards itself as being repelled by the CI so to speak, and which has lost all confidence in the latter, nevertheless still hopes to reach some agreements with it. They did not utter a single word against the Stalinist crimes. They also requested the delegates to participate in the Amsterdam-Ployel Committee. The great progress of the ILP consists merely of its definite break with the Second International. But it must be emphasized that the ILP is still far from a Marxist ideology. For example, in the discussion on the world situation, its delegate denied the class character of the British state, "because it aids the unemployed". To be sure, the ILP will have to go through the experiences of many more setbacks before it will take the road to the new International. The Dutch organization gives the impression of a revolutionary party with precise principles, although it still proceeds somewhat mechanically in its development. Generally speaking, however, it must be admitted that it gives evidence of the real spirit necessary for mass work. It has all the elements of a genuine revolutionary party.

The Swedish group is thoroughly opportunistic. In the discussion, it combatted not only Stalinism, but Leninism as well. (There is too much talk of the workers and too little of the petty bourgeoisie; in the case of war it is necessary to defend the democratic states against the Fascist states, etc.). The Swedes were against all resolutions containing obligatory actions. They did not fight against the social democracts at all; on the contrary, they had only praise for their own social democratic government and declared their intention of forming an electoral bloc with the social democrats in the next election. It is quite certain that this group will go over to the Second International. It belongs to the London Buro because it does not bind them to anything. It carries on its own, terribly opportunistic policy.

The Spanish Federation seems to have great influence in their country (6,000 members) and has fighting tradition behind it. But I got the impression that it is moving away from Communism and headed for the Second International. Its delegate declared that he preferred the Second to the Third. It took a position against the new International and defends its own slogan of "organic unity", without adding "on a revolutionary basis". But it is difficult to tell how far it has gone in this direction.

The Doriot organization is a compact group (2,500 members). In a number of questions, Doriot stood up rather well. He declared his opposition to both the Second and Third Internationals, but he also opposed the Fourth. He is for "organic unity" based on "revolutionary principles". It is hard to distinguish whether he means that unity must be achieved on the basis of revolutionary principles, or whether he imagines that the revolutionary principles will develop of themselves as a result of unity. His revolutionary principles are, in any case, a trifle shady. Not once did he have recourse to Lenin. In my opinion it is hard to foretell the direction Doriot will take.

The Austrians and the Italians did not represent any real forces. The former are only beginning to take on a political character. The Maximalists have lost a great deal. I believe that if there is no revival of the labor movement they will return to the Second International. As it is, they are already propagating today "organic unity" without any conditions.

The first report on the world situation (SAP) was correct in general, but was hardly anything more than a repetition of old truisms. Both the report and the resolutions failed to give any indications for practical action. The only indication of this kind which it did contain was the one on the necessity of building a new International. But on the insistence of the ILP and the Swedish organization, this point precisely was struck out of the test. There was not much discussion on the whole question. Only the Swedish delegate made some amendments, e.g., we should not say that the proletarian revolution will annihilate Fascism because that may frighten the petty bourgeoisie, etc. Sneevliet made several important statements on the "liberation of the colonial peoples".

The second report, that of the ILP on the war danger, enjoyed a more ample discussion. This report, in spite of its omissions and its lack of consistency (those are characteristic of the ILP) showed some progress, nevertheless: complete break with national defence; no differentiation between democratic and Fascist states; no differentiation between defensive and offensive war; in all cases civil war and fraternization of the soldiers. But they avoided saying anything of the false policy of the CI on these questions and of the criminal foreign policy of the USSR. The Swedes, Doriot, and several other groups declared against unconditional defence of the USSR. The Swedes are against any concrete directives in case of war, because "all directives given up to now have failed".

On the question of the new International, two resolutions were presented; one by the Dutch which clearly expressed the necessity for a new International, the other by the SAP, which says that the new International can only be realized in the process of practical work. The whole conference, with the exception of the Dutch and the Austrians, adopted the SAP resolution, in spite of the differences mentioned above. The conference ended with the vote on this resolution, indicating the place for the resident secretariat and working out a plan for a larger conference.

The hope that the Lefts in the Second International would create an anti-war committee jointly with the London Buro was not realized. Zymromski said quite clearly: "The Communist and socialist opposition ought to go back to their respective Internationals and work for organic unity". Pivert said the same thing a little bit more diplomatically: the work should be continued but the London Buro would be wise to enter into the Second International in order to avoid great difficulties.

The delegate from the Lefts in the Labour Party said that the ILP ought to return to the LP, that outside of the great parties no action is possible and that they would not collaborate with parties who are outside of the Second International.

Only the Belgian Lefts, who represented the anti-war committee, declared their readiness to collaborate in this committee. But this, too, was achieved only through a dangerous compromise. No one took the floor against the Belgian who demanded that the resolution declare against all war. They also said that they do not distinguish between the USSR and the capitalist countries (no reply).

Finally, the SAP itself appeared to be of the opinion that it is possible to reach revolutionary action by means of opportunist slogans. The conference was concluded with the election of an anti-war committee (Doriot, a German and a Spaniard).

There was also a letter from Chmurner (Polish Left Bund) who stressed the great value of ideological clarity, "because a small group that has achieved such clarity can often exercise a great influence, e.g., the International Communist League of Poland before the turn toward the SFIO ... the new orientation was harmful not only for the ICL but also for the Lefts in the Second International. That can also be felt in the meetings of the Bund".

I am among the Polish comrades who are not in agreement with the recent turn to the SFIO. I believe that Vidal made a mistake there. He only saw the united front as a point of departure for the revolutionary reawakening of the masses, and he failed to foresee the demoralization the two bureaucratic cliques would bring into effect. Vidal feared that we would be isolated in the midst of new revolutionary upswing. But instead of that we have the collapse of the united front and the deception of the masses. And, as a result of the turn, our organization has been weakened.

I think it would be advisable to follow the example of our Dutch organization and to enter the London Buro and work for our ideas inside of it. I attended the conference as a guest, to verify the correctness of my views.

---

[1] Conference of the London–Amsterdam Bureau, or IAG. (trans.)

CENTRIST COMBINATIONS AND MARXIST TACTICS
A Letter to the Polish Comrade V.
28 February 1935
by Crux [Leon Trotsky]
From *Writings of Leon Trotsky 1934–35*
Pathfinder Press, New York

I have read your letter about the conference of the organizations of the IAG
with great interest and profit, for your report proved to be really revealing.
But I must say from the very start that the conclusions you draw from the
facts that you so correctly observed appear to me to be one-sided and even
false. You are at once an opponent of the entry of the French section into
the SFIO and a proponent of the entry of the ICL into the IAG. You are
wrong on both counts.

From your own descriptions, it appears that we were confronted at the
sessions of the IAG only with diplomatic representatives of various centrist groups and tendencies oriented in various directions, and that every
one of these diplomats was particularly interested in not binding himself
to anything and was, therefore, inclined to be very liberal toward the others.
In other words, the prevailing principle was live and let live, or create confusion and let confusion be created.

The life of the IAG consists of the publication of documents from time
to time, which do not mean very much, and of conferences every year and
a half or so in order to prove that they are not sectarian, i.e., that, in con-
tradistinction to the cursed Bolshevik-Leninists, they are not at all inclined to inconvenience one another. Thus the IAG becomes an asylum for conservative centrist diplomats who do not wish to risk anything and who prefer
to let the omnivorous historical "process" take care of the most burning
problems of our times. Should the above-mentioned "process" succeed,
perchance, in creating a new, good Fourth International with steady posts
for the diplomatic gentlemen, then the latter will most obligingly condes-
cend to recognize the accomplished fact. But up to that time, they would
like to leave the door open. Perhaps the Second and Third will merge after
all and thus produce from both of these mutually complementary bankruptcies a new and flourishing firm. It will never do to spoil such an opportunity for oneself. Particularly must one avoid being pinned down to distinct
principles, because our epoch is much too uncertain and the principle much
too inflexible and, on top of that, there are those Leninist hotspurs who

are always there to wave under your nose the contradiction between principle and action.

You have observed very well that the people from the SAP, whose spirit dominated the conference, made quite radical speeches in which they advanced our principles quite passably, in order all the better to snap their fingers at these same principles when the time for the adoption of decisions came around. You remark very aptly that this is indeed classical centrism itself. When it is a matter of an honest, naively centrist state of mind of the masses, it is possible, under favorable circumstances and a correct policy, to hold one's own and to push the masses forward. But when one is confronted only with the leaders, and when these leaders are "classical" centrists, i.e., conniving centrist speculators, then very little can be expected from such a labor community, which is neither laboring nor community. To win five young workers in the SFIO for Marxist ideas is a hundred times more important than to vote on innocuous, i.e., deceptive, resolutions or even to record one's vote against them within the four walls of these conferences.

Such gatherings of solid bureaucrats, particularly when they come from different countries, often make a very imposing impression. It's best "to be there". One is not so "isolated" and, with aid of God, one can gain influence and prestige.—What a naive illusion! One possesses only that power that one conquers, i.e., the power of revolutionists welded together with clear ideas.

What is your objection to our turn in France? You quote from a letter of a representative of the Left Bund (Poland), in which it is quite correctly affirmed that a numerically small group can exert great influence, thanks to its ideological clarity. But from this indisputable fact you also draw the unexpected conclusion that the latest turn of the ICL is harmful to its growing influence and that the unfortunate consequences extend even as far as the Left Bund. How is that to be understood?

The strength of the Bolshevik-Leninists consists, you say together with the representative of the Left Bund, in the clarity of its ideas. Since you maintain that our influence has receded since the turn (which is a hair-raising untruth), it is to be assumed that our ideas had in the meantime lost their clarity. That is indeed the point in question. Has our French section since its entry into the SFIO become less determined, more confused, more opportunistic? Or has it maintained a completely irreconcilable attitude with regard to its fundamental position? That, my dear friend, is what you should decide for yourself, or else your whole judgment rests on a completely lopsided logical basis.

Since, you say, firmness in *principle and ideological clarity* determines the influence of the Bolshevik-Leninists, the change in our *organizational* methods has become fatal for the influence of our organization. That does not rhyme, dear friend. You can, of course, venture the opinion that the change in organizational methods (entry into the SFIO) was a departure from ideological clarity. That is quite possible. The only question is, is that really the case in this instance?

I maintain that none of our sections has as yet had the opportunity to formulate its ideas so sharply and to bring them so directly before the masses as our French section has done since it became a tendency in the Socialist Party. And if one is able to observe, then one must come to the conclusion that the entire life of the Socialist as well as the Communist parties is now determined or at least influenced, directly or indirectly, positively or negatively, by the ideas and slogans of our small French section.

I can very easily conceive that comrades in Poland or some other place who do not read French and cannot keep track of French life may be affected unfavorably by the bare fact of the entrance into the Second International. But in revolutionary policy, it is not the immediate impression that counts but rather the lasting effect. Should the entry into the SFIO prove fruitful for the extension of our influence, then the Polish and other comrades will have to revise their evaluation of the turn we made. The majority of comrades, as a matter of fact, have already done so. It is correct that a small group with clear ideas is more important than one that is, perhaps, large but heterogeneous. But we must not make a fetish of this phrase. For the small group must seek to create the necessary public for its correct ideas. And in doing this, it must adapt itself organizationally to the given circumstances.

You present the whole matter as if Vidal, frightened by the isolation of the French section, artificially invented the turn and imposed it upon the French section to the detriment of the whole movement.

In 1929 Vidal wrote to a Frenchman who accused the Left Opposition of sectarianism, as follows: "You point to individual groups of the Left Opposition and call them 'sectarian'. We ought to come to an agreement on the content of this term. Among us there are elements who remain satisfied to sit at home and criticize the mistakes of the official party, without setting themselves any broader tasks, without assuming any practical revolutionary obligations, converting the revolutionary opposition into a title, something akin to an Order of the Legion of Honor. There are, in addition, sectarian tendencies that express themselves in splitting every hair into four parts. It is necessary to struggle against this. And I am personally ready to wage a struggle against it, and not to be deterred, if need be, by old friendships, personal ties and so forth and so on."

The letter I quote from, which was written six years ago, then goes on to explain why the Bolshevik-Leninists carried on and had to carry on their work in sectarian form as a propaganda group under the given circumstances, after a series of great international defeats, and ends up with the prognosis that this stage will undoubtedly have to be surmounted – not without a struggle against those who want to deduce from the ideological treasures of our tendency the right to remain immovably conservative, until such time as historic development finally takes notice of them and cordially invites them to be good enough and take over the leadership of the working class. No, dear friend, it is not enough to have correct ideas. It is necessary to know how to apply them. How? There are no universally valid prescriptions for that. It is necessary to investigate the situation concretely in each instance, in order to furnish the power of the correct ideas with the most favorable organizational lever.

At the time of the split with the Brandlerites, a comrade from the Walcher group turned to me to ask my opinion of the prospective entry of the minority into the SAP (I believe it was in 1931). My reply was approximately the following: the entry into this left Social Democratic party cannot in any case be condemned itself. It is necessary to know in the name of what principles and aims you want to bring about this entry. Therefore, it is obligatory, first of all, to elaborate a clear and unequivocal platform of your own.

As you know, Walcher and his people did not proceed in this manner. They have played hide-and-seek with ideas and still do to this day. This is what we condemn them for, not for joining a *certain* Social Democratic organization in a *certain* political situation.

I am informed that a young SAP man declared at the conference of the IAG: The turn of the Bolshevik-Leninists in France is a confirmation of the SAP principles. Serious people can only get a good laugh out of that, because entry in itself proves nothing; the decisive thing is program and action taken in the spirit of this program after the entry. Insofar as they are represented in the SFIO, the SAP produces the effect of formlessness and lukewarm centrism. Our people act in the spirit of Marxist clarity and determination.

But Lenin said it is necessary to break with the reformists, and we are now entering a reformist organization. This manner of counterposing things is completely akin spiritually to that of the Bordigists and their disciple Vereecken, but has nothing in common with Leninism. Lenin proclaimed the necessity of breaking with the reformists after the outbreak of the war, the world war. He pitilessly demanded this of the centrists. At that time there were not in any country outside of the Russian emigration any consistent Bolsheviks. The leftward-turning elements to whom Lenin appealed were centrists, rooted in the Social Democracy not only organizationally but ideologically as well. It was to them that Lenin said: You must break with the reformists. But in order to be able to say that, the Russian Bolsheviks participated zealously in the internal life of the French, Swiss and Scandinavian Social Democracy.

Our great advantage over 1914 consists of the groups and organizations of hardened Bolsheviks that we have almost everywhere, which are internationally aligned and, therefore, subject to international control. They don't have to be convinced of the necessity of breaking with the reformists. They are faced with an altogether different problem: how can and should our small group with its clear ideas best get a hearing among the masses under present conditions? The situation is complicated and involved, so overrun with the remnants of old organizations that, while preserving absolute irreconcilability insofar as our principles are concerned, organizationally we must be very resourceful, very spry, very supple and very enterprising. Otherwise we will decay even with the very best ideas. In his correspondence with Sorge, Engels complains dozens of times that the English and German Marxists in America brought matters to such a pass that they transformed the liveliest theory, Marxism, into a sectarian faith under cover of which to be able to remain passive instead of intervening with all their force and determination in the stream of the living labor movement.

Look at Spain, dear friend. In the midst of all the tremors of revolution around them, the leadership of our section there distinguished itself during the whole period by its doctrinaire passivity. Individually, many of our comrades fought courageously. But the section as a whole distinguished itself more by "objective" criticism than by revolutionary activity. That is undoubtedly the most tragic example in the entire history of the ICL. And observe, it is precisely this section that to the present day remains completely intransigent toward the "opportunistic" turn in France.

In America developments took a different course. Our League has joined with the Muste organization to constitute an independent party. The organization participates eagerly in the actual mass movement and has considerable successes to its credit. And precisely for this reason, it has been able to show a clear understanding for the French turn, despite the difference in conditions and in the methods applied.

As Marxists, we are centralists. We are striving internationally also for the merger of the revolutionary forces. But as Marxists, we cannot be pettifogging doctrinaires, pedants. We always analyze the stream and adapt ourselves to every new situation without losing our identity. Therein lies the whole secret of revolutionary success. And we must master this secret regardless of the costs.

INDEX

Communist Party of Lithuania, 271
Communist Party of Poland, xi, 192, 195, 196, 247, 253, 254, 256, 265, 273, 281, 282; left-wing opposition forms in, xvi, xvii, 281-83; and Polish workers councils, 190-91; and Poale Zion, 196, 219, 221, 231, 283; and Uniteds, 196, 218; and trade-union influence, 196, 199, 213-14, 218, 274-75; and Combund, 196, 213, 214, 218, 247, 256; and union of Social Democrats and PPS-Left, 196; and October Revolution, 198; Jewish Central Bureau of, 198, 213, 218, 220, 234, 253, 273-74, 277, 283; and Polish-Russian War, 199-207; and Bund, 213-14; defends Radek and Brandler, 219; changes position on national and agrarian questions, 219-20; and minority faction, 231, 251-52, 253, 254, 271; and majority faction, 251-52, 253, 254, 259-60, 272, 289; decline of, 254-55; members of at Lenin School, 256, 257, 259-60, 266-67; purge of, 266-67, 271-72; attacks Jewish culture, 274; attacks Bund and Poale Zion, 274-75, 315; organizes adventurist strikes and demonstrations, 276-77; and Communist writers group, 282-83; expels Left Opposition, 284-85, 286, 289; cleans out Jewish members, 289; slanders and terrorizes Trotskyists, 290-92, 293-94, 315-316; extermination of leaders of, 317; dissolution of by Stalin, 317
Communist Party of the Soviet Union, 257, 258; *see also* Trotskyism
Communist Party of West White Russia, 214, 220, 239
Constituent Assembly, *see* Russian

Revolution of 1917
Consumer cooperative, 62, 68, 71, 80, 81, 84, 86, 91, 116, 122, 124, 125
Czechoslovak legions, 181

Daladier, Édouard, 324
Darwin, Charles, 50-51
David, 134-35, 142-43
Denikin, General Anton I., 260
Deutsch, Lev, 44
Deutscher, Isaac, 283, 284, 287, 289, 290, 293, 313, 317, 318
Diner, Moshe, 288
Dollfuss, Engelbert, 301, 306
Doriot, Jacques, 305-06, 312
Drucker, Avremel, 68, 121
Dua, Gershon, 219, 252, 254
Dubnov-Ehrlich, Sofia, 201
Duma, 47, 49, 67; Bolsheviks' attitude toward, 43, 77-78; and Mensheviks; 43, 77-78; elections to, 77, 78-79, 81, 100, 133; and Beilis trial, 119-20, 121
Duracz, Teodor, 217, 229, 313
Dzerzhinsky, Felix, 64 *n.*, 51, 219

Ehrlich, Henryk, 201, 204, 214, 316
Ehrlich, Shlomo, 288, 289, 293, 316
Engels, Friedrich, xii, 63, 327-28; critique of German Social Democracy by, 78; and *Origin of the Family, Private Property and the State,* 195
Epshteyn, Josef, 225
Esther (Maria Frumkina), 211
Estonian Putsch, 224
Eydl, 217

Falder, 297, 298, 300
Fascism, vs. Bonapartism, 236-37
Felix, 139, 144
56th Regiment (First Revolutionary